ORIGINS OF

DEMOCRATIC

CULTURE

PRINCETON STUDIES
IN CULTURAL SOCIOLOGY

──────────── EDITORS ────────────

Paul J. DiMaggio

Michèle Lamont

Robert J. Wuthnow

Viviana A. Zelizer

*Origins of Democratic Culture: Printing, Petitions,
and the Public Sphere in Early-Modern England*
by David Zaret

ORIGINS OF DEMOCRATIC CULTURE

PRINTING, PETITIONS, AND THE PUBLIC SPHERE IN EARLY-MODERN ENGLAND

David Zaret

PRINCETON UNIVERSITY PRESS

PRINCETON, NEW JERSEY

Library of Congress Cataloging-in-Publication Data
Zaret, David.
Origins of democratic culture : printing, petitions,
and the public sphere in early-modern England / David Zaret.
p.   cm. — (Princeton studies in cultural sociology)
Includes bibliographical references and index.
ISBN 0-691-00694-6 (cloth : alk. paper)
1. Democracy—England—History—17th century.
2. Civil society—England—History—17th century.   3. Public opinion—
England—History—17th century.   4. Great Britain—Politics
and government—17th century.   I. Title.   II. Series.
JN191.Z37   2000
302.2′244′094209032—dc21   99-25810

This book has been composed in Galliard

http://pup.princeton.edu

Printed in the United States of America

1   3   5   7   9   10   8   6   4   2

For Julie

Contents

Acknowledgments

IN AN EARLIER BOOK I dealt briefly with communicative issues in order to develop an explanation about change in the structure of English Protestantism. Even then I often found myself attracted more to peripheral issues, to literacy, debates, and printing, and to the look and feel of printed and scribal texts rather than to the religious issues inscribed in them. In the process of transforming the peripheral into a preoccupation, I have incurred many debts to fellow scholars, funding agencies, and my home institution.

Earlier versions of parts of this book have been presented at the Princeton University Colloquium on Religion and Politics, the Program in Social Theory and Cross-Cultural Studies at the University of North Carolina at Chapel Hill, the Mellon Seminar on Literacy and Political Culture at the University of Pennsylvania, the Symposium on Cultural and Economic Dynamics in Early-Modern England and Japan sponsored by the Achievement Project at Oxford University, at meetings of the International Sociological Association in Bielefeld, Germany, and at the Center for History, Society, and Culture at the University of California at Davis. A fellowship and a travel grant from the National Endowment for the Humanities, a grant from the Lilly Foundation, and a research leave fellowship and travel grant from Indiana University made it possible for me to conduct research on both sides of the Atlantic Ocean.

I am also grateful to historians who have provided encouragement and answers to questions, including Richard Blackett, Joad Raymond, Paul Seaver, the late Leo Solt, David Underdown, and Jeff Wasserstrom. My thinking on specifically sociological issues has benefited from conversations with Robert Antonio, Mabel Berezin, Jack Goldstone, and John R. Hall. In Bloomington, Thomas F. Gieryn has been a constant source of good advice. I am especially grateful to three other sociologists with well-known positions on some themes taken up in this study. They persisted in their support for this project in spite of my criticism of some of their ideas. Because they ought to be able to respond in kind as book reviewers, I will not list their names. The assistance of professional staff has been uniformly helpful at Duke Humfrey's Library, Oxford University; the Manuscript Reading Room of the British Library, the Public Record Office, and Dr. William's Library in London; and the Beineke Library at Yale University. At the Indiana University Library in Bloomington, Nancy Cridland, Diana Hanson, Polly Grimshaw, and Marty Sorury provided indispensable services and support.

My greatest debt of gratitude is owed to my wife, Julie Knost, and children, Anna ("Who's going to read this?") and Max ("Why so many pages?"). Not only have they provided continuous encouragement for this undertaking, but in many ways on every day they make me feel like the luckiest man alive.

IN REFERENCES I use the abbreviations, listed below, and also abbreviated titles or their British Library shelf marks for the Thomason Tracts or both. A microfilm edition of the Thomason Tracts, issued by University Microfilms International, uses these shelf marks, which are cross-indexed (in *The Thomason Tracts; 1640–1660* [Ann Arbor MI, 1981]) with the catalogue system *A Short-Title Catalogue of Books Printed in England . . . , 1641–1700*, ed. Donald Wing ([New York, 1945–51]). I also use short titles for other seventeenth-century printed texts and their entry number in Wing's catalogue or in *A Short-Title Catalogue of Books Printed in England . . . , 1475–1640*, ed. A. W. Pollard and G. R. Redgrave, updated and enl. by W. A. Jackson, F. S. Ferguson, and K. F. Pantzer (London, 1976–91). Microfilm copies of many items in catalogues by Wing, hereafter *Wing*, and by Pollard et. al., hereafter *STC*, are available in major research libraries.

I supply original punctuation and spelling of titles and verse but otherwise have modernized quoted material. London is the place of publication unless otherwise indicated for seventeenth-century texts.

MANUSCRIPT SOURCES

MSS Add	London, British Library, Additional Manuscripts
MSS Ashmole	Oxford, Bodleian Library, Ashmoleian Manuscripts
MSS Clarendon	Oxford, Bodleian Library, Clarendon Manuscripts
MSS Egerton	London, British Library, Egerton Manuscripts
MSS Eng. hist.	Oxford, Bodleian Library, English Historical Manuscripts
MSS Harl	London, British Library, Harleian Manuscripts
MSS JCC	London, London City Corporation, Journals of the Common Council
MSS Lansdowne	London, British Library, Lansdowne Manuscripts
MSS Nalson	Oxford, Bodleian Library, Nalson Manuscripts
MSS New College	Oxford, New College Library, Manuscripts
MSS Osborn	New Haven, Beinecke Library, Osborn Manuscripts
MSS Rawl	Oxford, Bodleian Library, Rawlinson Manuscripts
MSS Rep	London, London City Corporation, Repertories of the Court of Aldermen
MSS Stowe	London, British Library, Stowe Manuscripts

MSS Tanner	Oxford, Bodleian Library, Tanner Manuscripts
MSS Williams	London, Dr. Williams Library, Manuscripts
PRO *SPD* 16	London, Public Record Office, State Papers, domestic series, Charles I

PRINTED SOURCES

AJS	*American Journal of Sociology*
APC	*Acts of the Privy Council of England.* Edited by J. R. Dasent. 32 vols. London, 1890–1907.
ASR	*American Sociological Review*
CJ	*Journals of the House of Commons*
CS	*Camden Society*
CSPD	*Calendars of State Papers, Domestic Series*
D'Ewes I	*The Journal of Sir Simonds D'Ewes from the begining of the Long Parliament to the opening of the trial of the Earl of Strafford.* Edited by Wallace Notestein. New Haven, 1923.
D'Ewes II	*The Journal of Sir Simonds D'Ewes from the first recess of the Long Parliament to the Withdrawal of King Charles from London.* Edited by Willson Coates. New Haven, 1942.
ENT	*Elizabethan Nonconformist Texts.* Edited by Albert Peel and Leland Carlson. 6 vols. London, 1951–70.
HJ	*Historical Journal*
HLQ	*Huntington Library Quarterly*
HMC	*Historical Manuscripts Commission*
JBS	*Journal of British Studies*
LJ	*Journals of the House of Lords*
LL	*The Lisle Letters.* Edited by Muriel St. Clare Byrne. 6 vols. Chicago, 1981.
L&P	*Letters and Papers, Foreign and Domestic, of the Reign of Henry VIII.* Edited by J.S. Brewer, J. Gairdner, and R. H. Brodie. 36 vols. London, 1862–1932.
MA	*Mercurius Aulicus.* In *Newsbooks 1: Oxford Royalist,* vols. 1–3, edited by Peter Thomas. London, 1971.
ns	new series
os	old series
PJ1	*Private Journals of the Long Parliament, 3 January to 5 March 1642.* Edited by Willson Coates, Anne Young, and Vernon Snow. New Haven, 1982.

PJ2   *Private Journals of the Long Parliament, 7 March to 1 June 1642.* Edited by Vernon Snow and Anne Young. New Haven, 1987.

PJ3   *Private Journals of the Long Parliament, 2 June to 17 September 1642.* Edited by Vernon Snow and Anne Young. New Haven, 1992.

P&P   *Past and Present*

PP Elizabeth   *Proceedings in the Parliaments of Queen Elizabeth.* Edited by T. E. Hartley. Leicester, 1981.

PP 1610   *Proceedings in Parliament 1610.* Edited by Elizabeth Foster. 2 vols. New Haven, 1966.

PP 1625   *Proceedings in Parliament 1625.* Edited by Maija Jansson and William B. Bidwell. New Haven, 1987.

PP 1626   *Proceedings in Parliament 1626.* Edited by William B. Bidwell and Maija Jansson. 4 vols. New Haven, 1991–96.

PP 1628   *Proceedings in Parliament 1628.* Edited by Robert C. Johnson and Mary F. Keeler. 6 vols. New Haven, 1977–83.

RP-S   *Stuart Royal Proclamations.* Edited by James Larkin and Paul Hughes. 2 vols. Oxford, 1973–.

RP-T   *Tudor Royal Proclamations.* Edited by Paul Hughes and James Larkin. 3 vols. New Haven, 1964–69.

Rushworth   John Rushworth, *Historical Collections of Private Passages of State.* 6 vols. London, 1721.

ser.   series

SPD   State Papers, domestic series. Public Record Office, London.

ORIGINS OF

DEMOCRATIC

CULTURE

CHAPTER ONE

Introduction

PUBLIC OPINION is a central yet elusive aspect of democracy that several generations of scholars have explored as they pursued different questions about the cultural moorings of democratic governance. Three decades ago, when research on democracy examined prospects for new nations carved from colonies in Africa and Latin America, a key issue was the relationship between democracy's institutional arrangements and supportive cultural developments in the rise of "civic culture," "psychological modernity," and "value generalization."[1] Globalization and the demise of state socialism have renewed scholarly interest in these issues, although different concepts guide current research on democracy's communicative foundations. One line of work revives the eighteenth-century idea of civil society[2]–a societal community whose axial principle of solidarity demarcates it from political and economic realms based on power and money. Studies of civil society emphasize the centrality of public opinion in politics because opinion is held to be the principal link between the democratic state and civil society. So does research on the public sphere,[3] whose current status and future prospects are topics of lively, cross-disciplinary debates among social scientists and philosophers.

Although widespread agreement exists over the importance of public opinion for democratic governance, our understanding of its origins as a factor in politics is shrouded in confusion and controversy. In chapter 2 I survey widespread disagreement over every conceivable aspect of the early public sphere: the date of its appearance, the social background

---

[1] Gabriel Almond and Sidney Verba, *The Civic Culture: Political Attitudes and Democracy in Five Nations* (Boston, 1965); Daniel Lerner, *The Passing of Traditional Society* (New York, 1964); Talcott Parsons, *The Evolution of Societies* (Englewood Cliffs, NJ, 1977).

[2] Jeffrey Alexander, ed., *Real Civil Societies* (London, 1998); Craig Calhoun, "Nationalism and Civil Society," in C. Calhoun, ed., *Social Theory and the Politics of Identity* (Oxford, 1994); Jean L. Cohen and Andrew Arato, *Civil Society and Political Theory* (Cambridge, MA, 1992); John A. Hall, ed., *Civil Society* (Oxford, 1995); Thomas Janoski, *Citizenship and Civil Society* (Cambridge, 1998); Adam Seligman, *The Idea of Civil Society* (New York, 1992).

[3] Jürgen Habermas, *Structural Transformation of the Public Sphere* (Cambridge, MA, [1962] 1989). More recently, see Jürgen Habermas, *Between Facts and Norms* (Cambridge, MA, 1998), p. 299.

of its participants, and the extent to which exclusionary practices contradicted universalistic ideals of inclusion and open debate. Divergent ideological commitments are one source of disagreement over these issues. Radical critics of liberal democracy trace the origins of the public sphere to imperatives of capitalist development. Proponents of liberal democracy are more likely to cite structural differentiation and Protestant religion, while feminists point to patriarchal assumptions among capitalist men. These accounts of origins are not infrequently a foil for politically charged claims on the current and future prospects of the public sphere.

Another source of disagreement is methodological in nature. Writings by philosophers and social scientists on the public sphere highlight the intellectual tendencies of the hedgehog, who, unlike the fox that knows many things, seeks answers in discovering one big secret. The hedgehog's predilection for overly broad generalization appears in scholarly accounts whose big secret is that the early public sphere was an accretion of the bourgeoisie, capitalism, the Enlightenment, patriarchy, Protestantism, modernity, or some other grand category. Hedgehog approaches underwrite disagreement, already sufficiently fueled by ideology, because they promote an excessively speculative mode of analysis. Its practitioners, in undergraduate parlance, follow a "laid-back" version of the sociology of knowledge that cites affinities or parallels between epochal events, categories, or trends (e.g., capitalism, Protestantism, differentiation) and any of the many attributes of the *concept* of a public sphere—between, for example, economic competition and a marketplace of ideas or the sanctity of conscience and free speech. Though communicative issues—for example, modes of textual reproduction, rhetorical conventions, distribution and reception—are central to any concept of the public sphere, little empirical work on these issues guides research on the early public sphere. And when the public sphere is analyzed in isolation from these communicative issues, it becomes an extremely elastic concept, and our knowledge of its origins flows more from speculation on the relevance of epochal trends and events than from empirical study of what, after all, is the ultimate dependent variable in this line of inquiry.

Yet empirical referents exist for the concept of a public sphere and its history. They appear when inquiry into the communicative origins of democracy descends from the higher regions of culture and ceases to explore writings by Locke, Smith, Rousseau, Kant, and other luminaries of the Enlightenment as indicators of communicative practices that constitute the modern public sphere. If we want empirical evidence on the early public sphere, we must attend to communicative practices by a larger group of speakers, writers, printers, petitioners, publishers, and readers. We must study how individuals talked, argued, sang, wrote, read, and petitioned about public issues, and how this changed, not only in salons and universities, but in alehouses, shops, and churchyards. For this, the way has been cleared by historians who in recent years have explored many communicative issues pertaining to media, rhetoric, and reception.[4] These issues have been pursued in historical studies of printing, news, and politics in early-modern France and colonial America,[5] as well as in England.[6] References to media, rhetoric, and reception routinely appear in sociological studies of the *modern* public sphere,[7] but in accounts of the early public sphere they vanish behind interpretations of formal writings by Enlightenment philosophers and Protestant theologians. Use of these sources unites an otherwise heterogeneous collection of studies that is riddled with disagreement over key issues pertaining to the development of a public space in which appeals to opinion become central to politics.[8] These disagreements are inevitable principally because relying on texts from the summit of high culture as evidence for studying the birth of public opinion is like looking the wrong way through a telescope—the withering criticism advanced long ago by Peter Laslett against novels as a source of data for social history. The indirect path, reading philosophers and theologians, might be justified *if* no better sources existed for political communication among ordinary persons in the past. Yet such evidence exists, more or less abundantly, for many different types of political communication.

[4] On this development, see Lynn Hunt, "Introduction: History, Culture, and Text," in L. Hunt, ed., *The New Cultural History* (Berkeley, 1989), pp. 1–22.

[5] E.g., Jack Censer and Jeremy Popkin, eds., *Press and Politics in Pre-Revolutionary France* (Berkeley, 1987); Roger Chartier, *The Cultural Origins of the French Revolution* (Durham, NC, 1991); Jeremy Popkin, *Revolutionary News: The Press in France, 1789–1799* (Durham, NC, 1990); Jeffrey Sawyer, *Printed Poison: Pamphlet Propaganda, Faction Politics, and the Public Sphere in Early-Seventeenth-Century France* (Berkeley, 1990); Michael Warner, *The Letters of the Republic: Publication and the Public Sphere in Eighteenth-Century America* (Cambridge, MA, 1990).

[6] For developments up to 1660, see Sandra Clark, *The Elizabethan Pamphleteers* (London, 1983); Cyndia S. Clegg, *Press Censorship in Elizabethan England* (Cambridge, 1997); A. D. T. Cromartie, "The Printing of Parliamentary Speeches, November 1640–July 1642," *HJ* 33 (1990); Richard Cust, "News and Politics in Early-Seventeenth-Century England," *P&P* 112 (1986); Sheila Lambert, "The Beginning of Printing for the House of Commons,1640–1642" *Library*, 6th ser., 3 (1981); Joad Raymond, *The Invention of the Newspaper: English Newsbooks, 1641–1649* (Oxford, 1996). For after the Restoration up to 1700, see, G. C. Gibbs, "Press and Public Opinion," in J. R. Jones, ed., *Liberty Secured? Britain before and after 1688* (Stanford, 1992); James Sutherland, *The Restoration Newspaper and Its Development* (Cambridge, 1986); Harold M. Weber, *Paper Bullets: Print and Kingship under Charles II* (Lexington, KY, 1996).

[7] E.g., Ronald Jacobs, "Civil Society and Crisis," *AJS* 101 (1996): 1238–72.

[8] In addition to items in notes 2 and 3 above, see Leon Mayhew, "In Defense of Modernity," *AJS* 89 (1984): 1281–87; Elisabeth Noelle-Neumann, *The Spiral of Silence: Public Opinion—Our Social Skin* (Chicago, 1993), pp. 69–87.

Far more is concealed than revealed by studies of the early public sphere that overlook direct evidence on political communication and, instead, rely on philosophical and theological texts. In chapter 2 we shall see that this has led many scholars to associate the early public sphere with elite, eighteenth-century developments, most notably the rise of bourgeois society, leavened by the Enlightenment as the prototype for open, critical debate on public issues in civil society.[9] But the "invention" of public opinion as a political force occurred well before the Enlightenment, in a more popular social milieu, a consequence not of theoretical principles but of practical developments that flowed from the impact of printing on traditional forms of political communication.[10] The rationality and normative authority of public opinion appeared in English politics, unevenly to be sure, long before they were celebrated in writings by Enlightenment philosophers. During the English Revolution (1640–60) these practical developments led to precisely those democratic tenets—for example, the importance of consent, open debate, and reason for the authority of opinion in politics—that current scholarship describes as intellectual discoveries of the Enlightenment. Hence, empirical knowledge of the origins of our democratic culture will not be advanced by interpretations of philosophic or theological texts in order to establish the Enlightenment or Protestant religion as a prototype of the democratic public sphere.

When developed empirically, research on the origins of the public sphere confronts the following questions. When and why did political communication cease to be governed by norms of secrecy and privilege? How did invocation of public opinion become a central feature of political discourse? In pursuing these questions, my goal is not simply to attack hedgehogs. The point is not to discredit theoretical reflection on the origins of democratic culture, but to sharpen it, to bring it into closer proximity to contemporary historical scholarship. Toward this end, English history is "the model case" for studying developments in political communication that eventuate in the birth of the public sphere.[11] The shift from norms of secrecy to appeals to public opinion at the level of communicative practice in mid-seventeenth-century En-

---

[9] In addition to items in notes 2 and 3 above, see Reinhard Bendix, *Kings or People? Power and the Mandate to Rule* (Berkeley, 1978); Robert Wuthnow, *Communities of Discourse* (Cambridge, MA, 1989).

[10] For an earlier version of this thesis, see David Zaret "Religion, Science, and Printing in the Public Spheres of Seventeenth-Century England," in C. Calhoun, ed., *Habermas and the Public Sphere* (Cambridge, MA, 1992), pp. 221–34.

[11] Habermas, *Structural Transformation*, p. 57; and see Bendix, *Kings or People?* pp. 10, 12–13, 266–69; Reinhard Bendix, *Nation-Building and Citizenship* (Berkeley, 1977), pp. 86–87; T. H. Marshall, *Citizenship and Social Development* (New York, 1964), pp. 70–71.

gland occurred before comparable democratic initiatives in other Western societies.[12] Moreover, these practical innovations provided precedents for democratic ideas in Leveller writings and, later, in writings by Locke and others toward the end of the century.[13] Subsequently, these developments exercised great influence over reflection on politics in the French Enlightenment. Yet French philosophes warily regarded the English model of public opinion—unruly, relatively unconstrained by courtly manners—and preferred tamer, deferential discourse than that which flourished in a marketplace of ideas.[14] Here, then, is yet another reason for not using formal writings from the French Enlightenment as a source for exploring the origins of the public sphere.

For the case of England, the turn from theology and philosophy to communicative practice leads to the following point of departure for a new account of the birth of the public sphere. At the beginning of the seventeenth century, English politics afforded little place for public opinion. Political communication existed but was severely restricted by norms of secrecy and privilege, confined mostly to discussion among local and national elites. In Parliament, a customary right of free speech in the fifteenth century had evolved into a formal privilege under the Tudors. But disclosure of parliamentary debates was a crime. Popular participation in political discourse was limited to the receiving end of symbolic displays of authority. Though conflict was endemic to politics, and followed fissures between and within national and local communities, no "opposition," no parties, and no public space existed in which political factions competed in an open exchange of ideas. Yet by the end of the century, a privileged place for public opinion appears in liberal-democratic conceptions of political order, advanced by John Locke (1632–1704) and other Whig writers, such as Anthony Ashley Cooper, the earl of Shaftesbury (1621–83) and Algernon Sidney (1622–83). In

[12] Sawyer's analysis of propaganda and factional conflict in France between 1614 and 1617 shows that "pamphlets were designed to influence the perceptions and manipulate the behavior of an audience." *Printed Poison*, p. 11. But democratic models of the public sphere involve more than flows of information from the center to the periphery of the nation. Efforts to mobilize and invoke opinion in order to lobby political elites is crucial. This reservation also applies to descriptions of a public sphere in sixteenth-century England. See Clegg, *Censorship in Elizabethan England*, p. 222; Alexandra Halasz, *The Marketplace of Print* (Cambridge, 1997), chap. 5.

[13] This formulation of the relationship between the Levellers and Locke may meet objections advanced by G. E. Aylmer, "Locke no Leveller," in I. Gentles, J. Morrill, and B. Worden, eds., *Soldiers, Writers, and Statesmen of the English Revolution* (Cambridge, 1998), pp. 304–22.

[14] Keith Baker, *Inventing the French Revolution* (Stanford, 1990), pp. 173–78; Mona Ozouf, "'Public Opinion' at the End of the Old Regime," in T. C. W. Blanning, ed., *The Rise and Fall of the French Revolution* (Chicago, 1996), pp. 93–94.

examining the transition from communicative norms of secrecy and privilege to public opinion in English politics, we confront the *practical* origins of democratic culture: real-world communicative developments that made it possible for Locke and subsequent philosophers to uphold democratic conceptions of political order that presuppose the existence, rationality, and normative authority of public opinion.

At the core of democracy's formal philosophies and institutional arrangements lies the elusive idea of public opinion. Assuring the authority of opinion and limiting its volatile excess are principal goals of democracy's institutional arrangements, such the franchise and constitutional ground rules. Democratic governance is often associated with these visible arrangements, so much so that their development is often treated as coterminous with the history of democracy. Yet they are not the essence of the matter, for they presuppose the existence of free and open debate, a public sphere where political discourse derives from rival appeals to public opinion.[15] Public opinion in modern democracy is a specific type of vox populi, one that arises out of a "marketplace of ideas," whose authority for ultimately setting the political agenda derives from specific suppositions about the importance of consent, open debate, and rationality. That public opinion is in principle the prime mover of democratic politics is a commonplace observation. Yet unlike democracy's institutional arrangements and constitutional rules, public opinion defies easy description and explanation.

Like the commodity famously described by Marx as abounding in metaphysical subtlety, public opinion is a complex thing. This complexity reflects the dual nature of public opinion as a real and nominal entity. Nominally it is a discursive fiction; qua public opinion it collectively exists only when instantiated in discourse, when invoked by a politician, pollster, journalist, or social scientist in support of a contention about what the public thinks or desires. At the same time, real individuals participate in political discourse, as readers, speakers, hearers, and writers. This underlies the paradox, noted fifty years ago by Herbert Blumer, that public opinion research led to many technical improvements in methods but did little to dispel uncertainly and confusion over what public opinion is. The same situation exists today, according to Noelle-Neumann.[16] Compounding this complexity is the potential of the discursive fiction—public opinion invoked as a collective entity—to influence the opinion of individuals. One way to handle this complexity is an old convention in public opinion research: simplify matters with an op-

[15] See Alain Touraine, *What Is Democracy?* (New York, 1997), pp. 12–15.
[16] Herbert Blumer, "Public Opinion and Public Opinion Polling," *ASR* 13 (1948): 542–43; Noelle-Neumann, *Spiral of Silence*, p. 58.

erational definition that equates public opinion and the aggregation of individual opinions on public issues.[17]

Yet there is little novelty in the fact that today's opinion polls are inscription devices that transform individual opinions into their nominal counterpart and, in the process and after, often alter the former.[18] So were monster petition campaigns in the seventeenth century. Petitions and public opinion polls mediate between the real and nominal sides of public opinion.[19] Public opinion has always had close links to political propaganda, and its expression was never independent of organizational and rhetorical properties of practices used to represent it. In practice, the public sphere falls short of its ghostly idealization in political theory: universal participation, rational discourse characterized by symmetry and reciprocity.[20] This has led several generations of critics, from Lippmann to Derrida and Bourdieu, to conclude that public opinion is a sham and the public sphere "a conjuring trick," an ideological facade that conceals vast differences between reasoned debate and manipulation by spin doctors, between universal participation and limited access.[21] Scrutiny of this pessimistic conclusion is a subsidiary goal of this book. We shall see that such pessimism—so central a feature in current theoretical writings on the public sphere—relies on grossly unbalanced assessments of communicative change, mostly pertaining to the novelty and implications of commerce and textual reproduction, for which the empirical analysis in this book lends little support.

In arriving at these conclusions, this study of the shift from secrecy to public opinion reverses the priority accorded to theoretical over practical developments in early democratic culture. Public opinion was a factor in English politics long before philosophers extolled the idea of a civil society where politics emerge from appeals to the reason of private persons. The "invention" of public opinion was a practical accomplishment, propelled by the economic and technical aspects of printing,

---

[17] Floyd Allport, "Toward a Science of Public Opinion," *Public Opinion Quarterly* (1937): 23. See also Kimball Young, "Comments on the Nature of 'Public' and 'Public Opinion,'" *International Journal of Opinion and Attitude Research* 2 (1948): 387.

[18] See Susan Herbst, *Numbered Voices: How Opinion Polling Has Shaped American Politics* (Chicago, 1993), pp. 44–45 and passim.

[19] Bernard Manin, *The Principles of Representative Government* (Cambridge, 1997), p. 173.

[20] E.g., Habermas, *Between Facts and Norms*, p. 362.

[21] Bruce Robbins, "Introduction," in B. Robbins, ed., *The Phantom Public Sphere* (Minneapolis, 1993), p. viii; and see Pierre Bourdieu, "The Public Sphere Does Not Exist," in A. Mattelart and S. Siegelaub, *Communication and Class Struggle* (New York, 1979); Jacques Derrida, "La Démocratie Ajournée," in *L'Autre Cap* (Paris, 1991), p. 103; Walter Lippmann, *Public Opinion* (New York, 1922); Walter Lippmann, *The Phantom Public* (New York, 1927).

respectively, its relentless commercialism and its potential for efficient reproduction of texts. This occurred in the mid-seventeenth-century revolution, when contending elites used the medium of print to appeal to a mass audience, and activist members of that audience invoked the authority of opinion to lobby those elites. Ambivalence and other contradictory responses greeted this development on all sides—Royalist and Parliamentarian, Presbyterian and Independent. Though innovative, the development arose as an unreflective practice. Hence, I use quotations to signify that the "invention" of public opinion was an innovation largely disclaimed by its practitioners, a not unusual development that I call the paradox of innovation. A key issue in this particular innovation is the relevance of communicative changes associated with printing, not only for the *scope*, but for the *content* of political discourse. The relevance of printing and the concomitant growth in popular literacy has, of course, been noted in prior accounts of the early public sphere. But in these accounts communicative change associated with printing is conceived far too narrowly, in terms of the scope of political communication: facilitating more rapid, extensive dissemination of novel ideas. That print culture itself was a source of novelty—a point explored by historians of printing—remains unexamined.

Another critical issue is the divergence of historical scholarship on early-modern England and theoretical work in other disciplines on the origins of the public sphere. Social scientists and philosophers who find these origins in capitalist development or Protestantism rely on historical perspectives that revisionist scholarship forced professional historians to abandon or at least severely question. Historical revisionism represents a sharp reversal of great expectations, admittedly shared by this writer, about an imminent instauration in one area of interdisciplinary scholarship, an impending merger of historical research and social science.

While historical issues and data have acquired growing importance in many areas of social science, historical research has at many points turned away from social science. Nowhere has this turn been sharper than in the field of early-modern British history, where more than Marxist and Whig perspectives on long-term change were casualties of revisionism. In its emphasis on historical particularity and ideographic representation of the past as the prime duty of historians, the revisionist revolt against generalization proscribes pursuit of all *sociological* themes. To pursue them in studying the seventeenth century, argue revisionists, is to belabor anachronism.[22] Narrowing the gap between contemporary

---

[22] J. C. D. Clark, *Revolution and Rebellion: State and Society in England in the Seventeenth and Eighteenth Centuries* (Cambridge, 1986), p. 23.

historical scholarship and theoretical reflection is a subsidiary methodological goal of this study. A viable compromise between hedgehogs and foxes must occupy a middle ground between revisionist historiography, with its (unsustainable) goal "to return to the sources free of preconceptions,"[23] and sweeping theories of the public sphere that simply cannot be squared with individual-level observations offered by meticulous, revisionist scholarship. Revisionism is not unassailable. The birth of a public sphere in seventeenth-century England had antecedents, being neither an accident nor a product of elite maneuvers that emanated from idiosyncratic personalities and the problematic finances of the English ruling classes. We will not understand the origins of democracy's public sphere unless we can establish its links to long- and short-term changes in communicative media and practices, and place them in the wider context of social change in early-modern Europe. Yet this scholarly project just as much requires that we reject sweeping, insupportable explanations that emulate the hedgehog's use of concepts.

After reviewing these theoretical and historiographic issues in chapter 2, I begin in chapter 3 with traditional principles for communicative practice in English politics. In principle, political communication followed norms of secrecy and privilege that grew out of fundamental, uncontroverted assumptions about the nature of the political and social order. In practice, however, we shall see in chapters 4 and 5 that political messages traveled in all directions and took many forms in England. Long before the tumultuous events of the mid-seventeenth century, messages routinely circulated in oral reports and rumors, ballads, private correspondence, proclamation by herald and broadside, the posted libel, petitions, ritualized forms of restive behavior, political sermons, speeches by assize judges, scribal texts, printed propaganda, and other ways. At the same time, conventions governing political communication imposed strict limits on its exercise. Contradictions between principle and practice were numerous, for when contemporaries thought about political communication, they often overlooked that which was widespread in practice. Many licit channels of communication conveyed messages between the center and periphery of the political nation. At the same time, illicit but widely used channels conducted reports of news, the topic of chapter 5. Thus, political communication in prerevolutionary England exhibits great variation in terms of modes of transmission—oral, scribal, print—rhetorical conventions, licit or illicit status, and popular access. In general, an inverse relationship existed between access

---

[23] Kevin Sharpe, " 'Revisionism' Revisited," in Sharpe, ed., *Faction and Parliament: Essays on Early Stuart History* (London, 1985), p. x; and see Conrad Russell, *Unrevolutionary England* (London, 1990), p. x.

and substantive content of political discourse: access was greatest for purely symbolic displays of sovereign authority, least so for modes of communication that featured substantive discussions and debates.

These practices and their uneven relationship to norms of secrecy and privilege in political communication are the essential point of departure for studying the "invention" of public opinion. Due acknowledgment must be given to the range and complexity of traditional communicative practices in political discourse if we are to avoid substituting one set of sweeping generalizations with another. Claims about printing as the fountainhead of democracy rely on an untenable reductionism that hedgehogs would find congenial. The relevance of printing for the public sphere emerges in specific rhetorical and social contexts; it is not an inevitable consequence of "print logic."[24] Change in the scope and content of political communication flowed from the impact of printing on traditional communicative practices, such as scribal communication of news and petitioning. The "invention" of public opinion was not, then, an automatic consequence of print technology. Print culture, and not the Enlightenment, is a plausible candidate as *the* prototype for open debate in civil society. But this claim requires qualification, a balanced assessment that distinguishes between what was and was not unique in printing and print culture, between changes in quantity—where printing accentuated developments present in scribal modes of reproduction—and quality. For example, the coffeehouse culture in Restoration England, which Habermas specifically associates with the embryonic public sphere, relied for critical, accurate political news mainly on scribal modes of publication for political texts. "It is therefore in the sphere of inscription—the printed pamphlet and the scribal separate—rather than that of voice that we should be looking for the architecture of the public sphere."[25] That print and scribal publication were intertwined in complex ways should prompt additional care not to overemphasize the unmediated causal significance of printing for the public sphere.

Exploring print culture as a prototype for a political public sphere is the task of chapter 6. After it appeared in England, printing was quickly pressed into government service. Its technical superiority for textual reproduction commended it to English bishops who, otherwise wary of its implications for religion, created printed tax forms that helped them discharge their duty to collect annates, firstfruits, and other clerical taxes that, after the Reformation, flowed to Westminster and not Rome. At

[24] For criticism of technological determinism in studies of print culture, see Wendy Wall, *The Imprint of Gender: Authorship and Publication in the English Renaissance* (Ithaca, 1993), pp. 20–21; Warner, *Letters of the Republic*, chap. 1.

[25] Harold Love, *Scribal Publication in Seventeenth-Century England* (Oxford, 1993), pp. 194–95. A "separate" was a manuscript copy of a speech or news report.

this time, printing was routinely used to publish royal proclamations. It was also used to publish statutes enacted in Parliament, "especially in the important sense that they could be alleged in court without special pleading (which involved the production of a certified true copy)," and propaganda from Thomas Cromwell and his stable of writers who promoted religious policies of Henry VIII.[26] My reconstruction of links between printing and the public sphere begins with technical and social aspects of printing, and then moves on to the ensuing print culture, whose principal attributes—publicity, crass commercialism, evasion of censorship, popular readership—appear in literary and religious publications. In both the late-Elizabethan literary world and in religious debates occurring between Puritans, Separatists, and the ecclesiastical hierarchy, we find the same, distinctive attributes of print culture. In chapter 7 we encounter these same attributes in the political literature of the English Revolution.

Central to print culture is an alliance between commerce and controversy, forged by the interest of authors and stationers in producing texts for which popular demand exists. But, as noted above, printing's relevance for the birth of the public sphere goes beyond change in the *scope* and extends to the *content* of political communication. Competition among stationers is important for explaining changes in *scope*, when a flood of cheap texts and simple prose enlarged popular access to political debates and discussion. For explaining changes in the *content* of political communication, the heightened capacity of printing, relative to scribal culture, for reproducing texts is crucial for understanding how political discourse became oriented to the constitution and invocation of public opinion. The rise of a public sphere facilitated by printing is, then, a complex development because it encompasses public opinion as both a real and nominal factor in politics. Political texts claim the mantle of opinion to legitimate a legislative agenda. At the same time they thereby influence opinions of readers and open up possibilities for them to acquire knowledge, make judgments, and, when the printed text was a petition or announcement of a meeting, participate in activities intended to lobby legislators. In chapter 7 I analyze this alteration in the content of communication in terms of printing's imposition of dialogic order on conflict. Printing's technical capacity to reproduce texts led to the production of broadsides and pamphlets that referred to other texts, often accompanied by partial and, less often, full reproduction of referenced

[26] Arthur Slavin, "The Tudor Revolution and the Devil's Art: Bishop Bonner's Printed Forms," in D. Guth and J. McKenna, eds., *Tudor Rule and Revolution* (Cambridge, 1982), pp. 13–23; G. R. Elton, *Studies in Tudor and Stuart Politics and Government* (Cambridge, 1974–92), 3:105, 126–27; G. R. Elton, *Policy and Police: The Enforcement of the Reformation in the Age of Thomas Cromwell* (Cambridge, 1972), chap. 4.

texts. Readers thus confronted political texts that responded to prior texts, simultaneously referring to, excerpting from, and commenting on them. Though these texts prompted readers to arrive at "correct" conclusions, they derived rhetorical force from the presupposition that they reliably reproduced prior texts in order to appeal to the judgment of the reader. We shall see evidence of printing's imposition of dialogic order on political conflict in many categories of printed texts: pamphlets, newspapers, and petitions.

Once again, however, caveats are important. Scribal publication, too, had the potential to impose dialogic order on political conflict. In chapter 5 I present evidence of this from political accounts in diaries and commonplace books compiled in large measure by copies or summaries of manuscript copies of political texts. Private copying of texts was central to scribal modes of transmission for informal circulation of domestic news, which occurred in overlapping channels of oral and scribal communication. Copying became less necessary when printed domestic news became temporarily available, after 1640, when the Long Parliament disabled prerogative courts that had enforced censorship and commercial, serialized newspapers competed for readers. But during and after this development, rumors, ballads, private letters, and formal newsletters remained important vehicles for the informal circulation of political news and commentary. Thus, a balanced assessment of printing's impact on domestic news must accord equal importance to change and continuity in the transition from oral and scribal communication to textual transmission via printing. Production of printed texts of news was a quantitative extension of what was possible under scribal modes of transmission.

Petitions present a different story. Much of the evidence for the "invention" of public opinion in chapter 7 derives from inferences about the motives of writers and the political elites who subsidized their work in composing pamphlets and newspapers. Chapter 8 presents evidence on communicative developments outside the charmed inner circle of politics. After all, a democratic model of the public sphere presumes that political communication occurs in the political periphery, among ordinary members of civil society, and that a goal of their discussions and debates is to influence the decisions at the political center. Hence, petitions are crucial for understanding how printing facilitated the "invention" of public opinion. The impact of printing on petitions, unlike the transmission of news, led to change that was qualitative in nature, to abrupt discontinuities with traditional conventions that governed the venerable medieval device for registering grievances. Omission of this development is a critical flaw in prior accounts of the public sphere because petitioning in mid-seventeenth-century English politics provides an unparalleled empirical site for exploring how, long before the Enlightenment, public opinion began to mediate between the state and civil society. Petitions were not the only vehicle for political messages between the center and periphery; sermons, newspapers, and pamphlets, as well as official ordinances, proclamations, and declarations were also important. But petitions are an especially important source of evidence for studying the early public sphere because they are both a cause and indicator of other causes, such as printing and print culture.

Petitioning was a medieval communicative practice with rules concerning form and content. It was a privilege (in the medieval sense) that exempted petitioners from secrecy norms that otherwise prohibited popular discussion of political matters. The traditional petition referred local grievances to central authority; yet it did not load its message with normative claims about the "will of the people." Rules for petitions coexisted with more general norms of secrecy and privilege in political communication. During the English Revolution, new uses for printed petitions, as devices that invoked public opinion in order to lobby elites and influence the views of persons outside Parliament, provided the means by which appeals to public opinion broke through barriers of secrecy and privilege in political communication. Confronted by the problem of competition between petitions that advanced contrary opinions, some contemporaries upheld consent, reason, and representation as criteria of the validity of opinions invoked in public debate. Change in petitioning was, then, a practical precedent for "people's public use of their reason,"[27] a political development that Habermas and many other commentators assign to elite actors in the eighteenth century.

This practical precedent also led to new ideas. Some petitioners came to see the need for formal constitutional arrangements that would enforce the authority of public opinion. Innovation in petitioning thus fueled novel claims for the authority of opinion in petitions. Petitions came from associations of private persons, whereas tradition dictated that petitions on public issues be initiated by local elites in the name of corporate entities, for example, counties, guilds, and municipalities. Thus, another consequence of innovation in the practice of petitioning is the birth of the "party." Yet ambivalence bordering on denial best describes contemporary responses to innovative petitioning. Traditional rhetorical features of petitions provided a resource for denials of innovation. The same petition could be defended by supporters as a deferential, juridical, and spontaneous expression of grievance—the rhetorical form that depoliticized grievance in traditional petitions—and attacked by critics who made visible organizational practices that

[27] Habermas, *Structural Transformation of the Public Sphere*, p. 27.

contradicted apolitical appearances. Yet more than illogic or expediency underlies these reactions; they exhibit a pattern, shaped by communicative practices that have evolved in advance of supportive theoretical formulations.

In the epilogue, I tackle two themes. One concerns the aftermath of the English Revolution. My thesis that practical innovations in political communication preceded and prepared the way for democratic political philosophy leads to the following question: What is the relationship between events in the middle of the seventeenth century—for example, change in communicative practice and the politics of turmoil that led from civil wars, regicide, and creation to a republic to the Restoration in 1660—and the appearance of democratic conceptions of politics toward the end of that century? I argue that several developments after the Restoration prepared the way for liberal-democratic philosophies that put public opinion at the core of politics. The rise of toleration and natural religion, along with growing confidence in natural science as a means for overcoming religious differences, facilitated formulation of liberal-democratic philosophies by Locke, the earl of Shaftesbury, Algernon Sidney, and other Whig writers. During the English Revolution, a severely pessimistic appraisal of human nature in Puritan and sectarian religion was a principal reason for reluctance by political opponents of the Stuart monarchy to acknowledge innovative claims about subjecting politics to public opinion. The rise of natural religion in Restoration England overcame this obstacle because it allowed contemporaries to begin to untangle religion and politics even as they upheld the old precept that any adequate doctrine on political authority must encompass religion. In elevating reason over revelation, Whig writers, unlike their Puritan predecessors, were not obligated to assign divinely privileged status to any narrowly defined model of government. Locke and other writers could take definitive steps toward embracing the authority of opinion in politics because their religious commitments, though nominally Protestant, upheld an optimistic appraisal of human nature that did not preclude the priority of tolerance over revelation as a precondition for the pluralist pursuit of utility.

Finally, after jumping from the middle to the end of the seventeenth century, we leap to the present. The last theme pursued in the concluding chapter explores implications of this study for theoretical reflection on the contemporary public sphere. Debates over the current status and future of the public sphere often turn on accounts of its origins, which, we shall see, are not well anchored in empirical evidence on communicative developments in the early-modern era. Instead, these accounts rely on idealized descriptions of critical uses of public reason, often derived from self-promoting representations by eighteenth-century philosophers who celebrated their kingdom of reason. In critical theory and postmodernism, excessive pessimism on the modern public sphere is fueled by grossly unbalanced assessments of communicative change that attribute novelty in our era to rapid growth in commercialism and the capacity to reproduce texts. How, then, should we assess hypercritical perspectives on the public sphere in modern democracy that cite commerce and textual reproduction in media culture in order to explain why reasoned debate in public is now, if not extinct, an endangered species? Not only do these critiques wrongly attribute novelty to commercialism and textual reproduction in our era; they miss their constitutive role in the origins of reasoned appeals to public opinion in politics. That modernist accomplishment sprang precisely from those communicative developments that critical theorists and postmodernists hold responsible for the contemporary dissipation of reason. Empirical findings in this book flatly contradict this premise and militate against the pessimism that flows from it.

CHAPTER TWO

Theory and History

EVER SINCE MARX, key concepts in sociological theory have been tied to the supposition that English history is the modal case for exploring the rise of capitalism and democracy.[1] More than an Anglo-American variant of eurocentrism explains the persistence of this supposition in recent research on democratic developments in modernization. Comparative-historical studies have shown that development of a democratic public sphere occurred first in England and later served as a model in the transition from rule by kings to the mandate of the people in other societies. Positive and negative "demonstration effects" of prior developments in England have been described for public opinion in eighteenth-century France as well as for political developments in other nations.[2] England is also important for normative political theories of civil society and the public sphere that explore history in order to uncover opportunities for more universalism than what so far has been generated by modernization.[3]

However, theoretical reflection on democracy and modernization formerly occurred in closer intellectual proximity to historical scholarship than is now the case. Earlier in this century a near symbiosis between theory and history had two sources. First, much of the relevant historical research followed liberal or Marxist variants of the Whig view of history, whose philosophic underpinnings were similar to key assumptions in classical sociological theory. Historians produced teleological accounts of the rise of democracy in which English history appeared as the unfolding of parliamentary supremacy, toleration, and the rule of law. These democratic outcomes emerged from conflicts between "an-

[1] That the opposite supposition, English exceptionalism, more closely approximates empirical evidence is the thesis of an early revisionist foray against sociological theory. See Alan Macfarlane, *The Origins of English Individualism* (Cambridge, 1979).

[2] For France, see Keith Baker, *Inventing the French Revolution* (Stanford, 1990), pp. 173–78. More generally, see Reinhard Bendix, *Kings or People? Power and the Mandate to Rule* (Berkeley, 1978); Barrington Moore, Jr., *Social Origins of Dictatorship and Democracy* (Boston, 1966).

[3] Jean Cohen and Andrew Arato, *Civil Society and Political Theory* (Cambridge, MA, 1992); Jürgen Habermas, *Structural Transformation of the Public Sphere* (Cambridge, MA, [1962] 1989); T. H. Marshall, *Class, Citizenship and Social Development* (New York, 1964).

cients" and "moderns," rising and falling classes, tradition and reason, conflicts whose resolution expressed the inner logic of historical development conceived under the rubric of progress. Second, narrative accounts by Whig historians facilitated a cognate style of teleological reasoning among sociologists, most notably in the work of Talcott Parsons, who advanced the following gloss on the development of democracy: "In 17th-century England, differentiation of the religious system from the societal community required political changes."[4] Though critics now far outnumber supporters of this mode of structural-functionalist logic in contemporary sociology, the old Whig vision of history persists in current accounts of the early public sphere by social scientists and philosophers, who thematize the bourgeois nature of early democratic developments or early-modern England *en tout* and the revolutionary implications in Puritanism. Yet, as we shall see, these themes fly in the face of advances over the last decades in historical research. Proponents of the revisionist revolt against Whig historiography thus see revisionism as a liberation of historical scholarship from social science, and theory as a warrant for doing bad history, especially when it involves uncovering the roots of modernity in the soil of seventeenth-century history.

Of course, social scientists and philosophers will remain properly skeptical of revisionist epistemology, specifically its naive view of historical inquiry uncontaminated by general categories. This view, argues a principal bête noire of revisionism, supposes "that hindsight has grossly distorted the story we have hitherto been told."[5] Yet no amount of epistemological subtlety will provide sociologists and philosophers with a viable defense for theories whose substantive claims are flatly contradicted by individual-level observations amassed by revisionist historians. Fortunately, at least one path leads out of this impasse: to study political communication with the aid of empirical referents for key theoretical concepts and thereby develop balanced assessments of continuity and change in the rise of the public sphere. Research on many aspects of communicative practice—for example, modes of transmission, reception, rhetoric—is a large and growing area of interest among historians and has great relevance for advancing our understanding of the early public sphere. If the public sphere has referents other than the flattering self-image cultivated by Enlightenment philosophers when they thought about themselves,[6] or ethical maxims in modern normative

---

[4] Talcott Parsons, *The Evolution of Societies* (Englewood Cliffs, NJ, 1977), p. 145.

[5] Conrad Russell, *Unrevolutionary England, 1603–1642* (London, 1990), p. ix; cf. Christopher Hill, "Parliament and People in Seventeenth-Century England," *P&P* 92 (1981): 122–23.

[6] The intellectual conceit that critical thinking is an activity that occurs in regal isolation from other social activities antedates its apotheosis in the Enlightenment, e.g., in

political philosophy, they will be found in communicative practices for political discussion and debate. Such practices include tacit and explicit habits of thought, rhetorical conventions, and different modes by which political reports, commentaries, grievances, and other claims circulated in oral, scribal, and print communication.

A balanced assessment of continuity and change in communicative practices is essential for understanding the rise of a public sphere. Communication on political matters existed and took many forms long before the appearance of democratic innovations in practice or theory. These include proclamations that were printed on "broadsides," large single sheets designed to be affixed to a wall or post, along with homilies and sermons in churches, which taught the virtues of obedience and conveyed topical political messages. When judges of the King's Bench rode the assize circuit, they delivered explanations of royal policies to large audiences. Symbolic displays of authority were legion, in royal images that circulated on coinage, and in coronations, processions, and other occasions that used elaborate pageantry to convey lessons to subjects about the mutual duties that bound them and their rulers. Although such examples could be multiplied, it would be grossly anachronistic to equate traditional political communication and the concept of a public sphere. That concept refers not merely to opinions on public issues but specifically to the essentially *contestable* status of public opinions and their authority for ultimately setting a legislative agenda. In neither form nor content did traditional communicative practices in English politics—as we shall see, this also holds for elections—elevate the voice of the people to a position of normative authority. These practices were subject to norms of secrecy and privilege that precluded even the slightest intimation that politics ought to be subordinate to popular will.

Bringing history and theory into closer alignment also requires a resolution of the contradiction, noted above, between theories that rely on broad narratives of progress and historical research that, at the individual level, fails to disclose evidence of progressive intent. Indeed, this greatly understates the matter. Pervasive fear of change qua innovation is the dominant outlook of individuals, at all social levels, across the political spectrum, both in the early-seventeenth century and during the

---

Montaigne's description of his library: "There is my throne. I try to make my authority over it absolute, and to withdraw this one corner from all society, conjugal, filial, and civil." Michel de Montaigne, *Essays* (Stanford, 1958), p. 629. See also Roger Chartier, *The Cultural Origins of the French Revolution* (Durham, NC, 1991), p. 26; Anne Goldgar, *Impolite Learning: Conduct and Community in the Republic of Letters, 1680–1750* (New Haven, 1995), pp. 183–84.

midcentury Revolution. Here, I suggest, a little well-worn sociology provides needed guidance. Many studies of social change illustrate what I call "the paradox of innovation," instances of discontinuous change in which practitioners of innovative behavior do not acknowledge and even deny innovation. Although early-modern England is hardly unique, it provides some signal instances of this paradox, which are indispensable for assessing continuity and change in communicative practices at this time. The "invention" of public opinion in the English Revolution occurred at the level of communicative practice. Its inventors did not acknowledge the innovation, and with few exceptions they did not invest it with a principled foundation. Hence, I place quotation marks around "invention" when I borrow a phrase from Keith Baker's study, "Public Opinion as a Political Invention," in order to highlight differences between developments in eighteenth-century France and those analyzed in this book. In the former, public opinion was a linguistic innovation, a conceptual transformation that concealed continuities with older traditions of political authority.[7] In England the opposite situation occurred one century earlier: innovative communicative practices arose for which new words, like *public opinion*, were not coined.

THEORIES OF THE EARLY PUBLIC SPHERE

The importance of a public sphere is an old theme in social and political theories of democracy. Democracy's communicative underpinnings facilitate contestation among rival political interests, open debates that simultaneously constitute and invoke public opinion.[8] This appeal to public opinion is the ultimate source of authority in democratic polities for setting a legislative agenda. Hence, "the distinction between civil society and state . . . cannot fully account for what comes into being with the formation of democracy." Equally important is the rise "of a public space . . . whose existence blurs the conventional boundaries between the political and non-political."[9] The authority of opinion in the public

[7] Baker, *Inventing the French Revolution*, pp. 167–99; and see Mona Ozouf, "'Public Opinion' at the End of the Old Regime," in T. C. W. Blanning, ed., *The Rise and Fall of the French Revolution* (Chicago, 1996), pp. 98–110.

[8] Harold Lasswell observed that "the level of democratic attainment depends upon public opinion," and that public opinion exists only in virtue of debate. "Whenever a topic is beyond debate, the community no longer acts as a public." *Democracy through Public Opinion* (New York, 1941), pp. 20–21. When Walter Lippmann criticized this position, he noted that he was attacking a commonplace that held public opinion to be "the prime mover of democracy." *Public Opinion* (New York, 1922), p. 253. See also John Dewey, *The Public and Its Problems* (New York, 1927).

[9] Claude Lefort, *Democracy and Political Theory* (Minneapolis, 1988), p. 35; and see

sphere is not merely one attribute of liberal democracy but, rather, a precondition for many others, such as the franchise.

This point has been widely explored in influential studies of democracy—for example, in T. H. Marshall's account of the historical expansion of citizenship rights, which begin with civil rights, including communicative rights needed for a public sphere, and eventuate in political and social rights. It is a central theme in Habermas's analysis of critical uses of reason in public debates. It also receives due acknowledgment in recent comparative work on capitalism and democratic development. And it remains intact when distinctions are drawn between pure democracy and its representative variants that were adopted in England, France, and the United States.[10] The importance of the public sphere appears in structural-functional and neo-evolutionary theories that see growing societal complexity—differentiation—as a master trend in Western modernization. According to these theories, universalistic principles in the democratic public sphere—formal equality, tolerance, inclusion—are the integrative complement to higher levels of differentiation. This line of reasoning, fortified by cross-national comparative research, leads to the conclusion that success in institutionalizing democratic governance requires a supportive culture that underpins commitment to formal equality, civic participation, and tolerance.[11] Case studies pursued this theme, showing how the rise of political universalism in England followed a general trend in modernization toward "civic culture" and "value generalization."[12] In the revival of functionalist sociology by neofunctionalist writers, universalism in the public sphere continues to be understood as a secular extension of Protestant religion.[13] Many of these themes also appear in current work on "civil soci-

---

Leon Mayhew, "Political Rhetoric and the Contemporary Public," in P. Colomy, ed., *The Dynamics of Social Systems* (London, 1992), pp. 190–213.

[10] Marshall, *Citizenship and Social Development*, pp. 65–122; Habermas, *Structural Transformation*; Dietrich Rueschemeyer, Evelyne Stephens, and John Stephens, *Capitalist Development and Democracy* (Chicago, 1992), p. 44; Bernard Manin, *The Principles of Representative Government* (Cambridge, 1997), p. 169.

[11] Seymour Martin Lipset, "The Social Requisites of Democracy Revisited," *ASR* 59 (1994): 3–5, argues "that cultural factors appear even more important than economic ones" for democratic development (p. 5). For a different assessment of comparative data, see Rueschmeyer, Stephens, and Stephens, *Capitalist Development and Democracy*, pp. 41–78.

[12] Donald Hanson, *From Kingdom to Commonwealth: The Development of Civic Consciousness in English Political Thought* (Cambridge, MA, 1970); David Little, *Religion, Order, and Law: A Study in Pre-Revolutionary England* (Oxford, 1970). For the general pattern, see Gabriel Almond and Sidney Verba, *The Civic Culture: Political Attitudes and Democracy in Five Nations* (Boston, 1965); and Parsons, *Evolution of Societies*.

[13] E.g., Jeffrey Prager, "Totalitarian and Liberal Democracy," in J. Alexander, ed.,

ety," which stresses the importance of public opinion as the principal link between the liberal-democratic state and civil society.[14]

But after agreement on the importance of the public sphere and the utility of England as a modal case for studying its development, scholarly consensus vanishes. Though capitalism, the bourgeoisie, Protestantism, and differentiation are commonly cited as principal causes, references to these factors coexist with vast disagreement over when the public sphere appeared and precisely what in any of these causes had democratic implications for public life. Habermas delineates what may be the most widely held view when he traces the origins of the public sphere to the eighteenth century and to social elites, notably the bourgeoisie who participated in an elite world of letters.[15] Bendix, Parsons, and Wuthnow concur with Habermas on the eighteenth-century origins of the public sphere but not on the centrality of the bourgeoisie.[16] Marshall emphasizes legal imperatives of capitalist development and the involvement of the landed gentry in the eighteenth century. Earlier dates appear in other studies that locate democratic initiatives in the middle of the seventeenth century among the bourgeoisie or a broader grouping that includes the yeomanry and urban craftsmen as well as merchants. Change among the local gentry in the late-sixteenth century has been cited as the source of "a modern form of national politics, one in which individuals contested fundamental issues of governance."[17] Later dates for the birth of the public sphere appear in studies of the development of the newspaper and other news media. Alexander, Schudson, Giddens, and Gouldner place "the differentiation of a public sphere in the late

---

Neofunctionalism (Beverly Hills, CA, 1985), p. 188; Leon Mayhew, "In Defense of Modernity," *AJS* 89 (1984); Adam Seligman, *The Idea of Civil Society* (New York, 1992), p. 66.

[14] In addition to references in n. 2, chap. 1, see Ronald N. Jacobs, "Civil Society and Crisis," *AJS* 101 (1996); Lipset, "Requisites of Democracy," pp. 12–14; Margaret Somers, "Citizenship and the Place of the Public Sphere," *ASR* 58 (1993); Bryan S. Turner, "Citizenship, Social Change, and the Neofunctionalist Paradigm," in Colomy, *Dynamics of Social Sytems*, pp. 214–37.

[15] Habermas, *Structural Transformation.* See also Alvin Gouldner, *The Dialectic of Ideology and Technology* (New York, 1976), pp. 91–117; and the subsequent discussion in this chapter on the bourgeois public sphere.

[16] Reinhard Bendix, *Nation-Building and Citizenship* (Berkeley, 1964), p. 122; Bendix, *Kings or People?* p. 109; Parsons, *Evolution of Societies*, pp. 152, 168–73; Robert Wuthnow, *Communities of Discourse: Ideology and Social Structure in the Reformation, the Enlightenment, and European Socialism* (Cambridge, MA, 1989), pp. 218–19.

[17] Peter Bearman, *Relations into Rhetorics* (New Brunswick, NJ, 1993), p. 5; see also S. N. Eisenstadt, *Revolution and the Transformation of Societies* (New York, 1978), pp. 224–25; Mark Gould, *Revolution in the Development of Capitalism* (Berkeley, 1987); Jack Goldstone, *Revolution and Rebellion in the Early-Modern World* (Berkeley, 1991), pp. 125–34, 457–58.

eighteenth and early nineteenth centuries." Before this era, we are told, "political opinion remained almost exclusively within the realm of elite communication."[18]

Arguments about the religious sources of the public sphere exhibit no less variation than references to its class character. In contemporary sociology references to "revolutionary Puritanism," whose "revolutionary ideology" is held to have facilitated the rise of English democracy, is an article of faith.[19] But as they do with every class between the very bottom and top, contemporary sociologists cite every conceivable aspect of Protestantism to explain its link to universalistic values in the public sphere. This follows an intellectual tradition whose roots can be traced to the formation of sociological theories in the nineteenth century. Before Durkheim and Weber codified this tradition, Comte, Tocqueville, and Marx asserted that liberal-democratic ideology was a secular extension of Protestantism. This is implicit in Comte's negative remarks on revolutionary implications in "the dogma of unbounded liberty of conscience," explicit in Tocqueville's assessment of democracy. "Puritanism was not merely a religious doctrine," argued Tocqueville, "but corresponded in many points with the most absolute democratic and republican theories." For Marx, Protestantism was the ideology of the liberal bourgeoisie. In capitalism, "Christianity with its *cultus* of abstract man, more especially in its bourgeois developments, Protestantism, Deism, etc., is the most filling form of religion." Marx's analysis of English history depicted Puritanism as the ideology of the "bourgeois revolution" in the mid-seventeenth century. Later, after "the real aim had been achieved, when the bourgeois transformation of English society had been accomplished, Locke supplanted Habakkuk."[20] Subsequently, Durkheim and Weber placed more emphasis on Protestantism's unanticipated consequences, which, they argued, inadvertently promoted the rise of liberal-democratic politics. Both Durkheim and Weber found in Protestantism a radical individualism, admittedly neither foreseen nor

---

[18] Jeffrey Alexander, *Action and Its Environments* (New York, 1988), p. 207; Michael Schudson, "Toward a Comparative History of Political Communication," *Comparative Social Research* 11 (1989): 152, and see pp. 152–55; and see also Anthony Giddens, *The Nation-State and Violence* (Berkeley, 1985), pp. 210–211; Gouldner, *Dialectic of Ideology and Technology*, p. 95. Cf. Craig Calhoun, "Populist Politics, Communications Media, and Large Scale Societal Integration," *Sociological Theory* 6 (1988): 225, 229.

[19] Bearman, *Relations into Rhetorics*, p. 171; Goldstone, *Revolution and Rebellion*, p. 132, and see pp. 126, 273, 422–23; Gould, *Revolution in the Development of Capitalism*, pp. 222, 226–27, 284–85. A principal source for this view is Michael Walzer, *The Revolution of the Saints: A Study in the Origins of Radical Politics* (Cambridge, MA, 1965).

[20] Auguste Comte, *The Positive Philosophy* (London, [1830–42] 1896), 2:148–54; Alexis de Tocqueville, *Democracy in America* (N.Y., [1835–40] 1945), p. 33; Karl Marx, *Capital* (London, [1867] 1967), 1:79; Karl Marx, *The 18th Brumaire of Louis Bonaparte* (1852), in *Collected Works* (London, 1979), 11:105.

favored by Luther, Calvin, or other leaders of reform. Though unintended, Protestantism's corrosive impact on traditionalism unleashed
a growing individualism that buttressed claims on behalf of tolerance
and the right of individuals to act as autonomous agents in economic
and political life. On this point, at least, Durkheim and Weber are of one
mind, though they differ over the issue of whether religious developments are symptoms or independent causes of modern individualism.[21]
This issue continues to divide contemporary sociologists. Some see
Protestantism as a symptom, *pace* Gellner, who argues, "Democracy and
Protestantism reflect the abolition of fundamental political or cognitive
privilege." Others treat it is a cause but accord it varying degrees of significance. According to Lipset, "Protestantism's emphasis on individual
responsibility furthered the emergence of democratic values." Parsons
goes further in this line of thought: "The most important single root of
modern democracy is Christian individualism."[22]

But what specifically in Protestantism led to political universalism?
Contemporary sociologists offer many, inconsistent answers to this
question. A perennial favorite is the "priesthood of all believers," which
suggests a parallel between equality in religion and universalism in the
public realm of democracy. The "origins of the value-commitment
within Western democracies derive most broadly," according to this
view, "from the Protestant Reformation in which each person came be
seen as equally sacred in the eyes of God." This development, says
Robert Bellah, occurred as a secular extension and application of theological tenets to politics. "The 'priesthood of all believers' . . . was applied to secular politics in the course of the Puritan Revolution in England and eventuated in the secular democratic theory of John
Locke."[23] Other sociologists explain democratic culture as a secular extension of Protestantism by citing this doctrine or one of more of the
following: "justification by faith," "the communion of the saints,"
Puritan covenant theology, Calvinism, Arminianism, Presbyterian models of church order, predestination, asceticism, and the sanctity of
conscience.[24] This wide-ranging collection of causes is the inevitable

[21] For further discussion of this point, see David Zaret, "Religion and the Rise of Liberal-Democratic Ideology in Seventeenth-Century England," *ASR* 54 (1989): 166–67.

[22] Ernest Gellner, *Plough, Sword, and Book* (Chicago, 1989), p. 263, and see pp. 100–
112; Seymour Martin Lipset, *Political Man* (New York, 1963), p. 57; and see Lipset,
"Requisites of Democracy," p. 5; Talcott Parsons, *Sociological Theory and Modern Society*
(New York, 1967), p. 406.

[23] Prager, "Totalitarian and Liberal Democracy," p. 188; Robert Bellah, *Beyond Belief:
Essays on Religion in a Post-Traditional World* (New York, 1970), p. 68.

[24] Jeffrey Alexander, *Theoretical Logic in Sociology* (Berkeley, 1983), 4:130, 384;
Bendix, *Kings or People?* pp. 309–13; Stephen Kalberg, "Cultural Foundations of Modern
Citizenship," in Bryan Turner, *Citizenship and Social Theory* (London, 1993), pp. 98–99;
Little, *Religion, Order, and Law*; Mayhew, "Defense of Modernity," pp. 1281–82; David

consequence of methodological problems that I discussed in the previous chapter. Speculation is endless when texts by Enlightenment philosophers or Protestant divines are the principal evidence for democracy's cultural origins in sociological analyses that follow a hedgehog logic of explanation by citing parallels or affinities between great texts and epochal trends or structures.

Of course, it would be unwise to deny the importance of economic and religious factors in the emergence of a public sphere. Criticism of speculative, inconsistent references to capitalism and Protestantism as causes of the public sphere does not imply that we cease to think about capitalist development or religious change in early-modern Europe. After all, the "invention" of public opinion occurred during civil wars denominated by religious issues. And nowhere else in the early-modern era were capitalist principles—calculated assumption of risk based on entrepreneurial estimates of popular demand for competitively produced commodities—better exemplified than in printing. But the relevance of these religious and economic factors must be sought in their connection to specific communicative developments.

Scant *empirical* support exists for the claim that the public sphere was an extension of key aspects of Protestantism. We shall see that during the English Revolution different factions with starkly opposed views on religion followed similar practices in the competitive use of printed texts to appeal to public opinion. Consequences of these practices that spawned a public sphere include the dialogic imposition of order on political conflict, assertive claims on behalf of a right to petition, and growing authority claimed for opinions advanced in petitions. Religion is certainly not irrelevant for these developments, but its causal relevance should not be sought in speculation about affinities between attributes of Protestantism and liberal-democratic presuppositions. We shall also see that religious dissent in prerevolutionary England displays many of the economic and technical effects of printing that appear in political discourse in the 1640s. These include growing popular access to debates over purely religious issues—Puritan demands for liturgical reform—marked by the imposition of dialogic order by printing. Hence, the relevance of religion for the public sphere lies in linkages to communicative developments. Beyond this, the affinity alleged to exist between religion and democratic culture is a classic instance of a spurious relationship, where the religious and political variables of interest display the same economic and technical effects of printing.

Martin, *A General Theory of Secularization* (New York, 1979), pp. 25–29; Parsons, *Evolution of Societies*, p. 132; Seligman, *Idea of Civil Society*, pp. 66–70; Edward A. Tiryakian, "Neither Marx nor Durkheim . . . Perhaps Weber," *AJS* 81 (1975): pp. 24–25.

This criticism also holds for class-centered analyses that stress the centrality of the rising bourgeoisie or, more generally, capitalist development for the early public sphere. When these claims displace interest in the capitalist organization of early-modern printing and commercial motives in print culture, the problem of spuriousness arises in sweeping, implausible assertions about the bourgeois nature of the early public sphere or early-modern England *en tout*. As I noted above, the essential point of departure for current accounts along these lines is the celebrated study by Jürgen Habermas, composed as his *Habilitationsschrift* in 1961, *Structural Transformation of the Public Sphere*. The continuing importance of this early work by Habermas derives from its historical and institutional model of the public sphere. Taking England as the paradigmatic case, Habermas's historical-institutional model represents an advance over earlier writings by critical theorists, whose descriptions of the eclipse of reason and the ensuing collapse of progressive politics derive from interpretations of broad movements in social and political theory. Moreover, the historical-institutional model of the public sphere presented in *Structural Transformation* anticipates a fusion of Marxism and neo-evolutionary theories that view differentiation as a master trend in history.

Habermas explains growing universalism in public discourse in terms of its potential for securing social integration under conditions of growing system differentiation. Unlike functionalist and neofunctionalist writers, however, Habermas attributes little importance to religious developments as a source of universalistic discourse in a public sphere.[25] Instead, he relies on an orthodox Marxist analysis of structural requisites of capitalist development. This shows how fragmented sovereignty in feudalism, with its conditional restraints on property, was superseded by structural transformations in early-capitalist development that differentiated a private realm—civil society—from a public realm of sovereign authority. The outcome was centralized sovereign authority in the nation-state, capital as private property, and, in the wake of these developments, the public sphere as the mediator between these public and private realms of capitalist civilization. "The bourgeois public sphere may be conceived above all as the sphere of private people come together as a public; they soon claimed the public sphere regulated from above against the public authorities themselves, to engage them in a debate over the general rules governing relations in the basically privatized but publicly relevant sphere of commodity production."[26] The hallmark of this public sphere—more rational, critical habits of thought—make it "a

[25] Habermas, *Structural Transformation*, p. 266.
[26] Ibid., p. 27.

sphere of criticism of public authority." Moreover, "the medium of this political confrontation was peculiar and without historical precedent: people's public use of their reason."[27] What facilitates critical use of reason, says Habermas, is the institutional autonomy of the public sphere. In part, its autonomy depends on boundaries between it and the state; otherwise, the public sphere lacks leverage to influence political decision making. Yet the public sphere's capacity to support rational, critical debate just as much depends on boundaries between it and the rule of capital in civil society. "The rational-critical debate of private people in the *salons*, clubs, and reading societies was not directly subject to the cycle of production and consumption, that is, to the dictates of life's necessities."[28]

Here Habermas reiterates an old theme in critical theory: the opposition between culture and civilization, respectively, as realms of freedom and necessity. This old theme in German philosophy had, earlier in this century, been developed by Alfred Weber and also by the first generation of critical theorists, most notably Adorno, Horkheimer, and Marcuse. They attributed the capacity for critical reason to bourgeois culture's isolation from material civilization. Only in virtue of this isolation was survival possible for critical ideas whose premises contradicted the exploitative and instrumental logic in material civilization. Yet the same historical forces that created the bourgeois public sphere later led to its demise when, in advanced stages of capitalist development, market forces expanded into hitherto inviolable realms of culture. Mass culture destroys the public sphere's autonomy, for when discursive processes follow the logic of commodity production, the public sphere ceases to exist.

Since publication of his thesis, Habermas's analysis of the public sphere has undergone several conceptual revisions. But the model of cultural dynamics in modernization clearly survives the "linguistic turn" taken by Habermas over the last two decades. The critical rationality associated with the bourgeois public sphere reappears in theories developed around the key categories, first, of work and interaction, later, instrumental and communicative rationalities. This latter distinction departs from the bleak pessimism of the first generation of critical theorists who, Habermas argues, erred in equating rationalization with instrumental rationality.[29] In communicative rationality Habermas finds the immanent source of universalism that he, and the older generation of critical theorists, had attributed to high bourgeois culture. The distinction between culture and capitalist civilization is replaced by Ha-

---

[27] Ibid., pp. 27, 51.   [28] Ibid., p. 160.
[29] Jürgen Habermas, *The Theory of Communicative Action* (Boston, 1987), 2:372–403.

bermas's analysis of differences between the instrumental logic in "the self-steering of functional systems" and "the lifeworld potential for self-organization and for the self-organized use of the means of communication."[30] Hence, the source of public reason is not merely a specific historical development, the bourgeois public sphere, but, more generally, communicative reason in the lifeworld: the universality of validity claims that, he argues, implicitly attach to speech acts when they are intended to secure intersubjective agreement. Unlike instrumental reason, "Communicative reason does not simply encounter ready-made subjects and systems; rather, it takes part in structuring what is to be preserved. The utopian perspective of reconciliation and freedom is ingrained in the conditions for the communicative sociation of individuals."[31] Here, in place of the historical-institutional model of the public sphere in his earlier work, Habermas relies on a Kantian category, the ideal speech situation as a regulatory concept, in order to develop the rational foundations for morality and the public sphere in speech.

Yet after this linguistic turn in critical theory, profound continuities remain. Habermas describes problems formerly associated with the demise of the public sphere in terms of the "colonization" of "lifeworlds" by "systems," which blocks the unfettering of the rationality potential inherent in communicative action. This analysis restates at a higher level of abstraction earlier arguments about mass culture's assault on the bourgeois public sphere, but now it has a more general formulation. Older claims about the institutional autonomy of the bourgeois public sphere as the basis for critical use of reason reappear in more recent work by Habermas when he discusses the spontaneous emergence of public spheres over specific issues—a public sphere is "a structure that stands on its own and reproduces itself *out of itself*" (original emphasis).[32] In this context, spontaneity signals that "a rationalized lifeworld supports the development of a liberal public sphere." The same communicative reason underpins both the public sphere and the lifeworld—formerly though imperfectly understood as the private realm. And the principal historical example offered by Habermas as evidence for this development is "the bourgeois public sphere" in early-modern Europe.[33]

Of course, Habermas is not solely responsible for the fact that seldom does sociological discussion of the early public sphere fail to reference its capitalist origins or bourgeois character. His earlier thesis in *Structural*

---

[30] Ibid., p. 364.

[31] Jürgen Habermas, *The Theory of Communicative Action* (Boston, 1984), 1:398.

[32] Jürgen Habermas, *Between Facts and Norms* (Cambridge, MA, 1998), p. 364, and see pp. 380–84; Habermas, *Theory of Communicative Action*, 2:364–65.

[33] Habermas, *Between Facts and Norms*, pp. 366, 382.

Transformation is broadly congruent with traditional Marxist views on democracy and, in its particular details, is not entirely original.[34] Moreover, the centrality of capitalist development for the public sphere is a key theme in other influential accounts, most notably T. H. Marshall's analysis of the historical expansion of citizenship rights, first outlined in a short essay published in 1949. Marshall attributed this expansion—from civil rights of association and communication to political rights such as the universal franchise and, lastly, social rights pertaining to economic welfare—to legal imperatives at different stages of capitalist development. The importance of Marshall's analysis for Anglo-American studies of citizenship has been noted,[35] which is equivalent to Habermas's influence on studies of the public sphere by continental scholars. Such distinctions, however, have faded, due in part to the growing international stature of Habermas, which prompted the belated publication of an English translation of his *Öffentlichkeit* thesis and a companion book of essays that explored its utility and relevance.[36]

Several sources thus lead to current thinking on the early public sphere as an accretion of capitalism. Yet this thesis, though now admirably cosmopolitan, runs counter to prevailing views among historical specialists who do not think that interests and conflicts associated with an ascending bourgeoisie were central to revolutionary politics and democratic developments in early-modern England. If the thesis refers to the social composition of participants in the English Revolution, we shall see that revisionist scholarship requires that we reject it. Only by labeling virtually all participants "bourgeois" can the thesis be defended against evidence amassed by revisionist scholarship. If the thesis refers more broadly to central tendencies in English historical development, then supportive empirical evidence becomes displaced by a *post hoc ergo propter hoc* line of speculation on links between capitalist development and innovation in communicative practices: for example, the public sphere appeared when England was undergoing capitalist development; therefore the public sphere was bourgeois because it advanced interests that, by definition, corresponded to the dominant class in capitalist society. And when "it"—communicative practices that constitute the public sphere—is not an object of empirical study, the line of reasoning becomes as irresistible as it is fatuous. Thus we return to the impasse

---

[34] For an interpretation of the English coffeehouse, the French salon, and the concomitant growth of a reading public as evidence of the bourgeois origins of "public opinion as a prominent factor in politics," see Hans Speier, "Historical Development of Public Opinion," *AJS* 55 (1950): 380–82.

[35] Somers, "Citizenship and the Public Sphere," p. 590; Turner, "Contemporary Problems in the Theory of Citizenship," pp. 6–8.

[36] Craig Calhoun, ed., *Habermas and the Public Sphere* (Cambridge, MA, 1992).

between theories of the public sphere and contemporary historical scholarship.

Up to now, this impasse has not been problematic because it has been concealed by serene confidence in the evident and proven status of claims about the bourgeois nature and capitalist underpinnings of the early public sphere. "Marshall's view of citizenship," writes Michael Mann, "is essentially true—at least as a description of what actually happened in Britain." For Fredric Jameson and Stanley Aronowitz, a key issue is whether principles of the "bourgeois" public sphere are implicitly universal, as Habermas contends, or inherently constrained by narrow interests and the cramped vision of a particular class and gender. That Habermas correctly describes "the cultural-technical context in which the public of the bourgeois public sphere was constituted" remains unquestioned.[37] A recent study of extant writings on the sociology of citizenship critically observes that, following Marshall, "most scholars assume that the legal requirements of an emergent capitalist society were chiefly responsible for the birth of modern citizenship rights."[38]

The thesis of the capitalist origins of the public sphere also gains support from the fact that scholars associate it with different historical claims. It can mean that "bourgeois rights of civil and political membership" were necessary for capitalist development; and yet, *pace* Giddens, the relationship between "bourgeois rights" and class conflict may be "double-edged."[39] From this we can conclude that no simple relationship exists between social class and the early public sphere, that different social classes at different moments promoted its development, and that citizenship and social class can be opposing principles—a central theme in Marshall.[40] In its simplest form, the capitalist thesis holds that the early public sphere was bourgeois because its participants or the societies in which it arose were bourgeois. In acknowledging that little evidence shows that participants in the early public sphere were bourgeois, Calhoun dismisses the claim "that what made the public sphere bourgeois was simply the class composition of its members. Rather, it was *society* [original emphasis] that was bourgeois, and bourgeois society

---

[37] Michael Mann, "Ruling Class Strategies and Citizenship," *Sociology* 21 (1987): 339–40; Fredric Jameson, "On Negt and Kluge," in B. Robbins, ed., *The Phantom Public Sphere* (Minneapolis, 1993), p. 48; Michael Warner, "The Mass Public and the Mass Subject," in Robbins, *Phantom Public Sphere*, p. 238–39. See Stanley Aronowitz, *Dead Artists, Live Theories, and Other Cultural Problems* (London, 1994), p. 312.

[38] Somers, "Citizenship and the Public Sphere," p. 588.

[39] Turner, "Problems in the Theory of Citizenship," p. 7; Giddens, *The Nation-State and Violence*, pp. 208–9.

[40] Marshall, *Citizenship and Social Development*, p. 84.

produced a certain form of public sphere." Elsewhere, Calhoun cites the urban milieu as the specifically "bourgeois" attribute of the early public sphere.[41] Other descriptions of the bourgeois attribute of the public sphere have also been advanced. Wuthnow links the early public sphere in France to "a bourgeoisie of professional bureaucrats and office-holders."[42] Habermas cites the economic content of debates in the early public sphere, "debate over the general rules governing relations in the basically privatized but publicly relevant sphere of commodity production and social labor."[43] Yet none of these claims derives much support from empirical analysis of communicative change in seventeenth-century England, which, as we shall see, militates against all lines of inquiry that locate the birth of the public sphere in the eighteenth century and tie its appearance to institutional or cultural accretions of bourgeois society. Use of printed petitions to constitute and invoke public opinion in politics occurs in the middle of the seventeenth century, when it was neither limited to urban areas, reliant on a state bureaucracy, nor oriented principally to economic debates. The ineluctable conclusion, then, is that the emergence of a public sphere has few, if any, *direct* links to anything "bourgeois," although we shall encounter many indirect links—for example, in the capitalist organization of printing.

A closely related issue is the preoccupation in current scholarship with the restrictive scope and content of communicative practices in the early public sphere. Unmasking the ideological facade of the public sphere has long been a popular academic pastime. Today, old arguments about the bourgeois character and limits of the early public sphere take new forms in which, according to one proponent, "we now speak routinely of alternative public spaces and counterpublics" where subjugated discourse flourishes in working-class, female, and black communities. In this literature the public sphere described by Habermas and Marshall serves as a foil for showing how inequalities based on class, gender, and race preclude the realization of universalistic ideals.[44] Oddly enough,

---

[41] Craig Calhoun, "Introduction," in Calhoun, *Habermas and the Public Sphere*, p. 7, and see p. 42; Calhoun, "Populist Politics," pp. 225–27.

[42] Wuthnow, *Communities of Discourse*, p. 206.

[43] Habermas, *Structural Transformation*, p. 27.

[44] B. Robbins, "Introduction," in Robbins, *Phantom Public Sphere*, p. xvii; and see The Black Public Sphere Collective, *The Black Public Sphere* (Chicago, 1995); Geoff Eley, "Nations, Publics, and Political Cultures," in Calhoun, *Habermas and the Public Sphere*, pp. 289–331; Nancy Fraser, "Rethinking the Public Sphere," in Calhoun, *Habermas and the Public Sphere*, pp. 109–42; Elizabeth C. Goldsmith and Dena Goodman, eds., *Going Public: Women and Publishing in Early Modern France* (Ithaca, 1995); Susan Herbst, *Politics and the Margin: Historical Studies of Public Expression outside the Mainstream* (Cambridge, 1994), pp. 65–95; Oskar Negt and Alexander Kluge, *Public Sphere and Experience: Toward an Analysis of the Bourgeois and Proletarian Public Sphere* (Minneapolis, 1993); Iris Young,

these otherwise critical writings—many rely on sophisticated epistemological critiques from critical theory, feminism, and postmodernism—
credulously accept Habermas's account of the bourgeois origins of the
public sphere and thereby provide further instances of the discrepancy
noted long ago between lively debates over the fate of the public sphere
in the modern world and uncritical acceptance of Habermas's account
of its bourgeois origins in early-modern Europe.[45] It is also ironic that
this literature overstates exclusionary practices in the early public sphere,
for this obscures truly astounding claims by relatively humble citizens,
including women, to a right to participate in public debates.

A different view of the early public sphere—as a more popular, less
elitist phenomenon—arises when its history is developed empirically, in
terms of concrete communicative developments in popular as well as
elite cultures. To be sure, the difference is in degree, not kind. The turn
from speculative analyses that draw inferences about the early public
sphere from social categories—for example class or gender—to empirical study of communicative practices does not eliminate discrepancies
between universalistic claims and less-than-ideal practices. In its earlier
English and later French variants, the early-modern "public" never was
synonymous with "the people," any more than it is in modern democracies. Debate in the early-modern public sphere often invokes "the people" and involves persons drawn from remarkably diverse social backgrounds. But participants in those debates—even broadly construed as
speakers, hearers, writers, publishers, printers, readers—represent only a
subset of "the people." For the most part (we shall encounter significant
exceptions), participation in the nascent public sphere in early-modern
England depended on access to unequally distributed literary and economic resources that facilitated participation in print culture.[46]

Yet this last caveat affords little support for the claim that in its early
development the public sphere was an extension of learned culture to
which only social elites had access. Central to this claim is a view of
early-modern culture that underestimates the social distribution of literacy and draws an unsustainable distinction between elite and popular cultures. This, too, is a view long abandoned by historians,[47] but it

---

"Impartiality and the Civic Public," in S. Benhabib and D. Cornell, eds., *Feminism as Critique* (Minneapolis, 1987), pp. 63–64.

[45] Jean L. Cohen, "Why More Political Theory?" *Telos* 40 (1979): 71.

[46] Chartier, *Cultural Origins of the French Revolution*, pp. 21–37; Habermas, *Structural
Transformation*, pp. 31–43, 51–73.

[47] For a summary statement on this, see Roger Chartier, "Texts, Printings, Readings,"
in L. Hunt, ed., *The New Cultural History* (Berkeley, 1989), pp. 169–70. On the relevance
of this point for print culture in seventeenth-century England, see Harold Weber, *Paper
Bullets: Print and Kingship under Charles II* (Lexington, KY, 1996), pp. 8–10.

pervades contemporary writings on the public sphere and civil society that associate early liberal-democratic conceptions of public life with elite eighteenth-century circumstances, most usually identified as a bourgeois or a hybrid bourgeois-aristocratic world, the Enlightenment. "There is no doubt, at least as far as we are concerned, that the 'society' of the Enlightenment, constituting a new form of public life, was the prototype of the early modern concept of civil society."[48] But if we must choose *a* prototype, it should be print culture and not the Enlightenment. New forms of public life existed well before the elite eighteenth-century world of the Enlightenment, in innovative communicative practices that simultaneously constituted and invoked the authority of opinion in order to lobby political elites at the center and influence the views of individuals at the periphery of the political nation. These developments sprang up in the wake of communicative changes wrought by the printing press in Western Europe. Such changes spread rapidly, though unevenly, creating areas with surprisingly high levels of popular literacy and new public spaces in which religious authority and, subsequently, politics could become objects of discussion and debate.

One last caveat is important. The connection between printing and the birth of the public sphere has not been overlooked in current writings by sociologists and philosophers. For example, in *Structural Transformation* Habermas calls attention to the importance of printing—"the public sphere's preeminent institution"—for "the new domain of a public sphere whose decisive mark was the published word." Bendix devotes more attention to this point in his discussion of "intellectual mobilization" as an independent cause of democratic developments in modernization. Mayhew and Wuthnow refer to the new vocation of publicist created by pamphleteering.[49] Yet these remarks treat communicative developments in the printing revolution too narrowly, as a factor that facilitates change by disseminating new ideas more rapidly and to a broader audience. Historians of print culture in early-modern Europe have shown that novelty in the mode of communication can have intimate links with novel ideas.[50] Thus, the cultural impact of printing goes beyond issues of access and distribution. Printing of petitions as propa-

[48] Cohen and Arato, *Civil Society and Political Theory*, p. 87. See also Zygmunt Bauman, *Legislators and Interpreters* (Ithaca, 1987), pp. 26–35; Calhoun, "Introduction," pp. 7, 42; John B. Thompson, *Ideology and Modern Culture* (Stanford, 1990), pp. 109–14.

[49] Habermas, *Structural Transformation*, pp. 16, 24, 181; Bendix, *Kings or People?* pp. 256–58, 261–67; Mayhew, "In Defense of Modernity," pp. 1285–87; Wuthnow, *Communities of Discourse*, pp. 201–11; and see Calhoun, "Populist Politics."

[50] Elizabeth Eisenstein, *The Printing Press as an Agent of Change* (Cambridge, 1980), pp. 691–92; and see Roger Chartier, *The Cultural Uses of Print in Early Modern France* (Princeton, 1987); Robert Darnton, *The Business of Enlightenment* (Cambridge, MA, 1979).

ganda not only increased the scope of communication but also created novel practices that simultaneously constituted and invoked the authority of public opinion in political discourse.

Although I explore in the epilogue this theme and its implications for recent writings by Habermas on communicative rationality, it is important to observe here that Habermas's analysis of the early public sphere anticipates its subsequent fall, and that this anticipation shapes his assessment of the principal communicative development in the early-modern era: the printing revolution. Above, we examined Habermas's view that the public sphere ceases to be a viable forum for critical debate when it loses its institutional autonomy. "The model of the bourgeois public sphere," he writes, "presupposed strict separation of the public from the private realm." In its later stages, capitalist development destroys this separation, which occurs "to the extent that the press became commercialized." Habermas's conceptual framework thus led him to portray the early-modern press as a pristine extension of human reason. "A press that had evolved out of the public's use of its reason and that had merely been an extension of its debate remained thoroughly an institution of this very public."[51] This description, as we shall see, is very nearly the opposite of the reality of early-modern printing and print culture. Moreover, we shall also see that those developments which Habermas associates with the demise of reasoned debate in the public sphere—commerce and publicity—were not only central in printing and the culture of print but also in the early public sphere that arose when participants in the English Revolution relied on printed texts to constitute and invoke public opinion.

HISTORICAL REVISIONISM

The current impasse between theories of the public sphere and historical scholarship is largely a consequence of historical revisionism, which has demolished the underpinnings of historical perspectives that sustain these theories. At the core of revisionism is a blunt insight that militates against optimistic narratives of progress. The historical significance of revolutions is often less drastic than would be suggested by abrupt alterations in leaders, institutions, and policies that distinguish revolutionary from gradual change. More than cynicism about human nature and its potential for improvement supports this insight. We know, for example, that revolutionary regimes often follow a path that leads back to prerevolutionary antecedents. Restorations followed regicides in the English and French revolutions; Leninist regimes produced the

---

[51] Habermas, *Structural Transformation*, pp. 175–76, 181, 183.

monarchical cults of Stalin and Mao. Accordingly, revisionist scholars downplay the significance of major revolutions in history and emphasize the resilience of tradition concealed by narratives of progress—both in revolutionary ideologies and scholarly conventions for writing history. The history of revolution displays many marks of tradition's resilience: the social power of the English aristocracy was not broken by confiscation of Royalist lands in the English Revolution; French Catholicism survived Jacobin de-Christianization policies that extinguished its public practice by the spring of 1794; Confucian themes and tropes lay at the heart of Mao's delphic pronouncements.

Over the last two decades, revisionism has so dominated historical scholarship on early-modern England that it now resembles a graveyard for optimism about a convergence of historical and sociological scholarship. According to one proponent, the revisionist revolt opposed more than Whig and Marxist perspectives. It was "a salutary reaction against various forms of modernization theory." Or against any sociological explanation—as one critic of revisionist observes: "The Revisionists take it for granted that the failure of the traditional social interpretation [i.e., Whig and Marxist accounts] means the impossibility of *any* social interpretation."[52] Hence, revisionism rejects the interdisciplinary ideal of a synthesis between history and sociology. "The collapse of grand theories originating elsewhere in the academic world has allowed the effective reassertion of scholarly standards generated from within the historical profession." These standards are those advanced by traditional historiography: immersion in primary sources with the goal of *l'histoire événementielle*, "to return to the sources free of preconceptions."[53] In this context "preconceptions" refer to sociological concepts such as modernity, revolution, and class, whose use in studying the seventeenth century is held to be invariably anachronistic. Another anachronism is the concept of a political "opposition," because in both the early-Stuart era and Elizabethan England the importance of service to the Crown and patronage from royal councillors precluded formation of an organized opposition by MPs in Parliament.[54]

[52] John Morrill, *The Nature of the English Revolution* (New York, 1993), p. 35; Robert Brenner, *Merchants and Revolution* (Princeton, 1993), p. 645.

[53] J. C. D. Clark, *Revolution and Rebellion: State and Society in England in the Seventeenth and Eighteenth Centuries* (Cambridge, 1986), p. 23; Kevin Sharpe, "Revisionism Revisited," in K. Sharpe, ed., *Faction and Parliament* (London, 1985), p. x. Thomas Cogswell, "Coping with Revisionism in Early Stuart History," *Journal of Modern History* 62 (1990): 551, argues that revisionists "can derive a good deal of satisfaction from the knowledge that . . . they have at the very least forced a most distinguished body of scholars to abandon the pursuit of grand overarching theories and instead to ponder the facts."

[54] J. P. Cooper, "Introduction," in J. P. Cooper, ed., *Wentworth Papers, 1597–1628* (*CS*, 4th ser., 12, 1973), p. 7; Derek Hirst, "Court, Country, and Politics before 1629,"

Most generally, revisionist methodology relies on a related set of substantive claims advanced in recent historical research: that localism and loyalty to vertically integrated communities outweighed class divisions and religious commitments, even in the Revolution, when deference and patronage remained the common coin of politics.[55] This revisionist interpretation, concedes a leading critic, "is a powerful and coherent one."[56] It demolishes suppositions central to sociological accounts about the bourgeois nature of the English Revolution because, as a leading Marxist historian acknowledges, "it has yet to be shown that those who supported Parliament and those who supported the Crown . . . differed systematically in social class terms." When another observes, "Most historians reject the idea that the civil war was a class conflict," he can offer only the feeble response that "evidence of class hostility has proved impossible to ignore completely."[57] Suppositions about modernizing tendencies in Puritanism fare equally poorly. In contrast to references to revolutionary Puritanism in sociological accounts, revisionist writings ascribe Puritan opposition to Church and State in 1640 not to modern or democratic tendencies, but to their opposite: an aversion to innovation, which Puritans adhered to as much as, if not more than, their religious adversaries.[58]

Though sociologists can set aside revisionism's epistemological claims—we are properly skeptical about inquiry uncontaminated by presuppositions—empirical issues are more difficult. Invoking the inevitability of theory in empirical inquiry will not rescue sociological accounts of early democratic developments that were propelled by capitalist

---

in Sharpe, *Faction and Parliament*, pp. 105–37; Conrad Russell, *Parliaments and English Politics, 1621–1629* (Oxford, 1979), pp. 5–26; G. R. Elton, *Studies in Tudor and Stuart Politics and Government* (Cambridge, 1974–92), 3:158.

[55] E.g., Anthony Fletcher, *The Outbreak of the English Civil War* (London,1981); Mark Kishlansky, *The Rise of the New Model Army* (Cambridge, 1979); Mark Kishlansky, *Parliamentary Selection* (Cambridge, 1986); John Morrill, *Cheshire, 1630–1660* (Oxford, 1974); John Morrill, *The Revolt of the Provinces* (London, 1976); Morrill, *Nature of the English Revolution*; Conrad Russell, ed., *Origins of the English Civil War* (London, 1973); Russell, *Unrevolutionary England*; Conrad Russell, *The Fall of the British Monarchies, 1637–1642* (Oxford, 1993); Kevin Sharpe, *The Personal Rule of Charles I* (New Haven, 1992); Austin Woolrych, *Soldiers and Statesmen: The General Council of the Army and Its Debates, 1647–1648* (Oxford, 1987).

[56] David Underdown, *A Freeborn People: Politics and the Nation in Seventeenth-Century England* (Oxford, 1996), p. 5.

[57] Brenner, *Merchants and Revolution*, p. 643, and see p. 641; Brian Manning, *The English People and the English Revolution* (London, 1991), pp. 41–42.

[58] E.g., Patrick Collinson, *The Religion of Protestants: The Church in English Society, 1559–1625* (Oxford, 1981); Peter Lake, *Moderate Puritans and the Elizabethan Church* (Cambridge, 1982); Nicholas Tyacke, *Anti-Calvinists: the Rise of English Arminianism ca. 1590–1640* (Oxford, 1987).

imperatives, led by the bourgeoisie, or animated by revolutionary Puritanism. Little support for such claims exists in contemporary historical scholarship, even among "postrevisionists," who rightly point out that revisionism overlooks evidence of political conflict in early-Stuart England and reject the revisionist claim that this conflict had no social basis.[59] Nor do these claims gain added credibility from concessions by leading revisionists that antecedent social change may be relevant for explaining the nature as opposed to the causes of the Revolution.[60] The key shortcoming of revisionism, for understanding early democratic developments, lies elsewhere, in its tendency to dismiss the significance of major revolutions and emphasize the resilience of tradition. Revisionism overlooks the fact that institutional and political changes, with which revolutions have been most closely identified, are not necessarily the most fertile ground for exploring a revolution's historical importance. This may derive instead from long-term implications of less visible cultural changes in a revolutionary epoch. Innovative ideas and perspectives generated in a revolutionary context can subsequently facilitate gradual change in directions that were, literally, unthinkable in the prerevolutionary era.[61]

The "invention" of public opinion in the English Revolution illustrates this point. Political and economic changes during the revolution had no lasting impact on English society. Aside from constitutional legislation in 1641 that deprived the monarchy of important prerogative powers, little else survived the Restoration in 1660, which brought back the Stuart monarchy, the House of Lords, and the bishops. Fiscal weakness of the government—a source of chronic conflict before 1640—was not remedied; a state church perpetuated religious tensions by imposing significant penalties on noncommunicants, though some dissent was now tolerated; and, as noted above, the social power of the aristocracy was unimpaired by the revolution. Yet the same revolution produced innovative communicative practices that led to novel ideas on the political order, ideas that upheld important democratic principles that sprang from experience with using printed texts to constitute and invoke public opinion in contests between rival political factions. Precociousness

[59] E.g., Richard Cust, *The Forced Loan and English Politics, 1626–1628* (Oxford, 1985); Jacqueline Eales, *Puritans and Roundheads: The Harleys of Brampton Bryan and the Outbreak of the English Civil War* (Cambridge, 1990); Ann Hughes, *Politics, Society, and Civil War in Warwickshire, 1620–1660* (Cambridge, 1987); Theodore K. Rabb, *Jacobean Gentleman: Sir Edwin Sandys, 1561–1629* (Princeton, 1998).

[60] Fletcher, *Outbreak of Civil War*, pp. 407–8; John Morrill, "Introduction," in J. Morrill, ed., *Reactions to the English Civil War* (London, 1982), p. 4; Russell, *Unrevolutionary England*, pp. xvii–xix.

[61] Perez Zagorin, *Rebels and Rulers, 1500–1660* (Cambridge, 1982), 2:185.

marks this development. It occurred in a revolutionary context framed by millennial expectations, before democratic institutions had a sustainable social environment. Individuals advocating democratic principles were a minority within a minority, a small part of the activist core that supported Parliament in its struggle with the Crown. Proponents of these ideas were decisively defeated, first by Cromwell, later by the Restoration, their success checked by gross discontinuities between democratic ideas and prevailing assumptions about the irrationality of "the multitudes" that placed deference and patronage at the core of politics.

My analysis of public opinion as a practice that ran ahead of its expression in formal theories strikes a balance between factors that are unique to English history and long-term changes that exhibit patterns found in the history of other societies. The latter certainly includes economic, social, and technical aspects of printing and their implications for print culture and popular literacy. These were no more unique to England than, say, growth in market forces. But due acknowledgment must also be given to London's unusual position, compared to continental cities, as the uncontested political and printing center of a nation. Equally important were the collapse of government control over the press in the 1640s, England's unusually high level of literacy, and other contingencies that facilitated unanticipated innovations amidst civil wars. This was the context in which traditional practices for expressing grievances were creatively reworked in the pursuit of specific political ends that for the most part were not democratic. Political tactics by the Long Parliament, the king, the army, and divergent religious and political factions relied on printing to constitute and invoke public opinion and provided the impetus for a rethinking of the nature and role of vox populi in politics. From these practical precedents subsequently emerged new perspectives in which older presuppositions on the centrality of deference and the irrationality of commoners receded before a novel sense of confidence in the rationality of public opinion. Had public opinion not developed as a practice in the middle of the seventeenth century, subsequent theories by Locke and others that put the pluralist pursuit of utility at the core of politics would have literally been unthinkable.

THE PARADOX OF INNOVATION

Emphasis on the importance of unintended consequences further distinguishes the account advanced here from prior sociological work on the public sphere. The absence of a philosophic rationale for communicative change in the English Revolution, along with persistence of old traditions that placed deference and patronage at the core of politics, explains the ambivalent reactions of contemporaries toward political appeals to public opinion. This development was unintended, occurring initially at the level of practice where it was neither sanctioned nor anticipated by theoretical formulations. That this development was not the outcome of democratic creeds will be inferred from the uniform distribution of novel petitioning practices among all parties in the English Revolution, most of whom disavowed any democratic creed. In tracing the public sphere to a creative reworking of communicative practices, especially petitioning, this study supplies evidence for a widespread, though paradoxical, feature of innovation, which arises when individuals do not acknowledge innovative behavior in which they participate.

The paradox of innovation has different sources and assumes different forms across societies. In early-modern England, reluctance to acknowledge innovation derived from the view that it was antithetical to fundamental principles of social and political order. Revisionist historians have produced many descriptively dense studies that display the prevalence of deep, widely shared attachments to prevailing ideas, institutions, and vertically integrated communities in seventeenth-century England. At this time, "history was not the study of the past as we would understand it but a glass in which man might observe universal truths."[62] This was the point of departure for reflection on politics and religion, which appears in the wholly unexceptional view of an official with long service in early-Stuart government: "I ever held it safest in matters of government rather to improve the received ordinary ways than to adventure upon any innovation." Outside government, it appears in *The Anatomy of Melancholy*, first published in 1621, in which Robert Burton cites the "alteration of laws and customs" alongside oppression and other grievances that can afflict the body politic. "Innovations" are also among the bad consequences enumerated by Burton—these include theft, treason, and murder—that occur when a nation is governed by dissolute rulers."[63]

Puritanism supplied no reasons for a more benign view of innovation. The "master deviance of religious innovation" is a central theme in contemporary political language that linked Protestantism, Parliament, and patriotism as allies united against a Catholic plot to destroy English lib-

[62] Kevin Sharpe, *Politics and Ideas in Early Stuart England* (London, 1989), p. 41. Before he traveled overseas in 1614 to France, John Holles received the following fatherly advice: "all changes are dangerous, be they never so small, both body and mind be sensible of them." P. R. Seddon, ed., *Letters of John Holles* (*Thoroton Society Record Series* 31 1975), 1:53.

[63] Michael Young, *Servility and Service: The Life and Work of Sir John Coke* (London, 1986), p. 62; Robert Burton, *The Anatomy of Melancholy* (Oxford, 1622), pp. 68, 70.

erty.[64] Puritan preachers fueled the outbreak of the Revolution with grim warnings about innovation. "Take heed of innovating in religion," they preached. "Innovation has been ever held so dangerous that the fear thereof brought our prudent state to a pause." One cleric perceptively worried that "while we complain of innovations, we shall do nothing but innovate."[65] Even as "King Pym" in the Long Parliament and the earl of Strafford, the principal government minister of Charles I, fought their deadly struggle, they agreed "in an ideological rejection of change."[66] Few contemporaries would have been puzzled by a report from Rutland that it was "the innovating clergy" in the summer of 1642 who willingly read proclamations and declarations from Charles I but "none that come from the Parliament."[67] Innovation was, then, a sign of political malignancy. All sides invoked the "ancient constitution" and "primitive church" as models, respectively, for contemporary political and religious institutions. Accordingly, MPs ransacked medieval records for precedents to justify parliamentary initiatives against the monarchy. To be sure, such precedents could be challenged by questioning their probative value or utility for disputes over the nature and scope of the Crown's prerogative powers.[68] Yet the paradox of innovation involves more than mere veneration of precedent. The appeal to precedent springs from "anxiety to conceal the fact of unprecedented change." Even radical ideas were "frequently expressed in a phantasmagoric historicism like the Levellers' dreams of the halcyon days of Edward the Confessor."[69] Marx and Weber noted the paradox of innovation in seventeenth-century England: Marx, in remarks on traditionalism in the English Revolution at the beginning of *The 18th Brumaire of Louis Bonaparte*; Weber, in the claim that innovative economic orientations arising out of Puritanism were wholly unintended.

Seventeenth-century England may be a rich site for exploring the paradox of innovation, but it is hardly unique to this era. Following Edward Shils, we know that innovation can be stimulated by traditions that value

[64] Alastair Bellany, " 'Raylinge Rymes and Vaunting Verse': Libellous Politics in Early Stuart England, 1603–1628," in K. Sharpe and P. Lake, eds., *Culture and Politics in Early-Stuart England* (Stanford, 1993), p. 295.

[65] E177[11] (1641), p. 62; E179[7] (1642), p. 6.

[66] Russell, *Unrevolutionary England*, p. xvii.

[67] *MSS Nalson* 2, fol. 72.

[68] E.g., Clive Holmes, "Liberty, Taxation, and Property," in J. H. Hexter, ed., *Parliament and Liberty from the Reign of Elizabeth to the English Civil War* (Stanford, 1992), pp. 129, 141.

[69] Keith Thomas, *Religion and the Decline of Magic* (Harmondsworth, 1973), p. 504; Mark Kishlansky, "Ideology and Politics in the Parliamentary Armies, 1645–1649," in Morrill, *Reactions to the English Civil War*, pp. 164–65.

it. And Thomas Kuhn points out that an "essential tension" requires the successful scientist simultaneously to be a "traditionalist" and "iconoclast."[70] Recent studies of ethnicity arrive at the constructivist conclusion that "it is as common for traditional ethnic sentiments to be modified . . . as it is for recently introduced practices to be labeled as traditional."[71] Eric Hobsbawm describes "invented traditions"; Craig Calhoun, the "radicalness of tradition."[72] These examples lend support for the supposition that paradoxical features of innovation accentuate two general aspects of interpretative processes: first, a propensity to impose interpretative continuity on experience (even if continuity arises out of neophilia); second, the tacit nature of interpretative activity that sustains impressions of continuity (or normality). In the case at hand, the paradox of innovation arises from reluctance to acknowledge communicative innovation that violates communicative norms of secrecy and privilege in politics and more general social norms that predicate politics on deference and patronage.

Participants in the invention of public opinion in the 1640s never fully grasped the radically new assumptions about human nature implicit in this innovation. First, appeals to public opinion imply an optimistic assessment of human abilities, confidence in our capacity for improvement that separates Lockean liberalism from the broad Protestant tradition that emphasized the corruption and limitations of reason.[73] Second, public opinion in politics contradicts the then prevailing idea that irrationality inversely correlates with social rank, an idea deeply reflective of patriarchal and hierarchical principles in early-modern England. It is not surprising, then, that participants displayed ambivalent or contradictory views on innovation in political practices that involved appeals to public opinion during the English Revolution. Though printing facilitated innovative political practices in a context framed by constitutional and religious crises, these crises left undisturbed key presuppositions that shaped contemporary thinking on social and political issues: that deference is a prime social virtue and patronage the common coin of politics. Further complicating the situation is the fact that innovative

[70] Edward Shils, *Tradition* (Chicago, 1981); Thomas Kuhn, *The Essential Tension: Selected Studies in Scientific Tradition and Change* (Chicago, 1977), p. 227.

[71] Stephen Stern and John Cicala, "Introduction," in *Creative Ethnicity* (Logan, UT, 1991), p. xii; see also W. Sollors, ed., *The Invention of Ethnicity* (Oxford, 1989). I owe these references to Mitch Berbrier.

[72] Eric Hobsbawm, "Introduction: Inventing Traditions," in E. Hobsbawm and T. Ranger, eds., *The Invention of Tradition* (Cambridge, 1983); Craig Calhoun, "The Radicalism of Tradition," *AJS* 88 (1983).

[73] On the reformed tradition and reason, see John Morgan, *Godly Learning: Puritan Attitudes toward Reason, Learning, and Education, 1560–1640* (Cambridge, 1986), pp. 43–61.

communicative practices were not wholly discontinuous with the past. We shall see that contemporaries often found innovation where it was least evident. For example, they emphasized the unprecedented freedom of printers in the 1640s, forgetting that the Privy Council was unable to do much about circulation of news in manuscript form in the 1620s.[74] They also minimized far-reaching, substantive changes in political communication by confining their attention to rhetorical continuities. Deferential rhetoric in petitions concealed radically new uses for printed petitions as devices that allowed petitioners to invoke public opinion in order to lobby members of Parliament. Thus, there were many reasons for the ambivalence and confusion that greeted innovative practices that created the first democratic public sphere.

[74] Cust, *The Forced Loan and English Politics*, p. 151.

CHAPTER THREE

Secrecy and Privilege

> For the Actions of men proceed from their Opinions; and in
> the well governing of Opinions, consisteth the well governing
> of mens Actions. . . . It belongeth therefore to him that hath
> the Sovereign Power, to be Judge, or constitute all Judges of
> Opinions and Doctrines, as a thing necessary to Peace;
> thereby to prevent Discord and Civil War.
> (Thomas Hobbes, *Leviathan*)

IN EARLY-MODERN ENGLAND political communication was riddled with
contradictions between theory and practice. Political messages traveled
in all directions in prerevolutionary England, but contemporary reflection on the subject often overlooked that which was widespread in practice. In principle, no public space existed for discussion and debate on
public issues, which occurred in "councils," such as the Crown's Privy
Council or Parliament, where a customary though limited right of free
speech in the fifteenth century had evolved into a formal privilege under
the Tudors. Confined to Parliament, this privilege exempted MPs from
secrecy norms that prohibited debate on public issues but it did not extend beyond Parliament. For example, in debates over a response from
the Commons after Charles I imprisoned John Eliot for critical remarks
in the 1626 Parliament, members distinguished Eliot's case from the
case of Peter Wentworth, an MP imprisoned by Elizabeth in 1593. Eliot
delivered his remarks on the floor of the Commons—this was within the
scope of parliamentary privilege—but Wentworth and others met privately before Parliament convened, a clear violation of the norms of secrecy and privilege that confined political conversations to Parliament.[1]

Communicative practice, however, was another matter. From the
reign of Elizabeth onward, speeches and other parliamentary proceedings "were copied in larger quantities than any other kind of scribally
published text."[2] Despite norms of secrecy, members included accounts
of proceedings in letters to relatives and patrons, and recorded "abbreviated jottings of a diary" (see fig. 1). Formal newsletters appeared dur-

---

[1] *PP 1626* 3:244–46, 251–52, 270–71.

[2] Harold Love, *Scribal Publication in Seventeenth-Century England* (Oxford, 1993),
p. 9.

Fig. 1. Enlargement of part of a contemporary woodcut, *The True Manner of the Sitting of the Lords & Commons*, during the earl of Strafford's trial in Parliament in 1641. One earl (among seated members wearing hats) and three MPs, in the gallery immediately behind the earls, are shown taking notes of proceedings. Strafford is standing in the foreground, facing the clerks who also record the proceedings. 669f.4[12].

ing the 1626 Parliament, "aiming at a full narrative" of parliamentary proceedings. These circulated widely when the 1628 Parliament was in session and contained "full accounts, in grammatical and consecutive prose, of most of the main speeches."[3] Scribal reports of news covered contentious events in the Short Parliament (see fig. 2) and in the first session of the Long Parliament, when speeches were printed—a new development that was tolerated in spite of its evident breach of secrecy norms. When Oliver St. John complained about errors in a printed copy of a speech he delivered at a conference between the two Houses on

[3] Anthony Fletcher, *The Outbreak of the English Civil War* (London, 1985), p. xxv; Conrad Russell, *Parliaments and English Politics, 1621–1629* (Oxford, 1982), p. 389.

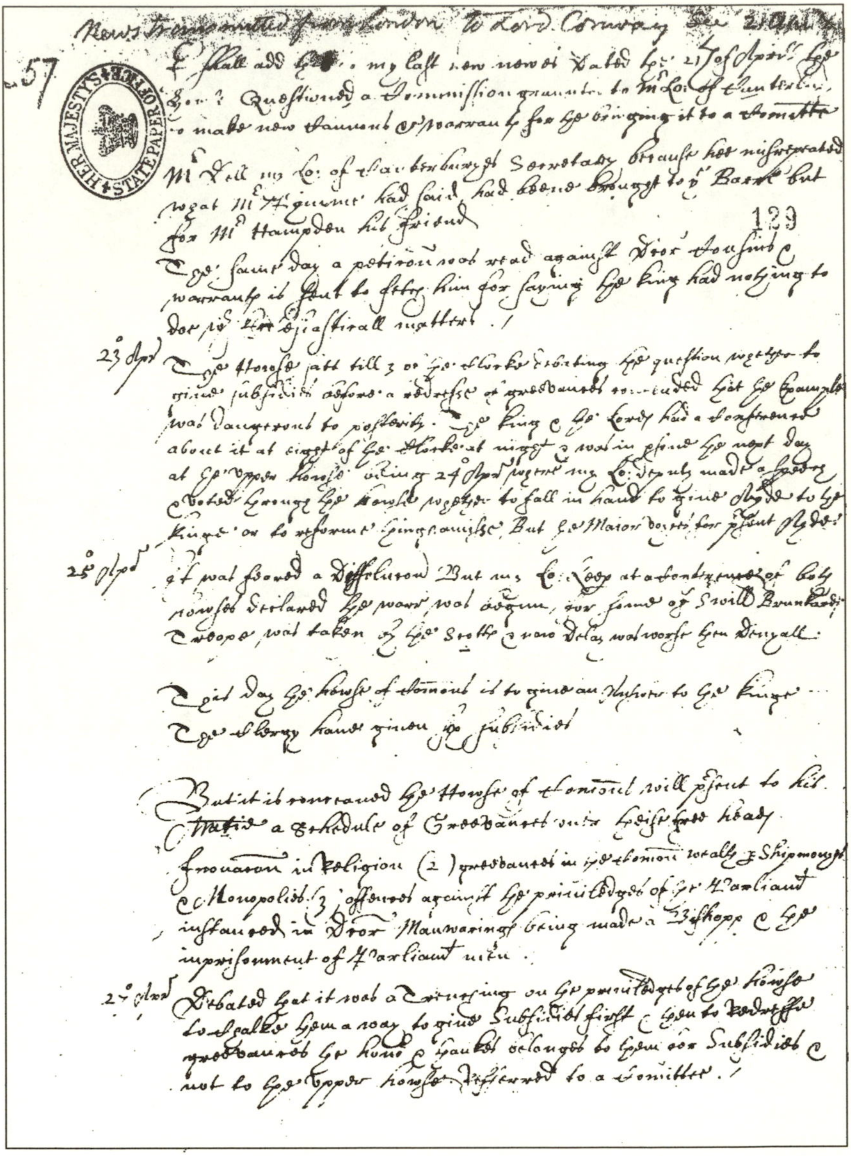

Fig. 2. Newsletter on events in the Short Parliament from April 21 to 27, 1640.

January 14, 1641, the Commons voted to have a "true copy" printed. Only a mild objection came from Simonds D'Ewes, a member noted for long antiquarian digressions on procedure, who invoked secrecy norms but invented a novel distinction between scribal and print publication. Fidelity to traditional norms of secrecy for proceedings in Parliament led D'Ewes to suggest that instead of printing the speech, members make scribal copies, which had been widely used to publish parliamentary proceedings.[4]

Discrepancies between principles and practices in political communication are neither surprising nor without precedent. After all, political communication is as old as connections between kingship, commemorative architecture, and coinage. Prompted by dynastic rivalry and domestic challenges to political stability, English monarchs used elaborate rituals in coronations and processions to convey political messages. In order to invest their rule with sacerdotal qualities during the Hundred Years' War, they borrowed sacred symbols and ritual formulas of Capetian kingship, which in the early-eleventh century had developed from "the continuing desire of the Capetians . . . to measure up to the ritual standards set by the German monarchs, masters of liturgical kingship."[5] Symbolic displays of regal authority were only one type of political communication in medieval England. Use of the pulpit to convey topical political messages was a common practice.[6] So were songs and poems that celebrated dynasties, recounted battles and insurrections, and lamented taxes and misdeeds by ecclesiastical or secular authorities. The prevalence of Latin, Anglo-Norman, and French in such songs and poems in the reigns of John (1199–1216), Henry III (1216–72), and Edward II (1307–27) indicates that they were intended for monastic refectories and baronial halls.[7] Gradual replacement of Anglo-Norman by English political songs and poems occurred under Edward III, stimulated by campaigns in the Hundred Years' War and, subsequently, during the War of the Roses, whose ultimate outcome was the Tudor dynasty.[8]

---

[4] *D'Ewes I*, p. 332; see A. D. T. Cromartie, "The Printing of Parliamentary Speeches, November 1640–July 1642," *HJ* 33 (1990): 23–44. Russell, *Parliaments and Politics*, p. 162, notes that members were given permission to copy a statement by the duke of Buckingham in the mid-1620s.

[5] John W. McKenna, "How God Became an Englishman," in D. J. Guth and J. W. KcKenna, eds., *Tudor Rule and Revolution* (Cambridge, 1982), pp. 27–31; Geoffrey Koziol, *Begging Pardon and Favor: Ritual and Political Order in Early Medieval France* (Ithaca, 1992), pp. 121, 128–29.

[6] R. B. Dobson, *Church and Society in the Medieval North of England* (London,1996), pp. 172–73.

[7] F. Furnivall, ed., *Political, Religious, and Love Poems* (*Early English Text Society*, os, 15 1866), pp. 1–42; T. Wright, ed., *The Political Songs of England, from the Reign of John to That of Edward II* (*CS*, os, 6, 1839).

[8] T. Wright, ed., *Political Poems and Songs relating to English History . . . from the*

These medieval precedents guided communication between the political center and the periphery of the nation under Tudor and early-Stuart rule. After succeeding to the throne following the death of Richard III in 1485, Henry VII solidified dynastic rule of the Tudors by frequent use of courtly and public spectacles that took many forms: festivals, the royal progress, civic pageantry, and more.[9] For subsequent Tudor and early-Stuart monarchs these practices continued to convey lessons to commoners about mutual duties that bound them and their rulers. Symbolic displays of sovereign authority also involved circulation of images. In 1600 Queen Elizabeth ordered that no "engravings in brass" of "the pictures of noblemen" should compete with those bearing the royal countenance. The most outspoken critic of Charles I's religious policies may also have been the most visible. In 1637, the bishop of Chester ordered destruction of portraits made by admirers of William Prynne, the Puritan martyr, on his journey to his prison cell in Caernarvon Castle. The failure of Charles I to ensure plentiful supplies of his image, along with his disinclination to allow subjects physical proximity to his person on public occasions, contributed to his unpopularity.[10]

Other modes of political communication were widely used by Tudor and Stuart monarchs. At his accession to the throne, Henry VII ordered the bishop of Lincoln to translate a papal bull that formally recognized Tudor reign—a summary published as a printed proclamation is one of the earliest instances of English printing. His successors routinely had proclamations printed on "broadsides," large one-sheet documents designed to be affixed to a wall or post. Preambles to public statutes that were printed and "distributed throughout the realm for public display" may have been, as Elton suggests, "the most effective form of printed propaganda" in support of religious changes ordered by Henry VIII.[11] Parliament was also useful for communicating with the nation. To promote his divorce from Katherine, Henry had "an embarrassed Thomas More" preside when favorable opinions on the divorce from universities were read aloud in the House of Lords in 1531. "After the proceedings

---

Accession of Edward III to that of Richard III (*Rerum Britannicarum Medii Ævi Scriptores* 14, 1859), 1:x; McKenna, "How God Became an Englishman," pp. 27–28, 30.

[9] Sydney Anglo, *Spectacle, Pageantry, and Early Tudor Policy* (Oxford, 1969).

[10] Leona Rostenberg, *The Minority Press and the English Crown* (Nieuwkoop, 1971), p. 83; Canon Bloomfield, "On Puritanism in Chester, 1637," *Chester Archaeological Journal* 8/9 (1871):283, 286–87; J. Richards, "'His Nowe Majestie' and the English Monarchy," *P&P* 113 (1986): 73, 77, 83–84.

[11] *RP-T* 1:6; Geoffrey R. Elton, *Policy and Police: The Enforcement of the Reformation in the Age of Thomas Cromwell* (Cambridge, 1972), p. 210. For a pardon to northern rebels, Henry VIII ordered his officers to "read the proclamation openly, and nail or fix a copy on the market cross, causing good espial to be made whether any man will pull it down." *L&P* 11, no. 956.

had been repeated in the Commons, More told MPs to report what they had heard to the counties."[12] Like their medieval predecessors, Tudor and early-Stuart monarchs ordered the clergy to instruct parishioners on the virtues of obedience; when occasion demanded, they ordered that sermons include topical political messages.[13] So did the Long Parliament when it seized the reins of power from Charles I.

Tudor and Stuart monarchs used judicial as well as religious activities to send political messages to their subjects. Assize sessions provided "important forums of publicity for the government."[14] In support of Henry VIII's religious policies, a secular official spoke at the Hampshire assizes in 1539, telling those present "how bounden the people were to thank the King for . . . setting forth God's word."[15] A Star Chamber "sermon" by the Lord Keeper on behalf of the king in the Privy Council was an address to judges of the King's Bench before they set out to ride their assize circuits. This provided a charge or guidelines for speeches on official policies that were to be delivered by judges at the commencement of assize sessions. Nominally directed to local justices of the peace, the judge's charge "could be an effective condemnation of the justices' shortcomings, a public pillorying of misfeasance before the eyes of the justices' inferior countrymen. It was also a powerful vehicle of propaganda acting through both the justices and the multitude attending assizes." The Star Chamber "sermon" given in 1600 by the Lord Keeper, Sir Thomas Egerton, tells the judges to urge local justices, among other things, to repress "libellers" and "discoursers and meddlers in Prince's matters." In 1603 Egerton informed the judges that James I wanted his first Parliament to find solutions to economic and religious grievances.[16] These political matters would have been topics whose informal discussion was an element of conviviality in the retinues and entertainment provided by local gentry for visiting assize judges. Here the context for political communication was occasions of "ceremonial, socializing, and legal business," accompanied by much "feasting."[17]

---

[12] Christopher Haigh, *English Reformations* (Oxford, 1993), p. 109.

[13] Peter McCullough, *Sermons at Court* (Cambridge, 1998).

[14] Cynthia B. Herrup, *The Common Peace: Participation and the Criminal Law in Seventeenth-Century England* (Cambridge, 1987), pp. 52–53.

[15] *L&P* 14. pt. 1, no. 775.

[16] Thomas Barnes, *Somerset, 1625–1640* (Cambridge, MA, 1961), p. 92; N. McClure, ed., *The Letters of John Chamberlain* (Philadelphia, 1939), 1:97; R. C. Munden, "James I and 'the Growth of Mutual Distrust': King, Commons, and Reform, 1603–1604," in K. Sharpe, ed., *Faction and Parliament: Essays on Early Stuart History* (London, 1985), p. 45.

[17] R. W. Ketton-Cremer, *Norfolk in the Civil War* (Hamden, CT, 1970), pp. 93–94; Diarmaid MacCulloch, *Suffolk and the Tudors: Politics and Religion in an English County, 1500–1600* (Oxford, 1986), pp. 23, 207.

PRINCIPLE

Although political communication took many forms, contemporary thinking on the topic did not accord legitimacy to anything resembling appeals to public opinion in politics. Access to a "public" space for discourse was a royal prerogative when it involved deliberation on laws, foreign policy, taxation, disputes among courtiers and aristocrats, and many other issues. Reinforcing this restricted model of political communication in prerevolutionary England were several widely shared, uncontested assumptions: that deference and patronage were core principles of political and social life; and that, at the hands of commoners, opinion was inherently irrational. The idea that irrationality inversely correlates with rank, a central theme in organic and patriarchal conceptions of politics, received added support from Protestant emphasis on the corruption of reason.[18]

Religion (Puritan or otherwise) supplied no basis for opposition to norms of secrecy and privilege in political communication. During the personal rule of Charles I, the dean of the Salisbury Cathedral could have cited either Richard Hooker or John Calvin to justify his order to preachers under his jurisdiction that "neither in your sermons, nor your private conversation, you intermeddle not with matters of state." In *Laws of Ecclesiastical Polity*, Hooker repeats Calvin's strictures that "private men" have no right publicly to discuss government.[19] Because they were tied to organic conceptions of the social and political order, secrecy norms prohibited not only seditious or disrespectful remarks but all public discourse that provoked division per se in religion or politics.

Prevailing communicative norms thus precluded anything resembling public debate. Such debate is the first of many corruptions cited in a petition—"The Supplication of the Commons against the Ordinaries"—ghostwritten by Thomas Cromwell and introduced in the House of Commons in 1532 for the purpose of furthering Henry VIII's control over the Church. This criticism was directed not at a specific doctrine but at inept management of conflict between religious reformers and conservatives, for "much discord, variance and debate has arisen and more and more daily is like to increase . . . to the great inquietation, vexation and breach of your peace." In the same vein, Cromwell requested the Lord Deputy of Calais to punish anyone who created "division and contention in opinion" or sowed sedition. Though the

[18] See John Morgan, *Godly Learning: Puritan Attitudes towards Reason, Learning, and Education, 1560–1640* (Cambridge, 1986).

[19] *MSS Rawls* C421, fol. 27; Richard Hooker, *Works* (Oxford, 1845), 1:102; John Calvin, *Institutes of the Christian Religion* (London, 1962), 2:656–67.

Lord Deputy admitted his inability to discern theological truth from error in debates between reformers and conservatives, no uncertainty attended his perception of the danger "to have any such opinions one against another."[20] Tudor proclamations against controversial religious publications often referred to violations of general communicative norms as well as to errors of a specific position, pointing out that "great inconvenience and dangers have grown . . . through the diversity of opinions in questions of religion." A proclamation issued by Elizabeth in 1573 against a pamphlet advocating Puritan reforms—*An admonition to the Parliament*—complained that these "books do tend to no other end, but to make division and dissension in the opinions of men." The queen also forbade "all her subjects of all degrees . . . to stir unquietness in her people by interpreting the laws of this realm after their brains and fancies."[21]

In prerevolutionary England, addressing the public on political issues was a prerogative of monarchs that contemporaries associated with publication practices by the Crown, such as proclamations. Persons who composed libels or challenges in private feuds were held to have usurped this prerogative when such writings were posted in public places or transmitted from one person to another. So Thomas Cromwell assured Henry VIII that "it has not been seen nor heard that any subject within this realm should presume to make proclamation." When James I prohibited dueling, he also denounced this aspect of aristocratic feuding as an invasion of "our special prerogative, as to take upon them to make any publication of their pleasure."[22] Implicit in these views are contemporary notions about publication that are not entirely foreign to ours. These associate publication with "a movement from a private realm of creativity to a public realm of consumption." Unlike in modern thinking, however, there is no supposition that publication involves printing.[23] A street where a ballad singer plied his trade or a post were "public places" that the Long Parliament sought to police in order to forestall publication of criticism.[24] Political commentary in scribal texts, such as private correspondence, violated norms of secrecy and privilege. After Oliver St. John sent a letter to the mayor of Marlborough that was

---

[20] R. B. Merriman, ed., *Life and Letters of Thomas Cromwell* (Oxford, 1902), 1:104; *LL* 5:152, 501–2.

[21] *RP-T* 2:5, 6, 375.

[22] *Letters of Cromwell* 1:349; *RP-S* 1:296. For examples of these practices, see *Letters of John Holles, 1587–1637* (Thoroton Society Record Series 31, 1975), 1:12; *Chamberlain Letters* 1:150–51; Alastair Bellany, " 'Rayling Rymes and Vaunting Verse': Libelous Politics in Early Stuart England," in K. Sharpe and P. Lake, eds., *Culture and Politics in Early Stuart England* (Stanford, 1993), pp. 285–310.

[23] Love, *Scribal Publication*, p. 36.   [24] *CJ* 5:73, 428.

critical of the Benevolence of 1615—a putatively "voluntary" contribution to the royal purse—prosecutors charged that St. John raised opposition "not privately, or in a corner, but publicly." When Puritan clerics circulated scribal texts with critical questions about new canons for the Church in 1640, opponents objected that they put the Church "upon the stage" and encouraged criticism "in public."[25]

Whatever freedom might attach to speech in Parliament had few ramifications beyond its walls because it was a privilege, an exemption from secrecy norms whose violation was grounds for imprisonment. "It was the Tudors' consistent policy to forbid the discussion of public affairs in private assemblies"—the offense of Peter Wentworth, noted above. Unauthorized disclosure of words spoken in Parliament was also forbidden. In February 1642 Sir Edward Dering was expelled from Parliament after he published his speeches and, worse yet, parliamentary passages that disclosed identities of other speakers by initials appended to their comments. Dering's offense, according to D'Ewes, was "the highest, greatest, and of the most transcendent nature that ever was committed by a member of this House."[26] Sedition and treason laws made politics a hazardous topic even for private conversation. The vagueness of these laws extended their scope to almost any utterance on public matters. It was treason to intend the death of an English monarch, which could occur in an act, a plot, or "by disabling his regiment, and making him appear to be incapable or indign to reign." So argued Francis Bacon in 1615, in a case that involved racking and other punishment, eventually fatal, for a hapless author of critical comments on royal policy.[27]

Contemporaries thought that public debate over political issues had inevitable, dire consequences for the political and social order because they understood the issue in terms of choice between reasoned debate in private and demagogic oratory in public. Positive consequences might arise from free speech only under very limited circumstances—when it occurred in "councils," for example, the Privy Council or Parliament. The "rigor of true reasoning" facilitated by free speech in such restricted settings was not possible "where a man is to speak to a multitude" and therefore he must have "a regard to the common passions" and rely on demagogic persuasion.[28] The point of departure for this reasoning was the study of classical rhetoric and history, and an uncontroversial as-

[25] T. Howell, ed., *A Complete Collection of State Trials* (London, 1816), 2:902; *MSS Rawl* C262, fol. 8

[26] J. E. Neale, "The Commons Privilege of Free Speech in Parliament," in E. B. Fryde and E. Miller, eds., *Historical Studies of the English Parliament* (Cambridge, 1970), 2: 165; *PJ1*, p. 253; Cromartie, "Printing of Parliamentary Speeches," p. 37.

[27] Howell, *State Trials*, 2:874.

[28] Thomas Hobbes, *Leviathan* (Oxford, 1909), p. 197.

sumption that had long dominated thinking on politics and society: that commoners constituted a "many-headed monster" whose irrationality precluded a role in politics. Reflection on this latter point in early-Stuart England was no different than it was in Tudor political culture, when Thomas Smith, the Elizabethan writer on the English constitution, explained that common people "have no voice or authority in our commonwealth, and no account is made of them but only to be ruled."[29] In this context, irrationality was not (as Locke would later argue) understood as a contingent condition, shaped by material and educational privations. Given prevailing organic and patriarchal presuppositions, claims by commoners to a "voice," to a right to participate in political communication, were necessarily perceived as irrational as a foot claiming the prerogative of a brain.

Secrecy norms in Tudor England thus were wedded to broader assumptions about the social and political order. This appears in a 1551 proclamation by Edward VI, which enforced statutes against "vagabonds, rumor mongers, players, unlicenced printers, etc." In it, the king commands his subjects:

> to live every man within the compass of his degree, contented with his vocation, every man to apply himself to live obediently, quietly, without murmur, grudging, sowing of sedition, spreading of tales and rumors, and without doing or saying of any manner of thing . . . that may touch the dignity of his majesty, his council, his magistrates or ministers . . . or in any wise contrary to his majesty's laws, statutes, or proclamations.[30]

When Edward VI's father confronted the Lincolnshire Rebellion and Pilgrimage of Grace in Yorkshire—the gravest domestic challenge to Henry VIII—a propagandist composed a tract against "seditious rebellyon" that flatly states, "It far passes a cobbler's craft to discuss what lords, what bishops, what councillors, what acts, statutes and laws are most meet for a commonwealth, and whose judgement should be best or worst concerning matters of religion."[31] This responds to Lincolnshire rebels who attributed unwonted innovations to the social upstart Thomas Cromwell and, accordingly, demanded that Henry select his councillors from the nobility. Another writer, Ralph Sadler, then secretary to Thomas Cromwell, drafted the king's response: "How presumptuous then are ye, the rude commons of one shire, and that one of the most brute and beastly of the whole realm . . . to find fault with your

---

[29] Christopher Hill, *Change and Continuity in 17th-Century England* (London, 1974), pp. 181–204; Thomas Smith, *De Republica Anglorum* (ca. 1565), bk. 1, chap. 24.

[30] *RP-T* 1:516.

[31] Richard Morison, *A Lamentation in Which Is Shewed what Ruyne and destruction cometh of seditious rebellyon* (*STC* 15185, 1536), sig. A4.

prince for the electing of his councillors and prelates."[32] In 1579, the price for presumptuousness was losing the hand that composed *The Dis-coverie of a Gaping Gulf Whereinto England is like to be Swallowed*, in which John Stubbs predicted dire consequences for England if Queen Elizabeth married the duke of Anjou, a Catholic. According to the royal proclamation that banned it, Stubbs's book brought the queen into discredit with her subjects and threatened "to prepare their minds to sedition, offering to every most meanest person of judgement . . . authority to argue and determine in every blind corner at their several wills of the affairs of public estate, a thing most pernicious in any estate."[33]

In the next reign, James I had Francis Bacon draft a 1620 proclamation against "lavish and licentious speech of matters of state." Bacon included "licentious discourses against the state" among "signs of trouble" that portended sedition in a later edition of his *Essays Or Counsels, Civill And Morall* (1625). The point was hardly novel. At this time the French ambassador in England reported, "It is a strange thing, the hatred in which this King is held, in free speaking cartoons, defamatory libels—the ordinary precursors of civil war."[34] Royal instructions given to the king's judges in 1622 cite the 1620 proclamation and note that "there is an unaccustomed and licentious boldness still used therein." Hence, the judges should admonish the king's subjects against "meddling with matters not appertaining to them" and to "lay such exemplary punishment" on persons who offend "by infusing any doubt or opinion of novelty or alteration in the church or commonwealth." The Privy Council closely monitored reports of offenders, directing judges, mayors, justices of the peace, the vice chancellor of Oxford, and others in handling cases. Enforcement of such rules affected not only lowly subjects. After reports of "unreverend and undutiful speeches" on Tudor queens by a barrister reached the Council, it ordered the Inns of Court to repress those who "lavishly enter into discourses of businesses of state, and especially touching the persons of princes."[35]

Control of political communication was aided by laws and proclamations directed against lavish speeches and speakers. Medieval statutes contained penalties for seditious rumors, including a key provision that facilitated their enforcement: imprisonment until a rumor's purveyor produced its source. A proclamation by Edward VI against seditious writings posted in public places states that any person who read them and "shall suffer the same bills to stand still or remain undestroyed . . .

---

[32] *L&P* 11, no. 780. [33] *RP-T* 2:449.

[34] *RP-S* 1:495, 496 n; Francis Bacon, *Works* (Boston, 1860), 7:123.

[35] *APC* 1621–23, pp. 153–54; 1623–25, pp. 19–20. For monitoring of cases, see *APC* 1621–23, pp. 81–82, 121, 134, 156–57, 357, 427, 483–84. For remarks on this by the Lord Keeper in his charge to assize judges in 1600, see *Chamberlain Letters* 1:97.

shall be taken and punished as the author."[36] Henry VIII enlisted superior and inferior officials and institutions in campaigns to stamp out unauthorized conversations on politics. Local officials were ordered to detect rumor spreaders; Privy Councillors were rebuked when they did not superintend this task in their local communities. In 1538 Cromwell drafted instructions to local courts of criminal jurisdiction, such as hundred courts, requesting juries to present persons who "sow . . . sedition, disorder, variance and trouble."[37] Detection relied heavily on informers, most of whom acted spontaneously, passing reports to a local official who relayed them up the chain of patron-client relations. Participation in this activity might be motivated by loyalty, fear, or desire for advancement. A would-be suitor to Thomas Cromwell declared that when "he or other true subjects know any person to write, preach or speak against the King," they would promptly report it.[38]

Thus, contemporaries saw nothing remarkable in proclamations and other published writings by James and Charles, who cited patriarchal political theory, the divine right of kings, and reasons of state to deny the legitimacy of public discussion of political issues. Though Charles I published accounts of decisions to dissolve Parliaments in 1625 and in 1626, "he was careful to explain that he was not *bound* to give an account of his 'Regall Actions' to anyone except God." He made the same point in 1628, 1629, and 1640: "Princes are not bound to give accompt of their actions but to God alone." An MP in 1626 echoed this point: the king "is only bound to give account to God of his doings." In the reign of Charles I's father, nearly identical words constitute a disclaimer at the beginning of a pamphlet issued by the royal printer that explains the decision to execute Raleigh in 1618.[39] James I regarded royal accounts of policy in much the same way that Calvinists thought about God saving souls: both were acts of grace. After dissolving the 1621 Parliament, James published a declaration that expanded on reasons offered in a previous proclamation for his decision.

> We were content [in the proclamation] . . . to descend many degrees beneath our self, first by communicating to all our people the reasons of a resolution of state. . . . And lastly . . . opening to them that forbidden ark of our absolute and indisputable prerogative, concerning the call, continuing and dissolving of Parliament.

[36] *RP-T* 1:523.

[37] *L&P* 15, no. 447; 16, no. 945; Elton, *Policy and Police*, p. 46.

[38] *L&P* 13, pt. 1, no. 819; and see Elton, *Policy and Police*, pp. 331–33.

[39] J. P. Sommerville, *Politics and Ideology In England, 1603–1640* (London, 1986), p. 34; *PP 1626* 3:251; *A Declaration Of The Demeanor And Cariage Of Sir W. Raleigh* (*STC* 20653, 1618), p. 1.

Matters of state, observed the 1620 proclamation drafted by Bacon, "are not themes or subjects fit for vulgar persons or common meetings."[40] For James and Charles, open discussion of policy was as an offense against divinely ordained monarchs, childish impudence against parental authority, which posed a security threat to the state.

> All Counsels would be overthrown
> If all were to the people known
> and to no use our counsel tables
> if state affairs were public babbles[41]

Above, we saw that the principal exception to secrecy norms in politics was freedom of speech in councils. For Parliament, this developed "from the fifteenth century, when free speech was a customary right, if a right at all, to the Elizabethan age, when it is a formal privilege, formally petitioned for, and formally granted" in a ritual between Speaker and monarch at the beginning of a Parliament. By 1593 the scope of this freedom allowed MPs "to say yea or no to bills . . . with some short declaration of his reason therein." By the 1620s, members regarded the ritual petition for free speech in Parliament as "no other but a declaration of our rights." The status of this freedom under Elizabeth was similar to the situation under her Stuart successors: a widely affirmed liberty for which no agreement existed on its meaning or limits. Elizabeth tried to limit speech in Parliament by prohibiting discussion of "matters of state," such as her marriage and succession. James, too, drew this distinction in an effort to limit discussion of foreign policy. Though this imposed "novel limits" on free speech in Parliament, it provoked only muted opposition there. A leading proponent of parliamentary privilege, Sir John Eliot, conceded that "mysteries of state," unlike grievances, were not fit topics for debate.[42] Though this allowed monarchs to punish in practice that which principle protected, the principle itself was well known. When the spread of Protestant books led the conservative bishop of Winchester, Stephen Gardiner, to remind the duke of Somerset of his promise, as Protector of Edward VI, to hold the line against further reform—"your Grace told me you would suffer no innovation"—"the bishop excused the blunt manner of his address with the

---

[40] *His Majesties Declaration* (*STC* 9241, 1622), p. 2; *RP-S* 1:495. For James I's proclamation on the dissolution of the 1621 Parliament, see *RP-S* 1:527–34.

[41] *MSS Rawl* D398, fol. 183v.

[42] Neale, "Free Speech in Parliament," pp. 161, 168; *PP 1626* 3:275; Russell, *Parliaments and English Politics*, p. 93 and see p. 141; *PP 1626* 2:315; Johann Sommerville, "Parliament, Privilege, and the Liberties of the Subject," in J. H. Hexter, ed., *Parliament and Liberty from the Reign of Elizabeth to the English Civil War* (Stanford, 1992), pp. 56–84.

plea, 'I beseech your Grace to pardon me, for I am like one of the Commons House, that, when I am in my tale, think I should have liberty to make an end.' "[43]

Parliament was only one instance of a council for which contemporaries thought free speech was essential. It applied as well to greater (e.g., the Privy Council) and lesser prerogative councils. The oath taken by Privy Councillors to James I enjoined secrecy and the obligation "in all things to be moved, treated, and debated in Council faithfully and truly declare your mind and opinion." That a council was a forum for open discussion of political matters also held for lesser councils. In 1534, Lord Lisle, the king's deputy in Calais, was warned not to discuss sensitive political news, "any matter or news ~~concerning the King's Highness or his Council~~" (the passage was deleted) "unless it be in the Council and in the Council Chamber" in Calais.[44] In this context, free speech in councils depended on secrecy norms to shield speakers from official disfavor. In defense of the privilege of free speech in Parliament, members cited medieval precedents, for example, a medieval petition from the Commons to Henry IV "that he will be pleased not to take any information of things out of the parliament but by the parliament."[45] Secrecy norms dictated that the official journal of the Commons not refer to speeches or debates or proceedings in committee, or identify sponsors of motions (though it names the presenters of committee reports to the House). Moreover, clerks responsible for the *Commons Journal* were not to allow written reports of events and words in the House to be disclosed to outsiders. In December 1640, debate ensued after the assistant clerk, John Rushworth, was observed taking notes in the Commons. He and the clerk, Henry Elsynge, were ordered to "suffer not copies to go forth of any argument or speech whatsoever."[46] But members freely took notes of proceedings. A woodcut entitled *The True Manner of the Sitting of the Lords & Commons*, made during the earl of Strafford's trial in 1641, shows two earls and at least seven MPs taking notes (see fig. 1).[47]

Free speech in parliaments was not seen as an end in itself—the modern view—but as a privilege with two purposes. First, as we have seen, it was thought necessary for effective deliberations in councils convened by a monarch. Hobbes conceded that "he that gives counsel to his sovereign . . . cannot in equity be punished for it, whether the same be

---

[43] J. Muller, ed., *The Letters of Stephen Gardiner* (Cambridge, 1933), p. 282 and see p. 392.

[44] J. R. Tanner, ed., *Constitutional Documents of the Reign of James I* (Cambridge, 1930), p. 132; *LL* 2:54.

[45] *PP 1626* 2:427–28. Quote is an MP's gloss of the petition.

[46] *D'Ewes I*, p. xvii–xviii.   [47] 669f.4[12].

conformable to the opinion of the most."[48] When Charles sought to stifle the Commons' attack on the duke of Buckingham, he reassured MPs that "his Majesty does not forget that the parliament is his council and therefore it ought to have the liberty and freedom of a council."[49] In debates on the scope of this freedom in the 1610 Parliament, members argued that "men's judgments are best guided and conducted when they are some way supported by the variety of opinion." And when granting the Speaker's petition for free speech at the opening of Elizabeth's first parliament in 1559, the Lord Keeper, on behalf of the queen, granted "liberty of speech for the well debating of matters propounded."[50] The opposition between contemporary views on the utility of debate in councils and in public could not be sharper.

A second reason for free speech is that parliaments and other councils were places to which petitioners could seek redress of grievances. The importance of councils as a destination for petitions led Sir Francis Bacon to recommend to all councils, especially the Privy Council, that they establish "set days for petitions," to give petitioners "more certainty for their attendance" and ensure sufficient time in other sessions "for matters of estate"—in other words, royal policy. Because parliaments received and transmitted grievances, the Speaker in his speech at the commencement of an Elizabethan parliament requested "that ancient privilege of freedom of speech that thereby the grievances of both Houses may be known."[51] The link between free speech in Parliament and its deliberations on grievances was a commonplace in contemporary political discourse. A Jacobean courtier and diplomat, Sir Charles Cornwallis, thought that "in monarchies, Parliaments were instituted" as a forum where "men might freely deliver their thoughts and advises in whatsoever they should find error of government or grievances in the commonwealth." It is a "confirmed privilege of parliament," argued Sir Edwin Sandys in 1626, "to complain of any subject whatsoever that is taxed for public grievances."[52] The right of subjects to send grievances to Parliament, and of Parliament to receive and respond to them in legislative remedies was undisputed, even by Hobbes, who held that the "best counsel . . . is to be taken from the general informations, and complaints of the people . . . who are best acquainted with their own wants."[53]

---

[48] Hobbes, *Leviathan*, p. 196.

[49] *PP 1626* 2:392.

[50] *PP 1610* 2:110; *PP Elizabeth*, p. 42.

[51] Bacon, *Works*, 12:151; *PP Elizabeth*, p. 652.

[52] J. Gutch, ed., *Collectanea Curiosa: Or Miscellaneous Tracts . . . from the Manuscripts of Archbishop Sancroft* (Oxford, 1781), 1:163; *PP 1626* 2:421.

[53] Hobbes, *Leviathan*, p. 272.

Still, communicative rights for grievance did not establish a public sphere. As we shall see, expression of grievance by petition was a privileged form of communication. Petitionary rhetoric portrayed grievance as an apolitical stream of information, devoid of any intimations about the supremacy of popular will in politics. In this perspective, to express grievance by petition was to enter a privileged communicative space, analogous to privileges that followed admission to the freedom of a corporation. Expressions of grievance had to appear as a direct, spontaneous communication from localities to the political center. In this context, spontaneity was the antithesis of faction. (The point has links to classical rhetoric that holds spontaneous utterances to have more probative value than premeditated ones.) The role of MPs in this process, then, was understood as a conduit. Hence, in his comments on grievances and parliaments, Cornwallis observed that members "are not to be thought to speak their own words, but those of their country."[54] In addition, the flow of grievances to the political center should not be diverted, that is, be made "public." Parliament had violated this precept, according to James I, when it issued the Apologetical Petition, a blatant appeal to public opinion over unresolved religious grievances, "tacitly implying our ill government in this point. And we leave to you to judge whether it be your duties, that are the representative body of our people, so to distaste them with out government." In the previous reign, Archbishop Whitgift complained about publicity given to a petition from Puritans in Kent who objected to his policies against clerical nonconformity. The petitioners "did not only deliver their objections to me, which had been tolerable, but they also gave out divers and sundry copies [. . .] to the manifest breach of the law." A printed Puritan petition to Elizabeth met with similar criticism because "it was not exhibited to her Majesty, as the title purported, but printed and scattered abroad in divers corners . . . to work in the common sort a dislike of the ecclesiastical state."[55]

Yet secrecy norms were not simply repressive, for they also provided a resource for asserting control over internal proceedings against royal encroachment. The presence of royal officials in both Houses meant that, in practice, monarchs could follow the course of parliamentary business. It "was not strange that the business of the House (which was so commonly spoken of abroad in the town) doth come to his Majesty's ear," observed Secretary of State George Calvert when, as an MP in the 1621 Parliament, he kept the Court informed of escalating concern

[54] Gutch, *Collectanea Curiosa* 1:163.

[55] Tanner, *Constitutional Documents*, p. 282; *MSS Lansdowne* 42, fol. 185v; Matthew Sutcliffe, *An Answer Unto A Certaine Calumnious letter* (*STC* 23451, 1595), sig. A4v.

among other MPs over the right of the Commons to debate government policies.[56] Just before Charles dissolved the Short Parliament in 1640, the Venetian ambassador reported, "The King . . . being carefully informed of everything with the object of putting a stop to these designs . . . sent for the members two days ago, and repeated with emphasis his request that they should vote without delay the subsidies he asked for, admonishing them not to spend time on other matters."[57] Of course, members knew about royal monitoring of House proceedings but "the fiction of secrecy, sustained by the privacy of the clerk's record, was nonetheless useful in maintaining the privileges of Parliament." After Charles I commented on a clause in a bill before the House for pressing of soldiers, members proposed a remonstrance that requested the king not "to take notice of any man's carriage of speeches concerning matters debated in the Parliament."[58] A century earlier, secrecy norms provided a weaker shield for free speech in Parliament. After a staunch Protestant member objected to reassertion of orthodox theology—the doctrine of real presence in the sacrament—a principal conservative advocate of orthodoxy, Stephen Gardiner, grudgingly acknowledged that, "being a burgess there, [the member] might well declare his mind and opinion." Yet Gardiner warned the member's patron, Lord Lisle, that his client faced close questioning about his views and about who might have suggested he air them in Parliament.[59]

Secrecy norms also had more than purely repressive implications for expression of grievances. For grievances from the people as well as free speech in councils, secrecy provided limited immunity to the general prohibition of public discussion of political matters, although much less for petitioners than for members of councils. In principle, the privileged communicative activity of petitioning allowed the periphery to communicate information to the political center, freely, without coercion. Petitioners sometimes affirmed their privilege as petitioners in order to fend off criticism from third parties. The right to petition did not create a public sphere; as a privilege it permitted petitioners to communicate directly to a petitioned authority. At the election of London MPs in 1640, "a petition was given by the multitude" to the elected members for delivery to Parliament. "Some of the people cried out to have this petition read out," but, after debate, this was voted down, "the major part by far . . . saying they would not have their grievances published but in Parlia-

---

[56] S. Gardiner, ed., *The Fortescue Papers* (*CS*, ns, 1, 1871), pp. 150–51; Tanner, *Constitutional Documents*, p. 288.

[57] *Calendar of State Papers . . . Relating to English Affairs, Existing in the Archives and Collections of Venice*, vol. 25 (London, 1924), p. 40.

[58] *D'Ewes II*, p. xix, 287.   [59] *LL* 5:546.

ment."[60] In 1643, readers would have readily understood the reasoning behind the complaint in the Royalist newspaper *Mercurius Aulicus* that publication of John Pym's observations on Charles I's response to a peace petition that the king had sent to London's Common Hall was "irregular, it not belonging unto them to take notice of his Majesty's answer unto the petition."[61] Petitioners used this logic to denounce printed attacks on their petitions. Independents held Presbyterian attacks on petitions before Parliament to be "contrary to the course of Parliament and the liberty of the subjects." When Independents used this tactic, Presbyterians objected to "obstructing the course of the people of England's free petitioning."[62] In this context, "liberty" and "free" can be understood only in terms of the medieval idea of privilege.

CONTRADICTIONS BETWEEN SECRECY NORMS AND POLITICAL PRACTICE

Although norms of secrecy and privilege prohibited public discussion of politics, necessity ensured that, in practice, political communication overflowed restrictive boundaries delineated by patriarchal, organic, and divine right theories of government. For example, successive governments followed these norms and principles and imposed extremely tight restrictions on printed accounts of domestic news in Tudor and early-Stuart England. Printed news in newsbooks covered foreign politics. For domestic news, readers of newsbooks had to be satisfied with lurid, nonpolitical topics, mostly miracles, monsters, and murders, supplemented by reports on ceremonial occasions for symbolic displays of royal authority, such as coronations and processions. Yet at the same time, substantive reports on domestic politics circulated widely, not only orally but, as we shall see in chapter 5, in many types of scribal texts. Scriveners sold copies of speeches and other documents as a business. Writers of weekly newsletters had diverse motives: some received hefty fees for newsletters with well-informed sources; others sent news as a token of friendship or as a service to powerful patrons. In these instances, secrecy and privilege gave way to imperatives of friendship, commerce, and patronage.

Political imperatives—for example, a government's need for favorable propaganda—also militated against the ban on printed domestic news.

---

[60] *MSS Add* 11045, fol. 128v.   [61] *MA* 1:50.
[62] E516[7] (1647), p. 11; E352[3] (1646), p. 9; E355[13] (1646), p. 36; E368[5] (1648), p. [259].

Proponents of an abortive plan for a weekly gazette in the reign of James I pointed out that printed news would "establish a speedy and ready way whereby to disperse into the veins of the whole body of a state such matter as may best temper it, & be most agreeable to the disposition of the head & principal members."[63] During the English Revolution, brute political necessity forced publication of printed domestic news. After the Restoration, Sir Roger L'Estrange, the principal censor of the press, assumed control over a licensed weekly newsbook even though, as a matter of principle, he opposed publication of printed news because "it makes the multitude too familiar with the actions and counsels of their superiors, too pragmatical and censorious, and gives them not only an itch but a kind of colourable right and license to be meddling with the government."[64] In allowing political expediency—the need to combat republican and dissenting opposition to the Restoration settlement—to overcome principle, L'Estrange provides a vivid illustration of the contradiction between principle and practice in early-modern political communication.

The contradiction, though not its acknowledgment, was widespread. It appears in many Tudor and early-Stuart proclamations when they provide brief explanations of circumstances that prompted their issue. Monarchs routinely obtained information on supposedly secret parliamentary speeches and proceedings, principally from royal officials who had seats in the lower House. Powerful courtiers also took steps to keep abreast with developments in a parliament. The complacency with which contemporaries viewed this activity in the reign of Henry VIII is similar to what we shall encounter in chapter 5 for the reign of Charles I. In 1532, after his recent elevation to the bishopric of Winchester and dispatch on an embassy to France, Stephen Gardiner wrote to Cromwell for news of developments in the 1532 Parliament. Cromwell justified his uninformative response—a cursory relation of a piece of religious legislation in the upper House—by the supposition that such news "by a multitude of your friends (who are far more secret and nearer the knowledge of the same than I am) be to your lordship already related and known."[65] The same point holds for a lesser council, the Calais Council, whose members by the act 27 H. VIII cap. 63 (1536) were bound not to disclose its deliberations: "ye shall effectually keep them secret, and not discover them in nowise in other form or manner." Yet Cromwell was kept well informed of these deliberations. So were other interested parties, such as Edward Seymour, the earl of Hertford, who closely

---

[63] William Powel, *John Pory, 1572–1636* (Chapel Hill, NC, 1977), p. 52.
[64] George Kitchin, *Sir Roger L'Estrange* (London, 1913), p. 143.
[65] *LL* 2:66; *Letters of Thomas Cromwell* 1:343.

questioned the Lord Deputy's servant on council deliberations over divisions between supporters and opponents of religious reform. Wisely, the servant feigned ignorance.[66]

The utility of such political intelligence for powerful persons, who used it to cope with treacherous Court politics, was one reason for violation of secrecy norms in councils. Another was the imperative to influence public opinion. At critical political moments this overrode secrecy norms for the Privy Council. Alarmed by mobilization of Catholic designs, foreign and domestic, against the reign of Queen Elizabeth in 1584, members of the Privy Council invented popular demands for a national association whose members took an oath to support England's Protestant rulers. "The Association was, in fact, a masterly piece of propaganda which served to bind the country to the Crown, to combat disorder, to focus the concerns of the political elite, and to achieve a dramatic and public attestation of loyalty to Queen Elizabeth." The pretext for creation of this association was the claim that the Council had received petitions from judges, municipal officials, "and certain Lords and gentlemen of divers counties" who allegedly "got knowledge" of a similar oath taken by members of the Privy Council. This fiction, evidently the work of the principal secretary of state, Francis Walsingham, conveniently overlooked the evident violation of secrecy norms for the Council.[67] Parliaments and early-Stuart monarchs also abridged secrecy norms when compelled by political necessity. In December 1621, amidst wrangling between James I and Parliament over its privileges, a letter from James I conveying his views—freedom of speech did not extend to foreign and dynastic policies and was not an ancient right but derived from royal grace—was read in the Commons and entered into its *Journal* with the stipulation "that everyone that will may have copies thereof." The Crown also connived at this flouting of secrecy norms by illicit scribal publication. Throughout the 1620s, confidential reports by ambassadors and secretaries of state leaked out of the Privy Council when it suited its purposes. "Contemporaries had no illusions about the confidentiality of these reports. In fact, the government even provided the Parliament men with copies and the encouragement to circulate them throughout the realm."[68]

Contradictions between principle and practice in political communication became especially acute when government policies underwent sudden shifts or reversals, such as England's foreign alliances in the

[66] *LL* 5:490–91, 496.

[67] David Cressy, "Binding the Nation: The Bonds of Association, 1584 and 1596," in Guth and McKenna, *Tudor Rule and Revolution*, pp. 220–21.

[68] Tanner, *Constitutional Documents*, p. 288; Thomas Cogswell, "The Politics of Propaganda," *JBS* 29 (1990): 195.

1620s. Political imperatives also overrode secrecy norms when policies were executed ineptly and called into question the competence of government, such as the Invasion of the Isle of Rhee in 1627 or military mobilization in the Bishops' Wars. Though James and Charles held that subjects had no right to explanations of royal policy, we have seen that they did just that in order to justify dissolutions of parliaments when unmanageable disputes eventuated in legislative gridlock. These contradictions between communicative principle and practice multiplied whenever political conflict escalated beyond control. Public relations initiatives at the end of the personal rule of Charles I responded to the government's inability to placate or repress the Scottish Covenanters or even to stop widespread distribution of printed political pamphlets from Scotland.[69] After the political stakes had been raised and redoubled by the outbreak of civil war, public relations initiatives include publication of *Mercurius Aulicus.* Now "the regime which had relied so heavily on suppression of the news itself set about capturing a nationwide audience with an enthusiasm and skill unprecedented in English journalism."[70]

Violation of secrecy norms did not only originate in the political center. Messages from the center to the periphery were prompted by the fact that domestic politics and foreign policy were objects of intense popular interest. In chapter 5 we will examine the nature and distribution of formal and informal channels in which news, rumor, criticism, and gossip circulated in England. Here it will suffice to point out that oral communication had long been and remained the principal medium for transmission of news. Often this occurred in taverns, inns, and alehouses, public spaces where the liberating effects of alcohol led to incautious expressions of political criticism. This activity was not entirely unrelated to developments that we have just surveyed in the political center. Parliamentary politics indirectly weakened secrecy norms by stimulating popular interest in politics and providing political leaders with motives for satisfying this interest, by illicit leaks of scribal texts, for example. This development led to an infusion of national issues in political perspectives among electors and ratepayers that, by tradition, seldom extended beyond the local community.[71]

Along with the growing salience of national political issues, there was more emphasis on the representative capacity of individual MPs. The

[69] *CSPD* 1639–40, pp. 515, 557.

[70] P. W. Thomas, *Sir John Berkenhead* (London, 1969), p. 56. See also Joad Raymond, *The Invention of the Newspaper: English Newsbooks, 1641–1649* (Oxford, 1996), p. 27.

[71] Richard Cust, "Politics and the Electorate in the 1620s," in Richard Cust and Ann Hughes, eds., *Conflict in Stuart England* (London, 1989), pp. 140–43.

idea that these were "public" persons who represented particular con-stituencies *and* the nation had medieval antecedents in claims that Par-liament was the representative body of the realm.[72] In the 1575 Parlia-ment, a member declared, "I am now no private person. I am a public, and a counselor to the whole state." Thomas Wentworth presumed that his constituents understood that he and other members in Parliament were "as you know, public persons."[73] The contemporary idea of an MP or magistrate as a "public person" was a commonplace, sufficiently so that it provided a metaphor for religious reflections on Adam or Christ as a representative person.[74] Growing emphasis on the representative ca-pacity of MPs had strong implications for political communication be-tween the political center and periphery of the nation. For example, members anticipated constituent reactions to developments in a parlia-ment. An important feature of a Tudor parliament was "its businesslike determination to show results." The same holds for early-Stuart En-gland, when members fretted over the probable apportionment of blame if political deadlock led to dissolution of a parliament. In the 1620s members anticipated negative local response to "failure to com-plete any satisfactory programme of legislation. The fear appears to have been of the reaction they would meet in the country when they came home."[75] A contemporary noted that this animated arcane maneuvers between the two Houses in 1628: "the study is who shall bear the blame of the rupture." Earlier, in the 1626 Parliament a member voiced this fear in debate over an issue that bedeviled parliaments from the ascen-sion of James up to the outbreak of the civil wars: to what extent should votes on revenues be linked to the resolution of religious, economic, and legal grievances? "And if we shall give away the people's money without having redress of our grievances, the country will blame us." During the 1621 Parliament, Thomas Wentworth spoke to his York-shire constituents and rebutted the objection "that we have given away your money and made no laws."[76]

[72] David Sacks, "The Paradox of Taxation: Fiscal Crises, Parliament, and Liberty in En-gland, 1450–1640," in P. Hoffman and K. Norberg, eds., *Fiscal Crises, Liberty, and Repre-sentative Government, 1450–1789* (Stanford, 1994), p. 21.

[73] Simonds D'Ewes, *The Journal Of All The Parliaments During the Reign of Queen Elizabeth* (1682), p. 241; J. P. Cooper, ed., *The Wentworth Papers, 1597–1628* (*CS*, 4th ser., 12, 1973), p. 80. See also Richard Cust and Peter Lake, "The Rhetoric of Magis-tracy," *Bulletin of the Institute of Historical Research* 59 (1981): 43–45.

[74] Christopher Hill, *Collected Essays* (Amherst, 1985–86), 3:300–319.

[75] Wallace T. MacCaffrey, "Parliament: The Elizabethan Experience," in Guth and McKenna, *Tudor Rule and Revolution*, p. 130; Russell, *Parliaments and English Politics*, p. 118.

[76] *Letters of John Holles, 1587–1637*, ed. P. R. Seddon,(*Thoronton Society Record Series* 36, 1986), 3:382; *PP 1626* 3:424; *Wentworth Papers*, p. 153; and see *PP 1626* 2:355.

This last point refers to widespread agreement that subsidies, on which the Crown was ever more dependent, should originate among the public persons assembled in the lower House of Parliament. Parliament's use of subsidy bills as a lever to promote new laws that resolved the people's grievance[77] also had implications for political communication, which appeared when members explained their proceedings on taxes and grievances to constituents.[78] When summer adjournment interrupted negotiations between the Crown and the 1610 Parliament over the "Great Contract"—a proposal to abolish many prerogative taxes in exchange for an annual subsidy—the Commons directed its members "in their several countries [counties] to take intelligence," that is, to ascertain local sentiment over the proposed deal. One member, John Holles, wrote in August to the Lord Treasurer that he was prepared to follow the directive "that first in this vacation we should feel the disposition of our countries thereunto, to the end with more general warranty we might proceed at our recess to a desired consummation." The next month he reported, "I find in the better sort a very sharp appetite, but in the plebs . . . a very uncertain temper," though they too were willing to contemplate advantages of a regular tax over the uncertain courses of disliked prerogative taxes, such as purveyance.[79] Another member of several parliaments thought it necessary to explain the rationale and course of proceedings that produced a levy on his constituents. When they assembled for collection of a "free gift" voted in the 1614 Parliament, Thomas Wentworth was prepared to describe: "1, the passages of the last Parliament; 2, ancient and late precedents; 3, the obligation binding us thereunto now more than ever; 4, and last, our own future benefit and comfort."[80]

Kings, royal officials, and members of Parliament were not the only persons for whom necessity forced a contradiction between principle and practice in political communication. Discussion of business pending in Parliament by interested parties outside its walls had always occurred and was a necessary adjunct to efforts by municipal and occupational corporations to secure their interests in Parliament. In the late-fourteenth century, aldermen and common councillors in London and Norwich sat on committees set up to discuss with MPs business that would be transacted in Parliament. Under Henry VIII, both London and York readied grievances "by drafting legislation they wanted passed." Thus, many precedents existed in 1640 for the decision by the

---

[77] This has medieval precedents; see Sacks, "Paradox of Taxation," p. 18.

[78] Clive Holmes, "Parliament, Liberty, Taxation and Property," Hexter, in *Parliament and Liberty*, pp. 149–51.

[79] *PP 1610* 2:292; *Letters of John Holles, 1587–1637*, pp. 513, 515.

[80] *Wentworth Papers*, p. 80, and see pp. 152–57 for similar remarks on the 1621 subsidy.

upper chamber of London's municipal government to establish a committee of six aldermen who "should at all convenient times during this session of Parliament meet together and inform themselves and consider all matters" affecting the City. Because these activities were thought to be vital for protecting local economic interests, it is hardly surprising that larger towns were not alone "in practising the mixed managerial arts of surveillance, canvassing, persuasion, propaganda and opposition." The borough of Sudbury in Suffolk "kept an eye on Parliament, in 1571 buying a copy of what its accounts describe as 'a bill that was entered against corporations' and in 1584 conferring with its legal counsel 'for matters to prefer into the Parliament House.' "[81] Though promoting local interests in Westminster may have necessitated intrusions into the veil of secrecy that shrouded Parliament's internal proceedings, contemporaries saw this as an unexceptional aspect of public life.

We are now in a position to see why such discrepancies between principle and practice in political communication were inevitable. Norms of secrecy and privilege were not simply repressive. They did facilitate expressions of grievance and some degree of parliamentary control over its proceedings. But they also were incompatible with other aspects of public life that grew out of imperatives that were as ordinary as they were necessary. Contemporaries expected political news and gossip from friends; patrons demanded it from clients. Scriveners sought sales. Municipal and occupational corporations advanced their interests by monitoring Parliament; so did monarchs and courtiers. Individual members of Parliament desired good public relations with local constituents. Governments wanted the same from the nation, especially when their credibility was damaged by ineptly executed or unpopular policies. Thus, a multitude of political and social imperatives lay behind communicative practices by rulers and subjects that violated norms of secrecy, even though contemporaries were no more prepared to question these communicative norms than the organic and patriarchal assumptions from which they flowed.

[81] A. R. Myers, "Parliamentary Petitions in the Fifteenth Century," *EHR* 52 (1937): 391; G. R. Elton, *Reform and Renewal* (Cambridge, 1973), pp. 77–78; M. A. R. Graves, "Managing Elizabethan Parliaments," in D. M. Dean and N. L. Jones, eds., *The Parliaments of Elizabethan England* (London, 1990), pp. 38–39; MSS JCC 39, fol. 162; MacCulloch, *Suffolk and the Tudors: Politics and Religion in an English County*, p. 46.

CHAPTER FOUR

Traditional Communicative Practice

MANY COMMUNICATIVE PRACTICES were part of politics in prerevolutionary England because, as we have just seen, both tradition and necessity set limits to the imposition of secrecy and privilege on political communication. In these practices, great variation existed in media, rhetoric, direction, and accessibility in flows of information between periphery and center of the political nation. Some traditional modes of political communication, such as symbolic displays of sovereign authority, moved in only one direction, center to periphery, and afforded little opportunity for popular participation beyond reception. Printed texts, sermons, and speeches at the opening of assize sessions conveyed messages from the center with more substantive content. Other modes of communication facilitated flows of information in the reverse direction. For petitions, this was by design. This was not the case for elections, although a gradual infusion of national issues in parliamentary elections in early-Stuart England brought more public discussion and debate to contests for seats than had occurred when voting followed the traditional pattern in which royal patronage and private canvassing among the gentry largely determined outcomes of elections.

Amidst the diverse forms of political communication at this time, one pattern is readily apparent: substantive content is inversely related to its accessibility. Nearly every adult could participate as a member of an audience for symbolic displays of power, but the forty-shilling franchise limited the electorate to a small, though not inconsiderable, proportion of male heads of households. Petitions and crowds constituted intermediary cases: both contained possibilities for influencing politics that were absent in purely symbolic displays, but access and autonomy were limited. Influential local leaders often initiated the process of drawing up petitions, gathering signatures, and presenting them to Parliament; and crowds were not coextensive with "the rabble." Another pattern exists in messages from periphery to center: these humbly conveyed information and did not include or intimate normative claims on behalf of subordination of politics to popular will. Rhetorical restrictions in traditional forms of political communication allowed vox populi to advance deferential requests whose satisfaction was the prerogative of a petitioned authority. No association existed between this activity and appeals to public opinion. Discussion of requests properly occurred in the councils of a petitioned authority, where, as we saw in the previous chapter, contemporaries thought reasoned debate could occur under conditions created by communicative norms of privileges and secrecy.

CENTER TO PERIPHERY

One of the oldest functions of political communication is to surround rulers with an aura, with intimations of links to transcendent powers. This occurs in ceremonies that symbolically display sovereign power, such as coronations, processions, and pageants. In early-modern England these were media for communication between the political center and the realm that provided a cultural frame in which commoners could understand reciprocal claims that bound them to their rulers. Regional and municipal rulers, too, used this mode of communication. The entourage and ceremony occasioned by entry of a regional magnate, the earl of Derby, into northwestern towns was "almost regal," attended with fireworks and military displays. This provided the earl with a useful backdrop when he confronted town burgesses for not being responsive to his wishes on whom they admitted, and upon what terms, to the freedom of the municipal corporation.[1] At this time, municipal citizenship was inseparable from the elaborate civic pageantry that defined and celebrated the identity and unity of larger towns,[2] most notably the Lord Mayor's show in London, which reached its zenith in the seventeenth century. Such symbolic displays of political authority constituted a public realm in politics not unlike a theater where applause is compulsory.[3] The advent of printing, far from discouraging this mode of political communication, extended it in new directions. "Both pageantry and the printed text could reduplicate the state's magnificent presentation of itself, but published accounts could also scatter local spectacle across the realm."[4] Moreover, printed accounts could be more accessible than the

[1] Barry Coward, *The Stanleys: Lords Stanley and Earls of Derby, 1385–1672* (Chetham Society, 3d ser., 30, 1985), pp. 132–33.

[2] Charles Pythian-Adams, "Ceremony and the Citizen: The Communal Year at Coventry, 1450–1550," in P. Clark and P. Slack, eds., *Crisis and Order in English Towns, 1500–1700* (London, 1972), pp. 57–85; D. M. Palliser, "Civic Mentality and the Environment in Tudor York," *Northern History* 18 (1982).

[3] Judith Richards, "'His Nowe Majestie' and the English Monarchy," *P&P* 113 (1986): 73–74, 77, 83–86; Clifford Geertz, *Local Knowledge* (New York, 1983), pp. 121–46; Peter Burke, "Popular Culture in Seventeenth-Century London," in B. Reay, ed., *Popular Culture in Seventeenth-Century England* (New York, 1985), pp. 43–44.

[4] Wendy Wall, *The Imprint of Gender: Authorship and Publication in the English Renaissance* (Ithaca, 1993), pp. 163–64.

original. Though it was not the first printed account of entertainment and speeches during James I's coronation in London, one by Thomas Dekker was vendable because it contained "those speeches that before were published in Latin, now newly set forth in English," a necessity because the "multitude is now to be our audience."[5] The novelty in this development lay in its dependence on authorial pursuit of profit and publicity—a central feature of print culture, as we shall see in the next chapter.

For sending more substantive messages to the nation, several medieval precedents existed. The commissioning of inventive historical accounts of a dynasty was a staple feature of medieval statecraft. "The ragged shape of the English chronicle, which by 1500 had become a kind of civic commonplace book, was well established before the advent of print."[6] Communicative practices of Tudor and early-Stuart monarchs also followed medieval precedents when they used the clergy to convey political messages in sermons. In the fifteenth century, comparisons of England and ancient Israel were "the stock rhetoric of parliamentary sermons," whose nascent nationalism depicted England as God's elect nation.[7] Political use of the pulpit was expanded and refined as an instrument of propaganda on behalf of the Reformation in the reign of Henry VIII. "Until the onset of the Reformation, Paul's Cross sermons were as a rule intended to declare some policy and were in measure supervised, but there was nothing like the control which Cromwell introduced." At this time "the pulpit mattered even more than the printing press" because printing's utility for propaganda lay in "supplying the right kind of arguments to the preachers."[8]

To gather popular support for the Henrician Reformation, Cromwell instructed bishops to require their priests to preach in support for the royal supremacy over the Church and opposition to the "bishop of Rome" (who was no longer to be called "pope"). Cromwell also reviewed sermons from individual preachers, instructions for sermons sent out by bishops, and even "verses" that the bishop of Winchester proposed to use for teaching children the virtue of royal supremacy. When a compliant archbishop forwarded the text of a sermon to be preached

---

[5] Thomas Dekker, *The Whole Magnificent Entertainment: Given To King James* (*STC* 6513, 1603), sig. B1v.

[6] D. R. Woolf, "Genre into Artifact: The Decline of the English Chronicle in the Sixteenth Century," *Sixteenth-Century Journal* 19 (1988): 325–26.

[7] John W. McKenna, "How God Became an Englishman," in D. J. Guth and J. W. McKenna, eds., *Tudor Rule and Revolution* (Cambridge, 1982), p. 32. For political sermons in medieval York, see R. B. Dobson, *Church and Society in Medieval North of England* (London, 1996), pp. 172–73.

[8] Geoffrey R. Elton, *Policy and Police: The Enforcement of the Reformation in the Age of Thomas Cromwell* (Cambridge, 1972), pp. 211, 213.

by a minor cleric, he suggested superfluously that Cromwell might "peruse, and add or take away as he thinks convenient." He also sent to Cromwell religious articles for preachers throughout England. "You may add other and take away what you please, or else make other articles all new; so that when they shall be devised exactly . . . you may cause them to be sent into every diocese, to be preached throughout all the whole realm."[9] The rhetorical style for these political sermons was often described as "sincere," which denoted not only loyalty but also a simple expository style, suitable to the task of influencing popular opinion. From York Cathedral, Cromwell received a report on preaching by the archbishop of York in favor of government policy: "It was in a plainer fashion than was ever heard there before."[10] Elizabeth, James I, and Charles I later followed similar practices. In response to the Northern Revolt in 1569, the Elizabethan Privy Council issued instructions on pulpit oratory that included "a long exposition of the glories and benefits of the queen's reign" for the use of preachers. King James ordered his bishops to "tune the pulpits" in order to harmonize state policy and growing public interest in foreign affairs that had been stimulated by the Thirty Years' War. His son, Charles, used the clerical hierarchy to cobble together "nationwide public relations campaigns" on behalf of the Forced Loan and the latest twist in a foreign policy, which threatened to commit England to war on two fronts, against France as well as Spain.[11] Following these precedents after it seized power, the Long Parliament appointed preachers to deliver fast sermons that described official policy in providential terms.

Political use of the pulpit was a jealously guarded resource. Charles I ordered Archbishop Laud to ensure that only "discrete & able men" preach before the assize judges and "that they forbear to meddle with the persons or men or anything prejudicial to the laws & present government."[12] At this time local Puritan elites in London and provincial towns sought to obtain control over the pulpit by raising funds for lectureships, which they hoped to fill with nonconforming preachers whose sermons on weekdays and Sundays would complement regular worship led by an episcopally appointed cleric.[13] Official hostility to this

---

[9] J. Muller, ed., *The Letters of Stephen Gardiner* (Cambridge, 1933), p. 66; *L&P* 14, pt.1, no. 173; *The Works of Thomas Cranmer* (Cambridge, 1846), 2:314.

[10] *L&P* 8, no. 994; and see Elton, *Policy and Police*, pp. 211–16, 232–34.

[11] Michael Pulman, *The Elizabethan Privy Council in the Fifteen-Seventies* (Berkeley and Los Angeles, 1971), p. 131; Thomas Cogswell, "The Politics of Propaganda: Charles I and the People in the 1620s," *JBS* 29 (1990): 195–96, 212. See also Peter McCullough, *Sermons at Court* (Cambridge, 1998).

[12] *MSS Tanner* 71, fol. 142r.

[13] See Paul Seaver, *The Puritan Lectureships: The Politics of Religious Dissent, 1560–1662*

initiative, which would place control over the pulpit within the reach of Puritan oligarchies, flowed from the fear that lecturers would value loyalty to lay patrons over obedience to the Church and State. "The meanest corporation among us, though consisting for the most part of apron men, have found opportunities to have their facies humored and their ears tickled by their hierling shepherds."[14] Puritan members of municipal and guild corporations led efforts to raise endowments for lecturers, so it is hardly surprising to learn that sermons by lecturers commended the election of such persons to municipal and national office. A staunch Puritan lecturer in Newcastle, Robert Jenison, reported in 1624 that the bishop of Durham was angry because Jenison in a sermon displayed partiality "concerning the choice of our burgesses for Parliament." In 1639, Jenison and a lecturer in Berwick—this town and Newcastle were critical to the security of the border between England and Scotland—were suspended by a government alarmed at the prospect of an alliance between Scottish covenanters and domestic critics in 1639.[15]

Printing had many ramifications for change that centralized and rationalized the Tudor state bureaucracy as well as for political communication. From its inception in England, printing had been quickly pressed into government service: to publish proclamations and statutes, print forms, such as receipts for taxes with blank spaces, and supply propaganda directly and indirectly to the nation. The technical superiority of printing for textual reproduction commended it to English bishops who, otherwise wary of its implications for religion, created printed tax forms that helped them discharge their duty to collect annates, first-fruits, and other clerical taxes that now flowed to Westminster and not Rome. By this time printing was routinely used to facilitate dissemination of royal proclamations; its use distinguished a public statute from a private act issued by Parliament.[16]

Use of printing by monarchs was nearly coterminous with the history of English printing. In the previous chapter we saw that one of the earliest instances of printing in England involved translation of a papal bull that recognized the reign of Henry VII. The government of his son mobilized authors and printers to justify the most abrupt and unpopular

---

(Stanford, 1970); Christopher Hill, *Society and Puritanism in Pre-Revolutionary England* (New York, 1967), pp. 79–123.

[14] Thomas Jackson, *Three Sermons Preached Before The King* (Oxford, STC 14307, 1637), p. 35.

[15] *MSS Tanner* 73, fol. 437v; *CSPD* 1639–40, pp. 11, 21, 77, 104–5, 183.

[16] Arthur Slavin, "The Tudor Revolution and the Devil's Art: Bishop Bonner's Printed Forms," in Guth and McKenna, eds., *Tudor Rule and Revolution*, pp. 13–23; G. R. Elton, *Studies in Tudor and Stuart Politics and Government* (Cambridge, 1974–92), 3:105, 126–27.

shift in official policy in early-modern England. This eventuated in a flood of state-sponsored publications that defended Henry VIII's claim to supremacy over the Church of England. Preserved among state papers are drafts of polemical treatises on religious and political issues, many clearly intended for popular consumption, such as a treatise rhetorically framed as a dialogue between a "doctor" and a "student" that defends the Reformation and attacks papal authority. When an observer in 1534 described initiatives in Parliament to deprive the papacy of revenues and appellate jurisdiction, he noted, "All his authorities be clean disannulled here, and daily doctors and great clerks make new books and write against his pomp."[17] The utility of printing for winning hearts and minds for the king's great cause was both direct and indirect. While it is difficult to assess the readership and impact of these printed tracts, "it does not matter so much that we cannot tell how many men may have read the pamphlets when we find preachers proving by the contents of their sermons that they had done so."[18] We shall see that this held for political events one century later, when, in the civil war between Charles I and the Long Parliament, both sides sent declarations and other printed texts to clerics, who were ordered to read them in church.

Printed proclamations often provide brief explanations of circumstances that prompted monarchs to issue them. One by James I that prohibited dueling states that "instruction ought to precede execution." Toward this end, "We thought it requisite to refer this proclamation to a more large discourse annexed," which was a printed pamphlet, a summary of royal reasoning by the earl of Northumberland.[19] In the previous chapter we saw that both early-Stuart monarchs used the medium of print to broadcast political messages when propaganda was urgently required to counter negative interpretations of foreign or domestic policies. In 1618 James closely supervised the writing of a printed declaration that justified the impending execution of Sir Walter Raleigh. This and the "haste" with which it was printed—the publisher "set 20 presses awork at once"—reflect concern with domestic opinion that rallied behind Raleigh's opposition to pro-Spanish policies.[20] Ten years later Charles I blocked Parliament's order, on June 10, 1628, to print the Petition of Right along with the king's second, more favorable answer to the petition, given on June 7. After Parliament adjourned, fifteen hundred copies of the petition and second answer were called in and destroyed, and a new edition was printed, with the earlier, equivocal answer given by the king on June 2 and supplementary material that held

[17] *LL* 2:66; *L&P* 11, no. 86, and see nos. 85, 1215, 1409, 1420.
[18] Elton, *Policy and Police*, p. 211.
[19] *RP-S* 1:304. For the pamphlet, see *STC* 8498.
[20] S. R. Gardiner, ed., *The Fortescue Papers* (*CS*, ns, 1, 1871), pp. 57–58, 67.

the king's assent to the petition had left his prerogative powers entirely intact.[21] Similar publication initiatives occurred at the end of the next decade as part of Charles I's ill-fated efforts to mobilize an army and impose religious conformity, as it was understood by him and Archbishop Laud, on Scotland. Unprepared administratively, militarily, or fiscally, the government experienced a public relations disaster in the Bishops' War. Because it could not hire mercenaries or call out whole militia units, it mobilized poorly supplied, incompetently led, impressed soldiers whose riotous behavior reinforced sympathy for the Scottish Presbyterians and suspicion about the government's intentions and competence.[22] In early 1640 the government embarked on public relations initiatives after Secretary Vane received well-founded[23] reports on these sympathies and suspicions and some advice: "some speedy remedy should be taken to give the whole kingdom true information." In March the Privy Council agreed on a proclamation that blamed the Scots for the current impasse and also on a "short treatise to be published, stating what his Majesty expects of his subjects of Scotland, and what he will grant to them." Both clearly aimed more at domestic opinion in England than at Scotland. Secretary Windebank remarked on April 11 that he had devoted much of the previous week to the writing of this treatise, "his Majesty having commanded my pen," which was now in press.[24]

In chapter 7 we shall see how political necessity during the civil wars between Charles I and the Long Parliament led both sides to produce an unprecedented flood of printed political publications. Yet other forms of communication remained important for sending political messages from the political center to the periphery of the nation—for example, a plentiful supply of engraved images of Charles I and his commanders competed with images of political and military leaders of the Parliamentary forces. The Long Parliament invented new symbols of authority to replace the privy and great seals used by the administration of the king, and it followed royal precedents in exploiting the political potential of the pulpit. But turbulent politics in the 1640s and 1650s also involved messages from the periphery to the political center. These, too, had

[21] Elizabeth R. Foster, "Printing and the Petition of Right," *HLQ* 38 (1974): 81–83.

[22] See Mark Fissel, *The Bishops' Wars: Charles I's Campaigns against Scotland, 1638–1640* (Cambridge, 1994). See also Kevin Sharpe, *The Personal Rule of Charles I* (New Haven, 1992), chap. 13.

[23] E.g., Conrad Russell, *The Fall of the British Monarchies, 1637–1642* (Oxford, 1991), pp. 84–90.

[24] *CSPD* 1639–40, pp. 503, 543; *CSPD* 1640, p. 21. For the pamphlet, see *STC* 9260 (1640).

many precedents. Only in view of the diverse forms of political communication that flowed in this direction in pre-revolutionary England can we assess the subsequent appearance of public opinion as a political factor.

PERIPHERY TO CENTER

Rulers had ceremonies, priests, printers, assize judges, and more for sending political messages. Other resources existed for political communication that moved in different directions. Highly ritualized forms of collective behavior afforded a limited opportunity for crowds to send messages to local and national rulers. Crowd behavior could be a passive extension of symbolic displays of authority or could involve extralegal means of limited violence. The latter appears throughout early-modern Europe, including England, where the "circumstances most likely to provoke popular political action . . . were ones involving an immediate threat to subsistence, such as the encroachment on common rights by enclosing landlords, or the failure of the magistrates to enforce protective market regulations."[25] Crowd behavior mobilized a semiautonomous body of opinion that nonetheless displayed an essentially conservative outlook on politics. Rhetoric and ritual in traditions governing unruly collective behavior limited expressions of grievance so that they did not appear to challenge fundamental premises of the political and social order.[26] Yet in early-Stuart England, new variations reflected growing political awareness among ordinary Englishmen. No longer was localism the only outlook expressed by crowd behavior: "A striking development of the early-seventeenth century is a gradual shift in focus of popular protests from localized grievances to issues of national importance." Already evident in the 1620s, this development accelerated in the civil wars and persisted after the Restoration (1660), when

[25] Michael Mullett, *Popular Culture and Popular Protest in Late Medieval and Early Modern Europe* (London, 1987), pp. 1–27; David Underdown, *Revel, Riot, and Rebellion* (Oxford, 1985), p. 107.

[26] Roger B. Manning, *Village Protests* (Oxford, 1988), pp. 1–2: "The rituals of protest employed by demonstrators frequently mimicked judicial ceremonies. . . . Even where popular conceptions of justice diverged from those of the governing élite, the former derived from the latter. . . . The employment of the customary symbols and rituals of festive misrule or affirmations of loyalty served to reassure the governors that the protestors were not challenging the social or political order." Cf. Susan Herbst, *Numbered Voices: How Opinion Polling Has Shaped American Politics* (Chicago, 1993), p. 62, who argues that modern opinion polls constrain expressions of opinion more closely than had early-modern riots.

politicized crowd behavior was a staple feature of London politics in the reign of Charles II.[27]

Scribal texts and anonymous publication techniques in collective mobilization resembled communication practices in less exceptional circumstances, when bills posted in public places might publicize an occasion for festive misrule by apprentices, a challenge in a feud, or a libel against a prominent public figure.[28] In the Lincolnshire Rebellion and the Pilgrimage of Grace in 1536–37 written communication served simultaneously as propaganda and a tactical resource for mobilization. The outbreak of revolt in Lincolnshire had been precipitated by rumors about further abolition of monasteries, confiscation of church goods, and crushing taxes. We shall see that these rumors circulated orally and in written form, on "bills" that were distributed throughout the shire and posted on church doors. Not only did these bills contain demands of the rebels—for example, restoration of the suppressed religious houses, removal of Cromwell and "heretical" bishops from positions of power—but also announcements of times and places for meetings of rebel hosts.[29] The mustering of rebels "was by means of divers bills and scrows set upon posts and church doors . . . and tost and scattered around in the country," reported Ralph Sadler. Bills also "were strewed about the market towns," a Lincolnshire rebel testified in the Tower.[30] Along with other rituals of popular mobilization, such as forced oath taking,[31] anonymously posted bills had links to collusive features of rebellions because they concealed elite participation. They also followed surreptitious publication practices commonly used for libels, which were often scattered in streets, left on stairways, or posted in public places. These methods were associated with both private and public disputes. In 1598, after a long feud led to bloody encounter with Gervase Markham, John Holles complained about his adversary's behavior: "at all the market crosses in Nottinghamshire, he set up most infamous libels and proc-

[27] Manning, *Village Protests*, p. 188; Underdown, *Revel, Riot, and Rebellion*, pp. 120–36. For crowd behavior after 1660, see Tim Harris, *London Crowds in the Reign of Charles II* (Cambridge, 1990).

[28] For writing practices in the 1381 rebellion, see Steven Justice, *Writing and Rebellion: England in 1381* (Berkeley, 1994), p. 29.

[29] *L&P* 11, no. 892, 1299; 12, pt. 1, nos. 163, 185, 1021, 1034, 1083. In the remote northwest town of Kendal, a bailiff who was "sworn to the commons" made copies of these bills and sent them to nearby villages for publication, *L&P* 12, pt. 1, nos. 425, 965, and see no. 786 for copying by a rector.

[30] A. Clifford, ed., *The State Papers and Letters of Sir Ralph Sadler* (Edinburgh, 1809), 3:362–63; *L&P* 12, pt. 1, no. 70.

[31] M. E. James, "Obedience and Dissent in Henrician England," *P&P* 48 (1970): 70–71.

lamations against me."[32] Libels with railing, humorous, or obscence verses on prominent persons often advanced a political point of view and were a staple feature of early-Stuart politics. They, too, relied on anonymous publication practices, although their circulation was abetted by reading and copying that "occurred in regular sociable contact."[33] Publication of scribal texts with polemical political messages in 1640 resembled libeling practices, for example, when anti-Scottish papers were "found in Newcastle streets" or when a "scandalous paper" critical of the new canons appeared on a post in the Ipswich marketplace or in London after the dissolution of the Short Parliament, when "many libels" were "set up on posts and found scattered in many places."[34]

Elections to seats in Parliament offered opportunities to forty-shilling freeholders for participation in political communication. Messages were conveyed not only by the outcome of a contest, but in debates that accompanied it. In 1642 one writer compared a meeting in Yorkshire called by Charles I in his quest for support to elections because the meeting "produced nothing but a confused murmur & noise, as at an election for knights of the Parliament (some crying the King, some the Parliament)."[35] This association of voting and political debate was a novel development. Up to and including many elections for the Short and Long Parliaments, voting was based on deference to local elites. In this setting, political choice involved informal discussion among the local gentry. Competition for places occurred privately, in letters that requested or offered support for candidates who were then acclaimed in essentially uncontested elections by electors who deferred to wishes of their local rulers, who in turn often had instructions from higher authorities. The importance of patronage and deference in determining outcomes of elections is well known.[36]

However, patronage and deference are not constants but exhibit variability in prerevolutionary England in the extent to which they subordi-

---

[32] *Letters of John Holles, 1587–1637*, ed. P. R. Seddon (*Thoroton Society Record Series* 31, 1975), 1:12; Lawrence Stone, *The Crisis of the Aristocracy* (Oxford, 1965), pp. 244–45, argues that the epidemic of dueling in England peaked between roughly 1590 and 1620.

[33] Alastair Bellany, " 'Raylinge Rymes and Vaunting Verse': Libellous Politics in Early-Stuart England, 1603–1628," in K. Sharpe and P. Lake, eds., *Culture and Politics in Early Stuart England* (Stanford, 1993), p. 291.

[34] *CSPD* 1640, pp. 518, 659; *MSS JCC* 39, fol. 84v.

[35] *The Diary of Sir Henry Slingsby*, ed. D. Parsons (London, 1836), p. 77.

[36] Richard Cust, "Politics and the Electorate in the 1620s," in R. Cust and A. Hughes, *Conflict in Early Stuart England* (London, 1989); Derek Hirst, *The Representative of the People?* (Cambridge, 1975); John K. Gruenfelder, *Influence in Early Stuart Elections, 1604–1640* (Columbus, OH, 1981); Mark Kishlansky, *Parliamentary Selection* (Cambridge, 1986).

nated local choice to central control. In the reign of Henry VIII, this subordination was extreme in both the canvassing and voting phase of elections. A Norfolk gentleman evidently had himself in mind when he promised Cromwell that at the election of county MPs for the 1539 Parliament he would "be there with his tenants and friends to give their voices to such as Cromwell shall indicate." Cromwell nominated two others and advised his suitor "to be conformable."[37] In 1536, town electors in Canterbury chose two burgesses to Parliament before the mayor received a letter from Cromwell, who conveyed the king's request that they elect other persons. A second letter followed, conveying royal displeasure and requesting that the town hold a second election to elect the king's candidates. And "if any person will obstinately gainsay the same," wrote Cromwell, "advertise me thereof that I may order him as the King's pleasure shall be."[38] More moderate exercise of influence was the norm in early-Stuart elections, illustrated by an electoral tactic for Edward Nicholas, a candidate for a seat in the Short Parliament as burgess for the port town of Sandwich. After accusations of Catholic sympathies damaged Nicholas's prospects, his aristocratic patron, the earl of Northumberland, requested the Admiral of the Fleet, Sir John Pennington, "to be personally present upon the day of the election" or, better yet, "the night previous . . . so as to procure for Nicholas as many voices as you can." In a port town there would be many electors eager to please an admiral.[39]

However, two developments altered the traditional pattern of elections. First, inflation enlarged the forty-shilling franchise, extending it to 30–40 percent of male householders. Second, national perspectives on politics weakened the electorate's traditional deference to local magnates. In the early-seventeenth century "emphasis on the fact of representation" and references to members of Parliament as public persons became commonplace. The concept of an MP as a public person was an extension of old notions that associated parliaments with redress of grievances. Pressure for change came from outside and within Parliaments. In the 1621 Parliament, opposition to traditional constraints on local choice arose from "growing resistance of some constituencies to outside members, and the fear of many members of the Commons that the quest of great men for additional supplies of patronage might lay elections unduly open to 'influence.'"[40] By 1640, elections were more

---

[37] L&P 14, pt. 1, nos. 672, 706.

[38] R. Merriman, ed., Life and Letters of Thomas Cromwell (Oxford, 1902), 1:125–28, 2:13–14.

[39] CSPD 1639–40, p. 569.

[40] J. H. Hexter, "Parliament, Liberty, and Freedom of Elections," in J. H. Hexter, ed,. Parliament and Liberty from the reign of Elizabeth to the Civil War (Stanford, 1992),

likely to be contested—the number of contested elections tripled between 1604 and 1624 and then doubled again by 1640. Gentlemen standing for election increasingly had to appeal to an electorate that "was gradually coming to think in terms of national issues." Many contests for seats in Parliament reflected traditional patterns, "expressions of the territorial power of aristocrats or gentry magnates. . . . But if it is a mistake to ignore the older form of electoral politics, it would be equally wrong to neglect the new. A broader, more independent electorate had been a striking feature of the 1620s, and it became an even more critical one in 1640."[41] Across England, reports on the 1640 elections cite unprecedented factionalism and vying for popular support. In elections to the Short Parliament, predicted one Norfolk gentleman, "It is likely there will be the greatest noise and confluence of man that ever have been heard or seen . . . for never do I think was there such working and counterworking, to purchase vulgar blasts of acclamation." At this time in Bristol a future member of the Short Parliament heard that "intelligence from all parts of England" indicated how those disaffected to the personal rule of Charles I "are disposed for their elections. . . . They are like to produce great factions in all parts." Rumors about one faction, "the Robins of the West," had reportedly "reached the Kings' ear." This reference to a popular Puritan faction, if David Underdown's detective work is correct, illustrates the Puritan dimension in reports on factionalism in elections to the Short and Long Parliaments. According to a report from Newcastle, "all the Puritans in our town are laboring to make Sir Lionell [Maddison] a Parliament man." In Sandwich, it was "factious nonconformists" who spread the rumor that candidate Nicholas had Catholic sympathies.[42] Growing factionalism among electors who were becoming somewhat less deferential was not limited to parliamentary elections. Local studies describe these changes in contests for municipal office in early-seventeenth century England.[43]

---

pp. 21–27; Russell, *Parliaments and English Politics*, p. 127; and see Cust, "Politics and the Electorate," pp. 143–51.

[41] Underdown, *Revel, Riot, and Rebellion*, p. 132, and see pp. 120–46; Hirst, *Representative of the People?* pp. 8, 30–35, 111, 153, 178–84; Kishlansky, *Parliamentary Selection*, pp. 12–18. Diarmaid MacCulloch detects in late-Tudor Suffolk a decline in the tradition of gentlemen instructing tenants how to vote. *Suffolk and the Tudors: Politics and Religion in an English County* (Oxford, 1986), pp. 334–35.

[42] Robert Ketton-Cremer, *Norfolk in the Civil War* (Hamden, CT, 1970), p. 111; J. Bettey, ed., *Calendar of the Correspondence of the Smyth Family of Ashton Court, 1548–1642 (Bristol Record Society* 35 1982), pp. 150–51; *CSPD* 1639–40, pp. 402, 561 and see p. 580; Esther Cope, *Politics without Parliament* (London, 1987), p. 186; *CSPD* 1639–40, p. 580; *HMC De L'Isle and Dudley*, 6:235; Underdown, *Revel, Riot and Rebellion*, p. 135.

[43] Peter Clark, "Thomas Scott and the Growth of Urban Opposition to the Early

Both patronage and factionalism in elections involved varying admixtures of oral and scribal communication. Patronage was requested and supplied in letters from great lords and powerful officials to local elites. To secure the election of a client for a borough seat in the 1572 Parliament, the fourth earl of Derby had a commendatory letter read before an assembly of Liverpool burgesses. After writs went out for elections to the 1614 Parliament, one observer remarked, "Here is much bustling for places in Parliament, and letters fly from great personages extraordinarily." For James I's first parliament, the Lord President of the Council of the North wrote as "supreme magistrate under his highness" in Yorkshire to a prominent member of the local gentry and requested that "you will give your voices of your selves and your tenants and such other friends as you can procure" for two candidates and "send me your present answer in writing."[44] Less imperious requests were common in letters among the gentry as candidates canvassed for support and in testimonial letters from the court, aristocratic patrons, local gentry, and clerics that were read aloud in support of candidates in both contested elections and those ruled by patronage. This not uncommon practice in early-Stuart elections appears to have intensified in elections to the Short and Long Parliaments of 1640.[45] Such literary practices were not confined to patronage from the powerful. In the disputed election of burgesses from Hastings to the Short Parliament, supporters of a losing candidate circulated writings as they "went about privately from house to house." Opposition to the election came from "the greater part of the freemen" of the town, whose "free voices" were not counted. Their opposition was stiffened by a letter from a defeated candidate that was read aloud in a private home just before twenty freemen demonstrated at the swearing in of one MP.[46] Sermons also sent messages as part of factional politics surrounding elections for the Short Parliament in 1640, when prominent Puritan preachers, such as Stephen Marshall, "preached often out of their own parishes before the election."[47]

Stuart Regime," *HJ* 21 (1978): 25; Richard Cust, "Anti-Puritanism and Urban Politics: Charles I and Great Yarmouth," *HJ* 35 (1992): 23; Jacqueline Eales, *Puritans and Roundheads* (Cambridge, 1990), pp. 7, 71, 94–95; John Evans, *Seventeenth Century Norwich* (1979), pp. 67–76; John Fielding, "Opposition to the Personal Rule of Charles I," *HJ* 31 (1988): 787.

[44] Coward, *The Stanleys*, p. 129; *Chamberlain Letters* 1:515; *Wentworth Papers*, pp. 47–48.

[45] Gruenfelder, *Influence in Early Stuart Elections*, pp. 196–97, 252, and see p. 199 on the 1640 elections: "The pens of a county's squirearchy must have been worn to the nub as the steady stream of letters pleading, exhorting, promising, and cajoling flooded from their desks as the search for voices went on, in some cases, right up to election morning."

[46] SPD 16/450/fols. 77, 173; *CSPD* 1639–40, p. 565; *CSPD* 1640, p. 3.

[47] *CSPD* 1639–40, p. 609.

Printing did not facilitate political communication surrounding elections in prerevolutionary England. This occurred later, in the development of party politics in late-Stuart England, when circulation of printed political texts—ballads, playing cards, and satirical prints as well as newspapers and pamphlets—was an important electoral tactic.[48] Just prior to the 1681 elections for the "Oxford" Parliament, a cover letter with copies of a Whig pamphlet sent through the posts, *The Certain Way To Save England . . . By A Prudent choice Of Members To Serve In . . . Parliament*, urged its recipients "to put yourself to the small charge of buying a parcel of them for your country people." A leading Tory polemicist, John Nalson, thought this was incompatible with the principle of free choice by electors of their MPs.[49] Such qualms would later be muted in Hanoverian England. By then, "election campaigns had an insatiable appetite for an unending stream of propaganda: advertisements placed in and letters written to the local press; posters; placards, cartoons and announcements . . . broadsides, handbills, songs, and squibs to circulate among the electors."[50] The element of publicity in these communicative practices is nearly absent in elections to Parliament in prerevolutionary England.

GRIEVANCES AND PETITIONS

Medieval Background

No communicative practice for sending messages from the periphery to the center had greater legitimacy than petitioning. Though prevailing principles of secrecy and privilege precluded popular discussion of political matters, they provided procedures for requesting favors and expressing grievance by petition. Contemporaries held these procedures to be venerable traditions, and they did not draw sharp distinctions between individual requests for favors and collective expressions of grievance. From the early Middle Ages onward, "the use of petitionary formulas was extremely flexible." Deference, humility, and supplication were inherent in the form and content of these formulas. "The great strength of petition was that it encapsulated the relationship of lordship and dependence that was the core of ideal political relations in a single, concise formula."[51]

---

[48] Harris, *London Crowds in the Reign of Charles II*, pp. 106–29, 153–55.

[49] [John Nalson], *England Bought And Sold* (*Wing* C1764, 1681).

[50] Frank O'Gorman, *Voters, Patrons, and Parties: The Unreformed Electorate of Hanoverian England, 1734–1832* (Oxford, 1989), p. 72, and see also pp. 139–40.

[51] Geoffrey Koziol, *Begging Pardon and Favor: Ritual and Political Order in Early Medieval France* (Ithaca, 1992), pp. 44–45.

In medieval England, receipt of pleas from petitioning subjects was a visible, time-consuming part kingship. In the fifteenth century, Lancastrian and Yorkist kings received several thousand petitions each year.[52] The same held for the business of parliaments, which met as high courts that received and tried petitions. More than sixteen thousand petitions went to parliaments from the thirteenth to fifteenth century. Predominantly juridical in nature, they conveyed complaints, decried miscarriage of justice, or requested relief from taxes, forest laws, and other regulations. In a three-week session, the 1305 Parliament dealt with nearly five hundred petitions, whose complaints and requests are inscribed on small pieces of parchment, with subsequent notations that indicate the prescribed remedy, if any.[53] Petitions were an acknowledged means for collective remonstrance that expressed popular grievances. Henry VIII's herald told rebellious commoners in Lincolnshire and Yorkshire that "ye might have forborne your unlawful assemblies, and sued him by petition declaring your griefs." Sending proclamations "to every market town" that the king was reviewing rebel petitions was a tactic used by Henry for "appeasing and quieting of the commons in the North parts."[54] In Jacobean England, conventional wisdom held that convening a parliament offered an occasion for traditional redress of grievances. This wisdom was agreeable to a leading conservative councilor to James I, the earl of Northampton, as well as to the king himself. In his journey south to claim the throne in 1603, James "was bombarded with an assortment of petitions" on secular and fiscal grievances, and he proposed to convene a parliament that "shall be chiefly assembled for the relief of all grievances of our people." This, Bacon later observed, was a principle of statecraft: "To give moderate liberty for griefs and discontentments to evaporate (so it be without too great insolency or bravery), is a safe way."[55]

The history of petitions to Parliament reflects growing complexity in medieval institutions. Unlike unevenly composed petitions in the reign of Edward I, petitions acquired a characteristic form under Richard II (for address and phrasing); their precision and elaboration often required use of scriveners and lawyers, whose fees for these services appeared in guild records.[56] By the early-fourteenth century, distinctions

[52] Charles Ross, *Edward IV* (New Haven, 1997), p. 304 and n.

[53] Frederic Maitland, "Introduction," *Rerum Britannicarum Medii Aevi Scriptores* 98 (1893): xxvi–xxvii, xxxii, lv, lxvii–lxxiii.

[54] *L&P* 11, no. 826, 1410.

[55] Linda Peck, *Northampton: Patronage and Policy at the Court of James I* (London, 1982), pp. 169–67; R. C. Munden, "James I and 'the Growth of Mutual Distrust,'" in K. Sharpe, ed., *Faction and Parliament* (London, 1985), pp. 44–45; Bacon, *Works* (Boston, 1860), 12:129.

[56] A. R. Meyers, "Parliamentary Petitions in the Fifteenth Century," *EHR* 52 (1937): 386–88.

were drawn between private petitions and parliamentary or commons petitions that raised "grievances regarded as being of common interest." This occurred as Parliaments added legislative to their original juridical functions. By the early-sixteenth century, however, a subsequent innovation superseded petitions. Legislation proceeded by "bill," which delineated the substance of a legislative act, and not by petition. Private bills were still called petitions,[57] and Parliaments continued to "petition" monarchs, most notably in cases of conflict between them. In the early-seventeenth century, MPs displayed keen awareness of the antiquarian nature of this use of petition, noting how humble overtones of petitions were appropriate for issues on which Parliament had little leverage. "We have fallen from a bill to a petition, and lower we cannot go," observed Wentworth in debates over how to oppose abuses in the exercise of the Crown's prerogative powers. The outcome was the 1628 Petition of Right.[58]

Petitioning Traditions in the Seventeenth Century

In early-seventeenth-century England, petitions were objects of popular knowledge, well suited to a hierarchical world in which deference and patronage functioned like money. The word *petition* was a common figure of speech, used literally and metaphorically to signify deferential request for favor or redress of a grievance. Letter writers seeking advancement or some other favor often described their request as a petition. "You know it is a petitioning age," one writer began, before outlining the requested favor.[59] On Sundays clerics explained that prayer was a petition to God and the faithful were humble petitioners. This petitionary metaphor had been used by Catholic priests before Puritan ministers used it to explain a key tenet of reformed religion: "Faith obtains, as a poor petitioner, what the Lord promises in special favor." Puritan laymen, too, used this metaphor. In 1639, Sir Robert Harley, who later was a prominent MP in the Long Parliament, instructed his son that fear of God "is the constant petitioner on your behalf at the throne of grace." A London tailor in 1636 asked John Winthrop in New England to "remember Old England in your petitions to the throne of grace."[60]

[57] Ronald Butt, *A History of Parliament: The Middle Ages* (London, 1989), p. 268; Elton, *Tudor and Stuart Politics* 3:118, 128, 132; G. O. Sayles, *The Functions of the Medieval Parliament of England* (London, 1988), pp. 48–57.

[58] *PP 1628* 3:582 and see 3:273; D'Ewes 1682, p. 645; *PP 1626* 2:427; *Wentworth Papers*, p. 75.

[59] *MSS Add* 61,989, fol. 26.

[60] John Ball, *Treatise Of Faith* (STC 1320, 1632), p. 247, and see pp. 136, 252; *MSS*

Allusions to literal and metaphorical petitions often overlapped. In the Northern Rebellion against Henry VIII, Catholic rebels sent their demands in a petition to the king and paraded with banners that depicted "the commonalty . . . making their petition to the picture of Christ" that he move the king to grant their petition. In the middle of the next century, Worcestershire petitioners sent Parliament a petition against proposals to abolish compulsory tithes "on the behalf of Jesus Christ, for whom we doubt not but you are daily petitioners."[61]

For defenders of royal prerogative, before and during the civil war, the petition was a congenial metaphor for thinking about constitutional issues. In this perspective, monarchs ruled and humble subjects petitioned. "When the subject's liberty is in question," declared the earl of Northampton in 1628, "I will creep upon my knees with a petition to his majesty with all humility. When the King's prerogative is in question, I will get upon my horse and draw my sword and defend it." In 1643 a Royalist writer invoked a long-antiquated procedure for legislation in describing the appropriate relation between monarch and parliament: the latter convened in order to "to propose, not to impose laws . . . they come to throw their petitions at his feet." For Puritan supporters of the Long Parliament, petitionary metaphor presented ungodly rebellion in a favorable light. In Lucy Hutchinson's account of the 1640 invasion by the Scottish Army, Scottish Covenanter soldiers were frustrated petitioners who "forced their way, after they had been refus'd to pass quietly by [the English army] with their petitions in their hands."[62] Contemporaries understood this use of petitionary metaphor, in which, observed James I in 1622, "the fair pretence of a dutiful petition" might conceal undeferential motives. A "humble petition" from the Commons could disguise a frontal assault on royal prerogative, just as a food riot might appear to some as an extreme form of petitioning.[63]

Worldly petitions in early-Stuart England requested many things: office, alms, and relief from debt, delay of justice, or imprisonment. Institutionalized means existed for sending them to the Parliament, Privy Council, and other seats of authority. Tuesday afternoons were set aside

---

Add 33,572, fol. 310; *Winthrop Papers* (Boston, 1929), 3:307. In the sixteenth century, this metaphor aided explanations of Catholic worship; *L&P* 13, pt.2, no. 571. In the seventeenth century, it was used by High Church opponents of Puritan ministers, e.g., John Shelford, *Five Pious And Learned Discourses* (Cambridge, STC 22400, 1635), p. 32.

[61] *L&P* 12, pt.1, no. 1001; E684[33] 1652, p. 8. For an Elizabethan example, see *An humble petition of the Communaltie* (Middleburgh, STC 7584, 1588), sig. B4v.

[62] *PP 1628* 5:526–27; James Howell, *A Discourse* (E61[14], 1643), p. 5; J. Sutherland, ed., *Memoirs of the Life of Colonel Hutchinson* (Oxford, 1973), p. 50.

[63] *His Majesties Declaration* (STC 9241, 1622), pp. 5, 7; Buchanan Sharpe, *In Contempt of All Authority: Rural Artisans and Riot in the West of England, 1586–1660* (Berkeley, 1980), p. 42.

by the Privy Council "to consider and give answer to suitors that shall prefer petitions." Later in the reign of James I, the Council specified detailed procedures for delivering petitions: immediately after councillors took their seats, to a clerk, passed on to a secretary of state, who then decided which ones would go before the Council.[64] At this time, a Parliament began with a medieval ritual, the appointment of receivers and triers of petitions. Petitions to kings were received by secretaries of state (if the petitioner had influence or money) or by the Court of Requests from poor suitors.[65] This last point calls attention to popular access to petitioning. Rich and poor alike petitioned; it was a popular activity because it provided a substitute for proximity and influence conveyed by wealth or connections to the Court. When plague threatened London in 1625, Sir Edward Coke argued that Parliament should establish no committees to receive petitions because of "the danger of infection by drawing the meaner sort of people about us." In a 1612 play by Thomas Dekker, the king declares:

> Tuesdays we'll sit to hear the poor-man's cries,
> Orphans, widows: our princely eyes
> Shall their petitions read . . .[66]

Incessant demands from rich and poor petitioners is why, in the reign of Charles I, "two gentlemen ushers were appointed to go before the king on state days to see that none thrust petitions into his hand."[67] Though understandable, this restraint was unusual. His father, James, "had been constantly beset by petitioners within his palaces, via back stairs and doorways, and without his palaces, even when hunting." So had been Edward III, three centuries earlier, when petitioners sought him out when he was hunting in the royal forests or fighting on the border.[68]

Petitions on every conceivable grievance went to all extant seats of authority and followed the tides of political fortune. When secretaries of state "no longer had access to the King's mind" in the reign of James I,

---

[64] J. R. Tanner, *Constitutional Documents of James I* (Cambridge, 1930), pp. 130, 132–33.

[65] Thus, the earl of Clare had a petition from a Nottinghamshire cleric exhibited against him, in a dispute over rent, at the Court of Requests. But when the earl was a petitioner, over a Star Chamber action against him for violating a ban on building in London, he sent his petition to Sir Francis Windebank, the principal secretary of state, after vetting it with the bishop of Lincoln, who "altered some pieces in it" in order to make it more acceptable to the king. *Letters of John Holles* 3:384–85, 495, 498–99.

[66] *PP 1625*, p. 220; Thomas Dekker, *If This Be Not a Good Play* (1612), in F. Bowers, ed., *Dramatic Works* (Cambridge, 1958), 3:132.

[67] Sharpe, *The Personal Rule of Charles I*, p. 199; and see Michael Young, *Servility and Service: The Life and Work of Sir John Coke* (London, 1986), pp. 106–7.

[68] Richards, " 'His Nowe Majestie,' " p. 80; W. M. Ormrod, *The Reign of Edward III* (New Haven, 1990), p. 57.

petitions for advancement and other favors "which had formerly flowed in to them in great abundance" now went to the bright star in the Jacobean court, the duke of Buckingham, "to the grievous loss of the regular officials in the matter of fees." Earlier in the reign of James, the flow of petitions supplies evidence of an alliance between Salisbury and Northampton as the dominant court faction.[69] Petitions came from corporate entities and individuals, who wished to convey public and private grievances, request favors, and enter pleas in juridical proceedings. Apprentices petitioned London's Court of Aldermen when marriage (a violation of apprenticeship indentures) blocked their admission to the freedom of the City; ten pounds would unblock it. A petition to the mayor and aldermen of Chester, who controlled a small school, complained about the incompetence of teachers who had ruined "a most flourishing school"; "to the general grief of us all, the spring time of our school is turned into an autumn, the little plants we send there are no sooner budded but blasted." Puritan aldermen in Norwich complained that "spit," "shit," and an occasional chair rained down on them from hostile clerics who sat in an overhead gallery in the town cathedral. Tailors sent petitions to the dean and chapter at Salisbury, protesting competition from persons who did not belong to their corporation and who practiced the trade on the chapter's property; if two were admitted at a "reasonable fine" to the corporation, the dean promised to evict the others. The earl of Warwick received a petition from America, from "one of my Negroes . . . that his wife may live with him"; the earl thought it "a request full of reason." In Thomas Dekker's play, "free-whores" petitioned for closing tobacco shops because they drew money from customers who "have now their delight dog-cheap, but for spending one quarter of that money in smoke."[70] The remarkable variety of petitioners and grievances in these examples points to the importance that contemporaries attached to the right to petition.

The Right to Petition

Contemporaries held strong views on the right to petition. It was "the indisputable right of the meanest subject."[71] When the Long Parliament met, in November 1640, a member attacked the Crown for seizing peti-

---

[69] Tanner, *Constitutional Documents*, p. 112; Peck, *Northampton*, p. 27.

[70] *MSS Rep* 54, fols. 47, 57, 90–91; *MSS. Rawl* C421, fols. 19, 20; John Evans, *Seventeenth-Century Norwich* (Oxford, 1979), p. 113; *MSS Harl* 2103, fol. 167; *MSS Eng. hist.* C1125, fol. 10; Dekker, *If This Be Not a Good Play*, p. 154.

[71] E341[5] (1646), p. 6.

tions delivered to Parliament and papers of members at the dissolution, last May, of the Short Parliament, reasoning that "the search of papers was a greater injury than the imprisonment of the body. For by that I suffer in my own person alone, but by the other, myself . . . and many petitioners might be drawn into danger, so as no man will either complain or let us know his griefs."[72] Though it was inappropriate to petition twice to the same authority over the same grievance,[73] the right to petition was noted even when persistent, possibly insane petitioners annoyed petitioned authorities.[74] As petitions poured into the Long Parliament, the patience of members reached the breaking point when receipt of a junior instead of senior fellowship prompted a disappointed professor at Cambridge to petition—but references to the Magna Carta stalled proposals to stop the receipt of more petitions.[75] In 1646, a Presbyterian petition that challenged Parliament's rule over the Church provoked heated debate in the Commons. Some saw this as contempt of Parliament but other members argued that petitioners "ought not be so charged for all the subjects may petition and show their reasons why freely."[76] Confronted by an insurgent Royalist movement in 1648, the Commons instructed a committee to frame an order against "all tumultuary meetings under pretense of petitions, with an assertion of the subject's liberty to petition in a due manner." The order refers to "the right and privilege of the subjects . . . to present unto the Parliament their just grievances, by way of petition."[77] Insurgent Royalists affirmed their right to present "just desires of the oppressed in a petitionary way (the undoubted right of the subject) and the very life of their liberty itself."[78]

Invocation of tradition lay at the core of contemporary thinking on the right of subjects to express grievance "in a petitionary way" and of the duty of officials to receive petitions. During the first civil war, both the commander of a Parliamentary garrison and the Royalist leader of Yorkshire troopers used similar arguments to justify their actions in forwarding petitions: this was a "duty" that "as a neighbor and countryman he is bound to do."[79] Modern ideas on individual rights are clearly irrel-

---

[72] *D'Ewes I*, p. 168. On the seizure of papers and petitions in May, see *CSPD* 1640, p. 112.

[73] *CSPD* 1639–40, p. 598.

[74] E.g., *PP 1628* 5:129, 131; John Spencer, *A Discourse of divers petitions* (E133[1], 1641).

[75] *D'Ewes I*, p. 415.

[76] M. Stieg, ed., *The Diary of John Harington, M.P.* (Somerset Record Society 74, 1977), p. 15.

[77] *CJ* 1646–48, p. 563, 567; *LJ* 1647–48, p. 273.

[78] 669f.12[20] (1648); and see 669f.12[33] (1648).

[79] H. G. Tibbutt, ed., *The Letter Books of Sir Samuel Luke* (Bedfordshire Historical Record Society 42, 1963), pp. 237–38; and see 152[1] (1642), p. [5].

evant to contemporary thinking on this issue, whose point of departure is a medieval conception of right. To petition is to enter a privileged communicative space, analogous to privileges that follow admission to the "freedom" of a municipal corporation. Petitions afforded subjects limited immunity to norms that otherwise restricted public commentary on political matters. These views accompanied otherwise novel developments in political petitioning during the English Revolution that we shall examine in chapter 8. For example, petitions against bishops and the episcopal church order were defended with the claim that "freedom . . . to make our grievances known is a chief privilege of Parliament." Radical agitators in the New Model Army invoked the rhetoric of "privilege" and "liberty" to defend their right to petition Parliament for redress of grievances.[80] But this customary language also appeared at the opposite end of the political spectrum, when Royalists protested efforts by Parliament to stop their petitions for the king and the Episcopal Church. A staple feature of Royalist ideology was the charge that the Long Parliament aimed at "arbitrary rule" when it interfered with Royalist petitioning, for example, in repressing petitions for peace in the winter of 1642–43 (see fig. 3).[81] This theme reappears in Royalist petitions in 1648 that defend the right to petition, "the birthright of the subject . . . once lost, must be succeeded with slavery and tyranny."[82] Royalists, army agitators, Puritans, and Levellers understood the right to petition in terms of extant tradition, as a medieval privilege and immunity. Its assertion by Royalists and conservative Presbyterians refers to the same "birthrights" that we associate with radical Leveller ideology.[83] Moreover, Levellers described the duty to receive petitions as Parliament's "own primitive practice."[84] Another traditional element in contemporary thinking on the right to petition was the petitionary metaphor in religion. Male and female Levellers used this to defend radical petitions, for "those in authority can in nothing more resemble God than in their readiness to hear and receive the complaints and petitions of any that apply themselves unto them." Women petitioners requested

[80] E146[24] (1642), p. 2; C. H. Firth, ed., *The Clarke Papers* (London, 1992), 1:56.

[81] In making this point in 1643, Royalists pointed out that Parliament had punished London officials who sought to quash Puritan petitions because "it was against the freedom and liberty of the subject not to permit them . . . to present their grievances in paper" E65[32] (Oxford, 1643), pp. 24–25; and see E67[23] (Oxford, 1643), p. 3; *HMC Cowper*, p. 311.

[82] E453[37] (1648), p. 1; and see E443[8] (1648), p. 3; E441[25] (1648), pp. 6–7; E447[18] (1648), sig. A2r.

[83] E355[13] (1646), pp. 12, 35; E422[9] (1648); E445[24] (1648), p. 4; E453[37] (1648), p. 1.

[84] E378[13] (1647), p. 9.

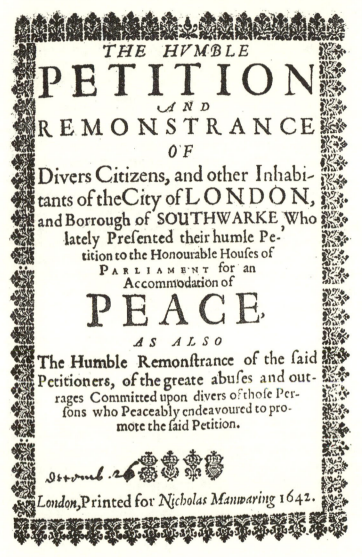

Fig. 3. London supporters of a peace treaty with Charles I defend their right to petition.

that Parliament not "withhold from us our undoubted right of petitioning, since God is ever willing and ready to receive the petitions of all. . . .
The ancient laws of England are not contrary to the will of God."[85]

Restrictions on Petitions

At first, it seems odd that the right to express grievance by petition was
so strongly entrenched in a society whose politics rested on deference
and patronage. But like other medieval rights, the right to petition was
far from absolute. Restrictions on expressions of grievance in petitions
provided only limited immunity against secrecy norms. No formal law
defined these restrictions, but their nature can be inferred from petitioning practices and from negative reactions to "factious" petitions that
violated conventions governing the rhetoric and content of petitions.
The rhetoric of petitions portrayed grievance as an apolitical conveyance
of information, principally by emphasizing *deferential, juridical,* and
spontaneous attributes of the grievance. Other restrictions further stipu-
lated that grievance should be local, directly experienced, and not critical of laws or indicative of discontent with authority.

Deferential rhetoric pervades petitions. Aided by juridical and religious metaphors, it portrays petitioners as "humble" suitors who "pray"
and "supplicate" for relief from grievances. Deference made petitions
equally appropriate instruments for communicating to God in religion
and worldly rulers in politics. Accused of subversion, a leader of Elizabethan Presbyterians denied that he and associates used any "means
besides prayer to God & petition to authority." Half a century later,
"theological and political" measures advocated by London ministers for
promoting the Presbyterian cause included prayer to God and petitions
to the Long Parliament.[86] Rhetoric in petitions restricted expression of
grievance so that it did not invoke or imply "popular will" as a source
of authority. In this form grievance appears as a neutral conveyance of
information that eschews prescribing solutions but leaves that to the
wisdom of the invoked authority. Lobbying—a principal motive for mobilizing public opinion in democratic politics—is prohibited. This appeared in a petition to the king from London in September 1640. Popular desire for convening a parliament had grown rapidly since the
dissolution of the Short Parliament, in May, and the subsequent military
fiasco that, by August, resulted in a Scottish army of occupation in the
northern part of the realm. To support calls for the king to convene Par-

---

[85] E579[9] (1649), p. 1; 669f.17[36] (1653).
[86] *ENT* 1:23; E273[18] (1644), pp. 5–6.

liament, the "humble petitioners" recited grievances about taxation, religion, and the alarming military situation, and reported that they had found "by experience that they are not redressed by the ordinary course of justice." Thus, they advanced their petition so that thereby "they may be relieved in the premises."[87] (The last phrase is still a term of art used by lawyers!) This rhetoric depoliticizes petitions by concealing the evident intent to lobby by petition, to promote preferred solutions to grievances, for this would signal contempt of authority. In response to George Digby's denunciation of a massive petition, the 1640 Root and Branch Petition that called for sweeping religious reforms, Nathaniel Fiennes argued that the London petitioners "come as humble suppliants, by way of petition" and "therefore [they] have done nothing, boldly or presumptiously." Later, London apprentices used this argument to deflect charges of presumptuousness from Fiennes and his allies in Parliament. "We come," they declared in a petition for peace in 1643, "to embowel our grievances . . . before you, not presuming to dictate to your graver judgments."[88]

Limited by deferential and juridical rhetoric, the right to petition granted only limited immunity to norms of secrecy and privilege in political communication. Permissible messages from the periphery to the political center did not include claims about the supremacy of popular will over petitioned authority. In debate over rival "peace" and "war" petitions from London citizens, a radical MP, Henry Marten, was reprimanded in the Commons "for saying that we ought to receive instructions for our proceedings from the people."[89] On this issue the view in Parliament was no different from the one in the leading Royalist newspaper, *Mercurius Aulicus*, on the impropriety of petitions perceived to be "directing in a manner what they would have done."[90] An extension of this point held that petitions should not take cognizance of business pending in Parliament because such lobbying violated the privilege of secrecy that surrounded parliamentary proceedings. "[A] great debate was in the House" in 1644 over "a seditious petition delivered in by some citizens of London." In prematurely thanking Parliament for passage of the self-denying ordinance that led to the formation of the New

---

[87] *Rushworth* 3:1264.

[88] *A Speech Of The Honorable Nathaniel Fiennes* (E196[32], 1641), p. 5; 669f.6[101] (1643). For Digby's attack on the petition, see *The Third Speech Of The Lord George Digby* (E196[30], 1641).

[89] *MSS Add* 31116, fol. 14.

[90] *MA* 1:107; and see *MSS Add* 31116, fol. 170; *MSS Harl* 166, fol. 216. In its 1648 declaration on the right to petition, Parliament reiterated a point made by the Commons in 1647 in opposition to a Leveller petition: "It is the right of the subject to petition. . . . It is the right of the Parliament to judge of such petitions." *CJ* 1646–48, p. 375; *LJ* 1647–48, p. 273; see also E427[6] (1648), p. 40.

Model Army, the petition erred "in taking notice of a vote passed in the House before it came to be made public in an Ordinance."[91] The next year Parliament reprimanded London's Common Council when, in March, it forwarded petitions from Presbyterian citizens that referred to ongoing deliberations over the Church. When these citizens subsequently promoted a new petition against Parliament's decision to vest disciplinary authority in lay commissioners (and not in presbyteries), they justified this step because "now the Ordinance [for lay commissioners] was passed, they had liberty to petition."[92] Contemporaries with varying political commitments acknowledged this restriction on petitioning. *Mercurius Britanicus*, a London newspaper aligned with the Independents in 1645, invoked it to attack a Presbyterian petition: it was "prejudicial and derogatory to the gravity and majesty of a Parliament; that when they are upon determination of anything, men should presume to instruct them." The point was often raised in debates surrounding competitive petition campaigns between Presbyterians and Independents.[93]

In addition to their deferential and juridical rhetoric, petitions appeared to be a *spontaneous* expression of grievance. In this context, the antithesis of spontaneity is faction. To explain this point writers used organic metaphor to compare expression of grievance by petition to the sensation of pain from an injured limb: "So questionless may the members of the body politic, finding themselves wounded or weakened . . . by humble petition sue unto the King and Parliament . . . the very heart and head." Just as pain spontaneously conveys information to the brain, petitions ideally were a spontaneous message, a neutral conveyance of information, devoid of normative claims for subordinating politics to popular will. The author of this point in a tract that defends petitions against bishops describes the right to petition in terms of "freedom of information."[94] Hence, petitions to Parliament were not held to violate contemporary norms of secrecy and privilege because petitionary rhetoric portrayed grievance as an apolitical flow of information on local conditions to the political center. When a constituent wrote to his representative in the Commons to urge him to promote sabbatarian legislation, a key issue for Puritans in the 1620s, he defended his action:

> because no man's eyes are able to see all things . . . to observe all the diseases and distempers of a commonwealth; it were therefore to be wished

---

[91] *MSS Add* 31116, fol. 179v; *MSS Harl* 166, fol. 151.

[92] *HMC Sixth Report*, pp. 104–5; *MSS Williams* 24.50, fol. 68.

[93] E308[5] (1645), p. 919; see also *CJ* 1645–46, p. 348; E323[2] (1646), pp. 44, 67; E340[5] (1646), p. 4.

[94] E146[24] (1642), pp. 2–3.

that every man who minds the public good would out of his private observations contribute somewhat to the right information of the knights and
burgesses on the state of their country.[95]

During the civil war, grievances from groups with different political
views were defended with this logic, which represented lobbying initiatives as information that was spontaneous, local, and apolitical. "Conveying information by the humble way of petitions" is how a Royalist
petition from Hereford described and defended a petition from Kent
whose defiant tone led to its suppression in 1642. So Levellers defended
the right "to frame and promote petitions, for your better information
of all such things as are . . . grievous to the commonwealth." Hobbes,
too, referred to "petitions or other informations of the people."[96] This
ingrained habit of thought was as old as it was widespread, appearing in
the title of Robert Crowley's 1548 tract, *An informacion and peticion
agaynst the oppressours of the pore Commons of this realm.*

Deferential, juridical, and spontaneous appearances in petitionary
rhetoric underpin the privilege of petitioning in this era. This rhetoric
deflects potentially fatal accusations of "faction" by diverting attention
away from the premeditation, dissidence, and organization that invariably lay behind petitions. Prevailing conceptions of the political order
abhorred faction. The ideal of organic unity made it difficult for contemporaries to think about political faction in terms other than sedition,
treason, or corruption. Thus, one tactic for discrediting a petition, or
prosecuting its promoters, was to expose that which petitionary rhetoric
concealed. This occurs in criticism of a cross-petition that defends a con-
formist curate from attacks in a prior petition from more than seventy
inhabitants of a Norfolk parish in Restoration England. With only four
signatures, the cross-petition sought to discredit signatures on the petition against the curate because "the whole management thereof, having
been carried on at taverns & coffeehouses" made them suspect.[97] Before
the advent of coffeehouses, other venues appear when organizational
details of a petition were exposed. A typical instance arises in questioning of promoters of a petition presented to the mayor and corporation
of Newcastle in 1640, just after the election of burgesses to the Short
Parliament. Evidence of the petitioners' factious intent is not simply
their religious, economic, and political grievances (respectively, anti-
Puritan policies, prerogative taxes, and threats to parliamentary privi-

[95] *MSS Lansdowne* 498, fol. 61. See also *CSPD* 1639–40, pp. 599–600 for a letter on
needed reforms, submitted just before the meeting of the Short Parliament.

[96] 669f.6[49] (1642); E428[8] (1648), p. 12; Thomas Hobbes, *Leviathan* (Oxford,
1909), p. 188; and see *CJ* 1645–46, p. 60; E304[17] (1645), p. 24; 669f.17[26] (1653);
Valerie Pearl, *London and the Outbreak of the Puritan Revolution* (London, 1961), p. 258.

[97] *MSS Tanner* 134, fol. 212.

leges) but comes from questions that elicit information on meetings in the homes of local merchants, where the petition was framed, copied by hand, and signed.[98]

Discrepancies between rhetorical appearance and reality in petitions arose not only from the organizational process of framing a text and gathering signatures, but from gaining suitable patronage and vetting the petition with lower-level officials before it was given to the petitioned authority. This, too, contradicted the appearance of spontaneity, yet its occurrence during the civil war[99] had many precedents. Bearers of a petition from Coventry over assessments for Ship Money "went first to the Lord Keeper for 'his direction,' and at his suggestion they revised their petition before submitting it to the Council." In 1605, petitioners on behalf of suspended Northamptonshire Puritan clerics repeatedly altered the text of their petition in meetings with members of the Privy Council in the office of the Lord Chamberlain, all to no effect. A final copy was "written fair," signed and delivered to the Lords, who took it to the king; they learned he disliked it, "and so delivered to us the petition again, to frame anew."[100] Instructions for organizing other Puritan petitions to James I—these requested harsh suppression of domestic Catholics—noted that five principal items in the petitions had been devised "with the advice and upon conference with the lords of the higher house of Parliament."[101]

In chapter 8 we shall see that massive petition campaigns in London in the 1640s often were organized by ward or parish, or in sectarian churches. In the countryside, organization might focus on assize and quarter sessions: informally, when political discussion among persons attending the sessions led to framing of a petition presented for endorsement by a grand jury; or formally, when canvassing for signatures by constables and parsons preceded presentment of a petition at the sessions. This was the source of many provincial petitions against policies of the Long Parliament: in 1642, against the attack on the episcopacy and on Crown control of the militia; in 1647, against heavy taxes, free quarter, and other military abuses; in 1648, against the vote to break off negotiations for a settlement with the king.[102] We shall also see that these

---

[98] *CSPD* 1639–40, pp. 600–604.

[99] Robert Ashton, *Counter Revolution: The Second Civil War and Its Origins, 1646–1648* (New Haven, 1994), p. 119.

[100] Cope, *Politics without Parliament*, p. 114; *HMC Beaulieu*, pp. 45–46.

[101] *MSS Rawls* D853, fol. 1.

[102] Ashton, *Counter Revolution*, pp. 117–18, 120–23, 148; David Underdown, *Pride's Purge* (Oxford, 1985), pp. 93–94, Underdown, *Revel, Riot, Underdown, and Rebellion*, p. 229; T. S. P. Woods, *Prelude to Civil War: Mr. Justice Malet and the Kentish Petitions* (Wilton, 1980).

and other petitions required close coordination and ample resources, for example, when organizers used printing as a tactical device to supply printed copies of a petition's text in order to facilitate its circulation for signatures. These developments magnified discrepancies between appearance and reality. What rhetoric portrays as a spontaneous expression of grievance was often quite the opposite. But political use of printed petitions in the 1640s only intensified an old discrepancy. One century earlier, the discrepancy appears in a petition against clerical corruption, *The Commons' Supplication against the Ordinaries*, which helped Henry VIII achieve control over the Church of England. Presented to the lower House, in 1532, in support of legislation to subordinate religious ordinances to lay control, it "took advantage of genuine concern over recent heresy proceedings to raise the question of prelatical power." Yet it had been drafted by Cromwell's clerks, revised by Cromwell, and promoted by him after his legislative program had stalled. Later that year Cromwell used the same tactic to secure passage of legislation that abolished payment of firstfruits to Rome.[103]

Moreover, the discrepancy between appearance and reality in petitions does not necessarily betoken manipulation with no popular sentiment behind it. Deceptive appearances provided petitioners with an important resource, enabling them to put an acceptable face on requests that might otherwise be perceived as factious. Puritan clerics had elevated this practice to an art, in orchestrated petitions designed to create "a false impression of spontaneous and general discontent." There was little spontaneity in petitions that protested efforts to enforce clerical conformity in 1584–85, in the early 1590s, and again at the accession of James I in 1603. The petition campaign in 1584–85 was anticipated in Suffolk by widespread circulation of a letter of protest to the Privy Council from ten leading members of the local gentry who complained about anti-Puritan prosecutions promoted by assize judges.[104] The principal adversary of these Puritans, Archbishop Whitgift, denounced their efforts to manipulate the appearance of public opinion in orchestrated petition campaigns. Whitgift would have been appalled by the petition campaign at the beginning of James's reign, conducted with the connivance of some MPs who reported that the new king thought the Puritan agenda for reform had little popular support. From London came instructions with a model petition: "that the contrary may appear, it is

[103] Merriman, *Letters of Cromwell*, pp. 96, 104–11, 133–34; Christopher Haigh, *English Reformations* (Oxford, 1993), p. 111.

[104] J. E. Neale, "Peter Wentworth," in E. B. Fryde and E. Miller, *Historical Studies of the English Parliament* (Cambridge, 1970), 2:261; MacCulloch, *Suffolk and the Tudors*, p. 208. See also Patrick Collinson, *The Elizabethan Puritan Movement* (London, 1967), p. 256; *MSS Rawls* D853, fol. 1.

thought good by some of credit . . . that noblemen, gentlemen & ministers . . . complain of corruptions & desire reformation in several petitions." But "to avoid the suspicion of conspiracy" these "petitions must vary in words." To this end recipients were told to insert local grievances in blank spaces provided explicitly for that purpose. Though these instructions focused on mobilizing the clergy and aristocracy, they also advocated a public relations campaign to enlist more popular support. "Besides this, the people are to be stirred up to a desire . . . of reformation . . . [by] often & zealous preaching . . . so also by godly, learned & well-tempered treatises printed & published before the Parliament." Yet these godly activists thought it credible to proclaim, "We mislike factious sermons and scurrilous pamphlets."[105]

This elaborate game of impression management by petition took a treasonable turn in August 1640, when twelve peers petitioned King Charles to summon what was to be the Long Parliament. The Twelve Peers Petition was coordinated with a petition campaign by the City of London and the gentry in the country, who sent petitions that also requested Charles to convene Parliament. Intelligence of the entire operation was passed to the Scots, then a hostile occupying army in the north of England; they too sent petitions with the same request.[106] Yet a county petition from Hereford that was part of this campaign never went to the king. Its framers feared, on September 19, that it would not arrive before an Assembly of Peers summoned to advise the king met on the twenty-fifth, and "if it come to his majesty after that day, it will savor of faction"![107] Toleration of such discrepancies, however, had long been part of English political culture, a consequence of traditional rhetoric in petitioning that concealed an essential tension between organization and spontaneity.

Other rules for petitioning further limited expressions of grievance so that they appeared as an apolitical conveyance of information. Though the right to petition pertained to individuals as well as collectivities, when grievance had a public complexion, petitions usually came from local corporate entities, guildhalls, wardmoots, common councils, and assize and quarter sessions. For private parties, petitioning on public grievances was liable to accusations of faction. Perceptions of faction were less likely when local authorities presented grievances as the unanimous view of a guild, county, or city. In addition, grievances conveyed

---

[105] *MSS Add* 38492, fol. 62; *MSS Add* 8978, fol. 17. For copies of these instructions in Northamptonshire, see *MSS Sloane* 271, fol. 20.

[106] P. H. Donald, "New Light on the Anglo-Scottish Contacts of 1640," *Historical Research* 62 (1989): 227–28.

[107] *MSS Add* 70086, unfoliated (draft of Hereford Petition).

by petitions were expected to be local, that is, experienced directly by petitioners: "a petition must be according to verity and particularity," noted Coke in the 1628 Parliament.[108] Violation of this precept underlay the negative response to an April 1640 petition from the trained band in Hertford: "It cannot be imagined that this petition was framed by those whom it concerns, but by some factious and indiscreet persons."[109] Other rules further separated the ideal petition from a public, ideological pronouncement. Petitions were not public documents because, as we saw in the previous chapter, secrecy governed the councils of a petitioned authority.

In addition, grievance in petitions was expected neither to criticize specific laws nor to imply popular discontent with government. Petitioning against a specific law or ruling often met with a harsh response. Among the reasons cited by James I for regarding Parliament's 1621 petition as an act of insolence was that the petition raised the issue of an impending Spanish match for his son, Charles, after the king had "made our public declaration already . . . directly contrary to that which you have now petitioned."[110] This view persisted after 1640. The same criticism leveled against persons who published "petitions . . . against the known laws and established government" of Charles I subsequently greeted petitions, such as radical anti-tithe petitions, that opposed policies of the Long Parliament."[111] Petitions for Puritan reform encountered this response at the beginning of the reign of James I when, in 1605, Viscount Cranborne warned Leicestershire gentry with Puritan sympathies not to proceed with a petition on behalf of clerics suspended for nonconformity. That year, Sir Francis Hastings was questioned by the Privy Council for his role in a Puritan petition from Northampton that was "seditious, malicious, factious," neither local nor sufficiently deferential. Hastings was a Somerset MP, and the petition proceeded by "combination of many hands against law" to allege "that a thousand [Puritans] are discontented." They were not "discontented," protested Hastings, but "grieved."[112] Later, army agitators used nearly identical words to defend a petition denounced by Parliament in 1647; there was no "discontent," only "grievances."[113] For us the distinction is meaningless. Contemporaries drew fine distinctions between apolitical conveyance of grievance by petition and factious discontent.

---

[108] *PP 1628* 3:480.   [109] *HMC Salisbury*, 22:131.

[110] King James, *Political Writings*, ed., J. P. Sommerville (Cambridge, 1994), p. 259.

[111] E112[26] (1642), p. 5; and see *Diary of John Harington*, p. 25; see also *Letter Books of Samuel Luke*, p. 281.

[112] *HMC Salisbury* 17:165–66; C. Cross, ed., *The Letters of Sir Francis Hastings* (Somerset Record Society 69, 1969), pp. 90–91.

[113] *Clarke Papers*, pp. 31, 36, 50–53.

Thus, petitioning exhibits many features of other types of political communication in prerevolutionary England. Though discrepancies between communicative practices and principles are widespread, the latter, at least prior to 1640, rested on organic and patriarchal assumptions about social and political order that were shared by nearly all contemporaries. Upheld by these assumptions, norms of secrecy and privilege imposed severe restrictions on popular discussion of political issues. When contemporaries thought about a public space for political communication, they often described it as an attribute of royal authority, a medium by which monarchs sent messages from the center to the periphery of the political nation in proclamations, instructions to preachers, judges, and writers, and symbolic displays of sovereign power in processions and other ceremonial occasions of state. Contemporaries distinguished between public and private aspects of communication, more or less as we do today. But communicative principles precluded the view that the public was a space for open discussion in which all persons had a right to participate. To be sure, well-established traditions provided paths for messages from periphery to the center, including ones with complaints and grievances. Yet these traveled in privileged channels that emptied into councils where discussion and debate occurred under conditions of secrecy.

Still, it would be a mistake to overlook evidence of change in political communication in prerevolutionary England. It occurs, not in fundamental assumptions about the nature of social and political order, but in growing emphasis on representative qualities of members of Parliament and in the infusion of national perspectives on politics at the local level. We also saw that more discussion and debate surrounded elections in 1640 than had previously occurred. And in chapter 5 we shall encounter several changes that made circulation of news by means of scribal publication more widespread before 1640. Nonetheless, an overall assessment is that continuity far exceeds change in principles and practices surrounding political communication in late-Tudor and early-Stuart England.

Yet only with reference to restrictive precedents of this era can we understand how printing in the English Revolution pushed political communication in new directions that today we associate with public opinion. We shall see how innovative communicative practices, which simultaneously constituted and invoked public opinion in order to justify political agendas, emerged from complex interactions between printing and traditional practices that we have surveyed in this chapter, especially petitioning. This development oriented political discourse to an anonymous audience of readers, made conflict between rival interests a central theme and thereby enlarged the substantive content of political messages, and led to the invention of public opinion when messages in printed texts invoked the authority of that which it constituted in print. When this occurred in the 1640s, appeals to public opinion did not emanate solely from Westminster as they had sporadically from early-Stuart Parliaments. After 1640 they were also an important feature in messages that traveled in the reverse direction, from the periphery to the center of the nation.

CHAPTER FIVE

News

> I hear new news every day, & those ordinary rumors of war,
> plagues, fires, inundations, thefts, murders, massacres, mete-
> ors, comets, spectrums, prodigies, apparitions. . . . A vast
> confusion of vows, wishes, actions, edicts, petitions, law suits,
> pleas, laws, proclamations, complaints, grievances, are daily
> brought to our ears. New books every day, pamphlets, coran-
> tos, stories. . . . Now come tidings of weddings, maskings,
> mummeries, entertainments, jubilies, embassies, tilts and
> tournament. . . . Then again, as in a new shifted scene, trea-
> sons, cheating tricks, robberies, enormous villanies in all
> kinds, funerals, burials, death of princes, new discoveries, ex-
> peditions; now comical, then tragical matters. Today we hear
> of new lords and officers created, tomorrow of some great
> men deposed, and then again of fresh honors conferred. . . .
> Thus I daily hear, and suchlike, both private and public news,
> amidst the gallantry and misery of the world.
> (Robert Burton, *The Anatomy of Melancholy*
> [Oxford, 1622], pp. 4–5)

"THIS IS AN AGE FOR NEWS." So begins a letter by a young military
officer who, after an inconclusive end to skirmishes with the Scots in the
Bishops' Wars, contemplates England's escalating political crisis in January 1641.[1] Street demonstrations in London heightened tension as the
Long Parliament and Charles I blundered down a path that eighteen
months later led to civil war. Events were unprecedented, but the comment on news invokes a false sense of novelty. Acute interest in news
existed a century before Burton wrote the epigraph, quoted above,
when we find Thomas Cromwell renewing "acquaintances" in a letter,
"supposing you desire to know the news current in these parts, for it is
said that news refreshes the spirit of life." Not yet a political insider—law
and the wool trade overshadowed his service to Cardinal Wolsey—
Cromwell still had news to convey as a member of the 1523 Parliament,
the first since 1515. At that time circulation of political news by private

---

[1] Frances Verney, *Memoirs of the Verney Family during the Civil War* (London, 1892),
1:179.

letters was limited to elites and those in service to them. Other practices satisfied popular interest in political news. As manager of the king's business in the 1523 Parliament, Cardinal Wolsey "found himself much grieved with the burgesses of this Parliament, for that nothing was so soon done or spoken therein but that it was immediately blown abroad in every alehouse."[2] Political news in oral reports, rumors, and ballads was then as much a fixture of everyday life as the inns and alehouses in which it circulated.

In Tudor and early-Stuart England both change and continuity were evident as printed news supplemented oral and scribal transmission of news, a tangible sign that "in the latter half of Elizabeth's reign, interest in news of many kinds was on the increase."[3] For foreign affairs, readers turned to inexpensive occasional news pamphlets. For domestic news readers had to be content with lurid murders, hideous monsters, miraculous occurrences, and accounts of coronations, processions, and other symbolic displays of political authority. More substantive reports of domestic politics circulated in manuscript form. Printed news in serial publications, also limited to foreign news, appeared in England in the 1620s, in *corantos*. A new development occurred shortly after Charles I summoned the Long Parliament in 1640: printed newsbooks, which "introduced regularity in length, exact periodicity, and the brief, unchanging title." These features of the newspaper did not, however, derive directly from imperatives of printing or print culture but from the source of copy used by printers for the earliest newsbooks, an illicit though widely available type of scribal publication, issued weekly, with narrative summaries of daily proceedings in Parliament.[4]

Throughout this era, popular interest in news appears in the common greeting "What news?" After circa 1500 this usage of *news*, according to the *Oxford English Dictionary*, became common and replaced *tidings* in references to reports of public occurrences or notable events. A line in a play composed by Dekker in 1602 that tells of a horse atop St. Paul's Cathedral in London who asks, "What news, what news abroad?" presumes familiarity not only with the equine stunt, but with the cathedral's function as London's emporium for oral exchange of news, twice daily, among walkers in the nave.[5] London was, of course, the

[2] R. Merriman, ed., *Life and Letters of Thomas Cromwell* (Oxford, 1902), 1:29, 313.

[3] Sandra Clark, *The Elizabethan Pamphleteers* (London, 1983), p. 86.

[4] Joad Raymond, *The Invention of the Newspaper: English Newsbooks, 1641–1649* (Oxford, 1996), p. 9, and see pp. 100–111. Cf. C. J. Sommerville, *The News Revolution in England* (Oxford, 1996), pp. 17–56 on the issue of periodicity and its origins.

[5] Thomas Dekker, *Satiromastix* (1602) in *Dramatic Works*, ed. F. Bowers (Cambridge, 1958), 3:319; Harold Love, *Scribal Publication in Seventeenth-Century England* (Oxford, 1993), p. 193. For the stunt, see N. McClure, ed., *The Letters of John Chamberlain* (Philadelphia, 1939), 1:118.

undisputed center for news. After expressing a desire "to hear from you," an Oxford letter writer in 1620 requests his recipient to "set pen to paper and send some news down from the place which is indeed the original of all news."[6] A century and a half earlier, the same request and its satisfaction appear often in letters between London and the Norfolk that record social and economic activities of an East Anglian landowning family, the Pastons, in the 1470s: "I pray you send me some tidings how the world goes."[7] Cynicism and greed in the conversion of flying tales into profitably printed news by stationers is the subject of Ben Jonson's 1621 satirical masque *News From the New World Discovered in the Moon.* Later that decade, a conservative cleric complained in a sermon before the king, "What news? Every man asks what news? Every man's religion is known by his news." The next decade a future archbishop, Thomas Sancroft, conveyed news to his brother in a jocular tone: after "News! News!" he retails the latest college gossip; after "Strange News!" he describes the recovery of a man, beset by fever, who was thought to have died. Next came political news: some of the king's judges "have declared for the country in the case of the Ship Money."[8] In 1642, "Master News" appears as a character in a dialogue with "Master Papist" in one of many polemical pamphlets that responded to Puritan proposals to pull down London's Cheapside Cross. "What news I pray thee?" asks Master Papist, who then learns from Master News that the cross is doomed—"Vox populi has passed this doom."[9]

Contemporary views on popular interest in political news ranged from neutral to negative. Some complacently lumped together ballads, newsbooks, and corantos in mildly dismissive references to popular interest in political news. Reporting on the military expedition to the Isle of Rhe in 1627, one letter writer described patriotic predictions of a revival of English martial honor "as the gazettes and ballads talk."[10] Many interpreted interest in news as a character flaw or negative sign of the times, among them playwrights as well as religious commentators with opposite theological principles. In 1626, a staunchly Puritan layman, John Bruen, lamented, "The world is now all ear & tongue . . . to hear & tell news; but the practice of religion is driven out of the world." An

---

[6] *MSS Rawl* Letters 41, fol. 44.

[7] J. Gairdner, ed., *The Paston Letters, 1422–1509* (Edinburgh, 1910), 3:57, and see 3:17, 37–38, 39–40, 41, 44, 59–60, 83, 85, 88–89, 92, 98–99, 104, 119, 122–23, 173, 192.

[8] M. A. E. Green, ed., *The Diary of John Rous* (*CS*, os, vol. 66, 1856), p. 44; *MSS Tanner* 70, fol. 164.

[9] Richard Overton, *Articles of High Treason Exhibited against Cheap-side Crosse* (E134[23], 1642), pp. 1–2.

[10] *Letters of John Holles, 1587–1637,* ed. P. R. Seddon (*Thoroton Society Record Series* 35, 1983), 2:362.

Arminian cleric included "news mongers" in his recitation of signs of corruptions in ancient Israel that now, in 1637, beset England. In the next decade, the Royalist newspaper, *Mercurius Aulicus*, calls Hugh Peter, a radical preacher, a "spiritual news monger."[11] Negative views on popular interest in news transcended media and persisted as printing acquired importance for circulation of news because, as we shall see, production and consumption of printed news had active connections to ballads and rumors. Unruliness and sensationalism equally characterized oral and print news in the mid-seventeenth century, when ballad writers obtained themes from printed news. Contemporary criticism of sensationalism in printed news—grotesque, improbable reports of a man "condemned for 27 wives," a woman who broiled her child "on a gridiron," and another who chopped hers "in pieces and baked it in a pie"—poked fun at ballad writers who ran to buy copies from news carriers, "found nothing of this true, [and] returned home again cursing the *Grubstreet News-Mongers*, who had so basely deceived them."[12] In the 1620s, publication of English corantos prompted denunciation of their producers and readers. The "coranto-coiner" lowered the prestige of print culture, and "vulgar" readers rashly presumed to be informed of foreign developments, hitherto the preserve of private letters among the gentry and aristocracy.[13]

Analysis of continuity and change in production and consumption of news must begin with oral communication. This was intertwined in scribal communication of news, in official dispatches, private letters, and commercial newsletters. Scribal communication had public dimensions—scribal texts were copied and read aloud in inns and taverns—and a critical edge that anticipated political discussions in coffeehouses in Restoration England. Though scribal communication was indispensable to the transmission of news throughout the nation, oral communication was the primary mode for transmission of news. In addition to restricted levels of literacy, the centrality of patronage in early-modern English politics put the court at the center of domestic news and the well-placed courtier or hanger-on at the core of an emerging profession of journalism. The nave of St. Paul's and bookstalls adjacent to the cathedral were principal meeting places outside the court where courtiers and citizens

[11] *MSS Add* 40,727, fol. 27v; Thomas Jackson, *A Treatise Concerning The Signes Of The Times* (Oxford, *STC* 14307, 1637), pp. 3, 7; *MA* 3:156. For playwrights, see Clark, *Elizabethan Pamphleteers*, p. 86.

[12] H. Rollins, ed., *Cavalier and Puritan: Ballads and Broadsides Illustrating the Period of the Great Rebellion, 1640–1660* (New York, 1923), p. 55, and see p. 43: "Composed partly by the same authors, printed, advertised and distributed by the same means, the early news-books and ballads came in for an equal amount of badinage and abuse."

[13] Joseph Frank, *The Beginnings of the English Newspaper* (Cambridge, MA, 1961), pp. 275–77.

gathered to exchange news, both foreign and domestic. This, too, anticipated political discourse in Restoration coffeehouses—these did *not*
provide English subjects with their first opportunity to be "drawn from
the isolation of lonely thought into a public world in which individual
opinion can be sharpened and tested in discussion with others."[14] Correspondence between Dudley Carleton and John Chamberlain indicates
that discussion of news in public places such as St. Paul's was nourished
by and was an outlet for scribal transmission of news. Because "court
news" was "more rife in Paul's than in the chamber of presence," Chamberlain, a descendent of London aldermen and ironmongers, could be
an amateur journalist whose near-weekly letters kept close friends informed of domestic and foreign news for three decades. Chamberlain
reassured Carleton, when the latter resided with the English ambassador
in Paris, that he did not expect his friend to send him "news or secrets,"
"especially as long as Paul's is so furnished that it affords whatsoever is
stirring in France, and I can gather there at first hand to serve my turn
sufficiently (saving for certain particulars) so that I shall not need to put
you to trouble."[15]

Taverns, inns, and alehouses were other public spaces for oral transmission of news and editorial comments on it. Not surprisingly, alco-
holic drink facilitated incautious expressions of political sentiments, so
much so that it is not always possible to distinguish political commentary on the religious and marital maneuvers of Henry VIII from outright
inebriation. Drunk and under the influence of evil spirits is the defense
offered by a spinster who, in 1535, distinguished between Queen Katherine, a "righteous queen," and Anne Boleyn, "a goggle-eyed whore."
Another examinant admitted he might have uttered indiscreet political
comments, but "if he so said, he was mad or drunk."[16] Indiscreet talkers
often offered "overcome with drink" as an explanation to officials who
were receptive to this defense.[17] Yet the strategy did not always work.
Henry VIII's Privy Council ordered one indiscreet talker to be "set on

[14] Lewis Coser, *Men of Ideas* (New York, 1965), p. 20; Love, *Scribal Culture*, pp. 193–
94, 203–5; and see Jürgen Habermas, *Structural Transformation of the Public Sphere*
(Cambridge, MA, 1989), pp. 30, 32–33.

[15] M. Lee, Jr., ed., *Dudley Carleton to John Chamberlain, 1603–1624* (New Brunswick,
NJ, 1972), p. 34; *Chamberlain Letters* 1:183–84. For more on "Paul's Walking" for ex-
changes of oral news, see Love, *Scribal Publication*, p. 193; Raymond, *Invention of the
Newspaper*, pp. 5–6.

[16] *L&P* 8, no. 196, 9, no. 74; and see 11, no. 407, 1328; 12, pt. 1, no. 567, 775; 13,
pt. 1, no. 94.

[17] *L&P* 12, pt. 1, no. 627; pt. 2, no. 13; T. Howell, ed., *A Complete Collection of State
Trials* (London, 1816), 2:878. Offenders thought to be "brain sick" did not suffer extreme
punishment. *APC* 1621–23, pp. 427, 483–84. For pleaders of this defense, see *CSPD*
1639–40, pp. 547–48; *CSPD* 1640, p. 487; *MSS Tanner* 63, fols. 66–67.

the pillory and warned, drunken or sober, to let no more such words escape him."[18] Beyond the liberating effects of drink, the importance of inns, taverns, and alehouses for political conversation reflects their prominence as nodes in the transportation network traversed by carriers and other travelers. These nodes were sites for conversations about the northern revolts in 1536. For reading and copying "bills" with demands of the northern rebels, inns and innkeepers may have been nearly as important as priests and churches connected to the revolt. Accused of spreading news of rebel demands, one gentleman pleaded that "the matter was so common" that "everybody had them," referring to scribal copies of demands and letters by the rebel leader Robert Aske. Moreover, he noted that these were disclosed in a response to the rebels in a printed tract commissioned by the government. Hence, when at supper in a tavern and asked "what were the demands of the rebels . . . I said it was in every man's mouth, and we were all true men there, so we might talk of it."[19] A century later, inns and taverns were nodal points for dissemination of news and political discussion of the Scottish Covenanter Revolt against Charles I. Imprisoned in February 1640 for reporting news on the revolt, Sir John Junes did not refer to a flood of Scottish pamphlets that inundated England; he had relayed "only such vulgar passages as he had heard and were the frequent discourse in all public meetings."[20] It would be difficult to overstate the importance of inns and taverns as venues for such public meetings. For example, customers of the Red Lion in Kettering, Northamptonshire, could learn from its proprietor about meetings of Puritan ministers at a rival Kettering inn, the Swan, in late August 1640. At the Swan, over twenty clerics from Northampton, Leicestershire, and Rutland dined, heard reports of the advance of the Scottish army into England, "had also a new book out of Scotland read amongst them," and discussed declarations from clerics in London and elsewhere who refused the oath in the new Book of Canons. The declaration of London ministers came from a weekly meeting, probably on August 6, of dissident ministers held at the Nag's Head Inn in London.[21]

In addition to public dimensions of nodes by which news circulated, these examples call attention to the considerable overlap of different modes for transmission of political news. A confluence of oral reports, scribal bills, and printed pamphlets flowed through both sacred and profane meeting places. In taverns, inns and alehouses, and churches and churchyards, scribal and printed texts of news were copied and read aloud. A prolific London writer of commercial newsletters, John Pory,

---

[18] *L&P* 16, no. 1281.
[20] *CSPD* 1639–40, pp. 453–54.

[19] *L&P* 11, no. 1231, 1405–6.
[21] *CSPD* 1640, pp. 564, 636, 638, 644.

obtained information at St. Paul's—unlike Chamberlain, he charged an annual fee—and also at the printshop of Nathaniel Butter and his partner, pioneer publishers of printed news in England. Butter's shop served as an informal headquarters for Pory, where his subscribers could contact him or leave his fees.[22] Satirical verse published at this time points to this overlap of oral and print transmission of news in references to advertisements for Butter's corantos:

> But to behold the wals
> Butter'd with Weekly Newes compos'd in Pauls.[23]

Prevailing practices for reading and selling printed texts further ensured that oral and print transmission of news remained in close proximity. Cheaply printed newsbooks and ballads were commonly read aloud in inns and taverns, where they were also sold by traveling chapmen. At fairs and country markets and on city streets, the performance of a ballad was a common technique used by singing peddlers to advertise broadside ballads, some on contemporary events. Highly partisan accounts of contemporary developments during the civil war and interregnum marked a departure from earlier broadside ballads whose expression of a nationalistic Protestantism was congenial to extant authorities.[24] Similar practices of distribution and consumption applied to lowly ballads and printed political texts. Toward the end of the personal rule of Charles I, a distributor of Scottish political pamphlets spoke to soldiers in Essex taverns who might want to purchase "books come from the Scots." Later, the Leveller leader John Lilburne frequented inns in order to talk politics and distribute his pamphlets.[25] Like taverns, bookshops were sites where printed, written, and oral modes of transmission for news converged. Clerical petitions and declarations by ministers in London and Northampton opposed to the 1640 Canons came to and from the shop of a London bookseller, who passed them around so that others could copy them. Oral and print transmission of news also mingled on the streets of London. In 1647 the House of Commons ordered a committee to draw up a bill "to suppress the publishing in the streets, by ballad-singers, pamphlets and ballads scandalous to the Parliament."[26]

The multiplicity of paths ensured not only widespread availability of

---

[22] William S. Powell, *John Pory, 1572–1636* (Chapel Hill, NC, 1977), pp. 55, 56, 57.

[23] Frank, *Beginnings of the English Newspaper*, p. 275.

[24] Natasha Würtzbach, *The Rise of the English Street Ballad, 1550–1650* (Cambridge, 1990), pp. 13–17; Tessa Watt, *Cheap Print and Popular Piety, 1550–1640* (Cambridge, 1991), pp. 86–87; and see Margaret Spufford, *Small Books and Pleasant Histories* (London, 1981), pp. 111–26.

[25] *CSPD* 1640, p. 647; Howell, *State Trials* 4:1336.

[26] *CSPD* 1640, pp. 619–20; *CJ* 1646–48, p. 73.

political news but timely distribution. Communication of military and political intelligence by government officials established the upper limit, which approached the speed of a man on horseback. At the time of the War of the Roses, military news typically took four days to travel from Exeter to London, 172 miles. This pace required relay systems and varied with the route and season; urgent messages could move even faster. During his campaign against the Scots in 1482, Edward IV set up a relay system of riders stationed at intervals of twenty miles in order to send messages from Newcastle to London in two days. Two days was the transit time for letters between Secretaries Windebank and Vane, stationed respectively in London and York, during the crisis occasioned by invading Scots and domestic opposition to the personal rule of Charles I in 1640.[27] In more tranquil times, official messages moved at a slower pace. When James issued a proclamation against dueling, he allowed forty days for its provisions to come into effect for persons who "by reason of their distance from the centers of direction cannot so speedily be made acquainted with our meaning as they that are at hand," though this may have been the king's estimation of time needed for the message to sink in. When alarm arose from a rumor that James I had been slain while hunting, a printed copy of the proclamation denying the rumor reached Kent within two days of the initial rumor.[28] County sheriffs played a pivotal role in the process of communication by proclamation. After the execution of Charles I, Parliament ordered rapid publication of its prohibition against anyone being declared king of England. The sheriff of Lancashire received the prohibition on February 2 and had it proclaimed in sixteen towns between February 4 and 10; by the seventh the sheriff of Norfolk had it proclaimed in eighteen major towns.[29]

Unofficial distribution of political information could not rely on relay systems, the post, and special messengers, which were official undertakings whose purpose was the security of the regime. Even so, the pace for unofficial news was not always slower than that of official communication in ordinary circumstances. Four days after a royal proclamation against "unthrifty games" was proclaimed in London in 1538, it was reported in an inn five miles from Bristol, when a traveler was asked by a tailor and others at supper, "What news at London." Six days was how long a letter writer thought it would take a priest returning home to deliver a letter from London to Cornwall in 1534. In 1535, only a few

[27] Charles Armstrong, "Some Examples of the Distribution and Speed of News in England at the Time of the War of the Roses," in R. W. Hunt, W. A. Pantin, and R. W. Southern, eds., *Studies in Medieval History Presented to Frederick Maurice Powicke* (Oxford, 1948), pp. 438, 452; *CSPD 1640*, pp. 56–57, 60–61, 68–69, 74–75, 84–85.

[28] *RP-S* 1:304, 134.   [29] *MSS Tanner* 57, fols. 520, 522–23.

days transpired between seditious words by a West Somerset artisan and a report to Thomas Cromwell. The report came from two justices of the peace, who had been informed by two local officials, a constable, and a tithingman, who had been contacted by three witnesses, two smiths and a husbandman. This vertical movement to higher levels of social and administrative authority is fairly typical of the path that brought informal political discussion to the attention of Cromwell in London. Moreover, we shall see that political rumors that inspired these exercises in detection spread across the country at nearly as fast a rate as their reports flew to London.[30]

Distribution of political news in scribal form had a slower pace. On February 11 a Shropshire cleric, Robert Horn, finished entries in his political journal for the 1621 Parliament, formally dissolved by James on January 6, 1622. The amount of material copied by Horn is not great—writing did not occupy much of the time between the date of events in Parliament and the date of their entry in Horn's journal. By January 8 Horn had copied the Commons Petition of December 3—it advocated supply for war with Spain, which James I desired, but opposed a Spanish match for his son, which infuriated Charles and led to an unexpected contest between royal prerogative and parliamentary privilege—the king's reply to the Speaker that same day, and a second petition from the Commons on December 9, which defended its "ancient liberty" for freedom of speech. Roughly four weeks lapsed between the date of the last reported event and the date by which copies of these documents were written in London, dispatched into the country, and received, read, and copied by Horn. This process took three weeks for subsequent events entered by February 11 in Horn's journal—the king's December 11 answer to the second petition, his letter of December 16 to Secretary Calvert, and the December 18 Protestation of the Commons, the text of which James tore from the *Commons Journal*. Horn's sources were scribal texts; by several entries Horn added the marginal comment "printed since."[31] Similar intervals exist for events in the 1624, 1625, and 1626 Parliaments and their appearance in Horn's compendium.[32]

Not surprisingly, these practices for scribal reproduction and circulation of political texts reappeared in the English Revolution. The most notable separate to emerge from domestic events of 1640 that eventuated in the calling of the Long Parliament was the Twelve Peers Petition.

---

[30] *RP-T* 1:266; *L&P* 13, pt. 2, no. 413; *LL* 2:252; Geoffrey R. Elton, *Policy and Police: The Enforcement of the Reformation in the Age of Thomas Cromwell* (Cambridge, 1972), pp. 331–32.

[31] *MSS Rawl* B151, fols. 40v–43 (December 3–9 events), fols. 43–46 (December 11 to January 6 dissolution).

[32] *MSS Rawl* B151, fols. 63v, 68v, 75, 80v, 83.

Presented on September 5, it requested that Charles convene a parliament. On September 9, a Northampton resident recorded in his diary that he "met with a copy" of that petition; the next day, a letter informed a member of the East Anglian landowning class, Sir Robert Crane, that he could see a copy, sent by the wife of the comptroller of the king's household to a female correspondent.[33] We shall see that mundane commercial and administrative practices, as well as ideological commitment, facilitated circulation of scribal political texts. Moreover, even after the rise of printed newspapers in the 1640s, printers relied on these scribal practices for obtaining news in a timely manner. After the Royalist newspaper *Mercurius Aulicus* began operations in Oxford in 1643, only a one-day interval separated a speech in the Long Parliament and delivery of a scribal copy by an informant to *Aulicus*.[34]

ORAL NEWS: RUMORS AND BALLADS

When popular discussion of public events, persons, and policies crossed the line from reporting to editorializing, it often took the form of rumor or prophecy. In this form, discussion of news by commoners could be an important political development—often ominous from an official point of view—that in turn made it an object of news in official reports. Most often this occurred when rumor involved deliberate disinformation in pursuit of a strategic goal or provided a focus for popular grievances. In the form of prophecy, political rumors were highly stylized prognostications, laden with references to animals, anagrams, and famous persons, real and imagined, such as Becket and Merlin, about the imminence of sudden change or disaster. Conventions of prophetic symbolism existed at the time of the Norman Conquest. These were used as a medieval political weapon, to inspire kings, justify wars, celebrate or denounce violent changes in regime, and as propaganda in the Wars of the Roses. Often this use of prophecy in the Middle Ages was instigated by rival elites and intended to control popular opinion. However, even before the reign of Henry VIII, prophecies had become more of "a pervasive popular discourse that challenged the official language of proclamation and statute." By the 1530s political prophecy had become the language of popular opposition to centralizing and reforming initiatives of the government, when popular disaffection for marital, religious, and political innovations by Henry VIII inspired prophetic intimations of a sudden change in reign. Royal officials sought to detect, repress, and

[33] *MSS New College* 9502, September 9, 1640 (unfoliated); *MSS Tanner* 65, fol. 112v.
[34] P. W. Thomas, *Sir John Berkenhead, 1617–1679* (Oxford, 1969), pp. 43–44, 48.

counter this development. This included publication of printed prophecies more to the king's liking, which was not a novel development.[35]

Successive governments had long been concerned not only with prophecy but, more generally, with all rumors on public matters. From the late-thirteenth century onward, several statutes spelled out penalties for purveying falsehoods,[36] such as imprisonment until a purveyor produced the informant. In letters to principal towns of the realm, Richard III prohibited spreading of rumors and "telling of tales and tidings whereby the people might be stirred to commotions . . . or any strife and debate arise between lord and lord, or us and any of the lords and estates of this our land." Part of official concern reflected the strategic value of rumor in wars. A proclamation in 1487 against "forged tidings" was directed against a propaganda campaign by Yorkist forces, rumoring the defeat of Henry VII, that caused reinforcements coming to Henry's aid to turn back. After establishing the Tudor dynasty, one of the earliest proclamations issued by Henry VII reiterated penalties by statute against "untrue and forged tidings and tales," for which offenders could be set on a pillory until they divulged their source.[37] His son and grandson, Henry VIII and Edward VI, later banned unfounded rumors of military victory and defeat, which led to the "impairing of his Majesty's service." Tudor monarchs discovered that rumors could also have economically dysfunctional consequences. After announcing a devaluation of silver coin at the end of April 1551, Edward VI's government issued a proclamation against "the spreading of false and untrue rumors" of further devaluations, whose effect was to send prices skyward.[38] Economic rumors could be political dynamite. Rumors about new, onerous taxes were persistent themes in popular opposition to religious and political reforms under Henry VIII in the second half of the 1530s. His government routinely used torture to extract information on sources of rumors from "seditious" talkers whose conversations came to the attention of Thomas Cromwell. In pursuing the source of rumors about new fiscal exactions on all "horned beasts," the earl of Southampton confidently promised Cromwell that he would convince a suspect "to tell where he heard it or else cause his body to suffer pain."[39]

Official concern with rumor, like prophecy, was a legacy of its promi-

---

[35] See Sharon L. Jansen, *Political Protest and Prophecy under Henry VIII* (Woodbridge, Suffolk, 1991), pp. 57–61, 152–54.

[36] 3 Edward I, c. 34 (1275); 2 Richard II, st. I, c. 5 (1378); 12 Richard II, c. 11 (1388); 37 Henry VIII, c. 10 (1545).

[37] Armstrong, "Distribution of News at the Time of the Wars of the Roses," pp. 433–34; *RP-T* 1:12–13.

[38] *RP-T* 1:329, 456, 528.

[39] *L&P* 13, pt. 1, no. 440; for efforts by the duke of Norfolk to repress this rumor in

nence in popular revolt. Richard III's warning, cited above, about the potential of rumors to ignite "strife . . . between lord and lord" reappears in Tudor proclamations that decry "false news" as an "occasion of discord . . . between the king, his people, or the nobles." Many proclamations for suppressing rebellion or pardoning participants link popular mobilization and the forging and spreading of news about official policies or developments at court.[40] Political rumors and prophecies "posed a special problem to the enforcement of policy" that constituted Henry VIII's break with Rome.[41] Their potential for transforming popular discontent into revolt appears in 1536–37, first in Lincolnshire, then farther north in the Pilgrimage of Grace, which opposed Henry's political innovations. Popular resistance was animated by rumors that the government intended to confiscate church goods, close churches, and impose draconian taxes on food, animals, and other items. The history of one rumor in the aftermath of these revolts is instructive. To dissuade his northern subjects from further disobedience, Henry sent the duke of Norfolk to overawe them with force, by "displaying of our banner," which proclaimed the rule of martial law. Under its rule Henry instructed the duke to exact "dreadful execution upon a good number of the inhabitants, hanging them on trees, quartering them, and setting their heads and quarters in every town."[42] A person of widespread interest, the duke inadvertently inspired a rumor when, after repeated complaints in the summer and fall of 1537 about "his old disease of the flux," the king granted his request to be relieved of his service in the north. On October 17, a report reached Cromwell of rumors that the king had died, "sprung by the hasty riding of the duke of Norfolk in post through Newark."[43] From Newark, the rumor spread rapidly, its progress recorded in letters to Thomas Cromwell. A friar questioned in Sussex on December 9 reported he picked it up in an "alehouse." Three days later, the abbot of Reading reported its arrival; the next day it was circulating in the east of Northamptonshire and Huntingtonshire, where it was traced to a husbandman who, on November 30, encountered the rumor at the house of a Leicestershire wheelwright, where he and companions on a short trip had stopped and "baited [fed] their horses." On December 16 the mayor of Oxford reported the rumor; one week later its source in Oxford was traced to a letter from the abbot of

---

East Anglia, see *L&P* 13, pt. 2, no. 52, 57, 84, 55, and see no. 1171 for an order that justices of the peace punish spreaders of this rumor.

[40] *RP-T* 1:388 and see pp. 21, 244, 246, 421, 426, 469, 476–77.

[41] Elton, *Policy and Police*, chap. 2.

[42] *L&P* 12, pt. 1 no. 479.

[43] *L&P* 12, pt. 2 no. 100, no. 935, and see nos. 229, 238, 650.

Reading to the abbot of Abingdon, who resided in or near Oxford. By January, the rumor, now in an elaborated version, was in Kent, where the king was reported to have been on his horse and to have seen "God's marks upon his hand and kissed them," praised God, lay twenty-four hours in a trance, and then died.[44]

Beyond its protean qualities, this episode illustrates several features of political news as rumor. First, markets, roads, shops, and eating and drinking establishments occupied a prominent place in the circulation of political rumors.[45] Second, oral and scribal modes of communication overlapped. Contemporary reports of political prophecies in the reign of Henry VIII often referred to "scrolls" or "rolls" and sheets of paper; both figured prominently in the transmission and sharing of these texts.[46] Third, as Elton points out in his discussion of the rumor of the death of Henry VIII, the government extended considerable effort to detect and punish the spreaders of political rumors. Commissioners appointed by Cromwell to uncover origins of the 1537 rumor of Henry VIII's death pieced together the multiple paths by which "loose and idle talk" spread rapidly from shire to shire.[47] This detective work was facilitated by laws, noted above, that allowed authorities to detain rumormongers until they revealed their sources.[48] The central government ordered local officials to detect rumor spreaders and expressed displeasure when Privy Councillors did not superintend this task in their local communities.[49] Whether or not this facilitated control over rumors is unclear. Punishment by ordinary courses of law—standing on a pillory, severing ears, and whipping—may have heightened public interest in a rumor, a possibility noted by one observer after two persons were sentenced in 1613 in the Star Chamber for spreading rumors about an impending toleration of Catholics: brutal punishment "breeds but more speech."[50] Given persistent official concern with political rumors, it is understandable why the first of several useful benefits cited in a 1621 petition for a royal patent "to print a Gazette or weekly occurrences" was "to settle a way when there shall be any revolt or back sliding in matters of religion or obedience (which common grows with rumors

[44] L&P 12, pt. 2, no. 935, 1185, 1205, 1208, 1220, 1252; 13, pt. 1, no. 6.

[45] See L&P 12, pt. 1, nos. 808, 1294; pt. 2, no. 121; 13, pt. 1 no. 58, 76, 107, 161, 354, 615, 715, 966, 1346; pt. 2., nos. 413, 1015; 14, pt. 1, no. 11; pt. 2, nos. 557, 1154; 15, no. 592.

[46] L&P 12, pt. 2, no. 1212; Jansen, Political Protest and Prophecy, pp. 2, 3, 4, 35, 40, 43–45, 53, 162–63.

[47] Elton, Policy and Police, p. 78, and see pp. 73–77.

[48] This may explain why an examinant, interrogated in 1539 for spreading rumors about new royal taxes, testified that his source was an elderly deaf woman. L&P 14, pt. 1, nos. 507, 553.

[49] L&P 15, no. 447; 16, no. 945.   [50] Chamberlain Letters 1:453.

among the vulgar) to draw them in by the same lines that drew them out, by spreading amongst them such reports as may best make for that matter to which we would have them drawn."[51]

Government concern with political rumor is just as evident in 1640, when it was associated with a new development: partisan elections to Parliament. On September 22, a small delegation of London citizens went to York and delivered a petition with ten thousand signatures to Charles I. It requested the king to convene what was to be the Long Parliament as a remedy for the war with Scotland and domestic grievances. On September 29, reports reached the king and readers of a newsletter about "a rumor spread by some factious spirits that on receipt of the Londoners' Petition he should publicly have spoken reproachful words against them." But a Puritan activist and London alderman, John Warner, reported the safe return of the petitioners to the city and noted "the King's answer to them very gracious." Did the rumor travel both ways, from York with the putatively reproached petitioners to London and back to York? More likely it originated earlier in London, after a majority of the City's aldermen refused to endorse it. The rumor may have worked against one alderman, William Acton, a staunch supporter of Charles I and senior member of the aldermanic bench who by tradition should have been elected mayor at the guildhall on September 28 but was rejected.[52]

Political rumors were only part of the larger stream of libels, songs, and popular verse in contemporary English culture. These other modes of expression, though predominantly nonpolitical, offered many opportunities to convey opinions on public events. For example, scribal publication of "seditious" rumors often resembled the practice of posting libels in public places. So common was this practice in feuds, in which accusations circulated in writing as well as in conversation, that it prompted a proclamation by James I, who disliked the public recriminations as well as the violence to which these sometimes led.[53] Surreptitious publication followed the same practices for libels in private duels and political libels. Bills scattered in streets, posted in shops and marketplaces, and hung on bushes published obscene libels against the duke of Buckingham in 1627 and, in 1640, declared disaffection for religious and political policies of the government at the end of the personal rule of Charles I. The content of political libels was variable: at the high end, verse couplets in Latin were read by a very small audience; most, how-

---

[51] Powell, *John Pory*, p. 52.

[52] *CSPD* 1640–41, pp. 84, 110; *State Papers Collected by Edward, Earl of Clarendon* (Oxford, 1767, 1773), 2:80, 117; *HMC Beaulieu*, p. 129; *MSS Harl* 383, fol. 88; Valerie Pearl, *London and the Outbreak of the Puritan Revolution* (Oxford, 1961), pp. 110–11.

[53] *RP-S* 1:296; see also *Letters of John Holles, 1587–1637* 1:12.

ever, were in English, with allusions to contemporary events and persons that might be evident to contemporaries or deliberately obscure. Not only were they distributed by the venerable practice of surreptitious posting or scattering in public; they accompanied reports of news in private correspondence and were copied in the same sociable contexts where they were often read aloud.[54]

The importance of libels for understanding how contemporaries published illicit political commentary is matched by that of verse and ballads for stylistic conventions. Like libels, poetry and song were important vehicles for political communication. Composed and recited in baronial halls and monastic refectories during the Middle Ages, they provided information on, for example, the Flemish insurrection in 1302 that destroyed the French army, intrigue and misdeeds among the ministers of Richard II in 1399, the reception of Edward IV at Bristol, and the beheading of an unpopular favorite of Henry VI, the duke of Suffolk. Here, too, oral and scribal modes of communication overlap. Though intended to be communicated orally, songs and verse were written on small scraps or rolls "for the convenience of the minstrel, who thus carried them about with him from house to house."[55] Songs were an important vehicle of political expression in Tudor England, when ballads expressed popular opposition to policies of Henry VIII or his ministers, especially Cromwell. For refusing to sing "Crummock" in an alehouse, one minstrel received a blow to the head. Another anti-Cromwell ballad was a revised version of an old song from the reign of Henry VI.[56]

Themes in most ballads were not political. Lurid murders, preferably laced with themes of sexual betrayal, were popular. So were panegyrics to the dutiful performance of occupations and lamentations over the decline of manners, hospitality, and other hallmarks of an idealized vision of a sedentary, agrarian world governed by deference, organized by patronage, and consecrated by devotion to God. Yet many ballads in the century before the civil war dealt with specific historical and political issues, although in this genre, accuracy in news was subordinate to moral instruction and authorial claims to authenticity.[57] When, like *Agincourt*, a ballad celebrated battles that shaped English history, it was

---

[54] Alastair Bellany, " 'Raylinge Rymes and Vaunting Verse': Libellous Politics in Early-Stuart England, 1603–1628," in K. Sharpe and P. Lake, eds., *Culture and Politics in Early Stuart England* (Stanford, CA, 1993), p. 291; and see chapter 4, note 34.

[55] F. Furnivall, ed., "Political, Religious, and Love Poems" (*Early English Text Society*, os, 15, 1866), pp. 5–11; T. Wright, ed., *The Political Songs of England from the Reign of John to that of Edward III* (*CS*, os, 6, 1839), pp. x–xi, 187–95; T. Wright, ed., *Political Poems and Songs Relating to English History . . . from the Accession of Edward III to That of Richard III* (*Rerum Britannicarum Medii Ævi Scriptores* 14, 1859), 1:363–86.

[56] *L&P* 12, pt. 1, no. 318; 13, pt. 1, no. 1346, and see no. 1054.

[57] Würzbach, *English Street Ballad*, pp. 146–62.

an "animated historical effusion." In Elizabethan England, ballads lamented Catholic conspiracies and extolled the executions of conspirators, such as Babington and accomplices in 1586:

> Next Babington, that catife vilde
> was hanged for his hier:
> His carcasse likewise quartered
> and hart cast in the fier.

The role of these ballads for the formation of English national identity appears in another ballad, which uses the occasion of a naval victory at sea—seizure of a Spanish warship—to denounce Spanish political intentions:

> . . . to deflower
> our virgins in our sight,
> And in the cradle cruelly
> the tender babe to smite
> Gods holy truth
> they meane for to cast downe
> And to deprive our noble Queene
> both of her life and crowne.[58]

A century later, ballads continued to be an important source of news during the Bishops' Wars, the civil wars of the 1640s, and the unsettled politics of the commonwealth. Roughly one hundred were registered in the entry book of the Stationers' Company in 1640, many on political topics, such as the convening of the Short Parliament and the Bishops' Wars. Commerce and patriotism inspired publication of these ballads. One prolific composer, Martin Parker, issued several that exhorted listeners to take up arms against the invading Scots, such as *News from New-castle*, composed after the seizure of that city at the end of August,

> Some other of our Cavaleirs,
> Were slaine and hurt, as it appears,
> About six hundred men outright,
> (Of horse and foote) were kil'd i'th fight,
> And of the Scots 'tis justify'd,
> As many if not more then dy'd;
> *Then let not faire, &c.*

Earlier in 1640 Parker wrote a ballad that described the royal procession in the opening of the Short Parliament on April 13. Such processions

[58] J. P. Collier, ed., *Broadside Black-Letter Ballads, Printed in the Sixteenth and Seventeenth Centuries* (New York, 1968), pp. 38, 84, 128.

involved expensive, elaborate pageantry witnessed by large crowds—
ideal subject matter for a best-seller. Set to the tune of "Greensleeves"
and accompanied by a woodcut of the procession, Parker's ballad was
completed by April 9, four days *before* the event; he relied on accounts
of prior processions in order to have printed broadsides for sales when
public interest in the event would be keenest!

> The order how they rode that day
> To you I will in brief display,
> In the best manner that I may,
>   For now my minde is bent
> To publish what my self did see,
> That absent (Loyall) hearts may be
> Parcipants as well as wee
> *Ith' joy oth' Parliament.*[59]

This admixture of journalism and ballading also appears in the work of
a commonwealth journalist, John Crouch, who treated ballads as a
source of sensationalistic news or filler. At this time, Sir John Berkenhead, formerly editor of *Mercurius Aulicus*, composed a satirical tract
that advertised for sale "an excellent new ballad, entitled *The life of a
souldier* to the tune of *No body else shall plunder but I*, by Major General
Lambert."[60] Broadside ballads on topical political events in this era had
roughly the same range of qualities generally associated with ballads as
a popular literary genre: nearly all made false claims to authenticity, to
being eyewitness accounts. Some were more inclined to sentimental
moralizing—in a ballad, licensed by the Long Parliament, the recently
executed Charles I laments his misdeeds. In other ballads, commentary
on persons and events was "irreverent, smutty and facile."[61]

The utility of ballads as a vehicle for propaganda derives from their
oral mode of delivery and the surreptitious publication practices for
written ballads. John Selden described ballads "as an important vehicle
of libel." Political ballads were often scattered about the streets, like the
libels, riddles, and verses that attacked Charles I's chief counselor, the
duke of Buckingham. Such libels, complained Attorney General Heath,
were "'the epidemical disease of these days,'" which festered in public
places and was spread by country fiddlers. In 1627, ballads and seditious
libels provided evidence of "national rejoicing at Buckingham's assassi-
nation."[62] In 1640, ballads and verse circulated in partisan campaigns to

---

[59] Rollins, *Cavalier and Puritan*, pp. 9, 78–79, 98.
[60] Ibid., pp. 55, 58–62.
[61] 669f.13[77] (1649); Frank, *English Newspaper*, p. 242.
[62] Würzbach, *English Street Ballad*, p. 249; David Underdown, *Revel, Riot, and Rebel-*

elect godly (i.e., Puritan) members to the Short Parliament. Surviving scribal copies of a ballad show that some contemporaries blamed factious Puritans for the dissolution of that Parliament. Later that year, written and printed ballads offered opposing views of the Scottish occupation of northern England.[63]

All three modes of communication—oral, scribal, print—overlapped in varying degrees in the transmission of political ballads, riddles, and verse. Print was less commonly used for these materials during the Bishops' Wars and Short Parliament than later, when ballads and verse subjected the Long Parliament to ridicule, as in "A Strange Sight to bee seene at Westminster."

> Within this house is to be seen
> Such a monster as hath not been
> At any time in England, nay
> In Europe, Africa or Asia
> Tis a round body without a head
> (Almost these 2 years) yet not dead.

This item first circulated in scribal form, was copied into commonplace books, and appeared in print years later.[64] Ballads in the 1640s and 1650s combine a modest degree of political sophistication with ballading's traditional cadences and claims to authorial eyewitness. In December 1642 two young men were reported by Ipswich authorities after they talked up the king's cause and displayed scribal copies of Royalist ballads in a tavern.

> O could I but spin forth some work of mine
> to make them hang themselves at every line
> When traitorous grace-high horse-born from a stable
> shall be exalted to a counsel table.[65]

Royalist and neutralist sympathies became ever more preponderant in surviving political ballads and verses from the 1640s and 1650s. The resurgence of Royalism and popular support for Charles after the end of the first civil war in 1646 may be responsible for this,[66] or it may reflect Puritan antipathy for the bawdy irreverence that had long been

---

lion (Oxford, 1985), p. 121; Kevin Sharpe, *The Personal Rule of Charles I* (New Haven, 1992), pp. 48–49.

[63] Sharpe, *Personal Rule of Charles I*, pp. 856, 875 and n, 903–4, 912–14.

[64] *MSS Rawl* poet 62, fol. 47v; Alexander Brome, *Rump, or, An Exact Collection Of The Choycest Poems and Songs Relating To The Late Times* (*Wing* B4851, 1660), sig. H1.

[65] *MSS Nalson* 2, fol. 208.

[66] See Robert Ashton, *Counter Revolution* (New Haven, 1994), pp. 197–207.

associated with ballads. Many ballads derided religious and political innovations superintended by the Long Parliament, such as abolition of Christmas festivities. In 1646 *The World Is Turned Upside Down* decried this Puritan initiative that had provoked yuletide riots.

> Listen to me and you shall hear,
> News hath not been this thousand year
> Since Herod, Caesar, and many more
> You never heard the like before.
> Holy-dayes are despis'd,
> New fashions are devis'd.
> Old Christmas is kickt out of Town.
> *Yet let's be content, and the times lament,*
> *You see the world turn'd upside down.*[67]

Royalist carols for Christmas day circulated widely in scribal copies in the 1640s, some of which were printed in 1654.[68] Details of the rebaptizing of thirty-nine persons in Essex appear in another ballad issued at this time, *The Anabaptists out of order*, which describes how Samuel Oates "rebaptized thirty-nine and drowned the fortieth." In addition to religious themes, oppressive taxes figure prominently in political ballads. Many decry Parliament's excise tax, such as *The Good-Fellow's Complaint*, which includes more irritability among women among the negative consequences of higher prices for "ale and beer" due to the excise.[69] Toward the end of the seventeenth century, the printed ballad as a genre declined as its functions were assumed by printed news and chapbooks. But the decline was gradual; as late as 1656 165 ballads were registered at Stationers' Hall in 1656.[70]

SCRIBAL NEWS

Private Correspondence

Transmission of news by private letters evolved as a literary practice as an extension of scribal practices animated by narrowly strategic purposes: diplomatic dispatches, military intelligence, official record keeping, and

---

[67] 669f.10[47] (1646).

[68] *MSS Rawl* poet 211, fol. 20v–21, 24–25, 34v–35v; Thomas Weaver, *Songs And Poems Of Love And Drollery* (*Wing* W1193, 1654). See also Rollins, *Cavalier and Puritan*, p. 326.

[69] Rollins, *Cavalier and Puritan*, p. 175, 207–8, 210.

[70] Spufford, *Small Books*, pp. 99–100; Würzbach, *English Street Ballad*, p. 241; Rollins, *Cavalier and Puritan*, p. 70.

business communications. By the fifteenth century, "governments of major powers" had "well-developed methods for procuring political information with reasonable celerity," which included spies, messengers, and official courier systems. Yet in England domestic news "circulating at any time in the kingdom was largely the product of private correspondence. From capital or camp letters radiated across the country." For monarchs and councillors, the stratetic value of news from "capital or camp" is evident. But such news could also have high survival value for commoners at this time. After hearing about the Lancastrian restoration, subjects discarded their Yorkist badges.[71] There were many reasons for acquiring political news. For persons with power or wealth, prudence dictated that they have timely, accurate news, especially if it pertained to developments at court and the course and outcome of sieges and battles. This appears in the well-known *Paston Letters*, which contain much strategic information: shifting alliances among notables and locations of their retinues; names on a 1494 list of the Knights of the Bath; a meeting between Henry VII and Philip, king of Castile, near Windsor in 1506; shifting dynastic fortunes in the War of the Roses.[72] Reports on less eventful political developments also appear in letters that describe maneuvering over elections and meetings of parliaments. "I pray you, cousin, that I may speak with you . . . and then I shall tell you tidings of the Parliament," writes Sir John Falstof to John Paston in 1455.[73]

The centrality of patron-client relations in politics makes it difficult to draw sharp distinctions between official dispatches of political intelligence to the Court—for example, summaries of reports from spies, common rumors, diplomatic conversations—and informal communication of news in private correspondence. During the reign of Henry VIII ambassadors and officials on the continent were reminded of the duty to supply news, to be "continually vigilant and diligent in writing to the King's majesty of all things and occurrences," urged "to exertion to gain news," and chided when they failed to supply sufficient, timely news.[74] They assiduously sent news,[75] but the official who received it might also be a powerful patron at Court who could facilitate

---

[71] Armstrong, "Distribution of News at the Time of the War of the Roses," pp. 431, 433, and see pp. 429–35.

[72] *Paston Letters* 1:263–68, 407–9, 416–17, 424–25, 2:5–6, 411–12, 3:3–5, 320, 384–85, 403–6.

[73] Ibid., 3:425, and see 1:126, 152, 157, 160–61, 337, 340–41, 377–78, 3:431, 435.

[74] *Letters of Thomas Cromwell*, 1:370; L&P 11, no. 469. A few years later, the French ambassador in London received instructions from Paris, informing him that he should supply reports of "all needful news; the office of a good ambassador is to write often and diligently what he hears." *L&P* 16, pt. 1, no. 1230.

[75] J. Muller, ed., *The Letters of Stephen Gardiner* (Cambridge, 1933), pp. 71–91; *LL* 3:285–86, 316–17.

requests for advancing their private interests, which not infrequently accompanied news reports. When Cromwell dominated the court of Henry VIII, the Lord Deputy in Calais was reminded by his agent in London of good practice: "that your lordship did procure ever the first news, although it were something the more to your cost and pains," because it would maintain Lisle's standing in court and "it would be wondrous thankfully taken."[76] In 1537 Archbishop Cranmer forwarded news he had just received from Germany for Cromwell's perusal, and then renewed a request that he raised a few months ago—could Cromwell get someone favored by Cranmer restored to his office in the Calais retinue?[77]

The strategic value of news for merchants and traders involved in international commerce made merchant communities in foreign lands important sources of political intelligence. For at least three centuries prior to the Reformation, the letter bags of merchants transmitted political news "more systematically than secular governments." Hundreds of newsletters sent by factors, clients, and servants to Fugger bankers in Augsburg in the second half of the sixteenth century conveyed intelligence of political developments, plagues, witch burnings, pirates, and more from around the world.[78] A century earlier, business and public news mingled in many surviving letters from the Cely family, whose principal members exported wool from London to the continent. The scope of news was narrow, mostly pertaining to military and political developments in the north of France and the low countries, and gathered with an eye toward its potential impact—war, inflation—on the trading activities of younger family members in Calais. On January 26, 1477, Richard Cely the elder reprimanded his son in Calais, George, that "you write not to me no letters of such tidings as you have at Calais, the which is much spoken of at London." He was unable to send trading instructions "for lack of understanding how it stands in the parties of the duke of Burgundy's lands and the King of France." Evidently the father had, in London, learned about the defeat and death of Charles the Bold, the duke of Burgundy (January 5), and seizure of his lands by Louis of France. Hence, he warned his son, "be not over hasty in sale and delivering of goods in Flanders."[79] The importance of news in letters from the Cely sons went beyond its utility for good trading decisions. Both Rich-

---

[76] *LL* 4:333, and see 339; *Letters of Thomas Cromwell* 2:3–4.

[77] *L&P* 12, pt. 2, nos. 592, 862;

[78] Armstrong, "Distribution and Speed of News at the Time of the War of the Roses," p. 441; G. T. Matthews, ed., *News and Rumor in Renaissance Europe: The Fugger Newsletters* (New York, 1959).

[79] A. Hanham, ed., *The Cely Letters, 1472–1488* (*Early English Text Society* 273, 1975), p. 10, and see p. 18.

ard Celys, elder and younger, bombarded George in Calis with reminders that, in exchange for his patronage of the family, Sir John Weston, Prior of the Knights of St. John, expected to be supplied with political news. In view of this, Richard the younger told George, "When you know any tidings for certain that you would write them to me," and then describes a recent gift from Weston, "a long gown cloth of his livery." From his father yet another reprimand: "I think you might write much more than you do, for my Lord of St. John's sends to me for tidings every week, for the which my Lord takes great pleasure," and "he is a courteous lord to me and to you and Richard."[80]

Sir John Weston expected to receive news from the Celys, just as Cromwell did from Lord Lisle and Archbishop Cranmer: as a service of clients or aspiring clients to patrons, an acknowledgment of past favors, a token of loyalty, and an accompaniment to current requests. In London, a chaplain who served as secretary to Cardinal Wolsey and was able to follow political developments sought to trade news for a favor. The motive behind his long letter of foreign and domestic news in 1518 to a northern earl, "remote from the political mainstream," appears in the last sentence, where he reminds the earl of a previous request for "timber." Two decades later, another letter writer thought that sending letters that reported persons who "write, preach or speak against the King" was a useful preliminary to requesting patronage from Thomas Cromwell. Just before the Short Parliament convened in 1640, Sir George Fleetwood wrote to the English embassador to the States at Hamburg, Sir Thomas Roe, reporting the summoning of Parliament and promising that "if ought fall in it worth your notice I shall weekly acquaint you." His promise was as unexceptional as the next line in his letter, in which Fleetwood requested Roe's aid to procure the assistance of a third party "in a money business." In 1643, a letter writer begins with an apology for enclosing a "tattered mercury" before reporting other news and then describing his desire "to place my wife in the Queen's bedchamber."[81]

The obligation of clients to monitor parliamentary developments appears to have arisen from their duty to protect the economic and legal interests of patrons. This appears in a report on the 1459 Parliament at Coventry, sent by John Bocking to John Paston and others: private bills (mostly pertaining to economic disputes) had been submitted "but none read, nor touching us." Bocking also boasts about his contacts,

[80] Ibid., pp. 24, 79–80, and see pp. 74, 103, 109, 164. The prior "ranked as premier baron in the rolls of Parliament." T. Stapleton, ed., *Plumpton Correspondence* (CS, os, 4, 1839), p. 267.

[81] A. G. Dickens, ed., *Clifford Letters of the Sixteenth Century* (Surtees Society 172 1957), pp. 39–40, 83; *L&P* 13, pt. 1, no. 819; *CSPD* 1639–40, p. 314; *MSS Nalson* 2, fol. 328; see also *Letters of Thomas Cromwell* 1:369.

"my Lord Privy Seal, and other good Lords," who will keep him informed of any relevant developments; "that and anything be, we shall
soon have knowledge." This monitoring of parliaments was a natural
extension of reports by Bocking on developments at court, for example,
"tidings" of the royal couple, meetings of the Council, and preferment
to high office.[82] It occurred in the reigns of Henry VI and Edward IV by
Bocking and others who conducted economic and legal affairs for the
Paston family. In the reign of Edward IV, Sir William Plumpton obtained news of events at Court from his agents in London; so did his
son, Robert, in the reign of Henry VII.[83] In the reign of Henry VIII,
Lord Lisle's man in London, John Husee, dutifully complied with requests for information on a private bill, which he supplied along with
extensive reports on public news. In the reign of Edward VI, news of
religious disputes and printed tracts swarming in London reached the
earl of Cumberland in a letter from a north-country cleric visiting London, who began with information on a bill introduced in Parliament by
the earl's adversary, Lord Wharton, that would deprive the earl of control over the office of the Westmorland sheriff.[84] This is the format for
the many surviving letters to Lord Lisle from his principal agent, John
Husee: the ebb and flow of Lisle's interests at Court or before judges
followed by news of public matters. Reports from London—arrests of
notables, appointments to and removals from royal office—were often
accurate and delivered to Lisle in Calais before they were publicly proclaimed at home.[85] Above we saw that Lisle's agent in London sent him
reminders "that your lordship did procure ever the first news," that it
was "requisite that your lordship use such discretion and diligence that
your news may be the first." In offering this advise, the agent worried
about competition from other clients who performed this service by
sending Henry VIII and Cromwell news of continental developments.
From the other end of the patron-client chain, Lisle was the recipient of
a promise from a member of his retinue, temporarily in London, "to
bring your lordship the first news."[86]

In addition to service, supplying news in private letters was also a
common practice as a conventional expression of friendship or filial
piety. The latter often appears in letters from sons in London to fathers
in the country. One begins, "Sir, I am ready to serve you with my pen

[82] *Paston Letters* 1:499, and see 1:127, 163, 377, 386, 387, 392, 403.
[83] J. Kirby, ed., *The Plumpton Letters and Papers* (*CS*, 5th ser., 8, 1996), pp. 38, 40,
135; Gairdner, *Paston Letters* 1:424–25, 426, 2:38–39, 51–52, 103–4, 110–11, 118–19,
134–35, 144–45, 148.
[84] Dickens, *Clifford Letters*, pp. 102–3; *LL* 3:318–19, 450, 454, 456.
[85] *LL* 2:116, 126, 147, 205, 257, 417, 437, 454–55.
[86] *LL* 2:158, 4:333, 339.

when there is any news stirring here in London." Such expressions of
filial piety were often leavened with fiscal distress; for example, John Paston the younger attached an urgent request for money to "tidings" at
the end of a letter in 1464. In the 1630s, a minor squire in Cheshire
received a stream of letters with domestic and foreign news from his son,
"who lived on the verge of the Court as a private secretary or tutor in
various great families." A plaintive reminder that his annual allowance of
five pounds would soon be due—"my expenses are necessarily very
great, and I shall have much to do to support myself in that manner as
is fit for my employment"—precedes a promise to send a "news sheet"
in another letter.[87] Obligations to include political news in private letters
extended to in-laws. Two months after the Long Parliament opened, a
London resident promised his father-in-law in Devon, "I know you expect to hear of the proceedings in Parliament, and to deny you that were
to deny the love and service I owe you." To his mother-in-law, Lady
Joan Barrington—the matriarch of Puritan gentry in Essex—Sir William
Masham wrote, "I cannot requite your love better than by relation of
our occurrences here," and supplemented his account with printed
newsletters. When Lady Barrington's son had no news to convey, he
apologized. When other sons neglected this duty, fathers complained.[88]

More evidence of expectations about sending news in letters exists in
rhetorical practices that acknowledge the writer has nothing to report,
for example, that there is no news other than that the king "hath kept
a royal Christmas" or is "merry," "in prosperous estate," or some such
soothing observation.[89] For a father in Yorkshire, a son's timely return
from London in 1544 meant he could add a postscript to a just-
completed letter: news of the Court and foreign affairs.[90] Apologetic remarks were a rhetorical commonplace in letters from writers with no
news to relate. Correspondents noted the advantage London afforded
for letter writers, especially when they found themselves at a distance
from the center of political news. At his family estate, John Holles lamented that rural life afforded news only of "buying and selling cattle
and corn"; hence, he could supply only stale news, "the fag end of the
news." The same apologetic comment appears in letters from John
Chamberlain, when residence as a guest at country estates impeded an
otherwise steady flow of newsletters. "Here grows no news," he writes

---

[87] *MSS Tanner* 66, fol. 100; *Paston Letters* 2:152–53; John S. Morrill, *Cheshire, 1630–1660* (Cambridge, 1974), p. 22; *MSS Add* 33936, fol. 1v.

[88] Eugene Andriette, *Devon and Exeter in the Civil War* (London, 1971), p. 199; A. Searle, ed., *Barrington Family Letters, 1628–1632* (*CS*, 4th ser., 28, 1983), pp. 43, 121, and see pp. 203, 211, 218; *Letters of John Holles, 1587–1637* 1:1, 2:221, 243.

[89] *Paston Letters* 3:33; *Letters of Thomas Cromwell* 2:162; *LL* 5:691 and see 2:188, 329.

[90] *Plumpton Correspondence*, p. 219.

in 1598 from Hertfordshire, unless he would stoop to tales about the harvest or "hawking, hunting, bowling or such like." There was no news in Oxfordshire in 1601, "unless I should tell how forward we be in harvest . . . or what a dearth and scarcities we have here of all manner of fruit but especially of plums." In 1606 in Hertfordshire he would have to resort to "stocking of trees, catching of moles or such other kind of husbandry" if he were to relate any news.[91]

How candid could reporters of news be in private letters? Compared to print publication, scribal modes of communication offered far more latitude for expressing one's opinion. But libels, ballads, satirical rhyme, and separates circulated anonymously; personal letters did not. Incautious expressions in a newsletter could land the reader in trouble, as happened to the recipient of newsletters in 1628 with "news of the times true enough, but so sauced with invectives against great men and the Parliament that every letter is a most dangerous satire."[92] Secrecy was requisite for letters with sensitive or critical information. In writing to his mother about the Battle of Barnet and other events leading to the restoration of Edward IV in 1471, Sir John Paston reminded her that the letter "must be secret."[93] Yet after Charles I banned further debate over the contentious issue of Arminianism and predestination, frank discussion of it continued in private letters between D'Ewes and his correspondent in Suffolk, Martin Stutville, and between clerics such as Thomas Gataker and Samuel Ward. Candor and a vigorous defense of Puritan reforms—these provoked ever more strident opposition from Queen Elizabeth—appear in letters of Sir Thomas Wood.[94] For the most part, writers of periodic newsletters relied on the discretion of readers. "I am so used to a liberty and freedom of speech when I converse or write to my friends that I cannot easily leave it," confessed John Chamberlain. Thus, he requested recipients of his newsletters not to share them with others—"and then there is no danger."[95] Writers practiced self-censorship on especially sensitive matters—few references to Sir Thomas More's name appear in English letters after his arrest[96]—and they sometimes explicitly acknowledged its necessity. In 1536 Lord Lisle in Calais grew exasperated by the refusal of his well-informed servant, John Husee, to send reports of the northern rebellions in Lin-

[91] *Letters of John Holles* 2:214, 267, 297, 357; *Chamberlain Letters* 1:44, 128, 239.

[92] J. Bettey, ed., *Calendar of the Correspondence of the Smyth Family of Ashton Court, 1548–1642* (*Bristol Record Society* 35, 1982), pp. 93–94.

[93] *Paston Letters* 3:5.

[94] *MSS Harl* 383, fols. 113–16; *MSS Tanner* 71, fols. 66, 68, 92, 102; P. Collinson, ed., *Letters of Thomas Wood, Puritan, 1566–1577* (*Bulletin of the Institute for Historical Research*, suppl. 5, 1960).

[95] *Chamberlain Letters* 1:59.   [96] *LL* 2:126.

colnshire and Yorkshire. "As for all the news . . . they are not to be written, as wise men hath showed me." This was on October 20, by which date reports reached Privy Council of the rising of a large rebel force that opposed commissioners sent from London to close down abbeys and collect taxes. On December 1, after the outbreak of the Pilgrimage of Grace in Yorkshire, Husee sent no news: "I trust your lordship will hold me excused, considering that this world is queasy, and I might perchance in writing of some put myself to displeasure and mean no hurt." "As touching news," he wrote four days later, "I trust your lordship will pardon me, for divers causes." Six days later, on December 11, he noted, "your lordship is displeased with me because I write no news," and offered the following rationale:

> I have written your lordship in my former letters the danger thereof . . . for if I should write it might chance that I thereby might put myself in danger of my life and also put your lordship to displeasure, for there is divers here that hath been punished for reading and copying with publishing abroad of news; yea, some of them are at this hour in the Tower.[97]

A century later, when conflict between Charles I and the Long Parliament's over control of the garrison at Hull threatened to precipitate war, a Royalist squire warned, "Its not safe to write any opinion of these high distractions."[98]

Given prevailing norms of secrecy in political matters, it is understandable that contemporary letter writers worried about incautious comments and careless recipients.[99] Fathers warned sons that even innocent words, once committed to paper, could haunt a writer years later. So Sir William Wentworth instructed the future earl of Strafford: "Letters to friends and strangers write as few as you can and let these be penned with so good discretion as you need not care though they were proclaimed in any time to come."[100] In reports on political developments fraught with danger, writers in the 1620s requested recipients to burn a letter after it was read. Simonds D'Ewes made this request to a Suffolk constituent for that part which describes attacks on the duke of Buckingham in the 1626 Parliament. "I desire you to keep to yourself" and not show it to others, "by separating this half sheet & burning it or concealing it, though there be nothing in it unlawful or unfit to be said." The same request accompanied reports of parliamentary

---

[97] *LL* 3:246–47, 252, 503–4, 534, 536, 551.

[98] B. Schofield, ed., *The Knyvett Letters, 1620–1644 (Norfolk Record Society* 20, 1949), p. 101.

[99] E.g., *L&P* 13, pt. 1, no. 850; *Chamberlain Letters* 1:453.

[100] J. P. Cooper, ed., *Wentworth Papers, 1597–1628 (CS* 4th ser., 12, 1973), p. 18; and see *Letters of John Holles,* 2:294, 314.

proceedings in the weekly newsletters that John Pory sold to subscribers. In 1638, a Puritan matriarch in Hereford admonished her son
in Oxford, "When you write by the carrier, write nothing but what any
may see, for many times the letters miscarry." The same advice went in
the next decade to a future archbishop, then a young correspondent,
after "your last letter came to be broken open." Its recipient wished it
had not contained references to controversial religious developments—
"the new dipping," that is, radical heresy. "For the future, write nothing
but what you & I should be willing all the world should see."[101] Fears of
reprisal for controversial subject matter were widespread among letter
writers. But in the principal forum for punishing expressions of political
opinion during the eleven years of personal rule by Charles I, no prosecutions occurred for this offense in private correspondence.[102]

Commercial Separates and Newsletters

Circulation of political news in private letters was a practice intertwined
in official intelligence gathering, patronage, and business communications. In the early-seventeenth century, this practice was augmented by
administrative, economic, and political developments. Formalization of
recording-keeping procedures by Parliament's clerks facilitated parallel
efforts by some members who circulated copies of speeches and summary narrations of proceedings. The latter had traditional and novel motivations: it was a service to aristocratic patrons whose support was often
crucial for election; it also reflected an emerging, partisan style of politics, which we encountered in chapter 4, nourished by the inability of
James I and Charles I to emulate Elizabeth's deft management of her
Parliaments. In the mid-1620s, John Pym sent the patron responsible
for his election to the Commons, the earl of Bedford, copies of his diary
of proceedings in Parliament, "which Bedford read and annotated with
scrupulous care."[103] At this time, the ascendance of Buckingham greatly
reduced the diversity of views within the Council, thereby denying opponents of government policy a channel of communication to the Court
and prompting, instead, appeals to public opinion. When this took the
form of scribal circulation of extensively described proceedings in the
1628 Parliament, it produced "a newly developed form in Parliamentary
reporting."[104]

---

[101] MSS Harl 383, fol. 32; Powell, John Pory, p. 54; T. T. Lewis, ed., Letters of the Lady
Brilliana Harley (CS, os, 58, 1854), p. 11; MSS Tanner 60, fols. 495v–496.
[102] Sharpe, Personal Rule, pp. 682–83.
[103] Conrad Russell, Unrevolutionary England, 1603–1642 (London, 1990), p. 209.
[104] Derek Hirst, "Court, Country, and Politics before 1629," in K. Sharpe, ed., Faction

Commercial forces aided the dissemination of news. Scriveners produced "separates," copies of political texts, most often speeches; and enterprising authors transformed the old practice of enclosing news in private letters into the more formal newsletter, sold for a fee. This "aristocratic news service" can be traced at least to the late-Elizabethan period, when England's earliest journalists sent newsletters to courtiers away from the Court.[105] Though John Chamberlain's principal motive was friendship in sending detailed newsletters to his small circle of associates, regular fees were the motive for writers of newsletters such as John Pory and Edward Rossingham. Pory used a stationer's shop as his business headquarters; Rossingham employed a scribe, who he once reported "has been drunk two days and a half," to produce his remarkably well informed newsletters. The future Charles II was advised to stop "such fellows as Captain Rossingham that made £500 a year with writing news to several persons." Pory received £20 per year for weekly letters to Lord Scudamore in the early 1630s. In 1640 Sir Robert Crane was told that, for subscribers such as the earls of Northumberland and Salisbury, Lords Say and Brooke, and others, Edward Rossingham, "writes not under twenty pounds per annum"—so princely a sum that the informant thought "tis scarce credible to report."[106] In view of the cost, it is not surprising that newsletters were copied and shared among several friends and relatives.[107] Commercial newsletters continued well into the Restoration era, when annual charges for weekly letters ranged more moderately from £3 to £6, perhaps because competition from less expensive printed news kept a lid on prices.[108]

Though prompted by economic and political motives, scribal publication of parliamentary proceedings in early-Stuart England relied on clerks in Parliament, who consumed vast amounts of paper in "scribbled books," subsequently redacted into rough drafts that eventuated in polished form as the official record, the journals of the two Houses.[109] A symbiotic relationship existed between official scribal practices and

---

and Parliament (London, 1985), pp. 115–16; Conrad Russell, *Parliaments and English Politics, 1621–1629* (Oxford, 1982), p. 389.

[105] Lawrence Stone, *The Crisis of the Aristocracy* (Oxford, 1965), p. 388.

[106] Powell, *John Pory*, p. 55–56; *CSPD* 1640, p. 33; Stone, *Crisis of the Aristocracy*, p. 389; Pearl, *London and the Puritan Revolution*, p. 95; *MSS Tanner* 65, fol. 78;

[107] E.g., Ann Hughes, *Politics, Society, and Civil War in Warwickshire, 1620–1660* (Cambridge, 1987), pp. 90, 122.

[108] Love, *Scribal Publication in Seventeenth-Century England*, pp. 9–11; Raymond, *Invention of the Newspaper*, p. 103.

[109] Elizabeth Read Foster, "The Painful Labour of Mr. Elsyng," *Transactions of the American Philosophical Society*, ns, 62 (1972): 21–25; Elizabeth Read Foster, "Staging a Parliament in Early Stuart England," in P. Clark, A. Smith, and N. Tyacke, eds., *The English Commonwealth, 1547–1640* 137–38, 139.

unofficial activities by members who compiled private diaries of proceedings and obtained copies of speeches, declarations, and other official statements for unsanctioned distribution. Diarists not infrequently relied on the clerks' rough notes, but the reverse also occurred. Keeping a private diary of proceedings in 1606–7 as an MP prepared Robert Bowyer for the tasks he assumed in 1610, when he became clerk of the Parliament, responsible for the *Journal of the House of Lords*. As a member, he compiled parts of his private diary by paraphrasing the record kept by the House clerk; in turn, he allowed the clerk to consult his notes and diary to fill in gaps in the official record. As clerk of Parliament, he shared transcripts of documents and the *Journal* with diarists such as Sir Simonds D'Ewes and the earl of Huntingdon. Three decades later, D'Ewes continued to rely on the clerk's records to fill in gaps in his diary. At the same time, the earl of Leicester's agent sought to repay a favor to the clerk when he requested that the earl return a copy of Charles I's second speech to the Long Parliament: before the clerk entered his copy in the *Journal*, he had lent it to Secretary Vane, who misplaced it.[110] Such scribal practices were an inevitable extension of another principal duty of the clerks that was a major source of income: supplying copies, for a fee, of documents. The customary rate was two shillings a sheet for copies of bills and speeches, with a different schedule of rates for private bills. Bowyers's assistant clerk received a third of fees for copies he wrote. In 1649, the clerk of Parliament was said to have earned five hundred pounds in fees.[111]

Unauthorized extensions of these official scribal practices supplied texts for the unofficial pipelines of political communication. If it was reasonable to offer Bowyer his regular fee plus "a piece of venison" for prompt compliance with Lord Say and Sele's request for a copy of a bill on religious reform, it was reasonable for a commercial writer of newsletters, like Rossingham, or an influential patron, like the earl of Leicester, to suppose that they or their scribes might, for a fee, have access to the rough notes and *Journals* compiled by the clerks.[112] Accounts of proceedings in the Short Parliament from April 21 to 27 in a Rossingham newsletter (see fig. 2) are nearly identical to passages of a manuscript entry book, preserved among the state papers, of proceedings of the entire Short Parliament.[113] That same month, the earl of Leicester, in Paris, sent a request to his agent that illustrates how powerful persons

---

[110] *CJ* 1610, 1:xxiii, xxvii–xxviii, xxx; D. H. Wilson, ed., *The Parliamentary Diary of Robert Boyer, 1606–1607* (Minneapolis, 1931), p. xv; *PJ1*, p. xv; *HMC De L'Isle and Dudley* 6:370–71.

[111] Foster, "The Painful Labour of Mr. Elsyng," pp. 10–11.

[112] *PP 1610* 1:28; *HMC Third Report*, pp. 12–14.

[113] *CSPD* 1640, p. 72, and see pp. 36–40.

took for granted the complicity of Parliament's clerks in facilitating access to its proceedings. The earl did not know the clerks in both Houses, "but if you can prevail with them, I should be glad that they would give you weekly a journal of all that passes remarkable in either House." These practices were hardly secrets. Other correspondents of the earl assume, correctly, that news of parliamentary proceeding would be sent "by divers Parliament men" or from Rossingham, "who, though not a member of that body, yet by his industry he is able to inform your Lordship of more particulars than most of those that sit in either of the Houses."[114] A special form of manuscript news was *Diurnall Occurrences or the Heads of Proceedings in Parliament*, the direct ancestor of the first serial newsbook.[115] This weekly summary of daily events in the Long Parliament was widely distributed in 1640 and 1641. Produced commercially by scriveners, it filled a gap: the narrative of proceedings in *Diurnall Occurrences* omitted speeches, for which inexpensive printed copies existed.

Unlike newsletters, "separates"[116] were discrete political texts, most commonly transcripts of speeches in connection with parliamentary proceedings, by monarchs, royal officials, and members, closely followed by declarations, petitions, remonstrances, articles and heads of accusations, and "private" letters between public persons. Like that of commercial newsletters, production of separates as a commercial enterprise overlapped with scribal practices of clerks and politicians. For Parliaments held in the 1620s preparation for a speech—not always did this eventuate in delivery—on an important issue might take the form of rough and polished notes in the diaries of MPs. In the Short Parliament, "Pym and Rous both spoke from scripts, which were made available for copying." Speaking from a script, technically prohibited, became more common during the Long Parliament; its practice "may indicate a desire to address an audience outside the walls."[117] Harbottle Grimston probably spoke from a script when he delivered a long speech on November 7, after which one member jotted in the margin of his diary, "This speech

---

[114] *HMC De L'Isle and Dudley* 6:245, 247.

[115] Raymond, *Invention of the Newspaper*, pp. 100–111.

[116] Richard Cust, "News and Politics in Early Seventeenth-Century England," *P&P* 112 (1986): 63–64 and passim. See also F. J. Levy, "How Information Spread among the Gentry," *JBS* 21 (1982); Love, *Scribal Publication*, pp. 13–22.

[117] Russell, *Parliaments and English Politics*, pp. 121, 123, 129 n, 227 n, 243–44 n, 341 n; Conrad Russell, *The Fall of the British Monarchies, 1637–1642* (Oxford, 1991), p. 107 and n. This desire was not limited to MPs. Though clerks had made a written copy of a speech delivered by the Lord Keeper at the opening of the Long Parliament, it was "commanded by his Lordship not to be divulged till he had perused it and perfected it," reported the earl of Leicester's agent. "When it is returned to the Clerk of the Parliament, I shall send [a copy] to your lordship." *HMC De L'Isle and Dudley*, p. 339.

get a good copy of. Mr. Grimston spake long and well." It also appeared in print. Another member, D'Ewes, made few entries for "set speeches" because he evidently assumed he could obtain manuscript copies.[118] Scribal copies of speeches by members satisfied requests for news from relatives, constituents, and patrons. For scriveners, such texts were sources of income and highly sought after. For example, considerable interest surrounded receipt of the king's answer to a London petition in Common Hall on January 13, 1643. The Royalist paper *Mercurius Aulicus* offers a jeering account of the arrest of "an audacious fellow" in the hall who wore the gown of a common council man. He was no spy, only "a scrivener's man" sent "to speak with one in the Hall about some money, and finding that there was no entrance to be gained but in such a gown, borrowed one to obtain his passage."[119] More likely, he was sent to take notes of the king's answer and the speeches in reply to it by Pym and the earl of Manchester.

Demand for separates followed the ebb and flow of popular interests. Judging by surviving copies, demand was greatest when separates covered formal occasions of high politics, such as a procession or opening speech in Parliament, or moments of acute conflict. Multiple copies of separates exist for petitions from the Lords and Commons in the early years of Elizabeth's reign that requested the queen to marry and settle the succession issue.[120] Many copies of separates survive for speeches, remonstrances, and petitions that mark high points of conflict in the 1620s between early-Stuart Kings and their Parliaments.[121] During that decade, separates could still be bought in London for an event in 1614 that raised the same issue which bedeviled relations between the Crown and Parliament in the 1620s, the 1614 trial of Oliver St. John, who refused to pay a benevolence, a levy not sanctioned by Parliament.[122] For the 1630s, survival of multiple copies of statements by judges at assize sessions on Ship Money is an indication of popular interest in debates and rumors over the topic.[123] So is the survival of separates that recorded the protests of two Cornish opponents of the forced loan in 1627. One was William Coryton, who recorded his exchanges with Privy Councillors in "A Relation of Soe Much as Passed Between the Lordes of the Counsell and Mr. Corinton at the Counsell Table." The other, more widely circulated separate was Sir John Eliot's "Petition from the Gatehouse," which cites statutes and other precedents to show the illegality

---

[118] *D'Ewes I*, p. 6 n, 336 n; E198[5] (1640) is the printed version of Grimston's speech.

[119] *MA* 1:47–48. See E84[14] (1643) for a printed copy of the answer to the petition.

[120] *PP Elizabeth*, pp. 44, 58.

[121] For the 1626 Parliament, see *PP 1626* 2:268, 323, 324, 291, 404, 432, 3:3, 58, 406.

[122] Richard Cust, *The Forced Loan and English Politics, 1626–1628* (Oxford, 1985), p. 155.

[123] Esther S. Cope, *Politics without Parliament, 1629–1640* (London, 1987), p. 116.

of the loan and his imprisonment. At "the height of interest in the Five Knights Case, Eliot's 'Petition' was to be found 'wandering amongst the subjects of Cornwall.'" Both items "were part of a co-ordinated campaign to publicize the moderate case for opposition."[124]

In spite of popular interest in the topics they reported, access to separates was limited. Personal connections expedited access, and, though commerce motivated scribal reproduction, copies were expensive. In the 1630s, for example, few domestic events stimulated more interest than judicial decisions in the trial of John Hampden after his refusal to pay a prerogative tax, Ship Money, created "the *cause célèbre* of the personal rule." Opinions of judges in the case "were widely circulated and well known." But the asking price for copies of one opinion, by a judge who broke with the majority and supported Hamden, was ten shillings. One letter writer, Sir William Dugdale, declined to buy a copy but instead sent his correspondent a copy of the decision, which he borrowed from a relation of the judge.[125] Still, the relatively high cost of commercial copies, the slow rate of reproduction, and dependence on personal connections for scribal political texts must be balanced against the widespread practice of sharing them and allowing copies to be made by interested readers. This opened up important channels of illicit communication. Circulation of banned books in manuscript form occurred along with separates. Sir Walter Raleigh's treatise on Parliament and its role in politics was influential in the 1620s but it was not printed in England until 1640. Before it was printed surreptitiously in Middleburg in 1628, it circulated as a separate and was read widely. So did inflammatory anti-Spanish tracts by Thomas Scot.[126]

Redundancy in scribal publication made it robust and exceedingly difficult to control. Different modes of scribal activities overlapped in any number of combinations. News in informal letters drew upon formal newsletters and separates; contemporaries compiled this material in collections[127] and incorporated it in commonplace books and diaries. A report on the Berkshire Grand Jury petition against the tax of coat-and-conduct money in the August 4, 1640, newsletter of Rossingham ended up in the diary of John Rous. Ballads and libels with political themes accompanied this flow of formal political texts.[128] It is hardly surprising that scribal publication of news persisted long after the uneven initial

[124] Cust, *Forced Loan*, p. 168, and see pp. 170–85 for separates that express opposition to the loan.

[125] Sharpe, *Personal Rule*, pp. 717, 725; W. Hamper, ed., *The Life, Diary, and Correspondence of Sir William Dugdale* (London, 1826), p. 184.

[126] Cust, *Forced Loan*, pp. 156–57.

[127] Cust, "News and Politics," p. 63; Hughes, *Politics, Society, and Civil War*, p. 89.

[128] Mark Fissel, *The Bishops' Wars: Charles I's Campaigns against Scotland, 1637–1640* (Cambridge, 1994), p. 132; Sharpe, *Personal Rule of Charles I*, pp. 695 n, 914 n.

appearance of printed news in the 1640s. The government could not stop that which contemporaries found useful for conveying political messages that dared not appear openly in print.

In many respects, scribal transmission of news anticipated important features of printed news that we shall examine in chapter 7. Both circulated in overlapping streams of commerce and sociability. For example, in 1644 the Reverend Ralph Josselyn reported that on a trip to Wethersfield, where he had "a good bargain of books," he also "saw some manuscripts" of events in the reigns of King James and Charles, probably scribal compilations of separates.[129] Though printed news was thoroughly permeated by commerce, publication of scribal news by scriveners was also a commercial undertaking. Other continuities also arose from the fact that printing's impact on circulation of news often enhanced tendencies already evident in scribal modes of publication. We shall see, for example, that one tactical use of printed texts in the 1640s was to disclose ongoing conversations and negotiations. Yet this also occurred under conditions of scribal publication, when in the 1620s discreet disclosure of confidential proceedings was undertaken by government officials.[130] Continuities also exist in the sensationalism of printed news and its tendency to highlight conflict and disorder in politics. While it undoubtably was "in the interests of newsmen to report in exaggerated detail all manifestations of disorder" in the 1640s and 1650s,[131] this observation also holds for news distributed by scribal publication in the 1620s. A fusion of religious and political issues in the false supposition that a necessary link existed between unparliamentary taxation and Arminianism was abetted by the misleading nature of scribal separates and newsletters. Readers of these texts alone would never perceive that, in virtue of the patronage at the disposal of powerful lords and the Court, "the majority of important political events took place outside Parliament."[132] Moreover, documents selected by copyists for scribal publication largely ignored the quotidian reality of politics, the mundane pursuit of profit and advancement by private individuals and corporate entities. Scandal and conflict were as prominent in scribal news as they later were in the printed newspapers of the English Revolution.

[129] A. Macfarlane, ed., *The Diary of Ralph Josselin* (London, 1976), pp. 22–23.

[130] See chapter 3, note 68.

[131] J. S. Morrill and J. D. Walter, "Order and Disorder in the English Revolution," in A. Fletcher and J. Stevenson, eds., *Order and Disorder in Early-Modern England* (Cambridge, 1987), p. 149, and see pp. 138, 147–50.

[132] Russell, *Parliaments and English Politics*, p. 1. On links between Arminianism and political issues, see Nicholas Tyacke, *Anti-Calvinists* (Oxford, 1990), p. 159.

CHAPTER SIX

Printing and the Culture of Print

MANY TRADITIONAL PRECEDENTS existed for political communication, but restrictive norms of secrecy and privilege in prerevolutionary England precluded a public sphere in politics. Movement in this direction required communicative changes that created public opinion as both a nominal and real factor in politics. In this chapter, I assess technical and social aspects of printing and the print culture that grew out of them for the "invention" of public opinion as a nominal entity, an authorial creation that exists in virtue of its instantiation in printed discourse. Public opinion in its other guise—debate and lobbying on public issues by private persons who read pamphlets or signed petitions—will be examined in chapter 8. Here we shall see how commerce and publicity, the twin imperatives of print culture, guided authors of a broad range of literary and religious printed texts that responded to the interests and intellectual capacities of a socially diverse reading audience in prerevolutionary England.

Many points of potential conflict existed between print culture and norms of secrecy and privilege in traditional modes of political communication. Print culture was a prototype for democratic models of the public sphere because it fostered discourse oriented to a virtual community to which widespread, though not universal, access existed. Transcending direct contacts between speakers and listeners in oral communication, and vastly exceeding the ability to reproduce texts by scribal publication, printing and print culture established a context in which it was possible for public opinion to be a factor in politics, both nominally as an object of discourse and also as a collection of readers, debaters, petitioners, and writers who participated in public discourse. Nominal and real aspects of public opinion have intimate links: appeals to public opinion are written and printed because (1) authors and publishers presuppose that a reading public exists and (2) popular literacy has developed to the point where this presupposition is reasonable. Hence, the connection between printing and the public sphere is as much social as it is technical in nature. Inherent in the production of printed polemical texts is the intention to address a virtual community of readers. Authors often signal this intention in introductory remarks to "the reader" that precede a text; so do critics who use printing to reproduce excerpts of a text along with critical comments on it.

These developments in print culture led to the imposition of dialogic order on political conflict. In print culture, political conflict assumed the form of a dialogue, in which opposing sides offered reasons to discredit adversarial claims in print—so much so that titles and fictive characters in political texts often appeared as authorial voices in their own right, an early-modern instance of the postmodern condition, signification run riot. Although imposition of dialogic order on conflict was possible in scribal modes of publication, print culture transformed restricted dialogue into a debate staged before a public, and it put simultaneous invocation and constitution of public opinion at the center of political argumentation. The technical potential of printing to reproduce texts thus had far-reaching cultural implications, as did assumptions by authors and printers about the audience for pamphlets, a new type of text often intended for readers drawn from nonelite classes.

Printing's technical potential to reproduce texts was inseparable from issues of literacy and its social distribution. To produce printed texts efficiently—that is, cheaply and quickly—presupposed sufficient popular demand for them. "Supply-side" factors may have been at work: greater availability of inexpensive printed texts may have prompted greater demand for them by stimulating popular interest in acquiring the ability to read. But equally, if not more, important were secular social and economic trends that contributed to steady growth in literacy rates. In addition to issues of literacy and popular taste, the organization of printing, bookselling, and censorship are also important. Printers had purely economic motives for printing popular categories of printed materials, such as pamphlets and ballads, and they worked under circumstances of, at best, political uncertainty. Here, too, technical and social issues converged. A registered press might issue illicit as well as authorized texts; fugitive presses could be moved and reassembled; and texts printed abroad were smuggled into England. All this made censorship a formidable task, especially when it was conducted under conditions of protracted political conflict.

PRESSES AND PRINTERS

Novel developments in print culture can be understood only if we grant equal importance to social and technical aspects of printing. Social aspects include the nature and distribution of literacy, authorial perceptions about readers, and competitive pressures generated by the quest for profit and fame among stationers and writers. Technical aspects include printing's potential for efficient, accurate reproduction of texts. At many points the social and technical are intertwined. Printing's technical potential for producing cheap books required a stable market for them, one constituted by a literate public. Early-modern printing was a capitalist enterprise that sold its products to a market of readers and depended less than did manuscript production on patrons. Nonetheless, important continuities existed between scribal and print reproduction.[1] Copying, circulating, and reading scribal texts coexisted with print culture and remained an important mode of communication for coterie literary production—Donne, Marvell, and other poets preferred scribal transmission—domestic news, private letters, libels, and more in early-seventeenth-century England. Scribal publication occurred at the instigation of authors, commercial agents, and users.[2] Long after the Restoration, circulation of scribal texts remained an important outlet for satirical, obscene, and seditious writings. For example, the government of Charles II prohibited publication of Algernon Sidney's *Last Paper*, in which he affirmed just before his execution for treason in 1683 the political doctrines in his *Discourses*. *Last Paper* was nonetheless "a spectacular success." It was printed after so many manuscript copies swarmed around London that "the government prohibition no longer served any purpose."[3]

Patronage, too, survived the rise of print culture—it even helped to legitimate printed texts[4]—but it became "more talismanic and less manifestly economic in nature." During the sixteenth century the economic significance of patronage for printing declined as "a more assured market was open to printers who were able to judge its needs."[5] Authors became attuned to the economics of text production. In the flourishing literary culture of late-Elizabethan England, popular literature and plays were composed by writers "who experience literature primarily as a saleable commodity," who were not "content with gratifying the taste or the caprice of some aristocratic dilettante" but sought "to meet the clamorous demands of a very varied public." These authors did not compose literature "as a fashionable pastime, nor yet as a sacred calling, but simply as the means of gaining a livelihood." Patronage, like scribal

---

[1] See N. F. Blake, *William Caxton and English Literary Culture* (London, 1991), pp. 73, 275.

[2] Harold Love, *Scribal Publication in Seventeenth-Century England* (Oxford, 1993), pp. 4, 46–83; Arthur F. Marotti, *Manuscript, Print, and the English Renaissance Lyric* (Ithaca, 1995), pp. 82–94, 246–47, 332–33.

[3] Jonathan Scott, *Algernon Sidney and the Restoration Crisis, 1677–1683* (Cambridge, 1991), pp. 343, 345. See also N. H. Keeble, *The Literary Culture of Nonconformity in Later-Seventeenth-Century England* (Leicester, 1987), pp. 110–11.

[4] Marotti, *Manuscript, Print, and the Renaissance Lyric*, pp. 294–96.

[5] A. S. G. Edward and Carol M. Meale, "The Marketing of Printed Books in Late Medieval England," *Library*, 6th ser., 15 (1993): 96; Collin Clair, *A History of Printing in Britain* (Oxford, 1966), p. 7.

publication, did not vanish but coexisted with newer commercial patterns. Hence, we need to be cautious about overly sharp literary distinctions between, for example, coterie and popular literature. Much aristocratic patronage descended on Ben Jonson, but he collaborated on productions for profit with the most "prolific" and "penurious" of the stable of playwrights-for-hire set on work by Henslowe for the Admiral's Company, Henry Chettle, and other popular writers such as Thomas Dekker.[6]

Yet after all these qualifications, the essential point remains: printing put commerce squarely at the center of textual production. Unlike that of scribal publication, the economics of text production increasingly involved calculation, risk taking, and other market behaviors in which printers oriented production to vague estimations of popular demand for printed texts.[7] Evidence of commercialism exists in one of the earliest broadsides printed in England, an advertisement printed by Caxton in 1477 that announced publication of a religious book, a missal, and the location where anyone desiring one "shall have them good cheap." Caxton affixed the phrase *Supplico stet cedula*—roughly, "Don't tear this down"—to the advertisement, which suggests that it may have been regarded more as a nuisance than a novelty.[8] Commerce and heightened technical ability to reproduce texts eventuated in a print culture that might fairly be described as a mass culture, if "mass" is scaled appropriately to the realities of early-modern Europe. By 1500, 35,000–40,000 editions of different works were published in Europe; thereafter, 150,000 to 200,000 new editions—that is, 75 million to 100 million individual books—appeared by 1600. Annual book production in seventeenth-century France was just over 1,000 titles in peak years; in England, over 2,000 titles appeared in 1642, stimulated by the outbreak of the civil war.[9] Fueling this output were technical developments that had stabilized by the mid-sixteenth century. Typefounding, compositors' tools, and the wooden printing press did not radically change until the eighteenth century.[10] Under these conditions, a compositor could compose about one sheet per day, and the daily rate of typographical print-

[6] Frederick Waage, *Thomas Dekker's Pamphlets, 1603–1609, and Jacobean Popular Literature* (Salzburg, 1977), 1:10, 21, 38; Harold Jenkins, *The Life and Work of Henry Chettle* (London, 1934), pp. 19–21.

[7] Love, *Scribal Publication*, p. 133, notes the small role this occupied in scribal production.

[8] Blanche B. Elliott, *A History of English Advertising* (London, 1962), p. 10.

[9] Peter Burke, *Popular Culture in Early Modern Europe* (New York, 1978), p. 250; Lucien Febvre and H. J. Martin, *L'Apparition du Livre* (Paris, 1958), pp. 377, 396–97; G. K. Fortescue, "Preface" to *Catalogue of the Pamphlets . . . Collected by George Thomason, 1640–1661* (London, 1908), p. xxi.

[10] Michael Clapham, "Printing," in C. Singer et al., eds., *A History of Technology* (Oxford, 1957), 3:377–411.

ing was about 500 sheets (both sides) per press (assuming two press-men).[11] In a quarto format—used for inexpensive tracts—a sheet was twice folded and yielded four leaves or eight pages. A survey in 1583 counted fifty-three authorized presses in London, though five more were operated by a rogue printer, John Wolfe. About the same number of authorized presses existed in the 1630s, excluding those in the King's Printing House and at Oxford and Cambridge. This corresponds roughly to a hypothetical output of one small book of twenty-four quarto pages per week for every eighty persons in England.[12]

Change in printing during the century before the outbreak of the English Revolution was economic and organizational, and not technical, in nature. Specialization occurred on many levels. Unlike England's earliest stationers, who practiced other occupations because the new craft provided only a precarious living, stationers in late-Tudor and early-Stuart England pursued an increasingly specialized profession in terms of printing and wholesale and retail operations. Divisions sprang up between wealthier and poorer printers. The Jacobean literary world relied on stationers who purchased rights to best-sellers and hastened them to market by dividing jobs into sections subcontracted to different printers. In the 1640s, Parliament relied on a few stationers who, for very large press runs, "simply organized printing or reprinting by other stationers."[13] The Company itself became, through ownership of rights to popular categories of printed items, a massive joint-stock enterprise, a collective book producer and wholesaler. Another change was the rising social status of individuals bound as apprentices from the reign of Elizabeth to the outbreak of the revolution.[14] Opportunities for profit in printing developed in concert with growth in popular literacy. "Money was to be made not from the ponderous folios of Caxton, or the learned books of Richard Pynson, but, as the commercially astute Wynkyn de Worde soon found out, by seeking to tap popular demand for small quarto books for schools." Still, large books could be moneymakers. After the Bible, the most venerated text among English Protestants was

[11] R. B. McKerrow, "Edward Allde as a Typical Trade Printer," *Library*, 4th ser., 10 (1929):140–44; see also Clapham, "Printing," p. 404.

[12] E. Arber, ed., *Transcripts of the Registers of the Company of Stationers of London, 1554–1640* (London, 1875–84), 1:248; Sheila Lambert, "The Printers and the Government," in R. Myers and M. Harris, eds., *Aspects of Printing from 1600* (Oxford, 1987), p. 11. Fifty presses printing five hundred sheets per day will produce about 1.2 million pages in quarto format in a six-day workweek. The population at the turn of the century in England was roughly 4 million.

[13] Sheila Lambert, "The Beginning of Printing for the House of Commons, 1640–1642," *Library*, 6th ser., 3 (1981): 59.

[14] Cyprian Blagden, "The English Stock of the Stationers' Company," *Library* 5th ser., 10 (1955); Cyprian Blagden, "The Stationers' Company in the Civil War Period," *Library*, 5th ser., 13 (1958): 1–2.

John Foxe's *Acts and Monuments,* a two thousand–page chronicle of the persecution of England's Lollard heretics and early Protestants. It was first printed in 1563 by a prominent stationer, John Day, who held lucrative patents giving him exclusive rights to several popular texts. Day invested large sums to produce this book and was well rewarded when it and subsequent editions sold out, according to his epitaph:

> He set a Foxe to write how martyrs run
> By death to life. Foxe ventured pains and health
> To given them light: Day spent in print his wealth,
> But God with gain restored his wealth again,
> And gave to him as he gave to the poor.[15]

This alliance of commerce and controversy appears in the careers of other stationers, such as John Wolfe, who developed the art of surreptitious printing in foreign vernaculars for "the dual purposes of commercial gain and political or religious propaganda." After organizing opposition among poorer printers to monopolies on profitable categories of texts held by prominent stationers, Wolfe embarked on a new career, in 1584 publishing prohibited erotic and philosophical writings—for example, Aretino's *Ragionamenti* and Machiavelli's *I discorsi* and *Il Prencipe.* To meet domestic demand for such texts, Wolfe became adept at publishing them with false imprints, which indicated that they had been printed on the continent (which the Index Librorum Prohibitorum made difficult). Use of false imprints served two purposes: it whetted the appetites of readers and helped Wolfe evade guild restrictions of the Stationers' Company. Wolfe's trade flourished after Lord Burghley, Elizabeth's chief minister, "recognized the value of having important documents on foreign policy translated and published in foreign languages," under false imprints, as political propaganda distributed abroad by English agents.[16] Printers at this time also sought to profit from domestic controversy. An investigation into publication of two letters, one by the disgraced Robert Devereux, the earl of Essex, the other by his sister, who pleaded the earl's case to the queen, revealed that this was not "done so much upon friendship or faction as upon hope of gain."[17]

---

[15] Clair, *Printing in Britain,* pp. 4, 7, 77. For de Worde, see Edwards and Meale, "Marketing of Printed Books." For economic calculation and vernacular printing by Caxton, see Blake, *William Caxton,* pp. 60–67.

[16] Denis B. Woodfield, *Surreptitious Printing in England, 1550–1640* (New York, 1973), p. 24 and see p. 46; Clifford Huffman, *Elizabethan Impressions: John Wolfe and His Press* (New York, 1987), p. 6: "Wolfe's move was one that characteristically combined desire for profit with the dissemination of new, different, and inherently interesting material for which, he sensed, his London readers were ready."

[17] N. McClure, ed., *The Letters of John Chamberlain* (Philadelphia, 1939), 1:96.

This last comment shows that some contemporaries understood the entanglements of commerce and controversy in print culture. Nearly a century after Wolfe's publication of pornographic and political texts, a collection of satirical petitions in 1677 included one from England's booksellers, "that when a dull, heavy book lies on their hands, it may be publicly burnt to promote the sale of it."[18] Commerce ensured a plentiful supply of controversial texts for which popular demand existed. To be sure, ideologically motivated printers existed and plied their trade. But the affinity for controversy in print culture was generally sustained by printers in search of profits, which is why commercialism in print culture came under attacks from all quarters. A catalogue of England's sins in a sermon delivered before Charles I by an Arminian cleric included printing and Puritan sermons: "Surely if the sins of this land . . . had been divided into ten parts, the transgressions of the pulpit and print-houses would have largely made up a tenth part." But the same hostility existed at the other end of the political spectrum, from the Leveller leader Samuel Chidley.[19]

Competitive pressures in early-modern printing took many forms. In 1586, when the Company of Stationers defended "privileges" in printing—licenses that granted holders an exclusive right to print popular titles or categories of books—they argued that no books would be printed without privileges because a printer invested money to produce a book, but "another that will print it after him comes to the copy gratis, and so may he sell better cheap than the first printer." Such competition also involved product differentiation: "Besides, the second printer may better the first . . . either by notes, tables, differences in paper or volume, which will also hinder the sale of the first printer's books." Half a century earlier a London merchant, Richard Grafton, advanced similar arguments when he asked Thomas Cromwell for a limited monopoly to sell a printed edition of the Bible. This was the "Matthew Bible," a large, annotated edition in which he and others invested large sums of money; "but now others are printing the same work in a lesser letter, intending to sell their little books cheaper than I can sell my great [book]."[20]

Commercial impulses in print culture shaped many features of literary culture in Elizabethan and Jacobean England. It was a common practice to borrow themes and fictional names, translate classics without acknowledgment, and even compose texts falsely attributed to successful

[18] *MSS Rawl* D924, fol. 242.

[19] Thomas Jackson, *Three Sermons Preached Before The King* (Oxford, STC 14307, 1637), p. 32; Samuel Chidley, *The Dissembling Scot Set forth in his Coulours* (E652[13], 1652), p. 10.

[20] Arber, *Transcripts of the Stationers* 2:805; *L&P* 12, pt. 2, app., no. 35.

authors. A minor poet, Phineas Fletcher, used only oblique references to acknowledge his reliance on Edmund Spenser, though this extended to "the style, the imagery, the philosophy, the vocabulary, the subject matter, the character portrayal, the prosody, and the wording, of parts of almost every Fletcherian poem." These practices must be understood in terms of prevailing conventions, which included "neither the word 'plagiarism' nor the attitude toward literary indebtedness denoted by the modern use of that word."[21] Veneration motivated Fletcher's appropriation of Spenser. But borrowing also had baser motives, disowned by Drayton, who averred, "I am no pickpurse of another's wit." A leading literary author, Thomas Nashe, accused a competitor, Gabriel Harvey, of misappropriating "the name of *Piers Pennilesse* (one of my books), which he knows to be most saleable, (passing at the least through the pikes of six impressions) to help his bedridden stuff to limp out of Paul's Churchyard."[22] Dekker cited the pursuit of fame by authors to explain why "the begetting of books is as common as the begetting of children." So did Robert Burton, who added the complicity of stationers: "the number of books is without number" because "mercenary stationers" have abetted "an itching humor, that every man hath to show himself, desirous of fame and honor."[23] Such perceptions gave rise to the stigma of print, invoked by authors who protested that they only reluctantly allowed publication. "It is not my ambition to be a man in print," declaimed Dekker. Like many authors, Nashe wrote that he permitted an unworthy work to be published only after a manuscript copy lent to a friend "progressed from one scrivener's shop to another, & at length grew so common that it was ready to be hung out for one of their signs, like a pair of indentures."[24]

LEGAL AND POLITICAL ISSUES

The transit of a text from writing to print was subject to legal issues as well as the motives of fame and gain. One was the absence of settled law on authorial copyright. Protestations by Nashe and other authors about

[21] Abram Langdale, *Phineas Fletcher* (New York, 1937), p. 132; Harold White, *Plagiarism and Imitation during the English Renaissance* (Cambridge, 1935), p. 120.

[22] Michael Drayton, *Ideas Mirrour* (1594), quoted in N. Burton Paradise, *Thomas Lodge: The History of an Elizabethan* (New Haven, 1931), p. 107; R. B. McKerrow, ed., *Works of Thomas Nashe* (London, 1958), 1:140.

[23] Thomas Dekker, *News From Hell* (1606), in A. Grosart, ed., *The Non-Dramatic Works of Thomas Dekker* (London, 1884–86), 2:87; Robert Burton, *The Anatomy of Melancholy* (1628), ed. T. Faulkner, Nicholas Kiesling, and Rhonda Blair (Oxford, 1989), pp. 8, 16 Thomas Dekker, *The Guls Horne-booke* (1608), in *Non-Dramatic Works*, 2:199; Thomas Nashe, *The Terrors of the Night* (1594), in *Works*, 1:341; and see H. S. Bennett, *English Books and Readers, 1603–1640* (Cambridge, 1970), p. 11, 61–66.

being forced into print were not always feigned. Legal right to a text was established by the act of entering a book's title into the register of the Stationers' Company, which conferred on a *stationer* an exclusive right to print it. Use of scribal publication to circulate texts thus exposed authors of nonliterary as well as literary texts to the peril of having an "imperfect copy" printed. In 1652, a technical treatise on use of a ruler in geometry, navigation, and astronomy was suddenly published after a recipient of an "imperfect copy" circulating in scribal form gave it to a printer.[25] The stationer who initially entered a book could assign this right to another; an active market existed for purchase and sale of such rights. One path to prosperity for printers was to buy rights to reprint proven winners. Thomas Pavier, a printer whose career began inauspiciously with pirated quarto editions of Shakespeare and cheap ballads, amassed great wealth by buying rights to Puritan devotional literature, such as *A Garden of Spiritual Flowers*, which appeared in 21 editions between 1609–1625.[26] Legal rights to specific texts and categories of texts also took the form of monopolies, created by Tudor and Stuart monarchs in letters patent that conferred an exclusive right to print lawbooks, Latin grammars, psalters, and so on. The King's Printer, who published proclamations and laws, acquired a monopoly for printing the Bible and used it to publish most of the more than 150 editions of the Bible that appeared between 1603 and 1640. Roger L'Estrange, the Surveyor of the Press in Restoration England, published the *Intelligencer* because, as the principal agent of censorship, he had a monopoly on licensed news.

Of course, there was a political dimension in controls over printing, which originated in treason and sedition laws that had been enacted without specific regard for the new craft.[27] In addition, specific licensing requirements provided the government with a mechanism for censoring texts. Political concerns were paramount in the evolution of these requirements, which ran in tandem with the formulation of *religious* policies of successive governments, Protestant and Catholic.[28] In the reign of Henry VIII, officials worried about the alliance between commerce and controversy: the competitive nature of printing, and not merely ideological commitment, propelled production of illicit religious texts.

---

[25] Samuel Foster, *Posthuma Fosteri* (E675[1], 1652), sig a2v–3; and see Love, *Scribal Publication*, p. 53.

[26] Gerald Johnson, "Thomas Pavier, Publisher, 1600–1625," *Library*, 6th ser., 14 (1992): 12–13.

[27] Extant law on libel and sedition readily lent itself to punishment of authors and printers, given the vagueness of what constituted these offenses. Much depended on a judge's characterization of intent, which could be inferred from an offending text.

[28] See Cyndia S. Clegg, *Press Censorship in Elizabethan England* (Cambridge, 1997), pp. 30–65, 222.

In 1539, the Protestant reformer Miles Coverdale complained to Thomas Cromwell about "ungracious Popish books," whose availability he attributed to desire for "lucre and gains" by London's stationers. At her accession in 1553, Mary, intent on returning England to the Catholic cause, issued a proclamation against public debate over religion that also cites commercial motives among stationers who issue

> lewd treatises in the English tongue concerning doctrine in matters now in question and controversy touching the high points and mysteries of Christian religion; which books . . . are chiefly by the printers and stationers set out to sale to her grace's subjects [because] of an evil zeal for lucre and covetousness of vile gain.[29]

The Injunctions for Religion issued at the accession of Elizabeth in 1559 included one that restricted printing because "there is a great abuse in the printers of books, which [who] for covetousness chiefly regard not what they print so they may have gain." The same point was made in the preamble to a bill for the regulation of printing exhibited in Parliament in the 1580s."[30]

This was the political context in which licensing requirements evolved. Henry VIII delegated licensing to unspecified councillors, when, in 1538, he ordered that all English books be examined "by some of his grace's Privy Council." More formal arrangements subsequently gave this task to specific ecclesiastical officials under terms specified by the Elizabethan Injunctions on Religion (1559) and the statute that created the ecclesiastical Court of High Commission.[31] A 1586 decree by the Star Chamber delegated the task of licensing to the archbishop of Canterbury and the bishop of London, and made the Stationers' Company subordinate to prerogative and not the common law courts in order to tighten political control over printing. The decree was quickly modified to allow the bishop's chaplains to license manuscripts, a step necessitated by the workload—one chaplain licensed more than 631 items between 1630 and 1640.[32] After receipt of a license—that is, written authorization to print on the manuscript—a stationer paid a nominal fee, entered the title in the official register at Stationers' Hall, then acquired a legal right to the text.

---

[29] *L&P* 16, pt. 1, no. 444; *RP-T* 1:6.

[30] *RP-T* 2:128; Albert Peel, ed., *The Seconde Parte of a Register* (Cambridge, 1915), 2:54.

[31] *RP-T*, 1:272, 2:128–29. For the statute, see 1 Elizabeth I, c.1.

[32] Arber, *Transcripts of the Stationers* 2:807–12; Bennett, *Books and Readers, 1603–1640*, pp. 40–41; Philip M. Olander, "Changes in the Mechanism and Procedures for Control of the London Presses, 1625–1637." (B. Litt. thesis, Oxford University, 1976), pp. 25–26.

In addition to licensing requirements, Star Chamber decrees in 1615 and 1637 set limits on printers and presses. Under the 1637 decree, twenty-three or twenty-four printers operated between forty-six and fifty-one presses.[33] In the 1640s, elimination of the Star Chamber and other prerogative courts had a predictable effect: the number of printers jumped to about sixty and unauthorized printing soared. Complaints over the latter often appear in records of the Long Parliament, which had difficulty controlling the press that it otherwise used so skillfully. In 1643 it gave the Stationers' Company greater control over printing because

> very many, as well stationers and printers as others of sundry other professions not free of the Stationers' Company, have taken upon them to set up sundry private printing presses in corners, and to print, vent, publish and disperse books, pamphlets and papers in such multitudes that no industry could be sufficient to discover or bring to punishment all the several abounding delinquents.

Parliament put forward several schemes to impose controls on printing that now broadcast news and a range of opinions "never before allowed outside the discreet pages of private newsletters." It failed to achieve much control until the autumn of 1649, when it revived the 1637 Star Chamber decree but added stricter rules that required printers to register presses and post bonds of three hundred pounds to ensure compliance with licensing authorities.[34] Subsequent renewal of these controls occurred in 1653 and, after the Restoration, in the 1662 Licensing Act. The latter was hardly novel. It prohibited unlicensed books, required registration with the Stationers' Company and the printing of the license at the beginning of a book, restricted selling to members of the Company, and set the same limits on master printers and presses (forty presses for twenty master printers) as in the 1637 decree, with no greater success in enforcing these restrictions. Roughly three to four times the number of authorized printers plied their trade between 1660 and 1700, often exceeding the two-press limit; unlicensed printing flourished and illicit texts were sold by venders who were not members of the Company.[35]

In theory, production and sale of printed texts was subject to guild controls of the Company of Stationers, which regulated apprenticeships, production capacity, prices, and legal rights to texts via its registration requirements. In addition, the government ordinarily depended on

[33] Lambert, "The Printers and the Government," p. 11.

[34] E106[5] (1643), pp. 3–4; Anthony Cotton, "London Newsbooks in the Civil War" (D. Phil. diss., Oxford University, 1971), pp. 258–94, 322; Clair, *Printing in Britain*, p. 138.[35] Keeble, *Literary Culture*, pp. 96–97, 128.

agents and resources of the Company to detect instances of unauthorized printing. Guild regulations on printing developed in a piecemeal fashion, prompted by economic and political concerns of stationers and the government. The Stationers' Company succeeded a guild that had represented limners (illuminators) and writers of text letters. Political concerns in the royal charter that established the Company in 1557 appear in references to "seditious and heretical books, rhymes and treatises [that] are daily published and printed." Once established, the Company aided government censorship, using its authority to search premises and shops and seize unlicensed texts and unauthorized presses. It also used this authority to defend interests of wealthy members, who had exclusive rights to print many categories of popular texts, by searching for illicit printing of popular texts by poor or unauthorized printers.[36] Economic interests led the Company to lobby for strict limits over the number of presses, which, like licensing requirements, were not unilaterally imposed by the government but often requested by Company officers, as in the case of Star Chamber Decrees issued in 1586 and 1637. Different interests guided the government and the Company: primarily economic, for stationers who wanted to maximize work for members of a profession subject to chronic overcapacity; primarily political, for government officials who worried that hungry printers might print seditious or schismatic texts.[37]

Raising political fears in order to maintain economic control was a venerable practice of the Company of Stationers. Though the tactic worked for stationers, it did not yield the government an effective instrument for stopping unauthorized printing, as we shall see. When stationers wanted to secure legislation for reviving the Company's authority to regulate printing in 1652, they printed jointly by subscription two pamphlets "for the service of the Parliament and commonwealth." Patriotic and pious goals of this service were to forestall "rebellion" and "provocation of divine vengeance" by prompting lawmakers to take action against Catholic books, whose titles the stationers provided. The date noted by George Thomason, a London stationer and avid book collector, on the title page of the first pamphlet, *A Beacon Set on Fire*, is September 21—the day when Parliament read an act for reviving old regulations on printing. *A Second Beacon* was published or bought by Thomason on October 4. Economic interests lurked behind patriotic sentiments in arguments for penalties for "abusers of printing," who turned out to be not only "sellers of popish books" but all "peddlers, hawkers, running mercurists" and others who competed with retailers

---

[36] Cyril Judge, *Elizabethan Book Pirates* (Cambridge, 1934), pp. 16–17.

[37] Lambert, "The Printers and the Government," p. 2; Judge, *Elizabethan Book Pirates*, pp. 44–60, for the instructive case of Roger Ward.

among the stationers.[38] Earlier, in 1643 and 1646, the Company had requested London's Common Council to take action to suppress this competition, persons "who do openly cry about the streets small pamphlets."[39] Evidently little had changed after the Restoration, when Sir Roger L'Estrange complained in 1663 that the Stationers' Company had "under color of offering a service to the public" gained control over printing but been ineffectual because they used it to protect their economic interests. Three years later, L'Estrange observed that when Stationers' agents seized a press used by a printer who printed a Catholic pamphlet, it was "not because of the character of the book, but because he was said to print their copies."[40]

AUTHORS AND SELLERS

Publishing afforded authors of printed texts three sources of income: from patrons, subscription projects, and stationers. Dedicating a text to a wealthy patron in the expectation of a gratuity was an old and common practice, but success was uncertain. More lucrative was the practice of publication by subscription. Developed to an art by John Taylor, in an era when stunts and wagers figured prominently in contemporary public life, a project began with a broadside announcing his intent to perform a feat—for example, to walk to Scotland without money, ride an inflated bladder on a river, and so on. Taylor invited subscribers to pay between 5s. and £1 in exchange for which they received a printed account of his feat. Profits required a knack for shameless self-promotion and derived from the difference between publication costs, assumed by Taylor, and subscription income plus revenues from sales of the pamphlet to the public.[41]

Payment from stationers reflected estimates of the market power of the latter. But in the absence of copyright law that established texts as literary property of authors, authors had little leverage when stationers acquired a right to a text by being the first to enter it into the Company's register. Authors did not receive royalties based on actual sales. Instead, a popular pamphlet writer in late-Elizabethan England might

[38] E675[14] (1642), pp. 78; E675[29] (1652), p. 11; *Weekly Intelligencer* E675[25] (1652), p. 606.

[39] *MSS JCC* 40, fol. 73v, and see fols. 78v, 184.

[40] Roger L'Estrange, quoted in Clair, *Printing in Britain*, p. 154; George Kitchin, *Sir Roger L'Estrange* (London, 1913), p. 172; see also Keeble, *Literary Culture*, pp. 108, 302.

[41] Taylor, a waterman, may have earned £450 for his 1618 walk to Scotland, a huge sum for a waterman, equal to rowing 200,000 passengers across the Thames. William Lamont, *The World of John Taylor the Water-Poet, 1578–1653* (Oxford, 1994), pp. 64–65. For public interest in stunts, see *Chamberlain Letters* 1:118, 247, 262.

receive £2, and authors such as Robert Greene and Thomas Nash, perhaps twice that amount, at a time when £20 was thought to be good annual compensation for parsons and college fellows. During the Restoration, Richard Baxter and John Milton were paid £10 respectively for *The Saints Everlasting Rest* and *Paradise Lost*. Ballad writing, though it had the least status in the literary hierarchy, was profitable. Some ballad writers earned more than playwrights did. For many authors whose writings passed through the press, payment was a few dozen free copies of their book. In between were writers, such as Henry Chettle, who earned a few pounds for a sole-authored play but more frequently earned only "a small proportion of that sum" for collaborative work in finishing up a play worked on by others.[42] At the bottom of the heap were "pot poets"—allegedly inebriated writers paid by printers to churn out sensationalistic prose on current events. When controls on printing disintegrated in the 1640s, a flood of printed reports and commentaries on domestic events issued from presses supplied by pot poets. For "scribbling a whole sheet" authors earned enough money to buy "a pot or a pipe, or perhaps (if it take) half a crown . . . if the knavish stationer do not cousen him of it." Credibility might be sought by distancing a text from mercenary motivations of such writers. "I deal not with pot poets nor such as write anything to get money," boasted one publisher.[43]

Friction was not uncommon in relations between authors and stationers. Comments on this have a familiar ring to them that points to the divergence of interest that inevitably attended ties between publishers and authors. I "myself as yet have not received, of 500 which were printed, past 14 copies sent me from the printer," grumbled a clerical author in 1626. "I have forty times more trouble in printing a book than I have in writing one," complained the eminent Cambridge philosopher Henry More in 1674; "it is like kicking and spurring of a tired jade or Cambridge Hackney; a man makes a great deal of do to little purpose." Over two decades his letters recorded frustration with many contingencies that delayed printing: founders might not deliver type; there were too few compositors; other, more vendable items were given precedence.[44] A printer's delay puzzled the late-Elizabethan writer Rob-

---

[42] Alfred W. Pollard, *Shakespeare's Fight with the Pirates and the Problems of the Transmission of His Text* (Cambridge, 1920), pp. 24, 36; Keeble, *Literary Culture*, p. 133; Natascha Würzbach, *The Rise of the English Street Ballad, 1550–1650* (Cambridge, 1990) pp. 20, 291; Sandra Clark, *The Elizabethan Pamphleteers* (London, 1983), pp. 25–26; Clair, *Printing in Britain*, pp. 155–56; Jenkins, *Henry Chettle*, p. 21.

[43] E675[7] (1652), p. 6; M.S., *Truth In Two Letters* (E83[11], 1642), sig. A1v; and see E143[6] (1642), sig. A2–3.

[44] *MSS Tanner* 73, fol. 29; M. H. Nicolson, ed., *The Conway Letters* (Oxford, 1992), p. 396, and see pp. 69, 162–63, 219, 222, 223, 306, 372, 387, 390, 429, 394–95. See also *A Vindication Of The Answer To The Humble Remonstrace* (E165[6], 1641), p. 221.

ert Greene: "marry, whether his press were out of tune, paper dear, or some other secret delay drive it off," Greene's manuscript remained "this twelve months in the suds."[45] Authors freely fixed responsibility for mistakes on printers. "As for errors of the press," wrote one to his readers, "blame the printer, not me." In turn, printers complained in notes to readers about the "ragged" or "very foul" copy submitted to them.[46] Another source of contention was the printer's compositor; he and not the author mostly decided matters such as punctuation and orthography. Authors were expected to proofread sheets at the print house.[47] In 1592 Thomas Nashe complained that many uncorrected errors would not have marred a new impression of *Pierce Peniless* if his printer "had not been so forward in the republishing of it." On behalf of printers, Henry Chettle, formerly an apprentice who had been admitted to the Stationers' Company before turning to a literary career, voiced irritation with a "common" custom: "when an author or translator (either ignorant or negligent) palpably err, then the printer (forsooth)" bears the blame in "a great *Errata*, calling the title, *Faults escaped in the Printing*."[48] At least one author, a cleric, shared the blame with his printer for mistakes, especially in Latin words: pastoral duties prevented him from attending the print house, the printer knew no Latin, and both "were not so thoroughly estated as to maintain a sufficient scholar" to proofread text.[49]

After an author's copy made it through the press, printed copies were sold in shops, originally clustered around St. Paul's in London and on Fleet Street. Like other aspects of the stationer's trade, selling was an increasingly specialized activity in the sixteenth century. Some stationers functioned as publishers, wholesalers who hired printers, such as the "ballad partners." These stationers were not printers but dominated the ballad trade in early-Stuart England by collaborating in publication and distribution.[50] At the high end of the retail trade were London bookshops, patronized by members of England's ruling elite, in deference to

[45] *The Complete Works in Prose and Verse of Robert Greene*, ed. A. Grosart (London, 1881–86), 12:7; see also Marotti, *Manuscript, Print, and the English Renaissance Lyric*, pp. 263–64.

[46] Bennett, *Books and Readers, 1603–1640*, pp. 210, 212; see also Edwin Willoughby, *A Printer of Shakespeare: The Books and Times of William Juggard* (London, 1934), pp. 90, 152–56.

[47] Percy Simpson, *Proof-Reading in the Sixteenth, Seventeenth, and Eighteenth Centuries* (London, 1935), pp. 2–19.

[48] Thomas Nashe, *Pierce Penilesse His Supplication to the Divell* (1592) in, *Works of Thomas Nashe* 1:153; Jenkins, *Henry Chettle*, p. 16.

[49] Edward Topsell, *The History of Serpents* (STC 24124, 1608), sig. A5v.

[50] Tessa Watt, *Cheap Print and Popular Piety, 1550–1640* (Cambridge, 1991), pp. 75–76.

whom "it was standard practice for new books to be published during the law terms, when London was crowded with people from the provinces." Individuals such as Sir Thomas Barrington and Lord Conway had accounts with a London bookseller, who sent religious and political texts, some perhaps ordered in advance.[51] Yet not much social status attached to even the high end of the profession. In 1622, one observer thought it a sign of difficult economic times "to see booksellers, stocking men, haberdashers . . . and other mean trades crept into the goldsmiths row."[52]

Booksellers outside London were an important part of the retail distribution network. A Suffolk cleric, John Rous, visited one in Bury; an Essex minister, Ralph Josselin, purchased books when he traveled to Wethersfield and Dedham; on other occasions, he asked acquaintances traveling to London to buy books.[53] A Shrewsbury bookshop kept by a disorderly printer, Roger Ward, in 1585 stocked ballads and inexpensive sermons. In York, John Foster had a more substantial stock in his provincial bookshop next to York Cathedral. At his death in 1616, he had 3,000 volumes. His wide variety of religious, educational, learned, and popular texts included 550 almanacs valued at one and a half pence apiece, a dozen copies of Aesops fables for half a shilling apiece, one folio of plays by Ben Jonson for ten shillings, and many religious tracts for a half to two shillings.[54] After the Restoration, the provincial book trade continued to disseminate all manner of licit and illicit books. Quakers had their own distribution network that, in 1664, covered York, Lincoln, Nottingham, Warwick, Huntingdon, Northampton, Hertford, Colchester, Bristol, and more—despite the fact that the Licencing Act of 1662 reconfirmed the restriction of bookselling to members of the Stationers' Company.[55]

At the low end of the retail book trade were provincial shopkeepers who sold cheap books as a sideline and itinerant booksellers who peddled their wares in London's streets and, in the provinces, at market towns, taverns, and fairs. Mostly they sold chapbooks—ballads, jestbooks, and other slender pamphlets that instructed and entertained.

[51] Lamont, *John Taylor*, p. 73; Mary E. Bohannon, "A London Bookseller's Bill, 1635–1639," *Library*, 4th ser., 18 (1937–38), pp. 417–46; *SPD* 16/450/fol. 33.

[52] *Chamberlain Letters* 2:460.

[53] M. A. E. Green, ed., *The Diary of John Rous* (*CS*, os, 66, 1856), p. 54; A. Macfarlane, ed., *The Diary of Ralph Josselin* (London, 1976), pp. 22–23, 36, 7.

[54] Alexander Rodger, "Roger Ward's Shrewsbury Stock," *Library*, 5th ser., 13 (1958); John Barnard, *The Early Seventeenth-Century York Book Trade and John Foster's Inventory of 1616* (Leeds, 1994).

[55] Keeble, *Literary Culture*, pp. 131–32; Margaret Spufford, *Small Books and Pleasant Histories: Popular Fiction and Its Readership in Seventeenth-Century England* (London, 1981), chap. 5.

Carriers, ballad singers, and coachmen also sold chapbooks. One knowledgeable observer at the end of the sixteenth century, Henry Chettle, claimed that printers of unauthorized, licentious ballads recruited peddlers "able to spread more pamphlets by the state forbidden than all the booksellers in London."[56] Distribution practices for ballads in the 1640s sent newsbooks and other inexpensive political pamphlets whizzing across the nation. A "mercury woman, a common dispenser of all kinds of dangerous pamphlets" is how agents of the Stationers' Company described an itinerant bookseller who was seized outside Westminster Hall, "her lap full of books." A critical account in 1641 describes how "suck-bottle," a hawker of political pamphlets, went from village to village, crying out, "Come buy a new book, a new book come forth."[57] This refrain of the itinerant peddler of cheap print was part of popular culture. Its utility as a trope appears in a Royalist ballad that satirizes Parliament's vote of "No Addresses" in January 1648 (a radical move to break off negotiations with the king). Beginning,

> Come, customers, come: Pray see what you lack,
> Here's Parliament's wares of all sorts in my pack,

the ballad, *The Cryes of Westminster*, pokes fun at Parliament's declarations and ordinances in references to the hawking of cheap print by wandering peddlers.

> Who buys the Parliament's Declaration against
>   the King? New, new, new.
> 'Twill surely unbind your eyes,
> That you may read a hundred lies.
>
> . . . .
>
> Buy a new Ordinance of the Commons
>   against stage-players: Newly printed, and
>   New-lye come forth."[58]

The supposition that peddling practices for printed texts were familiar features of everyday life and therefore useful for authorial purposes is but one instance of the way in the social milieu of popular literacy influenced the content of political texts.

---

[56] Henry Chettle, *Kind-Hartes Dreame* (*STC* 5123, 1593), sig. C2v. See also see J. P. Collier, ed., *Broadside Black-Letter Ballads, Printed in the Sixteenth and Seventeenth Centuries* (New York, 1968), viii–xii; Lamont, *John Taylor*, p. 73; Spufford, *Small Books*, p. 125; Watt, *Cheap Print*, pp. 76–77.

[57] *HMC Sixth Report*, p. 154; *The Downfall of Temporizing Poets, unlicenst Printers, upstart Booksellers* (E165[5], 1642), pp. 1–2.

[58] W. W. Wilkins, ed., *Political Ballads of the Seventeenth and Eighteenth Centuries* (London, 1860), 1:44 and 43–53.

POPULAR LITERACY AND READING

Popular print culture in early-modern England grew out of technical and social aspects of printing that we have so far examined. A flood of inexpensive printed texts was the consequence of competition among stationers who used printing's technical potential to produce for a wide spectrum of readers relatively inexpensive pamphlets, broadsides, and other printed texts. In England as on the continent, the cost of textual reproduction plummeted in the shift from scribal to print culture.[59] In the 1620s, a highly sought after separate, a scribal copy of a speech or other noteworthy piece of news, might command as much as 10s., whereas a printed newspaper, a coranto, sold for 2d.—a sixtyfold difference. A century earlier, Lollard heretics who valued the importance of reading vernacular Bibles paid 20s. to 55s. for manuscript editions of vernacular New Testaments, roughly the current price of a horse (about 34s.) or one hundred times the prevailing agricultural day wage rate. At this time, printed copies of Tyndale's New Testament in the 1520s had the same illicit status as scribal Lollard Testaments, but Tyndale's text cost only 3s. to 4s.[60] Small, illicit tracts in late-Elizabethan England, by Puritan and sectarian writers, were even cheaper, selling for the equivalent of one to one-and-a-half times the prevailing agricultural day wage rate. For example, Martin Marprelate's *Epistle* sold for 11d. and John Greenwood's *A Collection of Certaine Sclanunderous Articles Gyven out by the Bisshops* cost 8d. Prices were higher for contemporary Catholic texts: pamphlet literature cost 5s. to 17s., and Catholic Bibles cost between 16s. and 40s.[61] Half a century later the relative price of controversial religious and political texts was still lower. Since 1590 the agricultural day wage rate had increased about 40 percent but, due to the collapse of controls on the press, the price of dissident tracts after 1640 dropped to the level of the cheapest licit materials, such as ballads and newspapers. Sectarian pamphlets published by the radical printer Giles

[59] Elizabeth Eisenstein, *The Printing Press as an Agent of Change* (Cambridge, 1980), p. 46; Geneviève Hasenohr, "Religious Reading amongst the Laity in France," in P. Biller and A. Hudson eds. *Heresy and Literacy, 1000–1500* (Cambridge, 1994), p. 206. For relative costs of scribal and print reproduction in the late-seventeenth-century, see Love, *Scribal Production*, pp. 132–33.

[60] John F. Davis, *Heresy and Reformation in the South-East of England, 1520–1559* (London, 1983), pp. 58, 62; John Foxe, *Acts and Monuments of the English Martyrs* (New York, 1965), 3:597, 4:237; Alfred Pollard, *Records of the English Bible* (Folkstone, 1974), pp. 6, 44. For wage rates, see Peter Bowen, "Statistical Appendix," in J. Thirsk, ed., *The Agrarian History of England and Wales, 1500–1640* (Cambridge, 1967), p. 865.

[61] Leona Rostenberg, *The Minority Press and the English Crown* (Nieuwkoop, 1971), pp. 182, 206; *ENT* 4:107.

Calvert in the 1650s sold for 4d.; weekly newspapers usually occupied one sheet and sold for 1d., and Royalist newspapers sold for twice that amount. Broadside ballads defined the low end of the market, costing a halfpenny, roughly the cost of half a loaf of bread.[62] The low cost in printing simple texts facilitated the deluge of political declarations, replies, ordinances, petitions, and other materials that poured from printing presses during the 1640s. Parliament spent nearly as much (£30) for special messengers to distribute an ordinance for a day of public thanksgiving as it spent for printing ten thousand broadsides copies of the ordinance (£40), or roughly 1d. per broadside, the going rate for a broadside or small octavo pamphlet of eight pages, both of which consumed one printer's sheet to produce.[63]

The correlate to high volume and low prices was, of course, popular literacy. Measures of popular literacy indicate that the ability to read generally varied by social class, gender, and region. In early-modern England the ability to read was more widespread than the ability to write. Hence, "many more rural people could get through the text of a broadside ballad than could sign their names to a Protestation oath."[64] The ability to sign the 1642 Protestation Oath across different parishes varied from 17 percent to 38 percent. London in the mid-seventeenth century boasted an adult male literacy rate of 70 percent or higher; comparably high literacy levels existed in Bristol, England's third largest city. By the third quarter of that century nearly 40 percent of all adult males could read—a high watermark not seen again for nearly two centuries. In the century preceding the outbreak of the English Revolution in 1642, declining levels of illiteracy, including female illiteracy, followed an uneven but widespread pattern among artisans and craftsmen, yeomen and, in London, servants and apprentices. Opportunities for individuals to become at least semiliterate, to read but not write, existed in small villages where teachers who not infrequently were clerics without benefices offered intermittent schooling.[65]

Popular interest in acquiring literacy had several sources. First, it was a mark of social status. Second, economic developments prompted interest in acquiring literacy, as growth of market-oriented production implied greater use of contracts, bonds of debt, and other simple financial instruments in rural and urban areas.[66] Third, religion was important.

---

[62] Thomas Birch, *A Collection of the State Papers of John Thurloe* (London, 1742), 4:717; Würzbach, *English Street Ballad*, p. 20.

[63] Sheila Lambert, "Printing for Parliament, 1641–1700," *List and Index Society* 20 (1984): 2–3.

[64] Watt, *Cheap Print*, p. 7.

[65] For references, see David Zaret, *The Heavenly Contract* (Chicago, 1985), p. 36.

[66] Ibid., pp. 36–37.

Reading vernacular Bibles lay at the heart of Protestant religiosity (which partly explain why West European Protestant societies such as England and Holland had the highest levels of literacy in early-modern Europe).[67] Popular Protestantism involved a complex mix of semiliterate and literate practices. At the high end, reading was accompanied by keeping diaries, writing letters, and even composing simple treatises or taking notes at sermons—"pens walking at sermons" is how an Elizabethan cleric described worship in an area of Kent notorious for sectarianism.[68] Readers of a polemical pamphlet by the water poet John Taylor, whom we met above, would have understood the pun in the title page's reference (see fig. 4) to the author having taken notes of a ridiculous sermon by a sectarian preacher. Such practices coexisted with semiliteracy for a Dover mason, John Trendall, who in 1639 led craftsmen and women in sectarian worship. He often followed standard clerical practice. At one session, the mason "took his text from Isaiah 51:7 and raised two points of instruction thereupon. He then gave reasons thereof, and made application of the same." In other meetings, he preached on different biblical texts while a shipwright took notes. Yet Trendall was unable to write; he signed documents with a mark.[69]

Diversity characterizes the preferences of readers in popular print culture. Pious writings coexisted with inexpensive, often irreverent chapbooks, which, like their continental counterparts, the French *bibliothèque bleu* and Spanish *pliegos de cordel*, were "printed by the hundreds of thousands" and sold by itinerant peddlers.[70] English chapbooks edified and entertained; they were short, cheap, and dominated by merry tales, jests, romances, and lurid accounts of monsters, murders, and disasters. For the pious, a London bookseller published and sold for 2d. to 3d. chapbooks such as *The black book of conscience* and *The plain mans plain path-way to heaven*—as many as thirty-thousand copies of these two titles from 1651 to 1663. The latter item was an abridged version of *The Plaine Mans Path-Way To Heaven*, by Arthur Dent, that appeared in at least twenty-five editions before 1640.[71] Secular literature in popular pamphlets was also mixed; some writings were erudite and inaccessible, others "addressed primarily to those who were literate but not highly educated or sophisticated." In late-Elizabethan England,

---

[67] Burke, *Popular Culture*, p. 215.

[68] Peel, *The Seconde Part of a Register*, 1:118. For remarkable writing practices by artisans, see Paul Seaver, *Wallington's World: A Puritan Artisan in Seventeenth-Century London* (Stanford, 1985); MSS Rawl C765.

[69] *CSPD* 1639–40, pp. 81–83.

[70] Roger Chartier, *The Cultural Uses of Print in Early Modern France* (Princeton, 1987), p. 240; Burke, *Popular Culture.*, p. 253–54.

[71] Watt, *Cheap Print*, pp. 266–73; Spufford, *Small Books*, pp. 105–6.

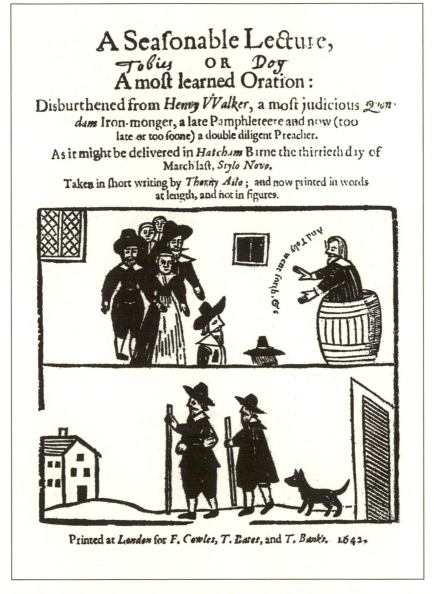

Fig. 4. Title page of satirical pamphlet that derides the sectarian preacher Henry Walker. Note the reference to the author (John Taylor) having taken shorthand notes of Walker's sermon.

popular writers included Henry Chettle, Thomas Dekker, Robert Greene, and Thomas Nashe. When he was not publishing texts with surreptitious titles, John Wolfe published work by Greene and induced Gabriel Harvey, an aspiring author bent on gaining a literary reputation as an upholder of high standards against Greene's popular style, to aim a bit lower, to prefer "one smart pamphlet of knavery, before ten blundering volumes of the nine muses."[72]

The popular element in secular literature has been defined in many ways, in terms of genre (e.g., ballads and jestbooks), commercialism, ambivalence toward the pamphlet as a licit culture form, the social status of writers, and more.[73] In terms of thematic and rhetorical complexity, cost, and authorial presumptions about the social status of readers and the cultural status of texts, a rough hierarchy existed. Like Dekker, Nashe, and Jonson, John Taylor put the productions of "lousy balladmongers" at the bottom, closely followed by producers of sensationalistic accounts of monsters, murders, and miracles. A measure of authorial respectability attached to jestbooks, prose pamphlets, plays, and nondramatic verse.[74] For Thomas Lodge, literary respectability "was to be gained only by the composition of non-dramatic poetry" and not by writing plays "to penny-knaves' delight."[75] Here, again, we should be wary of sharp distinctions. A prolific author of popular pamphlets, Henry Chettle, derided producers of ballads, "intruders into printing's mystery, by whom that excellent art is not smally slandered." Yet at least thirteen of his plays "dealt with themes on which ballads or chapbooks were already in existence." The same held for a jointly authored play by Greene and Lodge. Considerable sophistication on the part of readers was necessary to grasp ironic irreverence in Dekker's pamphlet *The Wonderfull Yeare* (1603), on the accession of James I to the throne and the visitation of the plague on London. But Dekker, too, composed jestbooks and incorporated that genre into his pamphlet. John Taylor had roughly 150 separate titles and over 500,000 individual copies to his credit, yet his satires and other writings contained "difficult allusions" and an "exotic vocabulary."[76] In the next chapter we shall encounter a

---

[72] Huffman, *Elizabethan Impressions: John Wolfe*, p. 111, and see pp. 99–111; Clark, *Elizabethan Pamphleteers*, p. 18.

[73] Waage, *Thomas Dekker's Pamphlets*, p. 5; See also Clark, *Elizabethan Pamphleteers*, p. 23; Alexandra Halasz, *The Marketplace of Print* (Cambridge, 1997), chap. 1.

[74] Lamont, *John Taylor*, p. 68. See also F. P. Wilson, "English Jestbooks of the Sixteenth and Early Seventeenth Centuries," *HLQ* 2 (1939); Würzbach, *English Street Ballad*, pp. 242–52.

[75] Paradise, *Thomas Lodge*, p. 85.

[76] Chettle, *Kind-Hartes Dreame*, sig. C1v; Jenkins, *Henry Chettle*, pp. 247–48, and see 14, 40, 161–64, 192, 234–35; Lamont, *John Taylor*, pp. 66–68; Waage, *Thomas Dekker's Pamphlets*, pp. 87–91; see also Watt, *Cheap Print*, p. 291; Paradise, *Thomas Lodge*, p. 154.

similar situation in the 1640s, when many printed political pamphlets blurred divisions between elite and popular culture.

A central issue in the stigma of print was the licit status of the pamphlet in print culture. Situated between broadsides and expensive folio books, the pamphlet catered to readers from diverse social backgrounds, for which university education and wealth were not prerequisites. The stigma of print flowed from hostility to the content and readership of pamphlets, both of which effaced boundaries between elite and popular cultural practices. This led authors to heap scorn on "ignorant dunces" and "every dull mechanic" who desired to read inexpensive printed texts.

> Readers too common, and plentiful be;
> For readers
> they are that can read a,b,c.
> And utter their verdict on what they doe view,
> Though none of the Muses they yet ever knew.[77]

Such complaints referred specifically to the low social status and rudimentary education of commoners who could read but whose formal education did not extend to grammar school and the universities. Popular readership, we have seen, was related to commercial imperatives in printing—another source of hostility to print culture. On this point, the contrast between transmission of texts by printing and coterie manuscript production could not be clearer for writers such as Ben Jonson, who "heaped scorn on the commercial enterprise" (though he participated in it) and objected "to the stationer's desire to reach a broad readership." For Nashe and Jonson, a distasteful combination of commerce and popular literacy appeared in the spectacle of "Goodman Reader," who "scarse can spell th'hard names," perusing title pages on a post—a common advertising practice of booksellers.[78]

Secular literature at the end of the sixteenth century bore the imprint of many features of print culture—blurred cultural boundaries, competitive pressures, and mixed readership for middlebrow pamphlets. But they had first surfaced in religious writings published earlier in that century. Unlike theological texts produced for clerics, scholars, and university-educated gentlemen, popular religious literature was marked by its

---

[77] Rachel Speght, *Mortalities Memorandum* (STC 23057, 1621), sig. A3v; see also Lamont, *John Taylor*, p. 68; Wendy Wall, *The Imprint of Gender: Authorship and Publication in the English Renaissance* (Ithaca, 1993), pp. 17, 57–58; Louis B. Wright, *Middle-Class Culture in Elizabethan England* (London, 1964), p. 97.

[78] Marotti, *Manuscript, Print, and the English Renaissance*, pp. 241–42; Nashe, *Terrors of the night*, p. 343; John Milton, *Poetical Works*, ed. Douglas Bush (Oxford, 1966), p. 173.

lower cost and intellectually more accessible content. The alliance of commerce and controversy animated publication initiatives as printers competed to satisfy popular demand for the original best-seller in print culture, vernacular Bibles. In Germany, a printed version of Luther's vernacular Bible first appeared in 1522, and, over the next two years, 14 authorized and 66 pirated editions were published. Tyndale encountered the same problem with his version of the English Bible. In all, sixty-four thousand copies of Tyndale's New Testament existed in England in 1530, among a population of 3.5 million.[79] Editions with official backing included, in 1539, the Great Bible—this refers to its size— and, in 1568, the Bishops' Bible. Unlike these Bibles, a quarto edition, produced in 1560 at Geneva and then in London after 1575, was often found at home. Christopher Barker purchased the privilege to print it, and from 1576 to 1600 he and his partners produced more than 50 editions. Another 90 editions appeared by 1644. Altogether more than a million English Bibles and New Testaments had been printed since the Reformation. By then, inexpensive Bibles sold for two to three shillings.[80]

Clues to the social composition and semiliteracy of many readers appear in epistles to popular religious texts published in the reigns of Henry VIII, Edward, Mary, and Elizabeth. Authors and translators refer to presumed readers as "simple" or "unlearned." Philip Gerrard's defense of Protestant Bible reading was intended for the "ignorant sort" of reader; Henry Barret calls his 1549 tract a "simple & illiterate treatise."[81] These references invoke the medieval equation *illiteratus* = *laicus*, persons outside the clerical world of Latin and university education. Vernacular religious pamphlets occupied a contradictory cultural location that could not be mapped onto the venerable distinction between *literatus* and *illiteratus*.

Though presumed readers of popular religious texts were commonly called "unlearned" or "illiterate"—also "rude," "simple," and "gross"—these labels refer not to illiteracy but to the lack of university education and the ability to read Greek or Latin. Hence, a vicar in 1536 denounced "schismatic English books" because they "deceive the unlearned."[82] Producers of popular categories of printed texts often referred to readers who were semiliterate. A biblical concordance pub-

[79] J. F. Davis, "Lollardy and the Reformation in England," *Archiv für Reformationsgeschichte* 73 (1982): 230; S. H. Steinberg, *Five Hundred Years of Printing* (Harmondsworth, 1966), pp. 142–44, 202.

[80] Clair, *Printing in Britain*, pp. 63–64, 97. Christopher Hill, *The English Bible and the Seventeenth-Century Revolution* (London, 1994), p.18.

[81] Henry Barret, *The armyng of a Christen Warrier* (*STC* 1499, 1549), sig. A3; Philip Gerrard, *A Godly Invective in the defence of the Gospell* (*STC* 11797, 1547), sig. A4.

[82] *L&P* 11, no. 970.

lished in 1550 begins with a table "expressing by plain letters the number of figures contained in this book"—the assumption is that readers understood roman but not arabic numerals. The title page to the English translation of Erasmus's *Decta spaientum* notes it is "good for all folkes to rede or to here redde."[83] Translators and paraphrasers of Scripture produced many vernacular religious texts, omitting difficult passages "as might be most meet and agreeing to the capacity of those that are simple." Anthony Gilby, who translated Beza's writings on the psalms of David for his "unlearned countrymen," was delighted by the thought that this was available to "now even the simplest poor man for a small piece of money."[84] The early Separatist leader Robert Brown presented his sectarian attacks on the Church of England "both to the learned and to the unlearned" in a treatise presented in four parallel columns. For the "unlearned," he recommended column 1; for the learned, who "seek deepness and stand on their methods and curious divisions," the additional columns provided "definitions" of entries in antecedent columns and "divisions" that subdivided the definitions.[85]

Seeking the attention of the "simple sort" in religious pamphlets was not limited to Protestant authors. Just before the English Reformation, Richard Whitford was only one monk who published "for the unlearned" simple guides that instructed the laity on proper conduct in religious and secular affairs. Thirty-two editions of Whitford's tracts were published between 1530 and 1538; *A Work for Householders, or for them that have the guiding or governance of any company* was his most popular book, having been printed eight times.[86] In that era, Sir Thomas More's career as a propagandist for orthodoxy began when Bishop Tunstal enlisted his aid in 1528, requesting that he publish "in English for the common man" arguments against the Protestant reformers. In *The Confutation of Tyndale's Answer* (1532–33), More sought to convince "the people unlearned" not to read "heretical" writings by Tyndale, Firth, and Barnes. Composed as a dialogue, More's work appeals explicitly to a popular audience: at its conclusion the goodwife of the Bottle of Botolph Warf rebukes Barnes, and More observes, "Lo, thus might a wise woman that could no more but read English, rebuke and confound Friar Barnes."[87]

[83] John Marbecke, *A Concordance* (STC 17300, 1550), sig. Aa5; Erasmus, *Dicta Sapientum* (Edinburgh, STC 10478, 1580).

[84] *The first tome or volume of the Paraphrase of Erasmus* (STC 2854, 1548), sig. B4; Theodore Beza, *The Psalmes of David* (STC 2033, 1580), sig A6; see also William Baldwin, *The Canticles or Balades of Salomon* (STC 2768, 1549), sig. A1.

[85] *ENT* 2:222–23.

[86] Christopher Haigh, *English Reformations* (Oxford, 1993), pp. 25–26.

[87] *Complete Works of More* (New Haven, 1973), 8:37, 896, 1139, 1265–66.

Many continuities link religious developments in the seventeenth century with communicative practices that we have observed in the emergent print culture of the prior century. The alliance of commerce and controversy continued to ensure a plentiful supply of texts on controversial matters. After Archbishop Sancroft's sermon of November 5, 1678, provoked widespread "murmurings"—it contained no reference to the popish plot—a stationer begged the archbishop for permission to publish his latest sermon because it would lift the stationer's lowly financial circumstances.[88] A half century earlier, a prolific Puritan cleric, Thomas Gataker, reported in 1625 that he was "looking over" a book he had published seven years earlier on a controversial topic: chance, lots, and card playing. This book was a response to *A Short And Plaine Dialogue Concerning The Unlawfulnes of Playing At Cards*, published in 1593 and reprinted in 1595 and 1600. After its author, James Balmford, replied in print to Gataker, in 1623, along with another reprinting of his 1593 text, Gataker's stationer sensed the existence of sufficient interest to justify a new edition of Gataker's book, and asked Gataker to prepare a new edition of it.[89]

The more common path to publication by Gataker and other Puritan clerics involved collecting spiritual advice in books intended for popular as well as elite readers, another extension of sixteenth-century developments. The blurring of distinctions between elite and popular culture in pamphlet literature is nowhere better illustrated than in the rise of a distinctively Puritan variety of religious literature. Popular demand for simple instructional treatises provided stationers with a reliable source of profit. From Newcastle, a Puritan lecturer, Robert Jenison, received a request by a stationer for permission to print his instructions on receiving communion, originally written in letters to his sister. "I was content to let him have them," wrote Jenison, "& to direct them to the ruder sort of my hearers."[90] Puritan writers cultivated a simple, expository style of preaching, designed as a casuistical guide for readers. Some compilations of sermons were reprinted dozens of times, such as *The plaine mans path way to Heaven*, by Arthur Dent. The most popular Puritan author was William Perkins, whose writings appeared in more than two hundred editions and reprints between 1590 and 1640. Almost as many printed items can be credited to other popular Puritan clerics of this era,

---

[88] *MSS Tanner* 314, fol. 14; John Spurr, "'Virtue, Religion, and Government'": The Anglican Uses of Providence," in T. Harris, P. Seaward, and M. Goldie, eds., *The Politics of Religion in Restoration England* (Oxford, 1990), p. 46.

[89] *MSS Tanner* 72, fol. 28.

[90] *MSS Tanner* 73, fol. 437; Robert Jenison, *Directions For Receiving The Lords Supper* (*STC* 14490, 1624). For publication of Edward Dering's catechism, see Willoughby, *William Juggard*, p. 189.

such as Henry Smith, John Preston, and Richard Sibbes.[91] Published most often in inexpensive quarto, octavo, and duodecimo formats, they cost one or two shillings, whereas folio volumes destined for libraries of wealthy patrons cost five to twelve times as much.[92] This literature was accessible to many lay readers. Its simple prose style—it lacked rhetorical polish and included few Hebrew, Greek, and Latin phrases—was well suited to manuals of practical divinity, whose compact style related technical points of divinity to the inner experience of regeneration for readers. Much the same also held, in terms of cost and authorial presuppositions about readers, for nonconformist literature in Restoration England.[93]

ILLICIT BOOKS

The affinity for controversy in print culture stemmed from commercial forces and existed long before its implications appeared in political texts in the 1640s. Prevailing norms of secrecy and privilege, along with more general assumptions about the organic nature of society, however, prompted secular and ecclesiastical officials to repress public controversy. To what extent, then, did censorship hinder the development of print culture as a prototype for a public sphere? We shall see that several factors limited the efficacy of censorship. The alliance of commerce and controversy greatly compounded difficulties faced by government censors and the Stationers' Company. We have seen that the government's interest in censoring controversial writings was often thwarted by their reliance on stationers to detect unauthorized printing. The flaw in this system of surveillance was that the interest of stationers in enforcing rules against unauthorized printing was variable and not always or even often congruent with official interests. Other factors facilitated publication of printed controversial texts, their publication spurred by greed, ideological principle, or both. Commercially minded book pirates and godly nonconformists used the same techniques for producing and distributing illicit texts. Both took advantage of the ability of a few persons to produce large numbers of printed texts on presses that might be registered (but otherwise used to produce licensed texts), unregistered and secretly concealed, or located abroad.

[91] Publication figures based on *A Short-Title Catalogue of Books Printed in England, Scotland, and Ireland . . . 1475–1640*, ed. W. A. Jackson, F. S. Ferguson, and Katharine F. Pantzer (London, 1976–86).

[92] Prices based on Bohannon, "A London Bookseller's Bill"; *SPD* 16/450/fol. 33v.

[93] Keeble, *Literary Culture*, pp. 132–43.

Purely commercial impulses animated book piracy in print culture and made illicit printing a common practice. Printing pirated texts was prompted by a large, recurring demand for some printed texts (e.g., primers), for which Tudor governments conferred lucrative licenses on individual printers, such as the one John Day and his son obtained in 1577 to the *A.B.C.* with the little catechism, metrical psalms, and other works.[94] Day's license was undermined by a massive scheme to produce pirate copies of the *A.B.C.*, the standard reading text for children. Conspirators advanced supplies to one Roger Ward, a poor printer, "to the end they might have the said books so imprinted the better cheap." Ward consumed twenty reams of paper and printed ten thousand copies, one sheet for each simple piece that was worth about a half pence. He sent fifteen hundred copies to Shrewsbury, where he had a bookshop, gave twenty-five hundred to one conspirator in exchange for paper, and used other copies to pay other debts. Ward's trial and imprisonment in 1582 did not deter others from pirating this and similar works on just as large a scale for the remainder of the decade. Many plays by Shakespeare and other writers appeared in pirated quarto editions, the text obtained either from actors or from a surreptitious copy taken by stenography.[95]

Unauthorized printing was difficult to repress because a surprisingly large proportion of printed materials did not follow licensing and registration requirements—perhaps a third of all copies printed in the early-seventeenth century were not registered or properly licensed. Half of all surviving ballads, the cheapest, most popular category of print culture, were not registered. The same situation existed in Restoration England.[96] When producers were detected, fines for printing an unlicensed or an unregistered book or both were often small sums, a few shillings (more for seditious materials) in Jacobean England; in the 1640s, admonishment and other light punishment was the most common sanction for unauthorized printing of parliamentary materials.[97] Moreover, opportunities for evasive, dissembling accounts by printers abounded. Accused in 1646 of publishing confidential papers of Scottish Commissioners, a prominent stationer, Robert Bostock, claimed that he was out

---

[94] Clair, *Printing in Britain*, p. 78.

[95] Arber, *Stationers' Transcripts* 2:754; Judge, *Elizabethan Book Pirates*, pp. 48–51. Seizure of "six or seven" presses in the 1630s did not deter a prolific printer of pirated primers; see Lambert, "The Printers and the Government," p. 17.

[96] Bennett, *Books and Readers, 1603–1640*, pp. 42, 45; Würzbach, *English Street Ballad*, p. 24; Keeble, *Literary Culture*, pp. 111–12.

[97] Bennett, *Books and Readers, 1603–1640*, p. 48; Joseph Frank, *Cromwell's Press Agent: A Critical Biography of Marchamont Nedham* (Lanham MD, 1980), pp. 27, 57; Lambert, "Beginning of Printing for the Commons," pp. 45, 48, 56–59, 61; Kevin Sharpe, *The Personal Rule of Charles I* (New Haven, 1992) p. 652. Fines were notably heavier in the reign of Charles II; see Keeble, *Literary Culture*, pp. 109–10.

of the shop when a "stranger" gave the papers to his wife, who then sent them to three printers. Servants of a radical printer, William Larnar, refused to answer interrogatories, "which tended, as they thought, to the disclosing of their master's secrets." Another printer flatly denied involvement in printing seditious books, but his wife was seized by agents of the Stationers' Company outside Westminster Hall, where she peddled "all kinds of dangerous pamphlets."[98]

Producers of illicit texts used techniques for concealing the origins of printed texts that were nearly as old as printing itself. These, too, reflect the alliance of commerce and controversy in early-modern print culture. Many pirated and controversial texts bear false imprints—title pages that wrongly attribute the location or identity of a printer. As was the case for John Wolfe's publication of prohibited erotic and philosophic writings, this widely used technique not only shielded the identity of the publisher, but also helped to stimulate sales. It was used for printed ballads that praised and condemned Thomas Cromwell in 1540. In 1555, the colophon of Queen Mary's printer was affixed to "a stinging satyr on the clergy and obliquely on the queen herself." False imprints appear on Dekker's 1603 pamphlet, *The Wonderfull Yeare*, in "an attempt to confuse authority and forestall reprisal until a profitable number of copies had been sold," and on pirated quarto editions of plays by Shakespeare issued by William Juggard.[99] In the 1640s false imprints shielded producers of printed news from detection and invested their work with credibility. Robert Bostock used one to indicate that speeches by the earl of Louden and papers of Scottish Commissioners had been printed in Edinburgh. A prominent London stationer, Thomas Underhill, requested readers of his accounts of civil war battles "that if they meet with anything in print, either feigned or scurrilous, with his name on them . . . not to believe that they are printed or published by him or his means, but by ungodly fellows, who usurp his name to credit their lies."[100] After Charles I made Oxford his headquarters in the fall of 1642, counterfeit Oxford imprints appeared on many Royalist pamphlets in order to protect London printers from reprisals by parliamentary agents. At this time a related trick in unauthorized printing of parliamentary documents was to include a previously published item that had the printed signature of the clerk of either House, thereby suggesting the whole pamphlet had been approved for publication. In

---

[98] *HMC Sixth Report*, pp. 111–12, 118, 154.

[99] E. Gordon Duff, *A Century of the English Book Trade* (London, 1948), p. xxiv; Clair, *Printing in Britain*, p. 68; Waage, *Thomas Dekker's Pamphlets*, pp. 48, 52, and see pp. 222–24; Willoughby, *William Juggard*, p. 3.

[100] E360[12] (1646); Fortescue, *Catalogue of the Thomason Tracts* 1:472; *Brave Newes Of the taking of the City of Chitchester* (E83[36], 1642), sig. A4v.

restoration England, frequency of false imprints in dissenting literature varies by denomination: low for Presbyterian tracts, progressively higher for Independent, Baptist, and Quaker tracts.[101]

Censorship was also evaded by the varying degrees of ease with which printing equipment, supplies, texts, and copy for the press could be moved. Even bulky presses and related equipment could be concealed and moved. In the 1580s, a printer of pirated texts and Puritan polemics concealed "a press and other printing stuff in a tailor's house near adjoining to his own and did hide his letters in a henhouse." After these were seized, he set up another press across the Thames in the house of a Southwark tanner.[102] At the end of that decade, production of Marprelate's scurrilous tracts—four were printed by Robert Waldegrave, a master of the Stationers' Company, at the home of a Puritan widow in East Mosely near Kingston-on-Thames—was possible because presses traveled, covered with hay in carts, across the midlands, eluding episcopal agents long enough to permit publication. A press traveled to Fawsley in Northamptonshire, to Coventry, and, after Waldegrave's departure for the continent, to "a low parlor" in a private home in Walston Priory, where new printers issued more Marprelate texts. After one more removal, to Manchester in the summer 1589, printers and their equipment were seized, but yet another Martinist tract issued from a press hidden at Walston.[103]

Printed texts were far easier to conceal and transport than presses. During the Bishops' Wars, the government utterly failed to stem the flood of Scottish political texts into England. A newsletter in March 1639 reported that Charles I had stopped the post from Scotland in order to interrupt communication between dissident allies in both kingdoms. But "this course does also prevent the bringing hither of Scotch pamphlets." In September 1640 Archbishop Laud received a report on a distributor of Scottish pamphlets in London who "lurk's about Greys' Inn," an associate or servant "following him with a cloak bag full of books."[104] Just as little success greeted efforts to stop importation of illicit English texts that were printed overseas. This operation used established techniques for smuggling, such as labeling illicit books "as other goods," abetted by persistent corruption among collectors, searchers, and undersearchers at English ports. After fining one searcher £200 for not seizing English Bibles and other religious texts, the High

[101] Lambert, "Beginning of Printing for the Commons," p. 60; Keeble, *Literary Culture*, pp. 112–13.

[102] Judge, *Elizabethan Book Pirates*, pp. 56–57.

[103] Collinson, *Elizabethan Puritan Movement*, pp. 139–40, 274–75, 391–96; Rostenberg, *Minority Press*, pp. 177–80.

[104] *MSS Add* 11045, fol. 3v; *CSPD* 1640–41, p. 62.

Commission sent a copy of his sentence to farmers of the custom, who were ordered to have it read to their subordinates. Yet, three years later, in 1638, the government learned that searchers of the customs continued to "frequently pass English books printed beyond the seas."[105] Although developed mainly for pirated texts of noncontroversial items, such as primers, book smuggling provides further evidence of the alliance of commerce and controversy in printing. Dutch and Flemish printers who catered to the flourishing trade in pirated materials also printed illicit sectarian tracts.

Puritan dissidents thus had several publication sources. In the early 1570s they used an unauthorized domestic press to publish several tracts advocating reform, such as Cartwrights's *Replye* to Whitgift's *Answere to the admonition*, and the *Second admonition*. After discovery of this press, Puritans had polemical Presbyterian tracts printed in Heidelberg. At this time, radical sectaries relied on oversea presses. In 1583 the government issued a proclamation declaring books by Robert Browne and Robert Harrison to be "seditious and schismatic"; both authors fomented "schism among his majesty's subjects, being persons *unlearned* [emphasis added] and unable to difference the errors therein contained." Their tracts were printed in Middleburg, capital of Zeeland, and include Browne's *Reformation without Tarrying for anie*, published in an edition of a thousand copies.[106] In the mid-1580s, Puritan writers again turned to a domestic press—it belonged to Waldegrave—and after it was discovered, they reverted again to overseas printers. Meanwhile, separatist writings continued to be printed in Amsterdam and Dort. Even after the imprisonment of three ringleaders, the government could not stop this practice. In prison, John Penry, John Greenwood, and Henry Barrow wrote manifestos and had them conveyed to Dutch printers.[107]

This last episode is but one of many in which manuscript copy from imprisoned authors was printed. In the 1630s, the government under the personal rule of Charles I had no more success in coping with the porosity of prisons, corruption among port searchers, and the connivance of printers. Imprisoned in the Tower, William Prynne published over a two-year period at least ten books![108] In the 1640s, the Stationers' Company could not stop unauthorized political printing. When Company pursuivants with a warrant searched a house for a press that printed a Leveller tract, *Englands Birth-right Justified*, they "were kept out by force, until at last, the doors of the house being by authority

---

[105] *CSPD* 1640, p. 400; *CSPD* 1635, p. 187; *CSPD* 1638–39, p. 258; and see Rostenberg, *Minority Press*, pp. 202–9.

[106] *RP-T* 2:501–2; Rostenberg, *Minority Press*, p. 191.

[107] *ENT* 3:210, 261, 4:106–7.

[108] Sharpe, *Personal Rule of Charles I*, pp. 651–52.

forced open, those that were at work got out at a window with a rope into a garden and escaped." The searchers seized the press and imprisoned a radical printer, William Larner; yet in jail he wrote several short tracts, all printed, that urged the public to read *Englands Birth-right*.[109]

Distribution networks for clandestine texts from the early years of the Reformation to the outbreak of the Revolution involved amateurs and professionals, united by shared beliefs or casual acquaintanceship. The trade in Tyndale's New Testament consisted of small quantities of books bought for reselling by merchants, clerics, Lollards, and aliens.[110] Illicit distribution of Catholic books did not quite fit this pattern but relied, instead, on more elaborate, centralized arrangements. Two hundred "new and handsomely bound" Catholic books were traced to a servant who worked in the household of successive Spanish ambassadors to the English court.[111] Above, we saw that distribution of Quaker books after the Restoration relied on a centralized network of agents. But before 1640, distribution of sectarian texts exhibited a different pattern, exemplified by the Marprelate episode, in which a cobbler transported printed sheets for Marprelate pamphlets from several locations in the midlands, where a printing press operated in secret, to a bookbinder in Northampton. Between six hundred and nine hundred copies of a Marprelate pamphlet were printed and sold in private homes of sympathetic laypersons, who included minor municipal officials, a widow, and deprived clerics. Separatist writings by Barrow, Greenwood, and Penry were printed in editions of two hundred to five hundred copies. One conspirator paid overseas printers for five hundred copies of two Separatist tracts, conveyed them to England, gave roughly half to Barrow and Greenwood, and sold the rest, presumably to recoup his expenses.[112] Reliance on "casual personal connections" and informal networks later also appears in the clandestine book trade for Puritan and Separatist tracts in the 1630s. In 1637, the chancellor of Norwich diocese reported to his bishop, Matthew Wren, that on a boat landed at Yarmouth two Puritan ministers, one of whom had been suspended by Wren, brought packages of a book by the Puritan martyr John Bastwick, four copies of which had been purchased by a "silly weaver."[113] Scottish pamphlets that justified

[109] Joseph Hunscot, *The humble Petition and information of Joseph Hunscot Stationer* (E340[15], 1646), pp. 5–7. E304[17] (1646) is *Englands Birth-right*.

[110] Davis, *Heresy and Reformation*, pp. 27, 43, 54–56, 59; Haigh, *English Reformations*, pp. 60–61, 63–66.

[111] *CSPD* 1640, pp. 256–57.

[112] Rostenberg, *Minority Press*, pp. 180–82, 204–5; *ENT* 4:107, 176; J. Payne Collier, ed., *The Egerton Papers* (*CS*, os, 12 1840): 173–74.

[113] *MSS Tanner* 68, fols. 1v, 9v–10. The book most likely was *STC* 1572. See also Stephen Foster, *Notes from the Caroline Underground* (Hamden, CT, 1978), p. 53.

the Covenanter Revolt in the First and Second Bishops' Wars were also distributed in small quantities by amateur conspirators.[114]

We are now in a position to appreciate why official control over printing had, at best, limited success. The government relied on the Stationers' Company, whose members had economic interests that militated against overly strict regulations, especially on the number of presses or on licensing and registration requirements. Star Chamber decrees in the reign of Charles I had just as little success against the Puritan press as did the Surveyor of the Press in the reign of his son against printers of Whig and dissenting texts.[115] Under favorable but often temporary circumstances, government officials enforced censorship—under the rule of Cromwell's Army, the Royalist press disappeared; when the Tory party regained control of the shrievalty, the office of London's sheriff, in 1682, most Whig newspapers ceased publication.[116] But these triumphs were short-lived. Ultimately, the Licensing Act of the Restoration, renewed in 1685 and 1693, lapsed and was not renewed in 1695, due to objections in the House of Commons that were "arguments of merchandise," that "were less libertarian than economic; licensing was an interference with freedom of production."[117]

APPEALS TO PUBLIC OPINION IN RELIGION TO 1640

Religious controversies in prerevolutionary England provide evidence of print culture as a prototype for the public sphere. New habits of thought cultivated by those reading printed religious writings had a corrosive impact on clerical authority and anticipated political developments in the 1640s. One source of this development was the probative value attributed by readers to the printed text, a consequence of a technical aspect of printing: its ability to reproduce large amounts of texts, accurately, in standard formats designed to appeal to the judgment of readers. In controversial issues, printed texts appealed to public opinion by putting before readers textual sources that supplied them with reasons and evidence for adjudicating debates. The assumption that printing reliably reproduced antecedent texts was amplified by the contemporary use of

[114] *CSPD* 1640, pp. 614, 622, 634, 647.

[115] Keeble, *Literary Culture*, p. 127; Lambert, "Printers and the Government," p. 17; Sharpe, *Personal Rule of Charles I*, p. 652.

[116] Tim Harris, *London Crowds in the Reign of Charles II* (Cambridge, 1990), pp. 154–55.

[117] Kitchin, *Sir Roger L'Estrange*, p. 129 n; Christopher Hill, *Collected Essays* (Amherst, MA, 1985), 1:54; see also Raymond Astbury, "The Renewal of the Licensing Act in 1693 and Its Lapse in 1695," *Library*, 5th ser., 33 (1978).

marginal notes and annotations.[118] Authors of inexpensive, intellectually accessible pamphlets on religious issues in the mid-sixteenth century supported their arguments by reproducing relevant scriptural passages, or supplying references to them, along with excerpts of textual passages that they sought to confute. A century later, this development in the 1640s propelled a political public sphere, when printed political texts referenced and selectively reproduced declarations, ordinances, statutes, and other texts in order to influence the opinions of readers. This was in sharp contrast to "the combination of the *litterae* with ceremony, ritual and a system of gestures" widely found in scribal texts in the Middle Ages, where the "text was considered not only as a sort of vehicle of factual information, but, and first of all, as part of a certain ritual infused with magic. Magic, ritual, sorcery seem to be the essence of the comprehension of the text."[119]

Here, two related points are important. First, the probative value attributed to texts in print was not limited to religious debates or other explicitly contentious issues. The printer in a 1621 masque by Ben Jonson exclaims, "See men's diverse opinions! It is the printing of 'em makes 'em news to a great many who will indeed believe nothing but what's in print." The same point appeared in a play by Shakespeare, again as satire: "I love a ballad in print . . . for then we are sure they are true."[120] The probity of print also arises in use of printing for bills enacted by Parliament. Only public and not private bills were printed, and only those bills that appeared in print "were regarded as public, especially in the important sense that they could be alleged in court without special pleading (which involved the production of a certified true copy)."[121] Second, publicity as much as probity was fostered by print culture. Cultural implications of printing's technical potential for reproducing texts moved in opposite directions, toward piety and pornography, self-seeking publicity and the critical scrutiny of arguments.[122] Publicity and media celebrity were prominent features of early-modern print culture, no less evident in Marprelate's attacks on pompous bishops than

[118] See Evelyn Tribble, *Margins and Marginality: The Printed Page in Early-Modern England* (Charlottesville VA, 1993), p. 161. Footnotes did not appear until the eighteenth century.

[119] Aaron Gurevich, "Heresy and Literacy: Evidence of the 13th-Century 'Exempla,'" in Biller and Husdon, *Heresy and Literacy*, pp. 105–6.

[120] Ben Johnson, *News From the New World Discovered in the Moon* (1621), in *The Complete Masques*, ed. S. Orgel (New Haven, 1969), p. 294; William Shakespeare, *The Winter's Tale*, 4.4.255–56. See also *The Fair Maid of the Inn*, in Fredson Bowers, *The Dramatic Works in the Beaumont and Fletcher Canon* (Cambridge, 1996), 10:617.

[121] G. R. Elton, *Studies in Tudor and Stuart Politics and Government* (Cambridge, 1974–92), 3:105, 126–27.

[122] Eisenstein, *Printing Press*, pp. 130, 228–30.

in the famous exploits of the water-poet, John Taylor, who was not the first to use print for self-promoting publicity stunts. Later, Sir John Gell, a Parliamentary officer in the civil war, was rumored to have "kept the diurnall makers in pension" in order to obtain press coverage. Gell was not an isolated case.[123] Wittingly or otherwise, William Prynne, the sour Puritan polemicist, became a media celebrity. In 1659 his celebrity was used against him in a satirical petition to Parliament that referred to the string of descriptive titles appended to his name on the title pages of his many pamphlets. Because Prynne had "such an athletic habit in the career of writing, that if he may not scribble and print too, he cannot live," the petition requested that he "have liberty to draw his own blood, and to write against himself; that William may have liberty to write against Prynne, Prynne against the esquire, the esquire against the utter barrister, the utter barrister against the Bencher of Lincoln's Inn."[124]

Probity and publicity in print culture conjointly appear in appeals to the judgment of readers in many printed texts in early English Protestantism. This development was at least implicit in the very act of printing vernacular Bibles, often explicit in religious pamphlets that advanced key tenets of early Protestantism. The title page of a simple tract attacking the Catholic mass contained the following appeal in the early years of the Reformation:

> Read me first from toppe to toe
> And afterward judge me a friend or a foe.

At the conclusion of another contemporary tract, readers were told, "if you will not believe us herein, search these scriptures following," and provided with the supporting references.[125] Similar appeals to readers appear in Separatist pamphlets in late-Elizabethan England and just before the restoration of Charles II in arguments against sectarian factionalism.[126] Critical remarks on Elizabethan Separatists and, later, on sectarian opponents of Charles I cite this use of textual reproduction in sectarian appeals to public opinion, in which dissidents "fill the margins of their books with such store of scripture that the simple might think

---

[123] For a precedent for Taylor's stunts, see Richard Ferris, *The most dangerous and memorable adventure of Richard Ferris* (*STC* 10834, 1590). For Gell, see Lucy Hutchinson, *Memoirs of the Life of Colonel Hutchinson* (Oxford, 1973), p. 68; see also Frank, *Cromwell's Press Agent*, p. 19.

[124] *To The Supream Authority ... The Humble Petition of the ... Well-affected* (669f.21[33], 1659).

[125] Antoine de Marcort, *A declaration of the Masse* (*STC* 17314, 1547), sig. A1; *An Epistle exhortatorye* (*STC* 10430, ca. 1549), p. [4]; and see *The dysclosyng of the Canon of ye popysh Masse* (*STC* 17626, 1548), sig. Aa4v.

[126] *ENT* 2:432, 5:29; *Irenicum* (E978[1], 1659), sig. A3.

they have even a cloud of witnesses against us."[127] Use of printing's ability to reproduce texts to appeal to the judgment of readers was not limited to sectarians. It appears in the publishing history of the first pamphlet by Separatist leader Henry Barrow, *A True Description Out of the Worde of God, Of the Visible Church*. First printed overseas in Dort in 1589 and several times thereafter in Amsterdam, it also was reprinted in two critical texts, in 1590 and 1613. The latter was Christopher Lawne's *Brownisme Turned the In-side Out-ward*, which uses a dual-column format, one side with Barrow's text, the other with Lawne's ridiculing commentary.[128]

Promoted by printing's capacity for textual reproduction, the imposition of dialogic order on conflict was a principal point of contention between opponents and supporters of reform at the onset of the English Reformation. Opponents decried criticism of religious practices by reformers who printed religious texts that supplied readers with the ultimate grounds of judgment. Stephen Gardiner, an apostle of religious conservatism, associated heresy and the work of paraphrasers and translators who produced these texts. "I lament to see the truth so abused . . . under the pretense of plainess." His misgivings focused on "unlearned" readers and "the facility and easy understanding of scripture, which many do arrogantly presume to have by themselves attained." Why, asked Gardiner in 1546, would the laity continue to defer to clerical authority if, as reformed clerics claimed, truth resided in vernacular Bibles?[129] For this point, important continuities exist across scribal and print culture. The centrality of printed Bibles in early Protestantism was an extension of practices in medieval heretical movements whose members typically displayed only the modest literacy of the "unlearned," such as continental Waldensians and English Lollards.[130] These were "textual communities," translocal entities whose organization was geared to the production, circulation, and reading of vernacular manuscripts.[131] The same negative consequences for clerical author-

---

[127] *The Church of England is a true Church* (*STC* 10398, 1592), p. 56; and see Richard Carter, *The Schismatik Stigmatized* (E179[14], 1641), p. 4.

[128] For Lawne, see *STC* 15323. For Barrow, see *ENT* 3:208–23.

[129] Stephen Gardiner, *A Declaration Of Such true articles* (*STC* 11588, 1546), sigs. F2–3, H2, L3. See also H. S. Bennett, *Books and Readers, 1475–1557* (Cambridge, 1952), p. 74; Miles Hogarde, *The displaying of the Protestants* (*STC* 13557, 1556), sig. K7; John Standish, *A discourse . . . whether it be expedient that the scripture should be in English* (*STC* 23208, 1555), sig. K2–3.

[130] For Waldensian literacy, see Garriel Audisio, "Were the Waldensians More Literate Than Their Contemporaries?" in Biller and Hudson, *Heresy and Literacy*, pp. 181–82, 185; Alexander Patschovsky, "The Literacy of Waldensianism from Valdes to ca. 1400," in Biller and Hudson, *Heresy and Literacy*, pp. 129–30.

[131] On the term *textual community* and its application to Waldensianism in the High

ity that conservative critics feared from the use of printing to spread Protestant beliefs had previously surfaced in English Lollardy, when lay heretics, with access to manuscript copies of the New Testament and Lollard sermons, averred that they "could hear a better sermon at home . . . than any doctor or priest could make at Paul's Cross or any other place."[132] Later, new textual communities appeared among Puritan artisans in London[133] and in new heretical movements, like the Familists, forerunners to the seventeenth-century Quakers. Scribal and print modes of publication nourished these communities. Before the Reformation and printed Bibles, "the market for Lollard books was good and was also well supplied." In Elizabethan and early-Stuart England, manuscript and printed editions of Familist texts circulated in London and the countryside. From Lollardy to Familism, the content of heretical literature and reading practices associated with it corresponded to the literary world of the "unlearned."[134]

Thus, at least some critical aspects of print culture represented amplifications of tendencies visible in scribal culture. But the vastly superior potential of printing to reproduce texts, in concert with slowly rising levels of literacy, led to unprecedented levels of public discussion and debate in homes, taverns, and other public places on religious issues. This situation appeared in complaints to the Privy Council on religious conflict in the early years of the English Reformation. Conservative clerics denounced lay readers of the New Testament, "especially those who explain it in taverns"; conflicts over this occurred between laymen, such as a brawl in a tavern when a minstrel urged a saddler to read the Bible.[135] When the government belatedly approved the printing of English Bibles, it ordered clerics to instruct parishioners to read them but not "be presumptuous in judging matters" and "not to reason about doubtful passages of the book in taverns and alehouses." These prohibitions were reconfirmed but did not dissuade commoners from these activities. This circumstance led to an act of Parliament (34 & 35 Henry VIII, c.i) that prohibited commoners from even reading the Scriptures—a futile effort, judging by the king's last speech to

---

Middle Ages, see Lutz Kaelber, "Other- and Inner-Worldly Asceticism in Medieval Waldensianism," *Sociology of Religion* 56 (1995); 100; Brian Stock, *The Implications of Literacy* (Princeton, 1983), pp. 88–240, 522. See also Eisenstein, *Printing Press*, pp. 131–32, 148–49, 443.

[132] Anne Hudson, *Lollards and Their Books* (London, 1985), p. 191.

[133] Seaver, *Wallington's World*, pp. 191–92, remarks on London sectarians, "Their literacy . . . freed these godly laymen from clerical dependence, as it did to a degree from patronage or kinship connections."

[134] Hudson, *Lollards and Their Books*, p. 182.

[135] *L&P*, no. 611; 13, pt. 1, no. 615; and see 13, pt. 2, nos. 253, 820, 1015.

Parliament, in 1545, in which he complained "how unreverently that most precious jewel, the word of God, is disputed, rhymed, sung and jangled in every alehouse and tavern." A contemporary proclamation against radical Protestant books indicated that not only Bibles but other texts were read by laypersons "who argue and dispute in open places, taverns, and alehouses."[136]

During the century before the outbreak of the mid-seventeenth-century civil war, discussion and debate stimulated by reading of printed texts became a hallmark of what we now call nonconformity. The tamer side of this development eventuated in the rise of household religion, a distinguishing feature of Puritan religiosity, in which householders were expected to provide religious instruction to their families. "The Reformation, by reducing the authority of the priest in society, simultaneously elevated the authority of lay heads of households."[137] Links to printing in this development existed on several levels. Printing supplied texts used in household worship, and, as we saw, debate in printed religious texts weakened the authority of clerics. In homes, taverns, and barns, discussion and debate that accompanied lay reading of religious texts was a prominent feature of sectarian religion at the radical fringes of the Reformation.[138]

Alongside this development there evolved a nascent public sphere in religion, constituted by debates over competing views on how best to organize English Protestantism. The principal issue was whether the liturgy established for the Church by the Elizabethan Settlement was fixed or represented a step on a path to further reforms. Initially, reformers restrained appeals to public opinion, directing their arguments to clerical opinion or to the collective opinion of England's governing elite. They also limited the scope of debate in a futile effort to detach religious disputes from questions about the larger political and social order. (Because of the established nature of the Church of England, religious controversies had inherent political ramifications.) For the most part, the laity were spectators to efforts by clerical reformers who used traditional levers of patronage to promote their cause.

In the first major Puritan controversy—over efforts in the mid-1560s to impose conformity on the issue of clerical attire—printed pamphlets were composed by and principally for clerics. The reformers' case against use of traditional clerical garments appeared in "the earliest puritan manifesto," Robert Crowley's *A briefe discourse against the outwarde*

[136] *L&P* 13, pt. 1, no. 1304; 20, pt. 2, no. 1031; *RP-T* 1:271.

[137] Christopher Hill, *Society and Puritanism in Pre-Revolutionary England* (New York, 1967), p. 446, and see pp. 443–81; Eisenstein, *Printing Press*, pp. 424–28; Seaver, *Wallington's World*, 33–34, 41, 79.

[138] Zaret, *Heavenly Contract*, pp. 100, 107, 118.

apparell and Ministring garmentes of the popishe church.[139] Distributed by dissident clerics to their congregations, this small tract met with a swift response, *A brief examination for the tyme, of a certain declaration, . . . refusing to weare the apparell,* written or commissioned by Archbishop Parker. Crowley responded with *An answere for the tyme to the examination,* and more tracts in defense of Puritan nonconformity also appeared in 1566, including several items that reprinted supportive texts from great churchmen of the past and contemporary continental reformers. The other side hastily prepared a printed tract with letters by Bullinger and other leaders of continental Protestantism who supported the English bishops. From London, Bishop Grindal reported success in dissuading some clerics and laypersons from leaving the Church, telling Bullinger, "Your letter . . . has greatly contributed to this result; for I have taken care that it should be printed, both in Latin and English." Restraint in this literature's appeal to public opinion also appears in a tract by Anthony Gilby, *To my lovynge brethren that is troublyd abouwt the popishe apparrell* (1566). Gilby reprinted a letter to William Cecil, a powerful member of the Privy Council, but deleted references to the queen. These were restored in another work, also composed in 1566, that Gilby held back from publication until 1573, *A Pleasaunt Dialogue betweene a Souldior of Barwicke and an English Chaplaine,* an influential polemical plea on behalf of nonconformity.[140]

In the 1580s, restricted controversies continued to be conducted in print by clerical authors, but with a new principal issue, the merits of Presbyterian models of church organization. The counteroffensive to this move included publication, in 1594 and 1597, of Hooker's *Laws of Ecclesiastical Polity.* At this time the circle of debate in printed polemics widened a bit. Presumed readers now included more than clerics in polemical Puritan pamphlets such as *The Unlawful Practises of Prelates Against Godly Ministers.* This pamplet was intended for Parliament and the classes it represented. So was *An humble petition of the Communalitie* (1588), whose epistle to readers noted the desire by reformers to communicate grievances to members of Parliament "and finding no other ways to perform the same, we desired that it might be done by the way of printing."[141] Separatist writers, such as Browne, Barrow, and

---

[139] Patrick Collinson,. *The Elizabethan Puritan Movement* (London, 1967), p. 77; and see M. M. Knappen, *Tudor Puritanism* (Chicago, 1966), pp. 198–211. See *STC* 6078 for Crowley's pamphlet.

[140] H. Robinson, ed., *The Zurich Letters* (Cambridge, 1842), p. 168, and see p. 175. For the printed items by Bullinger, Crowley, Gilby, and Parker, see *STC* 4063, 10387, 10388, 10390, 11888.

[141] *An humble petition of the Communaltie* (Middleburgh, *STC* 7584, 1588), sig. A1v. See also William Bradshaw, *A Triall Of Subscription* (Middleburgh, *STC* 24273, 1599);

Greenwood, wrote for an even broader audience—godly lay readers. Martin Marprelate's pamphlets aimed at all readers, godly or otherwise, and acquired instant notoriety as masterpieces of popular satire in which church officials were comical figures. One Marprelate tract has a running head—"Oh Read Over Dr. John Bridges, For It Is a Worthy Work"— that refers to a fourteen-hundred-page tome in which Bridges defends the church hierarchy. Puritan reformers did not welcome this sally on their behalf, though they were not guiltless, for Marprelate reiterated wittily and without tact the substance of Puritan critiques. Moreover, the same printer of solemn Puritan tomes had published Marprelate's scurrilous tracts and a blatant Puritan appeal to public opinion, *A Register, Contayninge Sundrie Memorable Matters Written by Divers Godly and Learned in Our Time*, whose collection of petitions, interrogatories, and letters provided a public record of encounters between beleaguered Puritans and Church officials bent on enforcing conformity to the Church of England.[142]

That religious controversy had acquired the character of a public debate appears in criticism by Francis Bacon of "this immodest and deformed manner of writing . . . whereby matter of religion is handled in the style of the stage." Significantly, Bacon's comment was directed against both Marprelate and his adversaries, such as Lyly and Nashe. Hired or at least encouraged to answer Marprelate in print and in kind, Lyly and Nashe in their anti-Martinist writings applied ridicule and satire to volatile topics, and prompted Bacon to conclude "these pamphlets as meet to be suppressed as the other."[143] Printing thus created conditions for placing debate over religious issues on—to use Bacon's metaphor—a stage. Reformers and their episcopal opponents often referred in printed exchanges to popular dimensions of their audience. A defender of the ecclesiastical establishment, Matthew Sutcliffe, gloated when an adversary, attacked as the secret author of the Marprelate tracts, responded in print, for it "was not wise to make himself the argument of the common people's talk."[144] Crowley's *Brief discourse against the out-*

Certaine Demandes With their grounds . . . by some religious Gentl. (Middleburgh, STC 6572.5, 1605); *Certaine Arguments To Perswade And Provoke The Most Honorable And High Court of Parliament . . . to speake for the Ministers* (STC 740, 1606); *The Unlawful Practises of Prelates Against Godly Ministers* (STC 20201, 1584).

[142] "The Puritans are angry with me," Marprelate notes, because "I am too open." William Pierce, ed., *The Marprelate Tracts, 1588, 1589* (London, 1911), pp. 118–19. See STC 10400 for *A Register*.

[143] Collinson, *Elizabethan Puritan Movement*, pp. 392–93; Tribble, *Margins and Marginality*, p. 121.

[144] Matthew Sutcliffe, *An Answere Unto A Certaine Calumnious letter* (STC 23451, 1595), sig a2v.

warde apparell, cited above, sought "to declare in writing, & to set forth
to be seen by all men, some part of the reasons & grounds of our doings." So did two Separatist collections published in 1590 for "the reading and view of all men." Like the Puritan *Register,* these provided another public record of correspondence and other exchanges between
Church officials and imprisoned Separatist leaders.[145]

Thus, by the end of the sixteenth century one aspect of growing lay
involvement in debates over religion involved production of printed
texts to put competing views before the reading public. Of course, this
had inherently political implications, given the established nature of the
Church of England. Subsequent events in the 1620s drew out these implications, as the tide of international politics turned against continental
Protestant regimes and a domestic crisis brewed over the influence of
Catholicism in the Stuart Court. Yet not until the English Revolution
did print culture leave its imprint on specifically political debates. Prior
to this point, appeals to public opinion on political matters relied mainly
on scribal modes of publication for circulating texts of parliamentary
speeches and protestations. Use of printing to publicize opinions on religious controversies occurred in the context of contestation over specific religious policies and not over the nature and purposes of the political authority that enacted those policies. Even among small radical
groups in the sectarian fringe of Puritanism, appeals to public opinion seldom touched on the fundamental issues of politics that would
subsequently be debated in a political public sphere during the English
Revolution.

[145] Crowley, *A brief discourse,* sig. A2v; *ENT* 4:108, 111, and see 103–262.

CHAPTER SEVEN

Printing and Politics in the 1640s

A POLITICAL PUBLIC SPHERE first appeared in the English Revolution. Both developments were unintended consequences of rapidly escalating conflict between Charles I and the Long Parliament, which convened in November 1640. Competing appeals to public opinion in politics occurred in a communicative context whose contours we followed in the previous chapter: high rates of popular literacy, an alliance of commerce and controversy in print culture, and ineffective control over production and distribution of printed texts. In this context, technical and social aspects of printing reoriented political discourse so that production of political texts became more closely attuned to the purpose of constituting and invoking public opinion. Printing's commercialism and its technical potential for efficient reproduction of texts were not unique to England, but several factors enhanced their potential for altering communicative practices. In the last chapter we saw that, compared to other nations, England had an unusually high level of popular literacy, promoted by the intimate association of Bible reading with the achievement of national identity. Moreover, London's position as the unchallenged political and publishing center of the nation was also unusual. Unlike France or the Low Countries, printing in England was not dispersed throughout market centers of the nation. Amsterdam rivaled London in terms of its diversity of religious and political opinion, but Amsterdam was not the center for printing and politics. Only in Oxford and Cambridge did a few presses exist outside London.

The confluence of these factors is why the midcentury revolution in England generated far more printed materials than other major early-modern revolutions had. In France, about 5,000 pamphlets, the Mazarinades, were published during the Fronde in the mid-seventeenth century. Thereafter, roughly 1,500 additional political pamphlets appeared during the personal reign of Louis XIV, averaging 20 per year from 1661 to 1698 and, in response to heightened international tensions, about 40 per year from 1699 to 1710. Nearly 600 political pamphlets appeared from 1566 to 1584 in the Netherlands Rebellion, the first early-modern revolt that created a republic. During the political turmoil in France from 1614 to 1617, caused by factional conflict between the administration of the queen mother and the prince de Condé, 1,200 pamphlets were printed. Earlier in France, the Wars of Religion from 1562 to 1598 produced "the first European Revolution wherein the press, the pamphlet and political propaganda played a vital role in events." Yet at the height of the Catholic League's insurrection against Henry III, in 1589, Parisian printers produced the greatest annual output on behalf of the League: 362 printed items; the next highest annual total, 157, was from the previous year.[1] This output is dwarfed by English printing from 1640 to 1660. Twenty-five thousand items appear in the Thomason Tracts, the largest single collection from this period, which still represents only half to two-thirds of what was originally printed. More publications appeared between 1640 and 1660 than in the prior history of printing in England, from about 1485 to 1640. The highest annual output was in 1642, when 2,134 items were published. In this era, press runs for pamphlets ranged from 500 to 1,500 copies—though 4,000–9,000 copies of some items were printed for Parliament.[2]

Change and continuity are both evident in communicative developments during the English Revolution. Routine publication of fast sermons delivered before the Long Parliament extended the tradition of using the pulpit to send political messages. Queen Elizabeth's government promoted surreptitious printing under false imprints to deceive foreign governments; in the 1640s and 1650s, this tactic misled successive English governments. Other continuities included printing's imposition of dialogic order on political conflict, which had precedents in religious controversies in late-Elizabethan England. The same alliance of commerce and controversy that animated earlier literary culture reappeared in the flood of political literature after 1640. And scribal transmission of news in separates and newsletters eventuated in printed newspapers. Yet amidst these continuities, profound change occurred in the content of political communication that streamed through pamphlets, declarations, newspapers, and petitions. Open appeals to public opinion on political matters became more important, and issued not only from the center but from the periphery of the nation.

---

[1] Richard Golden, *The Godly Rebellion* (Chapel Hill, NC, 1981), p. 162; Joseph Klaits, *Printed Propaganda under Louis XIV* (Princeton, 1976), p. 23; Philip Knachel, *England and the Fronde* (Ithaca, 1967), p. 78; Jeffrey Sawyer, *Printed Poison: Pamphlet Propaganda, Faction Politics, and the Public Sphere in Early Seventeenth-Century France* (Berkeley, 1990), p. 27; Perez Zagorin, *Rebels and Rulers* (Cambridge, 1982), 2:59, 106 n.

[2] Sheila Lambert, "The Beginning of Printing for the House of Commons, 1640–1642," *Library*, 6th ser., 3 (1981): 45; Sheila Lambert, "Printing for Parliament, 1641–1700," *List and Index Society* 20 (1984): 1–7, 21.

IMPOSITION OF DIALOGIC ORDER ON CONFLICT

The sheer volume of printed political texts has been noted in many studies of the English Revolution that point to links between politics and printing. However, these links are most often described in terms of printing's utility for producing many inexpensive texts.[3] This surmounted traditional limits on political communication by greatly expanding its *scope* and directing political discourse beyond contending elites to a larger, socially diverse audience of readers. In this view, political appeals to public opinion were facilitated by printing and motivated as a tactic by exigencies confronting contending elites who needed to mobilize popular support to fight a civil war. Thus, we learn from prior studies that printed political texts, such as petitions, were propaganda "intended for general consumption." Parliament "was deeply concerned about what may be termed 'public opinion,'" but so was the king. Both leaked information—details of negotiations, letters, and speeches—to partisan newspapers, such as the Royalist *Mercurius Aulicus* or the Parliamentarian *Mercurius Britanicus.* "As the political fissure widened, both sides engaged in systematic propaganda campaigns to influence public opinion, calling on sheriffs, mayors, and preachers to distribute official declarations."[4] Printing, then, has its place in prior historical accounts. But links between printing and politics cannot be adequately established if printing's implications for public opinion are conceived principally in terms of increased access to and dissemination of ideas. After commenting that "Parliament was surrounded by a forceful, observant public opinion that compelled it for the first time to act amid continual popular pressure," a historian observes, "the regime's collapse also liberated the press from any effective censorship."[5] Was the relationship between printing and public opinion merely contingent?

In its focus on printing's potential for more rapid and extensive dissemination of novel ideas, a limited appraisal of printing overlooks its implications for change in the *content* of political communication. That printing may have been a source of novelty remains unexplored other

---

[3] Joad Raymond, *The Invention of the Newspaper: English Newsbooks, 1641–1649* (Oxford, 1996), p. 82, observes that prior historical studies "emphasize the role of the press in lubricating the mechanisms of oppositional politics."

[4] Anthony Fletcher, *The Outbreak of the Civil War* (London, 1981), p. 198; Derek Hirst, "The Defection of Sir Edward Dering, 1640–1641," *HJ* 15 (1972): 193; David Underdown, *Revel, Riot, and Rebellion: Popular Politics and Culture in England, 1603–1660* (Oxford, 1985), p. 138, and see pp. 136–45; Lambert, "Beginning of Printing," pp. 44–45; P. W. Thomas, *Sir John Berkenhead* (Oxford, 1969), pp. 43–44, 48.

[5] Zagorin, *Rebels and Rulers*, 2:148.

than in connection with increased scope: by enlarging the circle of communication printed political literature encompassed new ideas from the discourse of the subjected.[6] Yet in addition to providing heightened access to political debates, the use of printing in politics left its mark on communicative practices that reoriented political discourse so that its production increasingly involved simultaneous constitution and invocation of public opinion. Explanations that refer only to issues of scope in explaining printing's implications for political developments overlook a crucial point: production of printed texts as appeals to public opinion was not limited to any one faction or subset of factions in the English Revolution. To be sure, political texts in the English Revolution exhibit great variation. Dense, antiquarian digressions were prepared for readers with a university education. Popular pamphlets might contain more accessible but carefully reasoned arguments, or perhaps nothing beyond ridicule and slander. Central to the appeal to public opinion in these printed texts is printing's imposition of dialogic order on conflict, a consequence of increased ability massively and swiftly to reproduce texts. Printed political materials—for example, formal documents such as declarations, ordinances, and laws along with polemical pamphlets, petitions, and scurrilous broadsides—encouraged readers to interpret conflict between king and parliament, and subsequently among parliamentary factions, as an ongoing debate.[7] Printed texts responded to prior texts, simultaneously referring to, excerpting from, and commenting on them. The cognitive content of referenced texts was variable, ranging from long prose passages to slogans, demands, names, puns, or images. Printed political texts invited readers to compare texts. Though they prompted readers to arrive at "correct" conclusions, printed political texts derived rhetorical force from the presupposition that they reliably reproduced prior texts that were offered up to the judgment of readers.

The imposition of dialogic order on political conflict in the mid-seventeenth century was not without precedent in print culture, as we saw in the previous chapter. But in the 1640s, it pervaded political discourse. Arguments between rival political factions obtained printed expression in a communicative space that was public, popular, and critical: public because it directed arguments to an anonymous audience of readers; popular in terms of authorial presumptions about the social composition of readers; critical because the imposition of dialogic order

---

[6] Christopher Hill, *A Nation of Change and Novelty* (London, 1990), pp. 24–55.

[7] Nigel Smith, *Literature and Revolution in England, 1640–1660* (New Haven, 1994), p. 139: "The Leveller view of failed negotiations between themselves, Army and Parliament is viewed as an account of texts (remonstrances, petitions, letters) not achieving their goals in politics."

on political conflict supplied readers with reasons and textual evidence for adjudicating rival political claims. Imposition of dialogic order on political conflict appeared in a preface to a Parliamentarian tract that enabled readers to understand its context of contestation: "A petition for peace is presented to the Parliament by some thousands of citizens; the petition finds a peaceable answer; and that answer (as I shall now set forth) is opposed by an unpeaceable reply."[8] The printing of texts in which political conflict appeared as a dialogue was not an emanation of Puritan or Parliamentarian convictions. It was practiced by supporters of Charles I and his bishops, such as the author of *Episcopal Inheritance. Or A Reply To the Humble Examination of a Printed Abstract of The Answers To Nine Reasons Of The House Of Commons Against the Votes of Bishops in Parliament.*[9] Readers encountered politics as a dialogue not only in polemical pamphlets but also in printed texts generated by petitioning. A Lancashire petition presented to the king at York in May 1642 supported the Long Parliament's request that Charles I return to London and Parliament, "the representative body of your kingdom." The king's response, in a hastily composed broadside, reprinted the offending petition and refers petitioners (and the reading public) "to the answer he has given to the *Declaration* presented to him at Newmarket, and to the petition presented to him the 26th of March last at York, wherein his Majesty says, you will clearly perceive that he is not gone but driven from his Parliament." Moreover, "His Majesty . . . recommends to your view and consideration his two messages and *Declaration* concerning Hull, and his message touching the reasons of his refusal to grant the militia [bill]."[10]

This imposition of dialogic order on conflict was aided by an aspect of printing that I discussed earlier, the probative value contemporaries attributed to printed texts. Readers were invited to compare texts, and certainly were prodded to make the correct comparison, but the rhetorical force of these productions depended on the presupposition that texts reliably reproduced prior texts. Henry Parker's 1642 broadside, *How Laws Are to Be Understood, and Obedience Yielded?* "became almost a proof-text to the Levellers, an antidote to Romans 13:1 cited in tract after Leveller tract simply by its place (p. 150) in Edward Husband's *An Exact Collection.*"[11] This promoted an immanent style of criticism that

[8] *Accommodation Cordially Desired* (E101[23], 1643), p. 1.

[9] *Episcopal Inheritance* (E132[29], 1641).

[10] *To the Kings most excellent Majestie. The humble Petition of . . . Lancashire* (*Wing* T1528, 1642).

[11] Michael Mendle, *Henry Parker and the English Civil War* (Cambridge, 1995), pp. 82–83.

cited arguments by adversaries in order to generate counterarguments. When Marchamont Nedham, now writing for the Royalist party, attacked Parliament after it vigorously rejected proposals in 1648 from its former ally, Scotland, he merely reprinted the Solemn League and Covenant, the 1643 oath that committed the two nations to a common policy.[12] Reproduction of an adversary's printed papers could facilitate efforts to collect money. In September 1640 Sir Henry Vane forwarded from York letters from the invading Scots with their demands and suggested these "be printed and published amongst you in the South . . . the better to induce a timely and vigorous supply." To galvanize support for the Royalist cause in 1644, *Mercurius Aulicus* printed "warrants and tickets" sent by an officer in Parliament's army to residents in Buckingham for money and supplies.[13]

The imposition of dialogic order on political conflict relied on printing's technical potential for textual reproduction and led to an unprecedented eruption of signification. In the English Revolution political culture in print is a pastiche, a representational kaleidoscope in which the relationship between the word and the world is just as tenuous as in the contemporary condition described as postmodernism. Real names, pseudonyms, titles of texts, and slogans are literary figures in their own right that assume authorial voice in political texts. We shall see that transformation of literary titles into authorial voices occurred often for printed newspapers, when the Royalist newspaper *Aulicus* accuses, pursues, and argues with *Britanicus*, a prominent, pro-Parliament newspaper. Inanimate objects also underwent this transformation. Proposals to demolish Cheapside Cross in London produced a flurry of pamphlets, pro and con, in which the Cross talks to other monuments, protests its innocence, and pleads guilty to the charge that it is a relic of superstition. Titles of polemical pamphlets were often transformed in this manner in extended exchanges of claims and counterclaims. After an Independent pamphlet, *Vox Populi, Or The Peoples Cry Against The Clergy*, denounced a 1646 petition from Norwich Presbyterians, it was answered by *An Hue-And-Cry after Vox Populi*.[14] This transformation of titles into voices also appears in texts with sophisticated political arguments. Much notoriety attached to Henry Parker's writings in 1642, in which he advanced an absolutist view of parliamentary sovereignty in order to justify the Militia Ordinance and other initiatives that undermined the military and political authority of Charles I. Issued

---

[12] Joseph Frank, *Cromwell's Press Agent: A Critical Biography of Marchamont Nedham* (Lanham, MD, 1980), p. 52.

[13] *CSPD* 1640, p. 47; *MA* 2:372–73.

[14] E352[7] (1646); E355[13] (1646).

anonymously, Parker's *Some Few Observations* and *Observations upon Some of His Majesties Late Answers* provoked more than a half dozen printed attacks on "the Observator." In taking up a literary cudgel on behalf of the king, a Royalist writer, Henry Ferne, did not specifically cite Parker's texts because he thought it sufficient to refer to "the Observator" as "the exemplar of 'all others that plead' for a right of resistance from the 'original of power' in 'the people.'" So did Robert Filmer in 1648, for whom "attacks on the 'Observator' required no special justification or explanation."[15]

Though the imposition of dialogic order on political conflict flowed from printing's ability to produce texts efficiently and rapidly, this was not inevitable. Imperatives of printing also magnified perceptions of chaos and disorder, especially when publishers and writers of printed news wanted to stimulate sales.[16] In addition, the dialogic dimension of argumentation only faintly appeared in many printed texts, adorned with crude woodcuts that rely on slander and sexual innuendo to convey a political message. These, too, poured from the printing presses, in inexpensive broadside and octavo editions that consumed just one printed sheet, such as the pro-Puritan tract, *The Answer To The Rattle-Heads . . . With many godly counsels to Doctor Little-wit: the composer of their former scurrilous and illeterate Pamphlet.*[17] Royalist and anti-Puritan writers excelled in producing pamphlets that combined satire and slander. Leading the way was the water-poet, John Taylor, whose publicity stunts we encountered in chapter 6. In the 1640s, his satirical barbs were as sharp as those aimed half a century earlier by Marprelate against bishops; and, like Marprelate, he often portrayed his adversaries as buffoons, frequently with metaphors of inversion, of a world turned upside down. Many writers with different political allegiances invoked these metaphors,[18] but Taylor was unrivaled in using them to skewer his adversaries. In *A Seasonable Lecture* he provided an exquisite spoof of a sermon by a former iron monger, the radical preacher Henry Walker, who mercilessly dissected every word of a line in the Old Testament apocryphal parable of Tobias and the angel ("So they went forth both, and the young man's dog with them." [Tob. 5:16]). The satirical force of this sermon on "Toby's dog" (see fig. 4) derives from its portrayal of the pious Walker as a social upstart and unconscious comic. This mocking criticism was a common theme in polemical pamphlets by Royalist writers.

[15] Mendle, *Parker and the Civil War*, pp. 90, 101.

[16] John Morrill and John Walter, "Order and Disorder in the English Revolution," in A. J. Fletcher and J. Stevenson, eds., *Order and Disorder in Early Modern England* (Cambridge, 1987), pp. 138, 147–49.

[17] E132[30] (1641).

[18] David Underdown, *A Freeborn People* (Oxford, 1996), p. 94.

> A Preacher's work is not to gelde a Sowe,
> Unseemly tis a Judge shoud milke a Cowe:
> A Cobbler to a Pulpit should not mount,
> Nor can an Asse cast up a true account.[19]

Crude woodcuts were common adornments of this literature that exhibits continuities with the broadside tradition of cheap print.[20] One illustration responded to Taylor's jibes by showing Taylor dangling from a rope; in another, the Devil defecates into the mouth of the water-poet, who is lying on the bottom of a boat (see fig. 5). The author of this last item, the preacher Henry Walker, had previously appeared on a title page of a Taylor pamphlet, in a woodcut that depicted Walker as excrement of the Devil.[21] Other woodcuts recorded enduring stereotypes of political actors: the close-cropped roundhead, the swashbuckling cavalier, a besieged king, a frantic sectary, and so on. Yet even this lowbrow literature was not uniform in terms of its cognitive content. Like many of Taylor's polemical pamphlets, a ballad printed in 1641 presumed fairly extensive knowledge of politics by readers. Directed against Archbishop Laud, the ballad *The Organ's Echo* expresses delight that "now he is in danger of an axe or a rope" (see fig. 6). But its expressions of coarse pleasure at Laud's plight occur alongside references to current political developments, including an elliptical one to a speech delivered in Parliament, and available in print, by Sir Edward Dering.[22] The same holds for sexual slander in a Royalist newspaper, the *Man in the Moon*, at the end of the decade. Henry Marten, a notorious republican member of the Long Parliament, was a "fornicator" whose radical convictions made him "stand up stiff" for the Levellers, but General Fairfax was a "cuckold general" because his antipathy to radical politics was ascribed to a strong-willed spouse, a patroness of Presbyterian clerics.[23]

The process of detecting links between printing and the dialogic imposition of order on conflict does not require that we overstate contrasts between scribal and print culture. After all, "the scribal medium must also be granted an inherent orientation towards a critical stance."[24] That scribal modes of communication could impose dialogic order on political conflict appears in manuscript copies of hostile "queries" by Puritan clerics opposed to canons adopted in 1640, which were widely

---

[19] E143[13] (1642); E176[7] (1641), pp. 2–3.

[20] Michael Mendle, "De Facto Freedom, De Facto Authority: Press and Parliament, 1640–1643," *HJ* 38 (1995): 323.

[21] E22[2] (1644); William Lamont, *The World of John Taylor the Water-Poet, 1578–1653* (Oxford, 1994), p. 145.

[22] 669f.4[32] (1641); see also Lamont, *John Taylor*, pp. 182–83.

[23] Underdown, *Freeborn People*, pp. 100, 102–3.

[24] Love, *Scribal Culture*, p. 293.

Fig. 5. Henry Walker responds to John Taylor in a pamphlet with a scatalogical woodcut that suggests the ungodly source of Taylor's inspired satires.

distributed, judging by the many surviving copies. One cleric criticized distribution of these documents that "are in every man's hand" because they blatantly appealed to public opinon by juxtaposing "questions" and the disliked canons: "you give the multitude the best encouragement you can give them, to question the Church."[25] In the previous chapter we saw that circulation of separates enabled readers in the 1620s to

25 *MSS Rawl* C262, fols. 6, 10v.

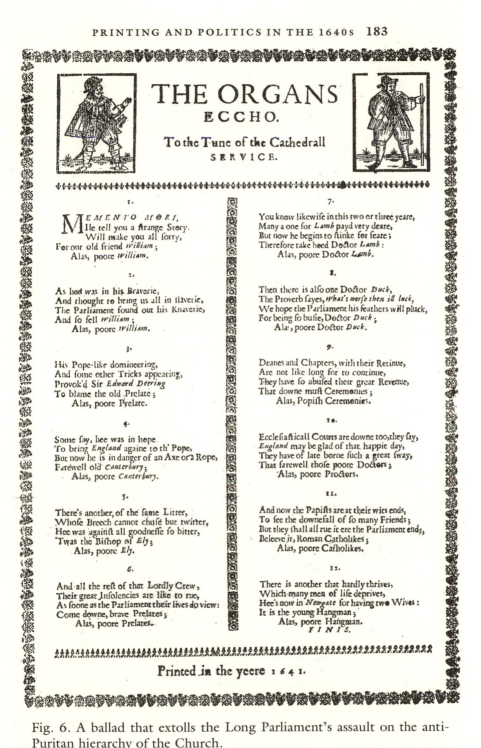

THE ORGANS
ECCHO.

To the Tune of the Cathedrall
SERVICE.

1.

MEMENTO MORI,
Ile tell you a ſtrange Story.
Will make you all ſorry,
For our old friend *William* ;
Alas, poore *William.*

2.

As hee was in his Braverie,
And thought to bring us all in ſlaverie,
The Parliament found out his Knaverie,
And ſo fell *William* ;
Alas, poore *William.*

3.

His Pope-like domineering,
And ſome other Tricks appearing,
Provok'd Sir *Edward Deering*
To blame the old Prelate ;
Alas, poore Prelate.

4.

Some ſay, hee was in hope
To bring *England* againe to th' Pope,
But now he is in danger of an Axe or a Rope,
Farewell old *Canterbury* ;
Alas, poore *Canterbury.*

5.

There's another, of the ſame Litter,
Whoſe Breech cannot chuſe but twitter,
Hee was againſt all goodneſſe ſo bitter,
'Twas the Biſhop of *Ely* ;
Alas, poore *Ely.*

6.

And all the reſt of that Lordly Crew,
Their great Inſolencies are like to rue,
As ſoone as the Parliament their lives do view:
Come downe, brave Prelates ;
Alas, poore Prelates.

7.

You know likewiſe in this two or three yeare,
Many a one for *Lamb* payd very deare,
But now he begins to ſtinke for feare ;
Therefore take heed Doctor *Lamb* :
Alas, poore Doctor *Lamb.*

8.

Then there is alſo one Doctor *Duck,*
The Proverb ſayes, *What's worſe then ill luck,*
We hope the Parliament his feathers will pluck,
For being ſo buſie, Doctor *Duck* ;
Alas, poore Doctor *Duck.*

9.

Deanes and Chapters, with their Retinue,
Are not like long for to continue,
They have ſo abuſed their great Revenue,
That downe muſt Ceremonies ;
Alas, Popiſh Ceremonies.

10.

Eccleſiaſticall Courts are downe too, they ſay,
England may be glad of that happie day,
They have of late borne ſuch a great ſway,
That farewell thoſe poore Doctors ;
Alas, poore Proctors.

11.

And now the Papiſts are at their wits ends,
To ſee the downefall of ſo many Friends ;
But they ſhall all rue it ere the Parliament ends,
Beleeve it, Roman Catholikes ;
Alas, poore Catholikes.

12.

There is another that hardly thrives,
Which many men of life deprives,
Hee's now in *Newgate* for having two Wives :
It is the young Hangman ;
Alas, poore Hangman.
FINIS.

Printed in the yeere 1 6 4 1.

Fig. 6. A ballad that extolls the Long Parliament's assault on the anti-
Puritan hierarchy of the Church.

compile selective accounts of political events. Thus, under conditions of scribal publication "the tendency of the news to concentrate on dramatic events affected the way in which the political process was represented." This tendency continued after the outbreak of the civil wars, when readers read and sometimes compiled selective accounts of public events that highlighted conflict in politics. Nowhere is this more evident than in the journals of a humble London wood turner, Nehemiah Wallington. But his task was facilitated by access to hundreds of printed texts for his selective reading of events, which depicted the struggle between Charles and the Long Parliament as a cosmic battle between forces of good and evil.[26]

PRINTED NEWS

Commercial production of printed news existed long before the outbreak of the civil wars. From 1588 to the end of the century, for example, more than one hundred small pamphlets, mostly of political news, were issued by one printer, John Wolfe, the pioneer in surreptitious printing of foreign vernaculars whom we met in the previous chapter.[27] Printed news in English had not yet acquired a serial format but was published in pamphlets throughout the sixteenth century. An early example is a simple tract with four leaves, *Hereafter ensue the trew encountre or Batayle lately don betwene England and Scotlande. In whiche batayle the Scottsshe kynge was slayne.*[28] Not until 1621 did printed news appear in England in a series, the inexpensive corantos, which cost twopence and supplied foreign news. A principal figure in this development was Nathaniel Butter, the figure satirized in Ben Jonson's play *Staple of the News* as an unscrupulous vender of news for money. Since 1605, Butter had published typical "grub street" fare: accounts of gruesome murders, pirates, foreign travel, and so on. Publication of corantos with foreign news by Butter built on his prior experience with these lowbrow publications.[29] Criticism of corantos raised literary and political issues. Some critics feared that cheaply printed news lowered the prestige of print culture. Government officials worried about its implications for commoners meddling in politics. But when, in 1632, the govern-

---

[26] Richard Cust, *The Forced Loan and English Politics* (Oxford, 1985), p. 151. For Wallington, see Paul Seaver, *Wallington's World: A Puritan Artisan in Seventeenth-Century London* (Stanford, 1985), p. 156.

[27] Denis B. Woodfield, *Surreptitious Printing in England, 1550–1640* (New York, 1973), p. 30.

[28] Colin Clair, *A History of Printing in Britain* (Oxford, 1966), p. 146.

[29] Leona Rostenberg, "Nathaniel Butter and Nicholas Bourne, First 'Masters of the Staple,'" *Library*, 5th ser., 12 (1957): 24–26.

ment banned corantos, Amsterdam printers took advantage of the situation and produced newsbooks for the English market.[30]

After the Long Parliament assembled in November 1640, domestic printing quickly flooded the market with printed accounts of news. Initially, these appeared irregularly in a traditional format, the small, inexpensive pamphlet with several news items that typically consumed one printer's sheet to yield eight octavo pages. A not untypical title page is *An Order From the High Court of Parliament . . . Also The True Copie Of A Seditious Paper . . . Likewise the Sermon which was preached . . . by a Brownist.* Other items mixed reports of high politics with the sensationalistic fare of traditional broadsides, such as a *Exceeding good Newes,* which described the Irish rebellion and "a prodigious birth" (see fig. 7).[31] News in pamphlets was the printed ancestor to the modern newspaper, which first appeared in November 1641, when John Thomas, a prolific publisher of inexpensive political literature, supplied readers with a narrative summary of proceedings in Parliament. Copy for the summary came from manuscript copies of the same that scriveners had produced commercially in response to public interest in events inside Parliament. Thus, the modern newspaper was invented when publication of serial domestic news emerged from an amalgam of news pamphlets and a very specific type of scribal publication.[32]

Serial newsbooks multiplied rapidly and varied enormously in terms of style and partisan affiliation. The king's cause was championed by *Mercurius Aulicus,* begun in Oxford in 1643 to counter pro-Parliament diurnals published in London. *Mercurius Britanicus,* Parliament's quasi-official response to *Aulicus,* reflected the anti-Presbyterian views of its editor, Marchamont Nedham. The *Moderate Intelligencer* adhered to a pro-army position and provided an outlet for Leveller ideas. Presbyterian politics received support from *Mercurius Civicus,* also begun in opposition to *Aulicus,* as well as from the *Scotish Dove* and the *Kingdomes Weekly Intelligencer* (see figs. 8–11). A new crop of mercuries sprang from weariness with taxes and civil strife in 1647, including *Elencticus, Melancholicus,* and *Pragmaticus,* the last edited by Nedham. These championed the cause of popular Royalism in a less lofty, more popular idiom than the one in *Aulicus.* Scatological and sexual slurs were favorite devices. For example, *Melancholicus* described the counte-

---

[30] Folke Dahl, "Amsterdam—Cradle of English Newspapers," *Library,* 5th ser., 4 (1949): 176–77.

[31] *An Order From the High Court of Parliament* (E181[1], 1641); *Exceeding good Newes* (E135[2], 1641).

[32] Raymond, *Invention of the Newspaper,* pp. 108–11, corrects accounts that attribute Thomas's newsbook to Samuel Peck and overstate the importance of corantos or newsletters. Cf. C. John Sommerville, *The News Revolution in England* (Oxford, 1996), pp. 6, 34–35.

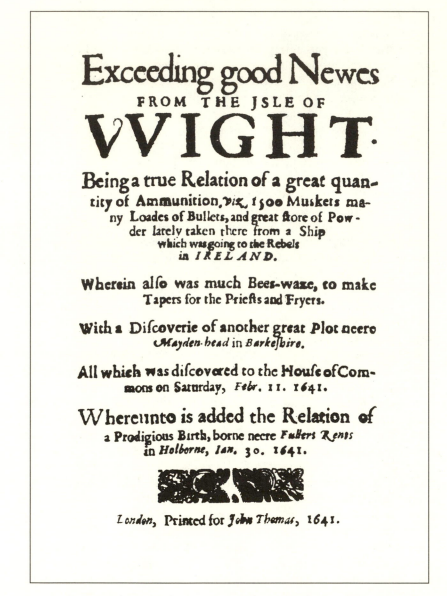

Fig. 7. A printed book of news that follows the format of a pamphlet.

nance of an MP as "in color like a piece of sooty bacon hanged seven years in the devil's arsehole" and taunted the mayor of London as a cuckold.

> The Lord Mayor rides on a bob-tailed horse,
>> So he does, so he does
> Whilst another rides his wife, that's worse,
>> How now cuz? How now cuz?

Two years later John Crouch's *Man in the Moon* relentlessly developed this idiom in order to assail enemies of King Charles and merry old England.[33]

Throughout this period, narrative summaries of proceedings in Parliament remained a staple of journalism and were supplemented by military reports after the outbreak of civil war. Prominent features of contemporary journalism also included descriptive embellishment (often from accounts reputed to have been written by private letter writers), editorial commentary, woodcuts, satirical verse, pornographic slander, and excerpts of speeches, messages, and petitions. The relative proportion of these raw ingredients varied in different serial newsbooks. Most were printed on a single sheet, sold for only a penny, and were published in weekly editions. By 1644

> any Londoner who wanted to read his newspaper in English had a dozen to choose from. On Monday he could select *A Perfect Diurnall*, *Certaine Informations*, or *Aulicus*. . . . Tuesday he had *The Kingdomes Weekly Intelligencer*; Wednesday, *The Weekly Account* or the newly revived *A Continuation* . . . and Thursday a choice between *Britanicus* and *Civicus*. Friday brought forth three papers. . . . On Saturday the reader either acquired *The True Informer* or went newspaperless. On Sunday, he rested.[34]

Purely political imperatives stimulated proliferation of English newspapers. "Ironically, in 1643 the regime which had relied so heavily on suppression of the news itself set about capturing a nation-wide audience with an enthusiasm and skill unprecedented in English journalism." This activity produced the Royalist newspaper *Mercurius Aulicus*. During its short existence, January 1643 to September 1645, it was challenged by no fewer than three rival newspapers and seventeen pamphlets expressly designed to discredit its version of events.[35]

---

[33] *Mercurius Melancholicus*, November 20–29 (E417[17], 1647), p. 77; December 18–25 (E421[10], 1647), p. 100. For Crouch, see Underdown, *A Freeborn People*, chap. 5.

[34] Joseph Frank, *The Beginnings of the English Newspaper, 1620–1660* (Cambridge, MA, 1961), pp. 56–57.

[35] P. W. Thomas, *Sir John Berkenhead* (London, 1969), pp. 28, 29, 56, 61.

This proliferation of newspapers also sprang from competitive pressures and the fact that journalists variously combined the roles of printer, publisher, and editor. Many papers were short-lived enterprises whose names were variants of popular series, either to achieve a polemical purpose or to promote sales. Here, too, commerce and controversy were entangled. From its inception, publication of serial domestic news was a cutthroat business, marked by piracy, publicity, and constantly shifting alliances among printers and publishers (see fig. 8). After editing the most popular Parliamentarian newspaper, *Mercurius Britanicus*, Marchamont Nedham took the helm of a royalist paper, *Mercurius Pragmaticus*. Nedham's talents made *Pragmaticus* "salable enough to attract counterfeits, and at least five times between June and December [1648] another *Mercurius Pragmaticus* tried to cut into Nedham's market." In the next decade, Nedham switched sides (again), became Cromwell's chief press agent as editor of *Mercurius Politicus*, and amassed a small fortune. Taking advantage of Cromwell's strict enforcement of censorship in the summer of 1655, *Politicus* secured a monopoly on printed news. Nedham "shortly thereafter raised his charge for a single advertisement from sixpence or a shilling to half a crown"; seven or eight advertisements appeared in each issue of *Politicus* and the *Intelligencer*, mostly for books, by John Milton and other approved authors, and medical services. His annual income from journalism exceeded five hundred pounds from 1655 to 1659, nearly double the highest salary paid to Milton, the regime's principal propagandist.[36]

Commercial forces in the production of printed news were hardly novel. As we saw in the previous chapter, pamphlet production had always been marked by the imperatives of commerce and publicity in print culture.[37] Another continuity between the pamphlet genre and printed news was that both were intended for a broad audience. Commercialism and a popular social milieu were prominent themes before and after 1640 in hostile commentary on "pot poets," a common term of abuse for inebriated writers hired by printers to churn out sensationalistic material on current events. One critic of printed news in 1641 plagiarized John Earle's 1628 description of a pot poet for whom

> the press is his mine, and stamps him now and then a six pence or two. . . .
> His works would scarce sell for three half pence, though they are often-

---

[36] Frank, *Beginnings of the English Newspaper*, pp. 246, 275; Frank, *Cromwell's Press Agent*, pp. 56, 107.

[37] Cf. Raymond, *Invention of the Newspaper*, p. 13, who argues that in the 1640s, "there rapidly developed a culture of the pamphlet, of which the newsbook was a central, driving feature."

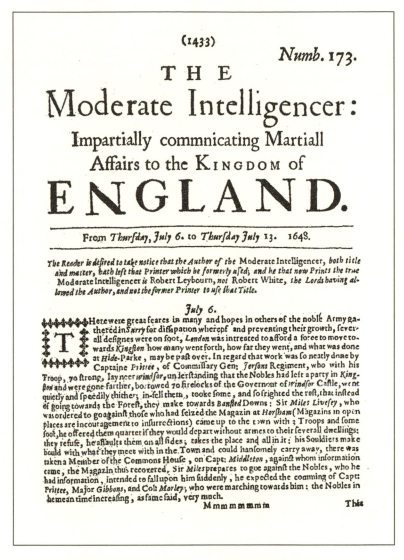

Fig. 8. A printed newspaper. Note the reference to the dispute over who prints the "true" version of the *Moderate Intelligencer*.

times given for three shillings, but only for the pretty title that allures the country gentleman. . . . His frequent works go out in single sheets, and are found in every part of the City, and then chanted from market to market to a vile tune . . . while the poor country wench melts like butter to hear them.

Clearly, the milieu of this activity defies description by simple distinctions between elite and popular culture. Though printed news was intended for the "country gentleman," the locations, persons, and practices involved in its production, distribution, and consumption were embedded in popular culture.[38] In the 1640s, principal figures in publishing, printing, and writing news included Henry Walker, who had served an apprenticeship to an ironmonger; Thomas Bates, son of a blacksmith; Jack Dillingham, formerly a tailor; and others who had been scriveners or were sons of yeomen—poor printers and "Bible-binders-turned-newsmongers," according to one recent account.[39] Their world straddled elite and popular cultures, like the milieu for the illicit trade in sectarian and seditious books in the 1630s that was inhabited by haberdashers, ironmongers, clerics, chandlers, and shopkeepers, bakers, and scriveners. This literate though nonelite culture was accessible to a humble artisan like Nehemiah Wallington, the London artisan who bought, read, and lent books by Bastwick, Prynne, and Burton.[40]

Who read printed news? Surviving evidence in letters from the gentry and clergy indicates that printed news was widely read and circulated among England's educated elite. Though Wallington's reading habits were exceptional, scattered surviving evidence indicates that "the readership of newsbooks was socially and geographically diverse, as diverse as any and probably all other publications."[41] Reinforcing this conclusion is the accessible rhetorical style of journalism and comments on the intended audience for printed political texts. Though the price of newspapers was low, news reports presupposed varying degrees of knowledge and sophistication by readers. In his 1650 prospectus to the Council of State for *Mercurius Politicus*, Marchamont Nedham proposed that it be "'written in a jocular way,' because 'Fancy . . . ever sways the scepter in vulgar judgement, much more than reason.'" Yet Nedham appealed to "vulgar judgement" in forty-four issues with political theory taken wholesale from his long pamphlet, *The Case Of The Commonwealth Briefly Stated*. Ultimately, he reproduced one-quarter of

[38] *A True Description Of The Pot-Companion Poet* (E143[6], 1642), sigs. A2–3. For Earle's account, see Louis Wright, *Middle-Class Culture in Elizabethan England* (London, 1964), p. 99. For other comments on or by pot poets, see *The Poets Recantation* (E142[13], 1642); E165[5] (1641); E83[11] (1642).

[39] Anthony Cotton, "London Newsbooks in the Civil War" (D.Phil. diss., Oxford University 1971), pp. 80, 104, 110–11, 148–49, 214–15; Mendle, "De Facto Freedom, De Facto Authority," p. 325.

[40] *MSS Tanner* 67, fol. 195; 70, fol. 183; Nehemiah Wallington, *Historical Notices of Events Occurring in the Reign of Charles I*, ed. R. Bentley (London, 1869), 1:xxxvii–xxxviii, xliv–xlv.

[41] Raymond, *Invention of the Newspaper*, p. 253.

the pamphlet in *Politicus,* omitting most Latin and Greek citations. At the same time, the first English writer who advocated a radical Machiavellian republicanism was also a proficient and vicious name caller. Serious reporting and commentary in contemporary journalism had not jettisoned the tradition of scurrilous irreverence in popular broadsides. When Nedham wrote for the Royalist side as editor of *Mercurius Pragmaticus,* he referred to Oliver Cromwell as "the Brewer, the Town Bull of Ely, King Cromwell, The Grand Seignior, Crum-Hell, Nose Almighty, Copper Nose."[42] (This did not prevent Nedham from becoming Cromwell's principal press agent in the 1650s as editor of *Mercurius Politicus.*)

In some respects, printing's impact on the production, distribution, and reading of news lead to incremental change, enhancing tendencies already evident in scribal modes of publication for news, for example, opening sensitive political debates and negotiations to the public. The Long Parliament experienced this problem on many occasions. In 1647 the Lords complained that a printer "printed some passages of this House which were sent to the House of Commons for their concurrence, before they were delivered to the House of Commons."[43] Yet such premature disclosure also occurred under conditions of scribal publication. In 1626, a scrivener sold a copy of the remonstrance from the Commons—this protested Charles I's order to cease attacks on Buckingham and move on to issues of "supply"—before it had been delivered to the king.[44] Continuity also existed in the sensationalism of scribal and printed news. Both highlighted conflict and disorder in politics. In this regard, there is little difference between the printed mercuries of the 1640s and news sold by scriveners in the 1620s. Even complacency over the availability of news had its precedents. In response to a mother-in-law's lengthy criticisms of his Royalist stance, one gentleman tartly denied, in 1643, "that I had need to be put in mind of such things as every diurnall tells us every week." Scribal news prior to 1640, though restricted in terms of access, was sometimes seen as a common, unremarkable activity. In 1626, D'Ewes begins a newsletter to a Suffolk gentleman by noting that he will relate news about the House of Lords: "Ordinary news I omit such I call Parliamentarie of the lower house and foreign. Such every man will tell you." In the 1640s complacency toward scribal and printed news appears in the use of newspapers to wrap fish and in Ashmole's use of the reverse side of a manuscript copy of a

---

[42] Frank, *Cromwell's Press Agent,* pp. 55, 87–88, 90–91; Jonathan Scott, *Algernon Sidney and the English Republic, 1623–1677* (Cambridge, 1988), pp. 110–12.

[43] *LJ* 9:131; and see *PJ2,* pp. 55, 57, 77.

[44] *PP 1626* 2:430.

civil war speech by the king to the Oxford Parliament: he worked out calculations for latitudes of different places.[45]

But routine printing of news also effected profound change in political communication. Print increasingly displaced private letters as the preferred medium for private and for even official communication of political news. Letters of intelligence sent to Edward Hyde during the civil war sometimes omit information on a development, "supposing you will be better informed thereof by divers papers sent out in print," or observe that no news merits notice except for what appears in an enclosed newspaper.[46] Because printed accounts of news often reproduced excerpts or the entire text of key documents, they reduced the tedium of copying such material in private letters when correspondents referred to printed matter that could inform the recipient of a letter more adequately than could the writer. In 1646 the master of a Cambridge college declared, I am "obstinately resolved to spot no paper with news whilst the penny worth from the press may outdo me."[47] Occasionally a printed edition of a text appeared while a correspondent labored to transcribe it in a letter. "The printer has now overtaken me," comments a letter writer in London as he transcribed petitions and other political texts related to events surrounding Charles I in York.[48] In his diary D'Ewes omits "particulars of his Majesty's answer because I assure myself that it will speedily be printed."[49]

Another advantage of printed news over scribal reports in private correspondence and newsletters was that weekly newspapers performed for readers, who may have been semiliterate, the same critical tasks that members of a learned culture performed when they consumed scribal texts. Due to the superior potential of printing for textual reproduction, the imposition of dialogic order on political conflict was laid before readers able and willing to spend one or two pence, whereas previously it was achieved by copying scribal texts into commonplace books and journals. Political competition among rival newspapers spurred this development. Many issues of *Aulicus* reproduced excerpts of passages from Parliamentary newspapers in order to discredit them by citing more recent, accurate reports on outcomes of military skirmishes. This practice emerged in stages, as journalists gained experience with printed news. *Aulicus* had been started in order to rebut pro-Parliament coverage of

[45] *MSS Tanner* 69, fol. 108v; *MSS Harl* 383, fol. 26; Frank, *Beginnings of English Newspapers*, p. 4; *MSS Ashmole* 830, fol. 279.

[46] *MSS Clarendon* 30, fols. 207, 302, and see fols. 217, 292v.

[47] *MSS Tanner* 60, fol. 354, and see *Tanner* 63, fol. 43; *Tanner* 66, fol. 234.

[48] *MSS Tanner* 63, fol. 43v; and see *Tanner* 60, fol. 178; *D'Ewes II*, p. xxii; *HMC Buccleuch* 1:300, 305.

[49] *PJ* 2:80.

MERCVRIVS AVLICVS,

Communicating the Intelligence and affaires of the Court, to the rest of the KINGDOME.

The fifty first VVeeke, ending Decemb. **23.**

SUNDAY. *Decemb.* 17.

 OU may remember this day three weekes, how the Rebels railed on us for telling the world what they doe on *Sundayes*. Their reason is (for some allow Them to be reasonable creatures) this day revealed by an Expresse from *Shrewsbury*; wherein it was certified among other particulars, that on *Sunday* last *Decemb.* 9. while His Majesties Forces were at Church, one of their Prisoners was missed by his Keeper, who searching for him, and looking through a cranny into the Stable, he saw a ladder erected, and the holy Rebell (busie at a Conventicle) committing Buggery on the Keepers owne Mare. The Keeper seizing on him, brought him instantly before Sir *Richard Levefon*, where being examined, he openly and plainly confessed the whole fact, for which they will speedily proceed against him, though the poore Keeper is like to loose his Mare, which (according to the Statute) must be burned to death.

This Truth hath too much horrour in it to admit of any descant, onely be pleased to subjoyne one passage which the

Ggggg   SCOTTISH

Fig. 9. The principal Royalist newspaper, *Mercurius Aulicus*.

(73) Numb. 10.

Be Wise as Serpents, Innocent as Doves.

THE
SCOTISH DOVE,
Sent out, and Returning;

Bringing Intelligence from the Armies, and
makes some Relations of other observable Passages
of both Kingdoms, for Information and Instruction.

*As an Antidote against the poisoned insinuations of Mercurius
Aulicus, and the errours of other intelligencers.*

From Friday the 15. of Decemb. to the 22. of the same.

OUr Dove sent out, hath (as becomes Innocency) carefully
returned at her time; and impartially made relation of truths
substantiall, and necessary; without envy to one, or flattery
to the other: yet contradicted by the Serpentine Malignity
of a venemous brood: *Mercurius Aulicus*, Master of the art of lying, Doctor of the Chaire of scorners, and false accusations, chiefe

K   Col-

Fig. 10. A leading Presbyterian newspaper, the *Scotish Dove*. Note the
reference to *Mercurius Aulicus*.

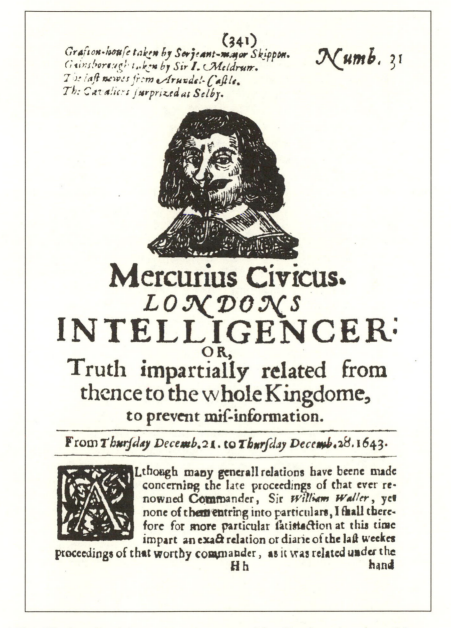

(341)

Grafton-house taken by Serjeant-major Skippon.
Gainsborough taken by Sir I. Meldrum.
The last newes from Arundel-Castle.
The Cavaliers surprized at Selby.

Numb. 31

Mercurius Civicus.
LONDONS
INTELLIGENCER:
OR,
Truth impartially related from thence to the whole Kingdome,
to prevent miſ-information.

From *Thurſday Decemb.*21. to *Thurſday Decemb.*28.1643.

Although many generall relations have beene made concerning the late proceedings of that ever renowned Commander, Sir *William Waller*, yet none of them entring into particulars, I ſhall therefore for more particular ſatisfaction at this time impart an exact relation or diarie of the laſt weekes proceedings of that worthy commander, as it was related under the

H h   hand

Fig. 11. Another important newspaper with a Presbyterian slant, *Mercurius Civicus*.

news. But not until the fifteenth issue of *Aulicus* did it provide readers with a list of specific errors in *Britanicus* and other London papers. After repeating this in the eighteenth issue, rebuttal lists in the twentieth and later issues became more elaborate, involving enumerated entries that offset claim from counterclaim by use of italic and roman fonts.[50] Many corrections of fact were quite trivial, though often leavened by humor, such as one in the November 18, 1643 issue: "4. *That Sir William Waller has only two men lightly hurt at Basing* (the rest were maimed and killed outright)." A list of such errors had as many as two to four dozen entries, especially in issues where *Aulicus* reports the birth of yet another London diurnal.[51] At its most elevated level, the imposition of dialogic order on political conflict in newspapers involved reprinting excerpts and texts of political documents. Sometimes this involved reproducing texts by adversaries. To counter a highly abridged edition of peace propositions—Parliament printed "only some few of their propositions, such as they thought would best take with the people"—*Mercurius Aulicus* reprinted them all.[52] At the end of the 1640s, newspapers provided readers with the text of radical petitions for legal reform, religious toleration, and abolition of tithes, along with responses to them, such as the dismissive one given by the Commons to women petitioners in 1649 who requested release of imprisoned radical leaders and requested that no laws on treason or capital crimes be enacted for offenses "that are not essentially destructive to civil society."[53]

At the same time, the impact of printing's ability to reproduce texts on the reporting of news led also in the direction of publicity and spectacle. Nowhere in print publication was the transformation of literary titles into authorial voices more common than in the realm of news. For example, in different pamphlets the principal Parliamentary newspaper, *Mercurius Britanicus*, is imprisoned, blessed, and chased by the principal Royalist paper, for example, in *Aulicus his Hue and Cry sent forth after Britanicus*.[54] Consigned to hell in *Mercurius Britanicus his Welcome to Hell*, the newspaper replies in *Mercurius Britannicus his Vision*.[55] *Aulicus*, too, receives rough treatment, when he is *worm'd for feare he should run mad and bite Brittanicus*. Both *Aulicus* and *Britanicus* are arraigned before disapproving judges.[56] Not surprisingly, the redoubt-

---

[50] *MA* 1:215, 257–58, 287–89, 369, 428–30. See E18[12] (1644), pp. 464–68, for an issue of *Britanicus* that rebuts two dozen items in *Aulicus*.

[51] *MA* 2:214, 399–402, and see 2:21, 38, 387–90, 399–402.

[52] *MA* 3:359.

[53] E529[21] (1649), p. 990; and see E529[1] (1649), pp. 2371–72; E529[7] (1649), pp. 927–28; E529[17] (1649), pp. 92–[9]3; E529[18] (1649), pp. 2442–43.

[54] E297[17] (1645); E316[17] (1646); E296[20] (1645).

[55] E378[5] (1647); E381[15] (1647).

[56] E27[13] (1645); E269[11] (1645); and see E298[18] (1645).

able John Taylor, whom we encountered earlier walking to Scotland, wades into the fray, in *Mercurius Aquaticus; or, The Water-Poets answer to all that hath or shall be writ by Mercurius Britanicus.*[57] Other newspapers participate as authorial voices when several hold *A Conference of the Grand Mercuries* and debate current political events.[58] This pamphlet literature provides a striking instance of the operation of commerce and publicity in print culture under conditions of political conflict and ineffective control. The result was an early-modern precedent for the postmodern condition. Production of printed news occurred under the communicative conditions that postmodernist writers attribute to advances in electronic media at the end of the twentieth century, where the "signifier becomes its own referent."[59] Distinctions between signifiers and the signified were attenuated by self-referential features in textual representations in the printed political literature of the English Revolution. The bewilderment that contemporaries may have felt when publication of political debates in printed texts eventuated in debates by prominent texts flowed from advances in the potential for textual reproduction. Arguably, the magnitude of this change was far greater in the transition from scribal to print publication than it has been for the subsequent transition from print to electronic media in the twentieth century.

PRINTED POLITICAL TEXTS

Like their scribal antecedents, printed political texts circulated and were read, privately and aloud, in public places such as inns and churchyards. In addition to conveying information, they served as political talismans, their possession taken, rightly or wrongly, to signal ideological affiliation. Printed political texts were objects of controversy in their own right. Conflict broke out between several parishioners, a constable, and the vicar of Stepney, who, after divine service, encountered in the churchyard readers of printed proclamations from Parliament. In the Essex parish of Radwinter, the curate, who was employed by a Laudian cleric, was confronted during divine service by a factious parishioner, a tailor who "came up to the reading desk & threw to the curate a base pamphlet . . . saying, there is reading work for you, read you that."[60] Clerics received Parliamentarian and Royalist texts with instructions to

---

[57] E29[11] (1644).　　　　　　　　[58] E422[14] (1648).

[59] Jean Baudrillard, *The Mirror of Production* (St. Louis, 1975), p. 127. See the epilogue below for more on this issue.

[60] *MSS Tanner* 62, fol. 211; *MSS Rawl* D158, fol. 43v. The pamphlet was probably E132[30] (1642).

read them to parishioners. Decisions about which to read provoked comment and conflict. When a Hereford cleric refused a gentleman's request to read a Royalist proclamation, he was shown "the King's order for the reading of it, in the frontispiece of the book." Another cleric, when brought competing texts from the king and Parliament, justified reading the former because "it comes from the King's own printer."[61] Proceedings against "malignant" clerics often include testimony from parishioners who describe what clerics did or did not read and how they read it. One curate read Royalist texts "with a loud, audible voice" and Parliamentarian texts "softly."[62]

Tactical use of printing for political propaganda went beyond publication of official declarations, such as those ordered to be read in churches. It also included production of pamphlets by writers who broadcast political arguments to a diverse audience of readers. Though some political pamphlets consisted of scurrilous and lewd attacks, others advanced reasoned but simple arguments designed for a socially diverse audience that included "unlearned" readers. Critical commentary on politics was not confined to highbrow publications. Evidence of the intent of authors and stationers to produce texts that straddled elite and popular cultures was often explicit. The title page to a 1641 pamphlet by Baillie, the Scottish commissioner, announced that it *is Framed of purpose for the capacity of the more simple sort of People.* The author of legal arguments against prerogative powers of the High Commission Court translated French and Latin passages that might "stumble the simple and such as be unlearned," as did the publisher of Lord Brooke's discourse on episcopal government. A cleric who composed a tract that advanced a staple feature of Parliamentary ideology—that fighting the king's army was no impediment to allegiance to the king— also wrote for an "unlearned" audience. "Let not the plainness of my style offend thee," he requested; he wrote so "that all that may read may understand, and therefore [I] have laid aside . . . all school terms and words of art."[63]

Publication of political pamphlets for both elite and common readers was a practice that transcended political and religious divisions. It was

[61] *MSS Add* 70106, unfoliated John Tombes to Robert Harley August 5, 1642; *MSS Rawls* D924, fol. 42v.

[62] *MSS Add* 15672, fol. 16v, and see fols. 8v, 12, 18v, 20, 22v, 24, 26v, 29, 32v, 37; *MSS Rawls* D924, fols. 192, 193, 194, 209, 211; Clive Holmes, "The Suffolk Committees for Scandalous Ministers, 1644–1646," *Suffolk Records Society* 13 (1970): 28, 35, 49, 51, 55, 64, 77, 82. For complaints about clerics who read only parliamentary texts see *MSS Add* 33572, fol. 296; *Add* 36913, fol. 140.

[63] D. Laing, ed., *The Letters and Journals of Robert Baillie* (Edinburgh, 1841), p. xcii; E156[19] (1641); Robert Greville, *A Discourse* (1641), in W. Haller, ed., *Tracts on Liberty* (New York, 1933), 2:119; Robert Austin, *Allegiance Not Impeached* (E42[12], 1644), sig. A2v–A3.

certainly not limited to upholding Parliamentary ideology or Puritan religion. Because the conservative, nonparty MP Clement Walker thought
that great interest existed for his critical history of the Independents,
published in 1648, he wrote "in a mixed style, in which . . . there are
some things fit to hold the judgments of the gravest; some things fit to
catch the fancies of the lightest, and some things of a middle nature,
applying myself to all capacities."[64] Royalist writers were just as explicit
about popular dimensions of their intended audience. One composed a
manuscript tract on the Sabbath, which portrayed Puritan concern over
its violation as hysteria intended to weaken popular affection toward
Charles. He noted that many learned treatises had already appeared on
his topic, to which he had little to add: "Yet happily I may illustrate the
difficulties . . . in a more familiar way to ordinary capacities." At Oxford,
Henry Ferne conducted an extended debate in print with William
Bridge, Henry Parker, and other defenders of the lawfulness of Parliament's resistance to the king. "Government is not the invention of man
but the institution of God," argued Ferne, who observed that "pleaders
for resistance" often rely on "the opinion of heathen writers, touching
the . . . derivation of the governing power from the people, as if they
had not scripture . . . to give them better direction herein." To provide
"better direction," Ferne addressed middlebrow readers, "the con-
scientious readers among the people," for whom he described different
arguments for resistance: one "framed more to the capacity of the vulgar," the other "cried up among the more intelligent of the party" with
"an appearing depth of reason." Fern also sought out the "misled people in this land" in another pamphlet. "I have therefore written it
plainly," he says, because "the learned through the land are sufficiently
persuaded."[65]

Of course, writers and stationers had purely self-serving motives that
led them to exaggerate printing's potential for influencing public opinion. But Parliamentary leaders in Westminster also "had a thorough
grasp of the importance of printed propaganda and rapidly became ex-
pert in its use."[66] So did their adversaries. Otherwise, how can we explain the expenditure of resources to maintain access to presses? When
Charles I rode north to Newcastle to confront the Scots in 1639, the
earl of Arundel, Lord General of the Army, "at once wrote off to the
Secretary of State for a printer and press to be sent to the town." After
Newcastle was taken in the resumption of the Bishops' Wars in 1640,

[64] Clement Walker, *The History of Independency* (E445[1] 1648), sig. A2r.

[65] *MSS Rawl* D1350, fol. 286v; Henry Ferne, *Conscience Satisfied* (Oxford, 1643),
sig. ¶2, *A Reply Unto Severall Treatises* (Oxford, E74[9], 1643), p. 13; *Resolving Of Conscience* (Oxford, *Wing* F800, 1643), sig. A2. On Ferne's intent to refute Henry Parker, see
Mendle, *Parker and the Civil War*, p. 101.

[66] Lambert, "Beginning of Printing," pp. 44–45.

the same hurried request came from York.[67] Following the king's flight from London in 1642, a press was quickly established "immediately after the King's arrival at York" in a room "at so short a distance from the royal residence, as to admit of a quick and unobserved communication between the King and his printer." For a brief period a press functioned in Shrewsbury, which the king entered in September, during the fall military campaign. After establishing the king's headquarters in Oxford, Royalist printing relied on the university's official printer, Leonard Lichfield. After surrendering himself to the Scots in 1646, the king summoned a York printer, Stephen Bulkley, who had printed many Royalist tracts until the city fell under Parliamentary control after the battle of Marston Moor in 1644, to Newcastle, where he issued tracts.[68] These practices were not, however, confined to the Crown. In May 1647 radical activists in London wrote to agitators in the army, telling them "if it be not thought on to have a press in the Army we are undone." This was arranged, and a Leveller printer arrived at army headquarters in May; in August he received twelve pounds for printing "proclamations & declarations." Fiscal accounts of the New Model Army contain outlays of money from August 1647 to the end of 1648 for printing remonstrances, declarations, and agreements: ninety pounds in August 1647, twenty the next month, ten the next.[69] The army's need of a traveling press ended, temporarily, when censorship fell under its control in September. Later, presses traveled with the army on subsequent campaigns led by Cromwell and by Monke.[70]

Multiple reasons prompted political printing. Its use was dictated when Parliament's adversaries preemptively published a political text. On March 12, 1642, members in the Commons fretted when they learned that the king's response to a parliamentary committee sent three days before with a declaration to him at Newmarket had been printed. MPs voted to have their declaration printed forthwith because "the King's message being printed, and not the Declaration, it might much reflect upon the Parliament."[71] Another use was to enhance a political reputation. Possibly to obtain better media coverage, John Pym obtained "an unusual warrant" for one hundred pounds to distribute as

[67] Clair, *History of Printing in Britain*, p. 151; *CSPD* 1640, p. 631.

[68] Robert Davies, *A Memoir of the York Press* (Westminster, 1868), pp. 36–39, 56, 69–70.

[69] C. H. Firth, ed., *The Clarke Papers* (London, 1992), 1:86; Austin Woolrych, *Soldiers and Statemen: The General Council of the Army and Its Debates, 1647–1648* (Oxford, 1987), pp. 44, 93, 200–201; Ethel Kitson and E. Kitson Clark, "Some Civil War Accounts, 1647–1650" (*Thoresby Society* 11, 1904), pp. 142–44.

[70] Thomas, *Sir John Berkenhead*, pp. 63–64.

[71] *CJ* 2:477; *PJ* 2:30. The king's message is E140[26] (1642); Parliament's declaration is E138[20] (1642).

"he shall in his discretion think fit"—this went to a prominent publisher of news, John Dillingham.[72] Printing was useful for combating rumors, such as the one reported by the sheriff of Yorkshire in 1642 that public support for Parliament in a county petition would be used in Westminster to justify withholding reimbursement for the county's militia expenses. The Commons responded with printed copies of a letter by its Speaker, who denied the rumor. Parliament's concern with printing extended to fairly minute details. Its order to proceed with publication of a declaration in 1646 "for taking off the misrepresentations of the Parliament and their proceeding to the people" instructed the subcommittee charged with the task "to take care it may be truly printed, in a fair letter and good paper."[73] These political concerns underlay the great quantity of texts printed by order and at the expense of Parliament or one of its Houses, which amounted to about 17 percent of all titles and editions printed domestically in 1642. Some items had press runs of nine thousand to eleven thousand copies, one for every five hundred inhabitants of the nation.[74]

Though ample domestic precedents existed, Parliamentary leaders may have learned about the importance of maintaining a stable of writers from commissioners sent from Scotland. When debate in London escalated over the nature and scope of episcopal authority, one writer, a minister employed by the commissioners, reported in February 1641: "The treatise I sent you of the *Unlawfulness of Limited Episcopacie* is answered. They have set me on a reply, which I have now ended. Readily, you may see it in print at once with a new edition of the *Canterburians*, much augmented."[75] Like their Scottish brethren, Parliamentarian leaders used money and patronage to employ political writers to justify their policies. In 1642 when MPs learned that a Royal message and proclamation to Parliament on the garrison at Hull was in print, the Commons entrusted its Committee of Safety to draw up an answer. But after the answer was brought into the House, D'Ewes observed inconveniently that the committee had relied on a printed work, "a pamphlet of observations," referring to Henry Parker's strident defense of parliamentary sovereignty. A few weeks later, Parker was appointed as

[72] Mendle, *Parker and the Civil War*, p. 21.

[73] G. Johnson, ed., *The Fairfax Correspondence* (London, 1848), 2:377–78; MSS Tanner 66 fols. 16, 293; E140[12] (1642); E140[18] (1642); *CJ* 4:512–13.

[74] Five hundred eighteen parliamentary papers out of a total of 2,968 items, according to Lambert, "Printing for Parliament," pp. ix, 1–2, 7, 21.

[75] Laing, *Letters and Journals of Baillie*, p. 303; and see Sheila Lambert, "The Opening of the Long Parliament," *Historical Journal* 27 (1984): 278: "The Scots knew all about political propaganda; the ministers who accompanied the delegation had been selected for their skills in this regard, and only secondarily to provide spiritual comfort to the Commissioners."

secretary to the committee, in which position, D'Ewes later noted, he "had a hand in . . . many seditious pamphlets."[76] This reciprocal relationship between patronage and publishing also appears just after the execution of Charles I in 1649, when a grateful Council of State rewarded the author of *The Tenure of Kings and Magistrates*—it invoked popular sovereignty to defend the regicide—with employment as Secretary for Foreign Tongues. In that position Milton continued as the regime's apologist, when, for example, he complied with a request for a response to *Eikon Basilike*, the Royalist panegyric, appearing in over thirty editions in its first year of publication, that presented the executed king as a martyr.[77]

Parliament's use of printing for propaganda extended practices that English monarchs had used for reaping political benefits from sermons. Many "fast sermons" that militantly Puritan preachers delivered before the Long Parliament appeared in print. The first two, by Stephen Marshall and Cornelius Burges, occurred immediately after the opening of the Parliament. In seven hours of preaching they advanced Pym's religious and political agenda in providential terms. Like Pym, they saw the policies of the Long Parliament as the principal defense against an ungodly alliance between Catholics and proponents of absolute monarchy. These and subsequent fast sermons "were quickly printed and much reported . . . as a means to keep parliament's ideology constantly in the forefront of Londoners' minds."[78] This also occurred at York after it fell under Parliament's control and a Puritan cleric, John Shawe, preached a sermon in late September 1644, when Fairfax and army officers swore allegiance to the Solemn League and Covenant. In an epistle to the copy of his sermon that was printed at York, Shawe apologized for problems due to the haste with which it was published. "I had only time to write it once over, so as the printer got it from me by pieces of sheets, as it was written." The reason for such haste was the need to cultivate support for taking the Covenant, which was ordered to be administered to municipal officials and citizens of York at the end of October.[79]

Instructions for printing political pamphlets that appealed to public opinion came not only from Parliament but also from county committees and military leaders. After a former MP, Sir Edward Dering, returned from Oxford in 1643, where he had fled following his defection from the Long Parliament, the County Committee in Kent required him

---

[76] *PJ* 3:208–9, 256; Mendle, *Parker and the Civil War*, p. 22. The king's message is E150[29] (1642).

[77] Christopher Hill, *Milton and the English Revolution* (New York, 1978), pp. 170, 172.

[78] Fletcher, *Outbreak of Civil War*, p. 345; John F. Wilson, *Pulpit in Parliament* (Princeton, 1969), pp. 36–46.

[79] Davies, *Memoir of the York Press*, pp. 72, 74.

to compose a public recantation of the tyranny and popery that reigned in Oxford. "This, sir, may be done in a little pamphlet, which will better sink into the common peoples' brain than any long volume." On more than one occasion the committee reiterated that what it wanted "might be no elaborate volume, but a pamphlet . . . which will satisfy the vulgar better than any elaborate piece of work, these being the men you have misled." Confronted by Edward King, a leader of a taxpayers' strike who had argued from the bench at a local session that assessments had no legal foundation, the County Committee in Lincolnshire had the relevant parliamentary ordinances "reprinted, and dispersed them into the several parts of this county" in December 1646, "which for the present gave some satisfaction." King responded, in February 1647, with *A Discovery of the Arbitrary, Tyrannicall, and illegal Actions of some of the committee of the County of Lincoln*, which, the committee reported in April, "rendered us, instead of patriots, oppressors of our county."[80] In 1641, Lord Fairfax's local agent recommended using the press to cultivate popular opinion: "it would give great satisfaction to the common people . . . and be an encouragement to them in paying their subsidies, if an act declaratory were passed in the Parliament, and published in print." One year later, he recommended that Parliament "employ some able pen" to cultivate right thinking on the issue of who controlled the militia. In 1645, a colonel bent on winning the hearts and minds of clubmen for Parliament told the Speaker, "It would much conduce to the perfecting of the work at hand, if we might have your declarations . . . our instructions, and other things . . . published in all places where we march, the country hardly believing you intend them either liberty or religion, especially since you take away the common prayer book." This last point about the prayer book is significant: suppression of the Book of Common Prayer by the Long Parliament had an especially inflammatory impact on popular opinion.[81]

Royalist officials and writers also displayed keen sensitivity to political uses of printing. In part, this involved negative reactions to the growing dexterity of Parliamentary leaders in using printed texts to influence public opinion. One government memo held printed copies of polemical exchanges between king and Parliament to be responsible for stimulating *popular* criticism of Royalist policy as insincere or temporizing:

And this they gather out of the printed speeches. Herewith give me leave to say that this liberty of printing everything exposes all our consultations and

---

[80] *MSS Stowe* 184, fols. 69, 73; *MSS Tanner* 58, fol. 39; E373[3] (1647); see also Clive Holmes, "Colonel King and Lincolnshire Politics, 1642–1646," *HJ* 16 (1973): 451–84.

[81] *Fairfax Correspondence* 2:104, 380–81; *MSS Tanner* 66 fols. 16, 293; *HMC Portland*, 1:237.

actions to the censure of the whole world. . . . Nothing but experience can impress what harm it does here, and how these publishings expose us to public scorn.

At the end of May 1642, a Royalist squire in London decried the centrality of appeals to the public in parliamentary proceedings. "Neither is there any proceeding in Parliament in any business but voting and declaring & courting of the people, and all little enough, if any man may judge, according to common discourse." Another Royalist writer denounced this reliance on printing and suggested that Parliament order all "declarations, messages, answers, replies, and such like weekly productions" be used by grocers to wrap produce, "which art will dispense them, not into every shire but into every house, so that no necessary business that requires paper would be done without them."[82]

In spite of many reservations about such practices, Royalists understood the necessity to use them and monitor their deployment by adversaries. This was part of the art of political intelligence. When Parliament debated the Vote of No Address—to break off negotiations with the king in 1648—a letter of intelligence from London informed Edward Hyde on February 10:

> now they are penning a declaration . . . which is to be published to the whole kingdom, to make his Majesty . . . to be more odious to the people. In the meantime . . . another scandalous & base book is set out by H[enry] M[arten] . . . whilst his Majesty's declaration that first was handed about in written hand, & now in print, is endeavored with all possible diligence to be suppressed.[83]

Royalist use of printed propaganda was not, however, merely reactive, that is, prodded by Parliamentary initiatives. It had been a part of statecraft for Tudor and early-Stuart monarchs, and, as we saw in chapter 4, was readily used to counter propaganda by the Scots. The assize circuit traveled twice yearly by judges provided an opportunity, just prior to the outbreak of fighting in 1642, for judges to distribute printed texts of their instructions, which justified Royal policy.[84] Royalists later exercised considerable initiative in establishing *Mercurius Aulicus*. Precedents for such public relations initiatives appear in Archbishop Laud's superintendence of the then principal defense of the Church of England,

---

[82] *CSPD* 1641–43, p. 70; B. Schofield, ed., *The Knyvett Letters, 1620–1644* (*Norfolk Record Society* 20 1949), p. 107; E179[18] (1642), p. 7.

[83] *MSS Clarendon* 30, fol. 290. Parliament's declaration, E429[9] (1648), appeared in print the next day; Marten's book, E426[2] (1648), in support of the Vote of No Address appeared on February 7; the printed version of the king's declaration, E426[5](1648), bears the date January 18.

[84] E108[7] (1642).

Episcopacie By Divine Right Asserted, composed toward the end of 1639 by the respected elderly bishop of Exeter, Joseph Hall—"the only bishop ever mentioned without disapproval by Nehemiah Wallington."[85] An orthodox Calvinist and defender of the Church establishment, Hall was an ideal author for deflecting attacks on the English Church from Scottish and domestic critics. Yet the final text of his defense of episcopacy emerged only after extensive correspondence with Laud. After reviewing a prospectus, Laud told Hall to send him "not the whole work together, but each particular head . . . as you finish it, that so we here may be the better able to consider of it, and the work come on the faster." Politics as much as theology guided Hall's construction and Laud's revisions. Hall acknowledged that many of the text's finer points, such as the concession "that the presbyterian government may be of use where episcopacy may not be had," were made "with respect to the present occasion." Just as Hall deferred to Laud's judgment of what "present occasion" demanded,[86] so did Bishop Morton, when he moderated attacks on Scottish Presbyterians and Romanists in a sermon before it went to press.[87]

When used as a political weapon, printing enlarged the range of tactics available to political elites in a legislative context and to activists outside Parliament who propelled the transformation of factions into parties. For leaders in Parliament, tactical implications of political printing created new options and strategies for negotiating agreements when, in 1641, coordinating printing plans with legislative strategies had become an art of politics. In early May, opponents of Charles I's principal minister, the earl of Strafford, adopted the traditional expedient of an oath—a protestation of loyalty to Protestantism, Parliament, and the king—as they struggled to manage a political crisis in London. Their efforts to bring the earl to the block occurred as the city was inundated with wild rumors of domestic Catholic conspiracies, foreign invasion by French forces, and an army plot. In addition, uncertainty existed over the response of Charles to public demonstrations and a massive petition campaign that called for Strafford's execution. Though Parliamentary leaders proposed the oath initially to cement resolve among MPs, efforts were quickly undertaken to impose it on the nation, only to encounter objections from the Lords, in May and July, to this political litmus test.[88] But printing provided the Commons with a viable option: in May the Protestation with a preamble was printed, along with an order from

---

[85] Conrad Russell, *The Fall of the British Monarchies, 1637–1642* (Oxford, 1991) p. 239.

[86] *CSPD 1639–40*, pp. 55–56, 87–88, 100.

[87] *SPD 16/437/fol. 87*; *CSPD 1639–40*, pp. 212–13.

[88] Fletcher, *Outbreak of Civil War*, pp. 15–16; Russell, *Fall of the British Monarchies*, pp. 294–95.

the Commons for printing both documents; in July, the Commons ordered the printing of its resolution that anyone who refused the Protestation was unfit to hold public office.[89]

This use of printing for completing an end run around legislative checks inherent in bicameral institutions reappeared later that year when the two Houses sparred over an order from the Commons against "innovations" in religion. This unilaterally implemented a Puritan purge by requiring parishes to remove crucifixes and superstitious images and to make other "reforms." After the Commons on September 8 published the order in an edition of 4,275 copies that cost £17, the Lords retaliated, on September 9, voting to print a prior order of January that had left divine worship as it was established by law. That day the Commons issued 1,937 octavo copies, at a cost of £7 15s. of a declaration that reaffirmed its order.[90] Thus, printing was already a highly contentious issue when, in November, the Commons debated the Grand Remonstrance. This historical narrative of "malignant" projects that imperiled the fundamental laws, liberties, and religion of England demanded specific reforms, including imposition of "discipline" in religion, removal of popish lords and bishops from the upper House, enforcement of anti-Catholic laws, and more. On November 19, Sir Edward Nicholas, who had kept King Charles well informed about the early-September episode of rival printing between the two Houses, reported that not only was the Remonstrance likely to pass, "it will be ordered to be printed without transmission to the Lords." He was not the first observer to note the intention to print the Remonstrance long before that move was proposed.[91] Nicholas's observation shows that not only parliamentary leaders had become knowledgeable about the political uses of printing—his report went to the king three days before the Commons took up the issue of printing the Remonstrance. When it did, the debate nearly provoked a riot on the floor. The matter of printing was left "undetermined" and was taken up on December 15, when William Purefoy moved that "there was no readier means to bring in money than to cause our declaration to be printed so that we might satisfy the people." After another long, contentious debate, the motion passed.[92]

Political printing during the English Revolution was often prompted

[89] 669f.3[2],[5],[6],[10] (1641). A London artisan copied the Protestation in his diary; R. Webb, ed., *Historical Notices of Events Occurring Chiefly in the Reign of Charles I* (London, 1869), 1:262–65.

[90] *CJ* 2:283, 286–87; *LJ* 4:391, 395; 669f.3[14],[17],[18] (1641); E171[13] (1641); Lambert, "Printing for Parliament," p. 2.

[91] W. Bray, ed., *Diary and Correspondence of John Evelyn* (London, 1857), 4:130, and see 132–33; *CSPD* 1641–43, pp. 163–64.

[92] *D'Ewes II*, pp. 186–87, 294; Fletcher, *Outbreak of Civil War*, pp. 155–56, 169; Russell, *Fall of the British Monarchies*, pp. 427–28.

by tactical considerations of contending elites and activists, which we have just surveyed. But the pursuit of profit and fame among producers of this literature was also important. Commerce and publicity, the twin imperatives of print culture, reverberated through political printing. Authors and editors displayed keen awareness of popular demand for printed political texts and measured success in terms of copies sold of their work. In 1642 Sir Edward Dering boasted that 4,500 copies of an important speech delivered by him in the Commons had been sold. "My book here is well liked," wrote Robert Baillie in December 1641, "and much searched for; all our copies are spent. A new edition from Amsterdam by my knowledge is come over."[93] Some contemporaries understood the commercial pressures that operated on the printing of political texts. Frank acknowledgment of the alliance of commerce and controversy appears in a simple pamphlet, a dialogue in which a "country gentleman" rebukes a London "citizen" for abusive Puritan rhetoric and in which Strafford is a "traitorous wretch," Archbishop Laud the "prince of Devils." Abashed, "citizen" points out that in London "you shall see divers writings, yea, and books printed, lying on many booksellers' stalls to be sold, that give them as bad language as I have done." Reminded that this undermines godliness, "citizen" cites the bottom line: "Well, sir . . . the printing and selling of such books has been a means to help many a poor man in London [during] these dead times of trading."[94] Another author charged that the flood of pamphlets with lurid accounts of murder and rape by Irish rebels against English settlers carried gross exaggerations by greedy writers seeking to inflate sales of their wares.[95] Commercial imperatives in political printing also impeded publication of religious truth, at least as it was propounded in an important series of tracts by "Smectymnuus." After Bishop Hall defended the Church of England in his January 1641 *Humble Remonstrance to Parliament* against demands for reform in the December Root and Branch Petition, Smectymnuus—that is, Stephen Marshall, Edmund Callamy, and other leading Puritan divines—published a response in February, *An Answer To A Booke entituled An Humble Remonstrance.* Yet not until June did the next item by Smectymnuus appear. On its final page, just above the errata notice, is an explanation:

> The Printer to the Reader. Courteous reader, We cannot but confess that the crowding in of many little pamphlets into the press has so many weeks detained this book, to the great grief of the authors."[96]

[93] L. Larking, ed., *Proceedings, Principally in the County of Kent* (*CS*, os, 80, 1862), p. xliii; *Letters and Journals of Baillie*, p. 284.
[94] *Sions Charity Towards Her Foes in misery* (E158[13], 1641) pp. 2, 3, 5.
[95] E134[3] (1642), sig. A2.
[96] Smectymnuus, *A Vindication Of The Answer To The Humble Remonstrace* (E165[6], 1641), p. 221.

These "little pamphlets" likely were items on Laud's imprisonment, Strafford's trial and execution, and the debate over the right of bishops to sit in the Lords, which might justly have been thought by the publisher to be more vendable than a complex 221-page tome.

Many other consequences followed from the intimate connection between commerce and political controversy. One was unscrupulous publication practices. Too many copies of one of Robert Baillie's books had been printed by a publisher, who, in an effort to unload unsold copies eleven years later, marketed it with a new, opportunistic title page, which proclaimed that it was *very useful to preserve those that are yet sound in faith, from the Infection of Mr. John Goodwin's great Book* (the latest threat to Scottish Calvinism). Another consequence was shifting opportunities to publish a text. When controversy waned, and with it potential sales, publishing interest declined. In 1656 an author complained, "No stationer will undertake to print books on divine right of particular church orders any more because that controversy lies dead among us, and few inquire for any books on that subject." Efforts to censor texts could backfire, by heightening interest in them. After an MP, Edward Dering, was ejected from the Commons for altering his views on religious reform in 1642, he justified his activities by publishing *A Collection of Speeches . . . in matter of Religion . . . now subjected to publike View and Censure.* This violation of communicative privileges of the House appalled members, who wanted to suppress the book but worried about provoking more interest in it. D'Ewes pointed out that if they called in all copies, "whereas it was now sold for some 14d., it would advance it to 14s. price and that it might besides hasten on a new impression of it."[97] Copies were publicly burned, with the same consequence that followed similar bonfires during the personal rule of Charles I: higher prices and greater demand for the text. In response to requests for Dering's book from relatives, a member of the Kent gentry—Dering had represented Kent—reported from London, "The book I could have bought for 14 pence last night, but now [after the order to burn it] a crown cannot buy it." However, he added, "You may easily come to the sight of it by some about Canterbury."[98]

Purely commercial imperatives produced a torrent of pirated and forged copies of speeches, petitions, and other controversial texts, visible evidence of the alacrity with which stationers and authors catered to popular interest in public events. The notoriety of William Prynne, arguably the most famous public Puritan figure of this era, led to publication

---

[97] *Letters and Journals of Baillie*, p. xcii; PJ 1:254–55. For Dering's book, see E197[1] (1642)

[98] D. Gardiner, ed., *The Oxinden Letters, 1607–1642* (London, 1937), pp. 286–87, 298; see also Sharpe, *Personal Rule*, p. 652.

of many inaccurate or false items attributed to him. One response was *An Exact Catalogue Of All Printed Books and Papers . . . by William Prynne.* Complaints about errors in forged and pirated texts were legion. Amidst widespread interest in the trial of Strafford, one MP warned his wife on May 20, 1641, "There are six several copies of Strafford's speeches, none very right."[99] Unauthorized publication often intensified pressure to publish by prompting public figures to declare their true views in authorized editions. One MP was forced to publish *A Speech Delivered in Parliament By Sir Benjamin Rudyard. Being none of those already in print*. References to unauthorized publication could also be pretextual, when they appeared on title pages for texts clearly intended for publication, especially petitions, such as *The Two Petitions of the County of Buckingham*, which was *Printed to prevent false copies*.[100]

INVOKING PUBLIC OPINION

How did contemporaries respond to the printing of news and polemical political texts? Was it possible to reconcile this development with traditional norms of secrecy and privilege? We shall see that answers to these questions involve the paradox of innovation. In assessing reactions to political printing in the 1640s, we must begin with the fact that contemporaries were not oblivious to communicative developments. Censorship of books was long considered a noteworthy event, judging by the frequency with which references to banning, censoring, and burning of books appears in letters and diaries during the 1620s and 1630s. In 1639 one writer informed his wife about two religious texts in press at two printing houses: "they were not permitted to print them till the licenser had expunged all passages that concerned Rome or opposing popery."[101] Reversal of this state of affairs after the Long Parliament met was equally noteworthy. One representative of the Scottish government in London was astounded by the lack of control over political printing: "You see what liberty is here, when such books dare bear the names of the author, printer, and seller." Later that decade, Royalist intelligence described how London printing "sends forth daily stores of pamphlets . . . some for the Army, but more against it. Indeed, there was never

---

[99] *An Exact Catalogue* (190[2], [1643]1660); Larking, *Proceedings in Kent*, p. 47. See also *Letters and Journals of Baillie*, p. 300; *Rushworth* 4:134.

[100] *A Speech Delivered . . . By Sir Benjamin Rudyard* (E198[28], 1641); *The Two Petitions of . . . Buckingham* (E181[29], 1642).

[101] *CSPD* 1639–40, p. 212. See also *MSS Tanner* 66, fol. 109; *Tanner* 67, fol. 126; *MSS Add* 11,045, fols. 27, 108; *MSS Egerton* 2716, fol. 276v; *HMC Portland* 3:42; M. A. E. Green, ed., *Diary of John Rous* (*CS*, os, 66, 1856), p. 5.

such liberty assumed as now."[102] Above, we also saw that contemporaries were keenly aware of the advantages of printing's efficiency for disseminating information, when letter writers commented on being "overtaken by the press."

Contemporaries also remarked on the content of printed political texts, especially when it took the form of an appeal to public opinion. Bitter controversy was provoked not only by specific political and religious positions but by use of printing to convey those positions before a reading public. Competitive appeals to public opinion issued from Parliament, and individually from both Houses, sometimes in opposition to each other; from the king and his supporters; from former members of Parliament who quit or were ejected from that body; from petitioners on behalf of local communities as they took sides or temporized; from municipal councils; and from political factions, religious sects, and the army. Contemporary reaction to these developments often sprang from perceptions of innovation that violated traditional norms of secrecy and privilege in political communication. In 1643, one MP explained why he had resigned his seat and joined the king in Oxford. After acknowledging his opposition to royal policies in earlier sessions of Parliament, he asked:

> In all those Parliaments did we ever see any declarations of both Houses against the King, or of one House against the other, printed and published to the people? . . . Did we ever see when anything had been proposed to and rejected by the House of Lords, the House of Commons notwithstanding proceed in it, and express their minds of it to the people?[103]

One year earlier, Edward Dering offered the same reasoning in explaining his decision to forsake the Long Parliament and join Charles I, who had removed his court to Oxford.

> Wherefore is this descension from a Parliament to a people? . . . And why are we told that the people are expectant for a Declaration? . . . When I first heard of a Remonstrance, I presently imagined that like faithful councillors we should hold up a glass unto his Majesty. . . . I did not dream that we should remonstrate downward, tell stories to the people, and talk of the King as of a third person. I neither look for cure of our complaints from the common people nor do desire to be cured by them.[104]

Dering's comments were a retrospective elaboration of arguments advanced against the Remonstrance of November 22, 1641. Though the

---

[102] *Letters and Journals of Baillie*, pp. 286; *MSS Clarendon* 30, fol. 66.

[103] E102[13] (1643), p. 5.

[104] Edward Dering, *A Collection of Speeches* (E197[1], 1642), pp. 65–66, 70.

Remonstrance took the form of a petition from the Commons to the king, its proponents embarked on novel courses in proposing that it be printed. "It appeared then," Hyde wrote several years later, "that they did not intend to send it up to the House of peers for their countenance, but that it was . . . an appeal to the people." This point was not evident only with the benefit of hindsight. When debating whether Parliament should proceed with the Remonstrance, supporters of Charles I reacted sharply to proposals for its publication, which would invest a venerable instrument of communication, the petition, with a new and ominous function. Culpepper argued that the remonstrance "should be addressed to the King, and not to the people. . . . We are not sent to please the people." Observers outside Parliament also noted the novelty in this development. In seeking to print the Remonstrance, its proponents in the Commons "desire not the concurrence of the Lords. Nor is it addressed to the King's [concurrence] as all remonstrances of grievances have ever been, but to the people." After Parliament voted on the text of the Remonstrance, comments by another observer highlight differences between the traditional petition and an appeal to public opinion: "the contestation now is whether to publish it in print to the public view or by petition to his Majesty."[105] Not surprisingly, Charles I objected to this development. Publication of petitions to him before he had given his reply was a gross violation of traditional restrictions on petitioning.[106]

These comments underscore a profound alteration in communicative practice, a break with traditions that confined expressions of grievances to privileged channels of communication that emptied into the secret councils of a ruler. Instead of indexing grievances humbly submitted to a monarch for remedy, the Remonstrance appealed to the public for support of a specific legislative agenda. Such appeals to public opinion, we saw, also animated the printing of declarations, pamphlets, and sermons, and they were not limited to conflicts between Charles I and the Long Parliament. They also arose in rivalries between the two Houses of Parliament, which led to unprecedented revelations of their internal proceedings and, as we shall see in the next chapter, in competitive petition campaigns conducted by Presbyterian and Independent politicians, Leveller activists, resurgent Royalists, and agitators and officers in the New Model Army. From the beginning of these developments, many contemporaries perceived that they violated traditional norms in political communication, as well as more general assumptions on the

---

[105] Edward Hyde, *History of the Rebellion and Civil Wars in England* (Oxford, 1849), 1:441; Russell, *Fall of the British Monarchies*, p. 427; *HMC Cowper*, p. 295; *CSPD* 1641–43, p. 170.

[106] E181[6] (1641).

centrality of deference in politics and on the social order as an organic body. Because they were unprepared to abandon these assumptions, Royalists and Parliamentarians in the early 1640s did not endorse novel communicative practices but, instead, regarded political appeals to the public as an illegitimate practice by adversaries. Certainly, neither side justified this activity in terms of principle. Gross discrepancies between theory and practice by both sides supply additional evidence of the paradox of innovation. To be sure, precedents for such discrepancies existed in prerevolutionary England, when surreptitious appeals to public opinion relied on scribal publication, a practice that required discretion. D'Ewes thought it less objectionable to allow members to make scribal copies of a speech than to sanction the printing of an authorized edition in order to correct errors in an unauthorized edition.[107] Subsequently, this connivance was impossible because, unlike scribal modes of publication, printing conveyed political information openly, as printed texts were set up on posts by booksellers and hawked in the markets and streets by peddlers.

One response to this development was to pretend that political elites were victims of printing. This theme appears in a pamphlet, *A Presse Full Of Pamphlets*, a condemnation of political pamphlets, whose title page describes its year of publication as "the Year of their Uncasing." Its author observes that there is:

> nothing more disgraceful to the proceeding of any court of judicature than to have the same spread over the world in unseemly and obnoxious papers. Secrecy in the agitation of government affairs has always been accounted good policy. . . . My intention . . . is no otherwise but to describe the abuse of printing, in publishing every pamphlet that comes to their press . . . even the proceeding of the House of Commons of Parliament; and the worthy members thereof are by the same exposed to the view of all men.[108]

Here the discrepancy between theory and practice disappears when the observer disregards or misses the fact that, as we have seen, "worthy members" were responsible for much of this publicity. The paradox of innovation also appears in comments by participants as well as observers, in denunciations of communicative practices by adversaries that overlook one's own participation in such practices. Though Simonds D'Ewes and Edward Dering ended up on opposite sides after Charles I fled from London, the same inconsistency attends their communicative practices. It appears in January 1642, when D'Ewes released for publication a copy of a speech in which he asserted that it was "the highest treachery and breach of privilege for any member of that House to wit-

---

[107] *D'Ewes I*, p. 332.
[108] *A Presse Full Of Pamphlets* (E142[9], 1642), sig. A1.

ness or reveal what was done or spoken in that House." A few months earlier, Dering delivered his spirited speech, partly quoted above, against printing the Remonstrance, in which he urged his colleagues in the Commons not to "remonstrate downward, tell stories to the people." Yet, as Conrad Russell points out, "Dering rather spoiled the effect by printing his speech."[109]

Contradictions between communicative practice and theory were exacerbated when political leaders began routinely to invest time and money in producing printed political texts. Tactical considerations led both sides to maintain stables of writers who composed political pamphlets and to support editors of newspapers—both intended for a very diverse audience of readers. Though Royalists and Parliamentarians were equally liable to accusations about violating norms of secrecy and privilege in political communication, perception of novelty was keenest when it applied to one's adversaries. In spite of the fact that leaders of the Long Parliament initiated the use of printing to appeal to public opinion, they and their supporters relentlessly attacked the violation of secrecy norms. "It is one of the greatest treacheries of state to divulge the secrets of either House . . . as the revelation of matters in deliberation before any determination," argued one writer in 1642, who claimed that this was mainly a Royalist practice and a cause of factions within Parliament. "Many things are penned and printed in papers under a royal name that are in this kind most unrighteous, and have caused, first, division in the Parliament, and then the desertion of that society." Leaders of the Long Parliament scorned the communication practices they so skillfully employed in disseminating its case to the nation. With exquisite ingenuity Denzil Holles denounced the Royalist publication of messages "in his Majesty's name . . . bitter invectives against the Parliament, to perplex it and engage it in the expense of time to answer them." So did Parliament collectively in its May 26 *Remonstrance*, which responded to a printed declaration with the Royalist account of the refusal to admit Charles I and his forces into Hull, whose garrison guarded a large magazine. In that *Remonstrance* Parliament complained:

> The great affairs of this kingdom . . . affords us little leisure to spend our time in declarations, and in answers and replies, yet the malignant party about his Majesty, taking all occasions to multiply calumnies upon the Houses of Parliament and to publish sharp invectives under his Majesty's name against them and their proceedings—a new engine which they have invented . . . to beget and increase distrust and disaffection between the King and his people.[110]

[109] *D'Ewes I*, p. xxi; Russell, *Fall of the British Monarchies*, p. 427.
[110] *Mercy And Truth, Righteousness and Peace* (E91[11], 1642), sig. A2; *The Speech of*

The rebuff offered to the king in his attempt to enter Hull signaled the growing inevitability of civil war and pushed the exchange of arguments in printed texts to new heights. Now "the paper war was at its peak," and, unlike in earlier exchanges, "the parties were openly appealing to the country for support."[111] This was the context in which Parliament's *Remonstrance* responded to the Royalist claim that "instead of giving his Majesty satisfaction, we published a declaration concerning that [Hull] business as an appeal to the people . . . which course is alleged to be very unagreeable to the modesty and duty of former times." Unable to deny the allegation outright, Parliament initially acknowledges the utility of innovation.

> And as for the duty and modesty of former times, from which we are said to have varied and to want the warrant of any precedents therein but what ourselves have made. But if we have made any precedents this Parliament, we have made them for posterity, upon the same or better grounds of reason and law than those were upon which our predecessor first made any for us.

Immediately thereafter, the *Remonstrance* qualifies the shift from precedent to reason. Its authors acknowledge the absence of any precedent for Parliament "setting forth declarations for the satisfaction of the people" but justify the appeal to the public by the magnitude of the threat to Parliament from malignant forces surrounding Charles I: "there were never any such monsters before . . . ever attempted to disaffect the people from a Parliament."[112] This moves the perception of innovation from parliamentary practices to monstrous conspiracies of their adversaries.

The contemporary habit of detecting novelty only in communicative practices by one's adversaries persisted in subsequent developments in the 1640s. When stalled negotiations between the Long Parliament and Scotland after the surrender of Charles I in 1646 prompted publication of speeches that presented Scottish views on the disposition of the king and a religious settlement, the London Independent Thomas Juxon noted approvingly, "The House resents this very deeply" that the Scots "go about to court the people."[113] Journalistic coverage of these events also shows how paradox of innovation sprang from the alacrity with

---

Denzil Holles (E200[48], 1642); *A Remonstrance Or The Declaration* (E148[23], 1641), p. 1.

[111] Russell, *Fall of the British Monarchies*, pp. 504–5.

[112] *A Remonstrance Or The Declaration*, p. 3.

[113] *MSS. Williams* 24.50, fol. 93. Juxton probably refers to publication of E360[20] (1646).

which contemporaries decried appeals to public opinion when they issued from political opponents. Divergent assessments of efforts to inform the public about negotiations between the Parliament, Scotland,
and Charles I appeared in the same week in two pro-Parliament newspapers. The *Weekly Intelligencer* praised the simple prose in messages from
Parliament to the Scots, for "plainness of speech or delivery is an evidence that they are not written or spoken with an intent to delude the
people, when [whereas] that which is printed with rhetoric may deceive
the people." Yet the *Moderate Intelligencer* decried this very activity
when it came from the king: "His Majesty's letter sent to the Parliament
is printed and dispersed. The people wonder at the condescension."[114]

These discrepant responses to communicative innovations that used
printed texts to appeal to public opinion exhibit a pattern. The pattern
is comprehensible if we recall the conspicuous absence of democratic
principles among principal political actors at the beginning of the civil
war in 1642 and for a good while thereafter. Political conflict occurred
while organic and patriarchal assumptions still dominated thinking on
the nature of social and political order. Norms of secrecy and privilege
in politics that grew out of these assumptions continued to guide contemporaries when they thought about innovative communicative developments. Inconsistency, then, was inevitable when, under conditions of
escalating conflict, political actors relied on tactics shaped by innovations in communicative practice that they were reluctant to acknowledge. The ensuing paradox of innovation was not merely a sign of political expediency. Expedient responses, to be sure, were legion. But
discrepancies between practice and acknowledgment also arose and acquired a specific form because innovative practices in political communication occurred before change in fundamental assumptions that guided
contemporary thinking on politics and society. We shall encounter the
same situation in the next chapter in ambivalent, inconsistent responses
by contemporaries to the use of printed petitions to appeal to public
opinion. In petitioning, however, discrepancies between communicative
practice and principle occurred not only at the political center but
among petitioners outside Westminster, for whom the paradox of innovation concealed innovations in political communication from the periphery to the center. These innovations replaced norms of secrecy and
privilege in petitioning with appeals to public opinion that were designed to accomplish a task that political leaders in Parliament often
found unsettling, lobbying on behalf of a legislative agenda that reflected popular will. Yet for this unwonted development they had largely
themselves to blame. In 1648, D'Ewes pointed to parliamentary uses of

[114] E369[2] (1646), sig. Ff1; E369[8] (1646), p. 823.

printing that we have surveyed in this chapter when he pondered radical arguments that "the same rule" which justified Parliament's right to critical judgments about Charles I also upheld a correlative right of "the people" to make critical judgments of Parliament. Why should "this new doctrine of the people's power," he asked, "now seem so strange to us, who have heard it formerly broached in the House over & over, besides the frequent printing of it in several pamphlets?"[115]

[115] *MSS Harl* 166, fol. 285.

CHAPTER EIGHT

Petitions

THE FIRST AMENDMENT to the U.S. Constitution concludes by upholding the right "to petition the government for a redress of grievances." To the contemporary eye, the reference to petitions seems archaic, far less central to the public sphere than are other communicative rights. But archaic appearances belie the historical significance of petitioning for the origins of democracy, especially for its public sphere, where political discourse arises from rival appeals to public opinion in a marketplace of ideas that has normative authority for setting a political agenda. In the seventeenth century, the "invention" of public opinion as a factor in politics emerged from the innovative use of printed petitions. This development superseded norms of secrecy and privilege in political communication. Yet it was a practical and not a theoretical innovation, an unintended consequence of communicative change that transformed petitioning and other traditional communicative practices. It not only increased the *scope* of political communication, but also altered its *content*, as production of political texts became oriented to an anonymous body of opinion, a public that was both a nominal object of discourse and a collection of individual writers, readers, printers, and petitioners engaged in political debates.

The special importance of printed petitions for the early democratic public sphere is that they were the principal means by which readers and subscribers participated in public debates, whose aim was to lobby elites on behalf of a legislative agenda. Before the English Revolution, however, traditions for petitioning did not involve appeals to public opinion. As we saw in chapter 4, norms of secrecy and privilege restricted expressions of grievance in the traditional petition to apolitical flows of information on local conditions to the political center. This was a privileged form of communication that did not contain or intimate normative claims about subordinating politics to popular will. In printing's transformation of these features of the traditional petition, we have an unparalleled empirical point of entry into debates over the rise of the public sphere. Petitions have the same illuminating potential for the study of communicative practice that murder has for a journalist, for whom the most interesting aspects often are not the murderous motives and deeds but the rhythms and activities of everyday life suddenly revealed in the harsh light of a homicide investigation. In this vein, I explore petitioning for evidence on communicative practices, rather than for the causes and social dimensions of the English Revolution, issues that have dominated prior study of petitions by historians.

The importance of petitions for politics in early-modern revolutions has long been recognized. Though the study of English history lacks the elaborate historiographic literature on petitions that exists for the French Revolution, petitions have nonetheless been an important resource in studies of the English Revolution. Divergent accounts of the English Revolution analyze the content and signatures of petitions for evidence on the ideology and social composition of different political groups. This use of petitions provides evidence for studies that emphasize class conflict and popular initiative in the revolution,[1] divisions between "court" and "country,"[2] and the centrality of "localism" and the "country community,"[3] as well as for work that militates against the revisionist emphasis on localism.[4] Petitions have been extensively used for studying politics in London,[5] the Long Parliament and the New Model Army,[6] the second civil war,[7] and nonconformity.[8] The rise and fall of the Levellers is a story recounted by summarizing petitions.[9] Studies ex-

[1] Brian Manning, *The English People and the English Revolution* (London, 1991), pp. 49–71, 120–30.

[2] Perez Zagorin, *The Court and the Country* (New York, 1970), pp. 104–5, 227–30, 290–92, 297–98.

[3] Alan Everitt, *The Community of Kent and the Great Rebellion* (Leicester, 1973), pp. 23, 60–64, 86, 89–90, 94–98; John Morrill, *Cheshire 1630–1660* (Oxford, 1974), pp. 45–55; T. P. S.Woods, *Prelude to Civil War* (Wilton Salisbury, 1980).

[4] Jacqueline Eales, *Puritans and Roundheads: The Harleys of Brampton Bryan and the Outbreak of the English Civil War* (Cambridge, 1990), pp. 114, 128–38; Clive Holmes, *The Eastern Association in the English Civil War* (Cambridge, 1974), pp. 25–28, 41–42, 44–47, 53–54, 245, 248–49; Ann Hughes, *Politics, Society, and Civil War in Warwickshire* (Cambridge, 1987), pp. 124–42.

[5] Robert Brenner, *Merchants and Revolution* (Princeton, 1993), pp. 311–14, 364–74, 396–98, 430–31, 436–37, 441–45, 470–80; Keith Lindley, *Popular Politics and Religion in Civil War London* (Aldershot, Hants., 1997); Valerie Pearl, *London and the Outbreak of the Puritan Revolution* (London, 1961), pp. 95–96, 108–9, 115–16, 130–31, 149–53, 173–75, 210–36, 252–56, 269–73; Valerie Pearl, "London's Counter-Revolution," in G. E. Aylmer, ed., *The Interregnum* (London, 1972), pp. 29–56.

[6] Mark Kishlansky, *The Rise of the New Model Army* (Cambridge, 1979), chap. 4, 7–8; David Underdown, *Pride's Purge: Politics in the Puritan Revolution* (Oxford, 1971), pp. 78–79, 93–95, 97–99, 107–10, 116–23; Austin Woolrych, *Soldiers and Statesmen: The General Council of the Army and Its Debates, 1647–1648* (Oxford, 1987).

[7] Robert Ashton, *Counter-Revolution: The Second Civil War and Its Origins, 1646–1648* (New Haven, 1994), chap. 4.

[8] Murray Tolmie, *The Triumph of the Saints* (Cambridge, 1977), pp. 130–39, 146–55, 169–78.

[9] For collections, see William Haller and Godfrey Davies, *The Leveller Tracts* (New York, 1944); D. M. Wolfe, *Leveller Manifestoes of the Puritan Revolution* (New York, 1967).

plore details of individual petitions,[10] rhetoric in petitions,[11] the role of women in petitioning,[12] and petitions in third party judicature.[13] Disagreement exists over the probative value of large-scale, countywide petitions as indicators of local opinion.[14] For army petitions, old claims about the influence of Leveller ideology have given way to an emphasis on the autonomy and spontaneity in grievances from soldiers.[15] Caution is well warranted in the use of petitions as historical evidence. In chapter 4 we saw that petitionary rhetoric concealed the organization of petitioning. In the 1640s, this rhetoric also minimized a petition's evident intent to lobby Parliament. Fortunately, these issues are illuminated by a metadebate over the propriety of petitioning, which accompanies substantive political disputes, in which contemporaries describe, attack, and defend petitions in their private letters, printed pamphlets, diaries, and newspapers. Evidence from these sources is crucial for drawing inferences that go beyond explicit claims by petitioners—a necessary step for analyzing the paradox of innovation. Appearances can be deliberately misleading in texts printed as propaganda. It is therefore incontestable that "petitions often do as much to obscure as to illuminate public opinion."[16] But patterns of deception and even outright forgeries (when known as such) are useful. Hence, corroborating evidence from other sources is indispensable, though it, too, can conceal much about petitioning. Journals of the House of Commons often record only a bland response to a petition that, like the May 1646 petition from London, provoked heated debate.[17]

Yet after all the scrutiny of petitions by historians, it remains unclear how and why petitioning changed in the 1640s and what the role of

[10] Anthony Fletcher, "Petitioning and the Outbreak of the Civil War in Derbyshire," *Derbyshire Archaeological Journal* 93 (1973); Woods, *Prelude to Civil War*.

[11] Elizabeth Skerpan, *The Rhetoric of Politics in the English Revolution* (Columbia, MO, 1992), pp. 73–77.

[12] Patricia Higgins, "The Reactions of Women, with Special Reference to Women Petitioners," in B. Manning, ed., *Politics, Religion, and the English Civil War* (New York, 1973); Ann Marie McEntee, " 'The [Un]Civill-Sisterhood or Oranges and Lemons': Female Petitioners and Demonstrators, 1642–1653," in J. Holstun, ed., *Pamphlet Wars: Prose in the English Revolution* (London, 1992), pp. 92–111.

[13] James S. Hart, *Justice upon Petition* (London, 1991).

[14] Cf. Everitt, *Kent and the Great Rebellion*, pp. 60–61; Anthony Fletcher, *The Outbreak of the English Civil War* (London, 1981), pp. 191–92; Hughes, *Politics, Society, and Civil War*, pp. 132–33, 136; Morrill, *Cheshire*, pp. 45–48; Underdown, *Pride's Purge*, p. 93, 110n; David Underdown, *Revel, Riot, and Rebellion* (Oxford, 1985), pp. 138–39.

[15] Kishlansky, *Rise of the New Model Army*, pp. 180, 189–90, 205–6; Woolrych, *Soldiers and Statesmen*, pp. 54, 59, 73–84.

[16] Underdown, *Revel, Riot, and Rebellion*, p. 231.

[17] *MSS Add* 31116, fol. 271; Bulstrode Whitelock, *Memorials of the English Affairs* (Oxford, 1853), 2:26; for a 1644 petition, see *CJ* 1643–44, p. 372; *MSS Add* 31116, fol. 179v, *MSS Harl* 166, fol. 151.

printing was in this development. On this point, for example, a currently authoritative account of petitions at the outbreak of the civil war is not helpful when it observes that petitions were quickly printed "as public utterances intended for general consumption." Critical questions go unanswered in this and other studies that direct our attention to the importance of petitions as propaganda in the rise of political factions in localities[18] and in adversarial party politics across the nation.[19] How did this most untraditional use of petitions come about, and what is its connection to printing and to democratic innovations in thinking on the political order? Political petitions in the English Revolution were indeed "public documents,"[20] but previously they were not. Political petitioning was not, as has been claimed, an extension or revival of well-accepted principles of petitioning.[21] This, too, overlooks changes that violated traditional restrictions on expressions of grievance in petitions. What remains to be examined, then, are new uses for petitions in the English Revolution, when printed petitions became a means to constitute and invoke public opinion. This development opened up traditional restrictions on petitions, which had been subject to the same norms of secrecy and privilege that more generally regulated political discourse. Permissible expressions of grievance in traditional petitions had little in common with modern conceptions of the public sphere as a forum for free and open debate over conflicting political goals because the relevant traditions were those of a society where political conflict and factions were understood as deviant behavior.

During the English Revolution change in petitioning wrought by printing established a complex relationship between petitions and public opinion. Printed petitions represent individual opinions, yet they are also a tool for their manipulation. This complexity reflects the dual nature of public opinion as a nominal and real entity. Nominally, it is a discursive fiction; qua public opinion it collectively exists only when instantiated in political discourse. Yet real individuals participate in political discourse as writers, readers, subscribers, printers, and promoters. Like today's opinion polls, petitions are devices that mediate between nominal and real moments of public opinion. Thus, to assert that inno-

[18] Fletcher, *Outbreak of the Civil War*, p. 198, and see p. 283; Eales, *Puritans and Roundheads*, p. 130; Underdown, *Revel, Riot, and Rebellion*, p. 138.

[19] Brenner, *Merchants and Revolution*, pp. 368–74, 436–50, 471–79; Kishlansky, *Rise of New Model Army*, pp. 78–90, 277–78; Pearl, "London's Counter-Revolution"; Underdown, *Revel, Riot, and Rebellion*, pp. 228–29; Woolrych, *Soldiers and Statesmen*, pp. 24–25, 168–71.

[20] Skerpan, *Rhetoric of Politics*, p. 73.

[21] H. N. Brailsford, *The Levellers and the English Revolution* (London, 1976), p. 189; Pearl, *London and the Puritan Revolution*, pp. 173, 229–30; Wolfe, *Leveller Manifestoes*, p. 261.

vative uses of petitions led to the "invention" of public opinion in the English Revolution involves two claims. First, petitions are important as propaganda, at least in the minimal sense that contemporaries valued them as devices to influence the opinions of persons within and outside Parliament. Second, petitions are an indicator of opinions; that is, they have some connection to debates in civil society and are not merely literary inventions foisted upon an unsuspecting public. Having established these two points, we can then examine links between printing, the paradox of innovation, and a transformation in traditional petitioning that led to new practices and ideas that put appeals to public opinion at the core of politics.

PETITIONS AS POLITICAL PROPAGANDA

Unlike traditional petitions, petitions in the English Revolution were an important source of political propaganda. Their prevalence reflects their utility as devices intended by promoters to influence public opinion and to lobby king or Parliament. Most petitioners, a Royalist writer later conceded, "were loyal men, yet in this epidemical petitioning time, they were also seized with the petitioning disease."[22] So widespread was this disease in the 1640s and 1650s that it is possible to construct a bald narrative of key events in terms of petitions, which I provide for the benefit of readers who may be unfamiliar with the history related in the rest of this chapter.

When the Short Parliament met early in 1640, it received county petitions with two principal grievances: anti-Puritan innovation in religion and prerogative taxation. One scribal publication of parliamentary proceedings provided a partisan account of the impact of these petitions on the Commons: "This day the petitions [were] read of Middlesex, Suffolk, Northamptonshire, which petitions stunned the Royalists more than anything."[23] At the abrupt dissolution of that Parliament in May, Charles I imprisoned one member who refused a Crown request for petitions and complaints pending before the Committee for Religion.[24] Late that summer subsequent petitions—the Twelve Peers Petition and others, like one from London citizens, inspired by it—requested the king to summon another Parliament. Behind these petitions was the threat of further military action by the Scots, who, after occupying

---

[22] John Nalson, *An Impartiall Collection Of The Great Affairs of State* (*Wing* N106–7, 1682–83), 2:841.

[23] E. S. Cope and W. H. Coates, eds., *Proceedings of the Short Parliament* (*CS*, 4th ser., 19, 1977), p. 234.

[24] *CSPD* 1640, p. 142; *Rushworth* 3:1167–68.

England's northern borders on August 28, coordinated their petitions with those of their English allies. When the Long Parliament met, widespread agreement among members existed over the need for modest religious and political reforms (limiting the power of bishops; the necessity of parliamentary consultation in fiscal and foreign policy). Members, who subsequently divided along Royalist and Parliamentary lines, arrived and presented county petitions that recited extensively solicited grievances. "Grievances are canvassed to the purpose," wrote a young man to his uncle in Devonshire, "and likely to be redressed; if you have any in Devon, put them forward." The practice of sending representatives to the Long Parliament "with a formal agenda of grievances" was widespread but not novel. Earlier that year Newcastle promoters of a strident petition intended for the Short Parliament—it denounced monopolies and "innovation" in religion—defended it by observing that one of their newly elected representatives "wondered that no instructions were given to the burgesses for their proceedings."[25]

Consensus dissipated as subsequent petitions sided with the Long Parliament or Charles I on the issue of control over the militia and the future of the Church of England. Some petitions came forward with as many as twenty-thousand signatures, though most county petitions had between three thousand to seven thousand signatures. The text and timing of some of these petitions in the early 1640s reflected the tactical plans of Pym and other managers of the Long Parliament. Both petitions and the plans behind them were objects of commentary by interested observers outside Parliament. On November 30, 1640, a west country minister received a letter with a copy of a clerical petition from Derbyshire ministers, a Wiltshire petition, rumors on contents of one from Lancashire, and the remark, "There is working in all parts, petition upon petition . . . presented to the Parliament . . . those liked best that fly highest."[26] In the winter of 1642–43 rival petitions for peace and war policies delineated the hardening positions of Royalists and Parliamentarians. Extensive approving reports of the peace petitions appeared in the first issue of the Royalist newspaper *Mercurius Aulicus*.[27] Petitions in the spring and summer of 1643 signaled the beginnings of an Independent faction, whose opposition to increasingly conservative Presbyterian policies led to competitive petition campaigns.[28] One by Presbyterians

[25] W. Trevelyan and C. Trevelyan, eds., *Trevelyan Papers III* (*CS*, os, 105, 1872), pp. 196–97; *CSPD* 1639–40, p. 603. For the initial consensus in Parliament, see John Morrill, *The Nature of the English Revolution* (New York, 1993), p. 4.

[26] *MSS Tanner* 65, fol. 209.

[27] *MA* 1:20–23.

[28] Unless employed in an explicitly religious context (e.g., Presbyterian discipline, Independent churches), the terms Presbyterian and Independent refer to political factions. These religious and political commitments did not always coincide.

in January 1646 "marked the opening of the great City campaign that determined the future course of the toleration controversy." Another in December 1646 "set off the chain of events that resulted in the final split with the army and, ultimately, the army's invasion of London in the summer of 1647."[29]

Attacks on the right of soldiers to petition Parliament politicized the New Model Army and prompted it into action, initially to rescue Parliament from a 1647 coup in London and, subsequently, to expel moderates from Parliament, in Pride's Purge, and demand execution of the king. In 1648, a letter of intelligence to Edward Hyde reports that "all counties will be set to appear in person with their petitions at Westminster, as they [the Puritans] did at the beginning of the Parliament [in 1640], which course did . . . give a great stroke to the benefit of that faction, & will conduce as much . . . now to the good of his Majesty." This refers to a petition campaign that galvanized growing hostility to Parliamentary absolutism and a resurgence of popular Royalism into an abortive counterrevolution that sealed the fate of Charles I.[30] During these years, a radical Leveller program emerged, the cumulation of ceaseless petitioning that increasingly focused on the unwillingness of Parliament to receive Leveller petitions. The commonwealth established by the execution of Charles I ended when Cromwell dissolved the purged (Rump) Parliament. In events leading to the dissolution, an August 1652 petition from the Council of Officers for radical legal, religious, and political reforms "is a key document, since eight months later Cromwell and the officers were able to justify their dissolution of the Rump largely because so little action had been taken on it."[31] Abolition of mandatory tithes was an especially contentious issue in commonwealth politics, which inspired rival petition campaigns between sectarian radicals and moderates who preserved the old Puritan vision of a comprehensive national church. Subsequent petition campaigns facilitated the fall of the Protectorate and the recall of the Rump Parliament.[32] In 1660, county petitions for assembling an unpurged Parliament rained down on General Monck as he marched his army to London and set in motion events leading toward the restoration of the Stuart monarchy.

The prominence of petitions in the English Revolution reflects the importance that contemporaries attached to them. As political propaganda, their utility for political leaders and activists derived in part

---

[29] Tolmie, *Triumph of the Saints*, p. 131; Brenner, *Merchants and Revolution*, p. 478; and see Pearl, "London's Counter-Revolution."

[30] *MSS Clarendon* 30, fol. 207; and see Ashton, *Counter-Revolution*, chap. 4.

[31] Austin Woolrych, *Commonwealth to Protectorate* (Oxford, 1982), p. 40.

[32] Austin Woolrych, "Last Quest for a Settlement, 1657–1660," in Aylmer, *The Interregnum*, pp. 189–92.

from the fact that petitions were objects of debate, curiosity, and commentary. Evidence on this is hardly conclusive, but what exists reveals widespread popular interest in petitions and petitioners. In London this was heightened by processions that took a petition to Parliament, sometimes accompanied by fleets of coaches or mounted riders. For petitions from a county, delivery in Parliament was the end point of a process that often began at assize sessions, where bitter debates might occur over petitions presented in open court to the grand jury for formal endorsement.[33] Perceptions of unprecedented popular participation in petitioning also heightened interest. In 1642, well before political petitioning had fully developed, one observer thought that "no time nor history can show that such great numbers of oppressed subjects of all sorts ever petitioned." This statement refers, in part, to a petition presented to the Commons by London's porters. Inside and outside Parliament, observers remarked on the "extraordinary nature" of this petition, from "the lowest and inferior sort of the people in the City," who "coming in [Westminster], all with white towels over their shoulder, delivered a petition with 1500 hands." The popular dimension of petitioning was among the providential signs that a godly London artisan, Nehemiah Wallington, saw in this and many other petitions delivered in to Parliament in January and February 1642. He recorded them in his diary "for the generations to come, that they may see and behold what our God has done in the stirring up the people of all counties, and of all sorts, high and low, rich and poor, of both sexes . . . that go up to Westminster . . . with their petitions."[34] The same sense of novelty also attaches to petitioners from the other side. A hostile report on a Cornwall petition that stridently upheld Royal prerogative and the established liturgy describes how a Cornwall cleric "solicited hedgers at the hedge, plowmen at the plow, threshers in the barns."[35] Satirical petitions mocked popular support for the Long Parliament from women, the insane, and, in one satire, "infants, babies and sucklings," who, observing that "all sorts of people . . . all degrees and conditions have petitions" before Parliament, so we "have therefore thought good, and according to our infantile understandings, to present to your grave consideration, these few lines." Among the satires recorded by the Royalist, anti-Puritan author of a commonplace book are references to cobblers, shoemakers, weavers, chandlers, and porters who signed a petition for religious reform because, in the words of the fictive peti-

[33] Woods, *Prelude to Civil War, MSS Clarendon* 31, fols. 37v–38.

[34] D. Gardiner, ed., *The Oxinden Letters* (London, 1937), p. 286; *PJ* 1:259, 265; *HMC Cowper*, p. 306; Nehemiah Wallington, *Historical Notices of Events Occurring in the Reign of Charles I*, ed. R. Bentley (London, 1869), 2:14.

[35] *The Buller Papers* (privately printed, 1895), p. 33; the petition is 669f4.[64] (1642).

tion's promoter, "we are not able to see great difference twixt a church & stable."[36]

Even before printing of petitions became a routine tactic in partisan politics—after Charles I's ill-fated attempt to seize five members of the Long Parliament on January 5, 1642—frequent references to petitions appear in letters and diaries in 1640 and 1641.[37] Keen interest in petitions appears in diaries kept by the London artisan Nehemiah Wallington, who compiled a numbered list of nearly one hundred petitions to Parliament between 1640 and 1642.[38] Diarists and letter writers in 1642 acknowledged the high stakes wagered by Kent petitioners who, at the spring assizes, promoted a petition that openly challenged key positions of the Long Parliament on religious and political issues.[39] In addition, surviving evidence provides tantalizing hints about the care with which petitions might be read. Some did this in order to uncover clues about the origins or true purpose of a petition. A newsletter in April 1642 reports that the king in York received a supportive petition and that the king "after gives an answer, both so concurring as if, some say, it was made by consent of parties." Another notes similarities in the Twelve Peers Petition and two petitions from the Scots. In the rise of factional politics three years later, petitions advancing the agenda of religious Presbyterians were subjected to such scrutiny. Amidst debates over an abortive Presbyterian petition circulating in London in September 1645, D'Ewes observed that "the petition was so cunningly penned as that it was not doubted but some of the Assembly [of Divines] had a hand in it." "Contrived by some Presbyterians" was Whitelock's appraisal of a subsequent Presbyterian petition in November.[40] Contemporaries were more likely to accord a petition only a causal reading if they thought it parroted grievances in other petitions. Observers in and outside of Parliament referred complacently to the repetitive qualities in

[36] *MSS Ashmole* 830, fol. 294; *MSS Rawl* poet 71, p. 21; and see E180[17] 1641; E404[30] 1647.

[37] *HMC Beaulieu*, pp. 129, 131, 134–35, *HMC Cowper*, pp. 272, 278, *HMC De L'Isle* 6:311, 332–33, 349, 371; *HMC Various Collections* 1903, 2:257–58; *HMC Egmont* 1905, 1:120; *MSS Tanner* 63, fols. 32, 43; *Tanner* 65, fol. 209; *Tanner* 66, fol. 181; Simonds D'Ewes, *Autobiography and Correspondence* (London, 1845), 2:242–43; M. A. E. Green, ed., *The Diary of John Rous* (CS, os, 66, 1856), pp. 91–94; T. Lewis; ed., *Letters of the Lady Brilliana Harley* (CS, os, 58, 1854), pp. 111, 113–14, 121; D. Parsons, ed., *The Diary of Sir Henry Slingsy* (London, 1836), pp. 56, 57, 66–67.

[38] Wallington, *Historical Notices*, 2:14–19.

[39] *MSS. Rawls* D141, pp. 25–26; *HMC Beaulieu*, p. 150–51; *HMC* Buccleuch, p. 295; *Letters of Brilliana Harley*, pp. 158; B. Schofield, ed., *The Knyvett Letters, 1620–1644* (*Norfolk Record Society* 20, 1949), p. 101; *Trevelyan Papers* 3:217.

[40] *HMC Beaulieu*, p. 148; *CSPD* 1640–41, p. 62; *MSS Harl* 166, fol. 265; Whitelock, *Memorials* 1:537.

county petitions in 1642, which, in news accounts and parliamentary diaries, are often described as "tending to the same effect" as ones previously presented.[41] But contemporaries were quick to remark on strong language, challenges to parliamentary authority, and strident demands in petitions. An unusually assertive passage in one county petition in 1642, a January 25 petition that Hertford petitioners proposed to send to the Lords, startled MPs because it reprimanded the House of Lords for "want of compliance by this honorable house with the House of Commons." "God's wounds, here is a petition indeed," remarked one MP. Others noted that the Hertford petition to the Lords had "not only what was expressed in their petition to this House but other particulars also, and that in too broad and plain terms."[42] Petitions from groups whose participation in politics was novel, such as the one from porters cited above, predictably attracted attention. By far the longest entry in a journal of political events from the end of the Charles I's personal rule up to 1644, kept by a Kent diarist, is a copy of a report in the *Kingdomes Weekly Intelligencer* of women petitioners for peace, who, on August 8, 1643, descended on Westminster after the Commons rejected peace proposals put forward by the other House, and returned the next day for a demonstration that ended in a violent fray with soldiers.[43]

Popular interest in petitions was not limited to persons who were able to read them. Petitions were read aloud and discussed in the same public places where oral, scribal, and printed news circulated, in churches, inns, and taverns,[44] often in conjunction with efforts to obtain signatures or marks. The assembling of parishioners on Sundays was a resource for these efforts, as was the parochial authority of clerics. All sides sought to enlist the pulpit to marshal support for petitions and thereby to persuade parishioners to sign petitions or assent to inclusion of their names on lists of supporters.[45] One Sunday in 1641, members of the Cathedral clergy in Chester announced "that there was something more to be done than reading of prayers." One cleric described the current Puritan petition campaign that aimed at abolishing the established liturgy, "to prevent which danger the nobility and gentry of this county have drawn a petition." Then the petition was read, and all who "had received any

---

[41] E201[23] (1642), p. 5, and see p. 2; *PJ* 2:2, 6, 23, 32, 38, 46.

[42] E133[15] (1642), p. 2; *PJ* 1:161, 171; and see *HMC Cowper*, p. 304. See *PJ* 1:402, where D'Ewes notes that a Sussex petition to the Lords, (E134[35], 1642), delivered along with one to the Commons on February 17, 1642, was unlike others in requesting that imprisoned bishops be denied bail.

[43] *MSS Rawl* D141, pp. 129–31; *Kingdomes Weekly Intelligencer*, August 8–15 (E65[11], 1643); Higgins, "The Reactions of Women," pp. 190–96.

[44] E.g., *MSS Tanner* 63, fol. 22.

[45] See Fletcher, *Outbreak of Civil War*, pp. 195–96.

benefit by [the Book of Common Prayer]" were asked to come "to the communion table and subscribe to the petition." Some left without signing and were challenged by a prebend who "asked the people what they meant to go out" when "most of the best of the city has subscribed to it."[46] In the winter of 1642–43, when "peace" and "war" petitions respectively delineated Royalist and Parliamentarian positions, an Essex cleric on Sunday "after he had read common prayer, . . . said unto the people there assembled, I will read to you the petition for peace, and the King's answer to it, & so began to read the scandalous petition." At this time another Essex cleric explained why he parted company with Stephen Marshall and other ministers who preached support for Parliament: to remain on good terms "I must turn my pulpit into Mount Ebal, and curse . . . all persons of what rank soever that have set their hands to the petition for peace."[47] After the emergence of factional politics in 1645, Presbyterian and Independent petitions received support from sermons whose delivery was coordinated with the drive to gain subscriptions. For a London Presbyterian petition in January 1646 "there was a sermon in every ward."[48] The other faction used Independent churches as organizational nodes for its petition campaigns. After Leveller petitions were burned on a Saturday in May 1647, a letter of intelligence to Hyde reports, "The next day . . . there was a sermon in Coleman Street [an Independent stronghold], a very passionate exhortation persuading the people to remain firm to the cause and to sign another petition of the like nature."[49]

As propaganda, petitions had different political objectives. Contemporaries saw propaganda value in petitions for influencing opinion outside Westminster. This development, as we shall see later in this chapter, was intimately linked to the printing of petitions, and it had profound implications for innovations in the content of political discourse. Well-founded presuppositions about popular interest in and access to petitions lay behind their use as political propaganda intended by all sides as an appeal to public opinion. Commentary on printed petitions sometimes referred to concerns with how a petition fared "with the people" and not just with Parliament,[50] especially in allegations that activists,

[46] MSS Nalson 13, fol. 66.

[47] Harold Smith, The Ecclesiastical History of Essex (London, 1932), pp. 85–86, probably referring to 669f.6[102] 1643; Edward Symmons, A Loyal Subjects Beliefe (E103[6], 1643), p. 62. Allegations about promotion of 1643 "peace" petitions appear in some parish petitions against "malignant" clerics. MSS Add 15672, fol. 10v; MSS Rawl D924, fols. 191, 193.

[48] MSS Williams 24.50, fol. 56v.

[49] MSS Clarendon 20. fol. 227v; and see Tolmie, Triumph of the Saints, pp. 144–72.

[50] John Tilsley, A true Copie of the Petition . . . of Lancashire (E352[3], 1646), p.8; and see Kingdomes Weekly Intelligencer, August 8–15, 1642, p. 227.

Royalist and Leveller alike, sought to to influence public opinion by presenting deliberately provocative petitions.[51]

Political leaders in Parliament used petitions to create the appearance of support for their policies. Like other printed political texts, petitions added new dimensions to the legislative maneuvering of political elites. Coordination of proceedings in Parliament and petitioning, often culminating in a timely procession of citizens bearing the petition to Westminster, was a political art practiced to perfection by John Pym. He also surreptitiously provided copies of petitions and his oratory on them to printers, who published pamphlets that advertised Pym's political prominence. This occurred in 1641[52] and again in 1642, when plans to wrest control of the militia from Charles confronted obstacles in the Lords, where only a third of the lay peers supported this move. The Commons then voted for a conference with the Lords on January 25 to take up "the London Petition, this day received, and other petitions from other counties." The "bitter" Hertfordshire petition that startled members for rebuking the Lords "for want of compliance" with the lower House also arrived that very day. At the conference, Pym read these and two other petitions, from Essex and Middlesex, as further evidence in support of arguments for ejecting popish and "malignant" Lords and for putting the kingdom in a posture of war by establishing parliamentary control over the militia. Pym's management of the conference extended to preparations for printing his speech and the petitions, which apeared in multiple editions.[53]

Insiders understood the propaganda value in this political use of petitions. In 1641 a massive petition from London citizens aided efforts in the Commons to overcome resistance in the other House to proceeding against Strafford by a bill of attainder. "The earl has many friends in the Lords, reported an MP on April 17. "To balance the Lords there is a petition preparing in the City with 20,000 or 30,000 hands subscribed." On the twenty-fourth the Commons received the petition with 20,000 signatures; five days later another MP wrote, "The London petition for expedition of justice is transmitted by us to the Lords, with a special enforcement of our own; upon which they have read the bill of attainder twice."[54] Pym's promotion of popular petitioning to ram leg-

---

[51] *A Narrative And Declaration Of the Dangerous ... Petitioning* (E446[25], 1648), p. 5; *The Declaration of the Well-Affected Non-Subscribers* (E453[17], 1648), p. 4; [John Price], *Wallwins Wiles* (1649), in Haller and Davies, *Leveller Tracts*, pp. 307–8; William Walwyn, *Walwyns Just Defence* (1649), in Haller and Davies, *Leveller Tracts*, p. 357.

[52] Joad Raymond, *The Invention of the Newspaper* (Oxford, 1996), pp. 108–9.

[53] *CJ* 2:394; *PJ* 1:164–65; Russell, *The Fall of the British Monarchies* (Oxford, 1991), pp. 468–9; John Pym, *A Speech Delivered At A Conference* (E200[21], 1642); *A true Copie of the Master-Piece Of all those Petitions* (E134[7], 1642); and see below, n. 105.

[54] *HMC Cowper*, p. 278; *MSS Osborn* fb. 94, no. 7.

islation past recalcitrant legislators inspired promoters of partisan petition campaigns in the middle of the decade. Presbyterian members of
London's Common Council produced drafts of petitions in 1647 and
1648 that they proposed to send to Parliament along with supportive
petitions from Presbyterian citizens that called upon the Common
Council to take this step.[55]

Petitioning also had propaganda value as a metaphor that facilitated
creative redescription of political violence. This could represent ungodly
rebellion in a favorable light. A devout Puritan woman, Lady Lucy
Hutchinson, described Scottish soldiers who invaded England in 1640
as frustrated petitioners: they "forced their way, after they had been refused to pass quietly by them [the king's opposing army] with their petitions in their hands." This logic reappears in the claim that Charles I had
not been driven from London in 1642 by unruly mobs; "it is manifest to
the contrary, for they went in a petitionary way, no law being to hinder
or prevent petitioners." Later in the decade, Presbyterians used this
logic to justify popular riots that propelled the abortive summer coup in
London in 1647, and the next year Royalists used it to describe counter-
revolutionary initiatives—for example, riotous behavior of Surrey petitioners—as the actions of frustrated petitioners, debarred from exercis-
ing hereditary rights by tyrants in Westminster.[56] Contemporaries were
not oblivious to the rhetorical trick in this redescription of political violence. They knew that petitioning could be an opening ritual in violent
confrontation, and a petition a disguise that put a deferential face on
demands that were factious or seditious.[57] This charge confronted Royalist petitioners for peace in the winter of 1642–43 and, later, John
Lilburne and other Leveller advocates of radical reform in religion, politics, and law."[58] Mutiny as the true design behind an episode of petitioning was often alleged during the Royalist counterrevolution of
1648. That year the Commons received a report on a Royalist mutiny in
Norwich, precipitated by Parliament's summons to its disaffected mayor
to come to London: "the ground of the business was a petition . . . to

[55] *MSS JCC* 40, fols. 236, 278v–279.

[56] Lucy Hutchinson, *Memoirs of the Life of Colonel Hutchinson* (Oxford, 1973), p. 50;
E86[4] (1642), p. 3; and see E16[10] (1644), p. 2; *The Case of the Impeached Lords, Commons, and Citizens* (E423[16], 1648), p. 7; E445[3] (1648), pp. 4–5; *An Impartiall Narration Of The . . . Late Kentish Petition* (E453[37], 1648), pp. 1–2; 669f.12[27],
[33],[34] (1648).

[57] Rebels in the Pilgrimage of Grace called their demands to Henry VIII petitions; see
L&P 12, pt. 1, nos. 44, 137, 370. James I denounced MPs who promoted parliamentary
privilege at the expense of his prerogative powers, "all of which they covered with . . . the
fair pretense of a dutiful petition." *His Majesties Declaration, Touching his proceedings in
the late . . . Parliament* (STC 9241, 1622) p. 5 and see p. 7.

[58] E245[24] (1643), p. 2; *A Declaration Of Some Proceedings of Lt. Col. John Lilburn*
(E427[6], 1648), p. 19.

the honorable House of Commons for the mayor's stay; but it seems the end was, by raising a force, thereby to make him stay. So the petition prayed; the multitude enforced . . . they were both birds of the same feather."[59]

Given the diverse uses of petitions as propaganda both within and outside the walls of Parliament, we can readily understand the attention to petitions given by political leaders. In intelligence reports sent to Hyde, we can follow the course of petition campaigns in events leading to the abortive Presbyterian coup in 1647 and the Royalist uprising of 1648.[60] The strategic importance attributed to petitions also appears in efforts to suppress those from political adversaries. On all sides this involved fine political calculation as well as brute force. Informed in September 1640 that citizens would soon present a London petition requesting the king to summon a Parliament, Charles I responded irritably to suggestions that he imprison its presenters when they arrived to see him in York, noting in the margin of a memo from his Council in London, "I could wish ye would show as much stoutness there as you counsel me to here." The next year the king requested London's mayor to suppress the anti-Strafford petition then circulating in the city, with instructions to "have a care to do that secretly as of himself, and not by any command from his Majesty." These issues also shaped political tactics by the king's adversaries in the Commons who were no more desirous than was Charles to appear publicly as an obstructor of the right to petition. That year a member of the Commons observed, "All art is used to keep petitions for episcopacy from being presented to the House."[61] In 1643 Presbyterian leaders enlisted an Independent cleric, Philip Nye, to work discreetly to quash radical plans to petition against the Solemn League and Covenant, which allied England with Scottish Presbyterianism. No trace of this appears in the official records of Parliament, but, not surprisingly, it is reported in *Mercurius Aulicus*.[62] Members of Parliament were often at the center of efforts to stop petitions. After Somerset representatives reported in June 1642 on a strident Royalist petition that was gathering signatures, Denzil Holles prompted the Commons to summon the petition's promoters as delinquents. In 1647 the Wiltshire County Committee asked Holles for instructions on suppressing a radi-

[59] Henry Cary, *Memorials of the Great Civil War* (London, 1842), 1:401; and see *A Narrative and Declaration* (E446[25], 1648); E475[24] (1648), pp. 4.

[60] *MSS Clarendon* 29, fols. 68, 72, 158, 161, 165, 227, 263; *Clarendon* 31, fols. 37v–38, 43, 56, 73, 77v, 77v 79v, 80, 83v, 85v 88, 99.

[61] *State Papers Collected by Edward, Earl of Clarendon* (Oxford, 1767), 2:117; *CSPD 1640–44*, p. 538; *HMC Cowper* 2:295.

[62] B. M. Gardiner, ed., *A Secret Negotiation with Charles the First, 1643–1644* (CS, ns, 31, 1883), pp. 5–6; *MA* 2:55–56.

cal petition. That year the House sent Essex members home to forestall a strident anti-army petition; and the County Committee in Essex was pleased with the news on plans to disband the Army because it would remove all cause for "complaint or petition." The committee promised Westminster that it would relay the news "to gentlemen and freeholders now at this time at the assizes"—a likely site for framing petitions. Next year, the Commons sent Surrey and Kent members to their counties, but they were unable to carry out instructions for stopping Royalist petitions for a treaty between Parliament and the king.[63]

PETITIONS AS INDICATORS OF OPINION IN THE PERIPHERY

Only part of the complex relationship between petitions and public opinion appears when we examine petitions as propaganda intended to manipulate public opinion. As propaganda, petitions nominally constitute public opinion as a means to influence the real opinions of individuals. But how important is the reverse movement? Do petitions have tangible links to opinions held at the individual level? Do they represent discussion and debate in civil society or are they merely literary productions, with no discernible relation to a public sphere? Answers to these questions require assessment of the importance of manipulation and outright deceit in practices that led to the framing, signing, and printing of petitions.

Manipulation and deceit were topics of contemporary speculation on petitioners as unwitting tools to further a hidden agenda. "A fair opportunity had the great ones to work their ends over other men's shoulders" is a skeptical view of the favorable reception accorded by Parliament for the 1642 petition from London's lowly porters.[64] *Mercurius Aulicus* charged that the war party in the Commons had allocated the lowly role of stooge to citizen petitioners in London; Levellers argued that the "malignant" faction in the House put London's Common Council in this role. Accommodation petitions to Parliament were "first contrived and plotted by themselves, and then cunningly laid to be acted in Common Councils."[65] The "element of charade" that a historian discerns in some county petitions in the early 1640s was also noted by contemporaries. After the king's failed attempt to arrest five Parliamentary leaders in January 1642, the first petition to protest this move came

[63] *LJ* 5:133–34; *PJ* 3:72; *MSS Tanner* 58, fol. 50; *CJ* 1646–48, pp. 130, 134, 563.

[64] *Persecutio Undecima* ([1648]1681), p. 3.

[65] *MA* 1:392; *Londons New Colours displaid* (E452[21], 1648), p. 2; and see *A Petition Presented . . . By the Royal Party in Sussex* (E522[38], 1648), p. 5

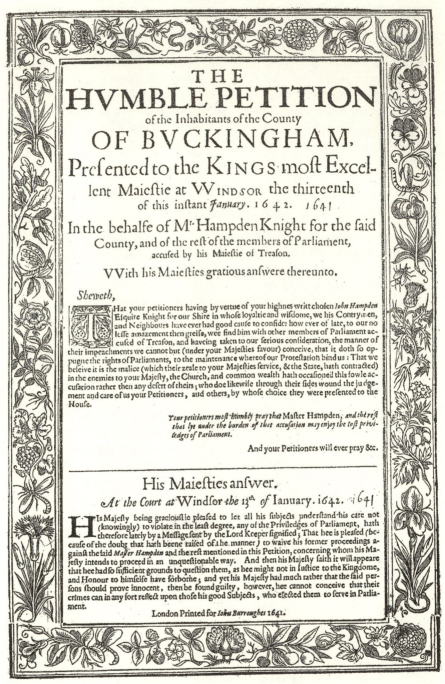

THE HVMBLE PETITION

of the Inhabitants of the County

OF BVCKINGHAM,

Prefented to the KINGS moſt Excellent Maieſtie at WINDSOR the thirteenth
of this inſtant *January*. 1 6 4 2. 1641

In the behalfe of Mr Hampden Knight for the ſaid
County, and of the reſt of the members of Parliament,
accuſed by his Maieſtie of Treaſon.

VVith his Maieſties gratious anſwere thereunto.

Sheweth,

THat your petitioners having by vertue of your highnes writt choſen *Iohn Hampden*
Eſquire Knight for our Shire in whoſe loyaltie and wiſdome, we his Contrymen,
and Neighbours have ever had good cauſe to confide: how ever of late, to our no
leſſe amazement then greiſe, wee find him with other members of Parliament accuſed of Treaſon, and haveing taken to our ſerious conſideration, the manner of
their impeachments we cannot but (under your Majeſties favour) conceive, that it doth ſo op-
pugne the rights of Parliaments, to the maintenance whereof our Proteſtation bind us : That we
beleive it is the malice (which their zeale to your Majeſties ſervice, & the State, hath contracted)
in the enemies to your Majeſty, the Church, and common wealth hath occaſioned this fowle accuſation rather then any deſert of theirs ; who doe likewiſe through their ſides wound the judgement and care of us your Petitioners, and others, by whoſe choice they were preſented to the
Houſe.

> *Your petitioners moſt humbly pray that Maſter Hampden, and the reſt
that lye under the burden of that accuſation may enjoy the Inſt priviledges of Parliament.*

And your Petitioners will ever pray &c.

His Maieſties anſwer.

At the Court at Windſor *the* 13th *of* Ianuary. 1642. 1641

HIs Majeſty being graciouſlie pleaſed to let all his ſubjects underſtand his care not
(knowingly) to violate in the leaſt degree, any of the Priviledges of Parliament, hath
therefore lately by a Meſſage ſent by the Lord Keeper ſignified ; That hee is pleaſed (be-
cauſe of the doubt that hath beene raiſed of the manner) to waive his former proceedings a-
gainſt the ſaid *Maſter Hampden* and the reſt mentioned in this Petition, concerning whom his Majeſty intends to proceed in an unqueſtionable way. And then his Majeſty ſaith it will appeare
that hee had ſo ſufficient grounds to queſtion them, as hee might not in Iuſtice to the Kingdome,
and Honour to himſelfe have forborne ; and yet his Majeſty had much rather that the ſaid per-
ſons ſhould prove innocent, then be found guilty, however, hee cannot conceive that their
crimes can in any ſort reflect upon thoſe his good Subjects, who elected them to ſerve in Parliament.

London Printed for *Iohn Burroughes* 1641.

Fig. 12. The first petition from the counties that protested the attempt
by Charles I to seize five members of Parliament in January 1642.

from Buckingham (see fig. 12). Skepticism greeted presenters who averred that, in conformity to traditional strictures on petitions, their petition was a spontaneous reaction to events; they were "not counseled thereto by any but hurried along with apprehensions of the dangers this honorable house was in." D'Ewes observed that the petition was already in print. Whitelock "did dislike this manner of petitioning," despite his support for the five leaders, suspecting that one of the five—John Hampden, a Buckingham MP—had orchestrated its promotion. Later that year, one organizer of the infamous Kent Petition of 1642, Sir Roger Twysden, met Sussex petitioners on the road, traveling with a county petition, who, he claimed, knew nothing about their petition: "the petition was framed already in town."[66]

Contemporaries underscored the danger of taking petitions at face value as indicators of local opinion in references to "parrot" petitions, local petitions that reiterated the substance of a London petition. Though Royalists used this tactic, parrot petitions were usually associated with the other side, as in the following cynical verse:

> Though set forms of prayer be abomination
> Set forms of petitions find great approbation.[67]

The most well known example of this is the 1640 Root and Branch Petition from London, whose call for sweeping Puritan reforms in religion set the agenda for subsequent county petitions. In presenting one from Kent in January 1641, Edward Dering, a prominent Kent MP, remarked that "if it were not the spawn of the London petition," it was "a parrot taught to speak . . . by rote calling for Root and Branch." Later, this charge was raised against Independent and Presbyterian petitions.[68] But historians point out that coordination per se "does not necessarily prove that a particular petition had no local support."[69] Coordination might impose national political perspectives on petitions from localities where opinion was insular and unideological. But the opposite also occurred, when a petition concealed sharp views at the local level that were

---

[66] Fletcher, *Outbreak of the Civil War*, p. 194; *PJ* 1:36; *The Diary of Bulstrode Whitelocke* (London, 1990), p. 130; "Sir Roger Twysden's Journal," *Archaeologia Cantiana* 1 (1858): 201. Twysden may have been referring to the two petitions from Sussex (E134[35], (1642) presented on February 17.

[67] *MSS Rawl* poet 62, fol. 51; for Royalist use of a London petition as a template for ones at the local level, see *MSS Clarendon* 29, fol. 72.

[68] Edward Dering, *A Collection of Speeches* (E197[1], 1641), p. 9; and see *A New Birth Of The City Remonstrance* (E350[12], 1646), p. 3; Tilsley, *A true Copie* (E352[3], 1646), p. 13.

[69] David Underdown, "'Honest' Radicals in the Countryside," in D. Pennington and K. Thomas, eds., *Puritans and Revolutionaries* (Oxford, 1978), pp. 195–96; and see Lindley, *Popular Politics and Religion*, pp. 153–54; Russell, *Fall of the British Monarchies*, p. 108.

inconvenient for political leaders in Parliament. The case of Dering and the Kent petition is instructive. In presenting it to Parliament, Dering boasted, "I dealt with the presenters thereof . . . until (with their consent) I reduced it to less than a quarter of its former length, and taught it a new and more modest language." His "modest" version substituted bland remarks on the countenancing of papists, entirely unobjectionable to the main body of opinion within and outside Parliament, for specific references in the original petition to highly contentious religious issues (e.g., predestination), moderated its vitriolic anticlericalism, and omitted a passage that denied the king to be above the law.[70] *Mercurius Aulicus* reported in 1643 that the Common Council in London ordered that a citizens' petition for more active prosecution of the war "be reviewed for the amendment of some expressions which could not but seem scandalous unto themselves." This was not the last time that the Council moderated citizens' petitions before sending them on to Parliament.[71] Leaders of the New Model Army moderated grievances in regimental petitions when they consolidated them in one master petition in 1647. And, in 1652, Cromwell revised a petition from the Council of Officers so that it merely echoed prior pledges of the Rump Parliament and did not insist that MPs name an early date for its dissolution.[72]

Though traditional patron-client relationships guided coordination between local activists and political leaders in Parliament, in petitioning this did not always work to imprint opinions from the center on petitions. Coordination facilitated sharp expression of local opinion in parish petitions that conveyed grievances over "malignant" clerics. These petitions were organized by local activists under the direction of prominent members in the Long Parliament, such as Harley, Dering, Barrington, and D'Ewes. A Hereford justice of the peace wrote to Harley for instructions on handling local complaints about a malignant cleric: "I am advised to prefer a petition unto the Parliament against him, and to that purpose have sent my man to solicit the business, if you think necessary."[73] Among the Essex papers of Barrington is a draft of a parish

[70] Dering, *Speeches* (E197[1], 1641), p. 9; and cf. 669f.4[9] (1641) and L. B. Larking, ed., *Proceedings, Principally in the County of Kent, in Connection with the Parliaments called in 1640* (CS, os, 80, 1862), pp. 30–33.

[71] *MA* 1:194. In December 1646 the London Common Council prepared a petition that, like many from that body, justified this step by enclosing prior citizens' petitions to the Council. The committee charged with the task of drafting the Common Council petition was "to alter, add or diminish . . . what they in their discretion should think requisite." *MSS JCC* 40, fol. 199v; *The Petition of the Lord Mayor of London and Common Councell* (E366[15], 1646), p. 2.

[72] Woolrych, *Soldiers and Statesmen*, p. 91; Woolrych, *Commonwealth to Protectorate*, pp. 41–42.

[73] *MSS Add* 70106, Kyrle to Harley [unfoliated]; see also *MSS Add* 70003, fol. 111; *MSS Stowe* 184, fol. 33.

petition with editorial revisions—for example, "they have ~~groaned~~ suffered"—and instructions for the parish activists: "You should do well to get as many hands to this petition as can be . . . & if you have heard the vicar or his curate preaching anything contrary to true doctrine, to agree upon the particulars among yourselves, that you may be able to prove it."[74] In view of subsequent proceedings, a quasi-juridical hearing before a sequestration committee that heard the testimony of witnesses, Barrington's advice seems sensible and should not be construed as an invitation for locals to commit perjury. Thus, directions flowed from the top down, but initiative in these matters came from below as well as above. When a complaint bogged down in Parliament, a local activist wrote to D'Ewes "to put you in mind of that petition and articles against the vicar of our parish, wherewith we have troubled you and you stand entrusted."[75]

In addition to the content of grievances in a petition, the issue of manipulation arises in connection with efforts to gather signatures to them. Here, too, appearances can be deceiving. Thousands of signatures on a petition might be a better indicator of the initiative and resources of its promoters than the extent of the petition's local support. Organizational initiative in rival petition campaigns between Royalists and Parliamentarians in the early 1640s enlisted the local gentry and clergy to act as whips, persuading tenants, parishioners, relatives, and servants to sign. Reinforcing suspicion of this possibility is the grouping of signatures by parish, with the resident cleric's name at the head of each group.[76] It is hardly surprising that allegations of fraud and deceit flew on both sides. Hyde claims that Puritan petitions for religious reform used a moderate text to get signatures that were subsequently appended to more radical petitions. Puritan activists said this about petitions from Cornwall and Chester that defended the established liturgy against "sectarian" proposals. Against one organized by Sir Thomas Aston it was said, "The hands of the men of Chester were not underwritten to this petition but to the subsequent brief declaration of the intent of the petition." Organizers of this petition responded with a parish petition whose signers affirmed their signatures.[77]

Few records shed light on individual decisions to sign a petition, so it is difficult to assess the relative weight of informed consent versus manipulation and coercion. References to popular debate and discussion over the merits of a petition are evidence that militates against the

---

[74] *MSS Egerton* 2651, fol. 98. [75] *MSS Harl* 383, fol. 199.

[76] Everitt, *Kent and the Great Rebellion*, p. 90; Fletcher, *Outbreak of the Civil War*, pp. 194–97; *Letters of Brilliana Harley*, p. 111.

[77] Edward Hyde, *The History of the Rebellion and Civil Wars in England* (Oxford, 1849), 1:286–87; *MSS Harl* 4931, fol. 118v; *MSS Add* 36913, fol. 131; *Buller Papers*, p. 31

supposition that little individual autonomy attended the signing of petitions. Laypersons sought advice from parish ministers, and newspapers and sermons advertised the readiness of clerics to discuss the merits of a petition then in circulation.[78] In addition, reports of conflict, resistance, and failed petitions indicate that ordinary persons did resist coercion by clerics and other local authorities. In 1642 a parishioner wrote to D'Ewes about efforts by his Isle of Ely vicar "to have my hand to a petition on the behalf of the bishops," claiming that the vicar "pressed me so far for my reasons of refusing, until some coarse language passed between us." In June of that year, an informant in Somerset reported a strident Royalist petition that "has been read in several places by the ministers in these towns" and was promoted by influential members of the Royalist gentry. He urged "that some way be thought on to nip this in the bud; for otherwise it will set us together by the ears. There are many earnestly for it, but as many violently against it." A few months earlier, a rumor that "prevails with the multitude" frustrated efforts by a local agent for Thomas Fairfax, a Yorkshire MP, to get signatures on a pro-Parliament petition. "I find the sense of the people poisoned with an opinion infused to them, that all who subscribe the petition, and none else, must contribute toward the maintaining of soldiers of the Trained Band." After the Yorkshire sheriff informed the Commons that the rumor spread among "divers country people of sundry towns," it voted to print a letter from the Speaker that denied the rumor, which, Fairfax's agent later reported, "had cooled the hot invectives against the Yorkshire petition."[79]

The context in which individuals encountered petitions in the 1640s was initially established by extant structures of civil society. Promoters of petitions organized their activities by wards, parishes, hundreds, and counties. They solicited signatures from potential subscribers in churches, taverns, inns, guild halls, and common councils and at quarter and assize sessions. In these venues rumors flowed, petitions were read, and their merits debated. Parish churches and assize sessions were crucial for petitions in the countryside. In London, wards were the organizational unit for the 1640 City Petition in support of the Twelve Peers Petition and the second London petition for religious reform in 1641,

---

[78] *Perfect Passages*, September 17–23 (E302[24], 1645), p. 380; Thomas Edwards, *Gangræna* (E323[2], 1646), p. 110; Thomas Ale, *A Brief narration of The truth* (E341[24], 1646), p. 3; *CJ* 5:436.

[79] *MSS Harl* 383, fol. 197; *LJ* 5:133–34; G. W. Johnson, ed., *The Fairfax Correspondence* (London, 1848), 2:377–79, 391; *MSS Tanner* 66, fols. 16, 293; see also *MSS Nalson* 13, fol. 66; Fletcher, *Outbreak of Civil War*, p. 289; *Oxinden Letters*, p. 232; *Perfect Occurrences*, March 30-April 27 (E529[21], 1649), p. 990; Underdown, *Pride's Purge*, p. 93.

for which local officials collected signatures in their own wards. Later this organization was used for Presbyterian petitions. For one in January 1646 clerical supporters provided a sermon in every ward; "all of them drove one & the same way."[80]

Yet even within these structures of everyday life, popular participation in London petitions made a decisive break with traditional practice. Petitions organized at the ward or parish level might bypass the mayor, aldermanic court, and common council—only they had authority to issue petitions on behalf of the City—and instead come forth in the name of the City's "inhabitants." The Privy Council complained about this development in London's 1640 petition that supported the Twelve Peers Petition "to which many hands . . . are endeavored to be gotten in the several wards. . . . And we cannot but hold it very dangerous and strange to have a petition framed in the name of the citizens, and endeavored to be signed in a way not warranted by the charters and customs of the City."[81] Leaders of an embryonic Royalist party subsequently advanced this criticism to oppose Parliament's endorsement of the mammoth Root and Branch Petition presented by London citizens on December 11, 1640. In urging the Commons to reject the petition and its Puritan agenda for religious reform, Digby, Hyde, and Falkland precipitated a long, contentious debate in February. Digby began by noting that he, too, disliked abuses in the exercise of clerical authority. If the petition followed tradition, he might pass over its excesses; if his colleagues intended "merely to make use of it as an index of grievances, I should wink at the faults of it." But novelty in its promotion was dangerous, an innovation in relations between governors and the governed that threatened the social order. Hence, Digby "looked upon it then with terror, as upon a comet, a blazing star raised and kindled out of the stench, out of the poisonous exhalation of a corrupted hierarchy." The petition was not from the City Corporation, "but from I know not what 15,000 Londoners" who presumptuously sought "to prescribe to a Parliament."[82] Digby's use of conventional imagery heard before in the Commons[83] underscored the popular innovation in petitioning that

---

[80] *MSS Williams* 24.50, fol. 56v, and see fol. 101v; 669f.10[41] (1645); Lindley, *Popular Politics and Religion*, p. 153; *MSS Nalson* 22, fol. 131; for the 1640 London Petition, see *MSS Add* 11045, fol. 121.

[81] *Rushworth* 3:1262.

[82] *The Third Speech Of The Lord George Digby* (E196[30], 1641), sig. A3v–4v, B2; *Rushworth* 4:170–72; *D'Ewes I*, pp. 334–40. See also Pearl, *London and the Puritan Revolution*, p. 214 n; for similar arguments about a 1641 petition from London citizens, see *CSPD 1641–43*, p. 191.

[83] In the campaign against Buckingham in 1626, Dudley Digges delivered a set speech on May 8, "comparing the Duke to a comet exhaled out of base & putrid matter," *MSS Harl* 383, fol. 32.

later was a central feature of factional politics. In 1646, citizens of London issued a petition in order to validate a prior petition from the municipal government! This reversal of traditional practice occurred in response to Independent allegations that the petition was "not the act of the City but of some few of the Common Council."[84] Similar developments occurred that year in Norwich, where, a decade before, a factious Puritan petition that opposed Bishop Wren's campaign against nonconformity split the municipal government and raised the same issue of representation cited by Digby for the Root and Branch Petition. "Although it be presented in the name of our corporation," complained one opponent to Wren, "not near half our aldermen" supported it. By 1646, Bishop Wren was gone, along with any pretense to unity among nonconformists. Now competing petitions from Independent and Presbyterian citizens actively lobbied the Common Council over proposed petitions from Norwich to Parliament.[85]

In these popular developments, private associations of individuals met in homes, inns, and sectarian congregations to debate and sign petitions. Growing reliance on printed information for organizing these petitions supplemented communicative contacts based on primary associations (e.g., residence, family). For example, in rival campaigns by petitioners for "peace" and "war" policies in the winter of 1642–43, opposing sides met in taverns and advertised meetings on small printed tickets posted in public places.[86] Petitioning in politics was now the organizational analogue to sectarianism in religion. Both the gathering of separatist congregations and petitioning cut across traditional residential affiliations of ward and parish, uniting individuals in voluntary organizations denominated by opinion.[87] Signatures to petitions from radical opponents of City Presbyterians were "gathered all about the suburbs . . . especially at conventicles and private meetings." Hostile and sympathetic accounts describe heated debates in private houses and taverns among religious and political Independents and Levellers over matters of principle and tactical issues, such as "different judgements for seasons of petitioning"—that is, whether it was tactically wise to proceed with a petition.[88] In this context, contemporaries invoked tradi-

---

[84] *The true Copy of a Petition* (669f.10[63], 1646).

[85] *MSS Tanner* 68, fol. 149v; *Vox Populi* (E352[7], 1646); *An Hue-And-Cry after Vox Populi* (E355[13], 1646); *Vox Norwici* (E358[4], 1646). On the 1636 petition, see John Evans, *Seventeenth-Century Norwich* (Oxford, 1979), pp. 91–94.

[86] *Certaine Informations*, January 23–30 (E86[35], 1643), p. 16; Pearl, *London and the Puritan Revolution*, pp. 233–34, 255; and see below, n. 117.

[87] Tolmie, *Triumph of the Saints*, pp. 139, 142.

[88] *Scotish Dove*, May 28–June 3 (E339[13], 1646), p. 676; *Walwyns Just Defence*, p. 351, and see pp. 352–53, 355; Thomas Edwards, *The Third Part of Gangræna*

tional claims for "our native right to meet together to frame and promote petitions" to justify activities that traditional norms of secrecy and privilege had proscribed as seditious faction.[89]

The point of departure for this development in petitioning was the encouragement given to mass petitioning by political elites, who saw this as a source of propaganda in the early 1640s. But when Levellers and army activists subsequently presented their petitions to Parliament, one member observed, "Petitions with multitudes of hands to them were now decried by those who formerly encouraged them."[90] In 1649, the Leveller leader Lilburne defended the many petitions undertaken by fellow radicals who merely "trod in the very path that they themselves (I mean both Parliament and Army) chalked out unto us," when, two years earlier, they impeached Presbyterian leaders "for traitors, for obstructing and prejudging of public petitions to the Parliament." Presbyterians advanced similar arguments. To defend their right to frame petitions that might discomfort those who wielded power, they cited the precedent of petitions from the army—these "had pleaded this to be the hereditary freedom of all subjects . . . freely to petition the Parliament without restraint"—and even earlier ones, "like those from the bishops and others in the beginning of this Parliament."[91] This was a common theme in attacks on the arbitrary authority of the county committee system and the army. An anti-army petition in 1648 cites the precedent of the petitioning at the beginning of the Long Parliament—it "gave a great stop to his Majesty's high proceedings against his subjects"—in order to justify "this our present petition . . . to make the like stoppage of such high proceedings from the subject against his Majesty." In 1658, promoters of the "good old cause," an abortive effort to rally support for parliamentary privilege and Puritan reform, defended their current petition campaign by asking, "Is this now become a crime? It was not accompted so in the time of the famous Long Parliament."[92]

(E368[5], 1646), p. [163]; George Masterson, *The Triumph Stain'd* (E426[18], 1648), pp. 9–10.

[89] [John Lilburne?], *A Lash for a Lyar* (E428[8], 1648), p. 12; see Edwards, *Gangræna* (E323[2], 1646), p. 44; *The Armies Petition* (E438[1], 1648), p. 7. West-country clubmen told Parliament that "their frequent meetings [were . . .] for no other end only . . . to represent their great grievances by this innocent & humble way of petition." *MSS Tanner* 60, fol. 196v.

[90] *Diary of Whitelocke*, p. 190.

[91] John Lilburne, *The Legal Fundamental Liberties of the People of England* (1649), in Haller and Davies, *Leveller Tracts*, p. 448; *The Case Of The Impeached Lords, Commons, And Citizens* (E423[16], 1648), p. 17; *The humble Petition Of The Inhabitants of Suffolke* (E377[4], 1647), pp. 1–2.

[92] *The Humble Petitions . . . of the Easterne Association* (E438[15], 1648), p. 13; *A True Copy Of A Petition* (E936[5], 1658), p. 7; see also E375[9] (1647), pp. 15, 17.

PETITIONS AND PRINTING

Popular developments in petitions during the English Revolution are inseparable from the connection to printing. From the adoption of printing in England until 1640, only a few petitions were printed. But after 1640 all sides quickly grasped the tactical importance of printing for publishing petitions as well as broadsides, declarations, pamphlets, and newspapers. For petitions, this development violated traditional rules that limited the expression of grievance to apolitical flows of information from the periphery to the political center of the nation. It also antiquated strictures against private meetings and the supposition that, for grievances on public issues, petitions ought to come from corporate entities, from municipal corporations and county assize sessions. By publicizing petitions, printing transformed them, orienting their production to readers of printed texts. In analyzing this development, we must distinguish between printing's impact on the *scope* and *content* of political communication in petitions. Printing facilitated greater access to petitions for readers and signers, and it transformed their content as petitions began to be used to place grievances before a public audience with the goal of influencing individual opinion about the merits of a broad political agenda.

The very act of printing signals their promoters' intent to increase the scope of communication in petitions. Printed petitions openly appealed to public opinion, unlike the traditional petition that conveyed grievance as a privileged form of communication from the periphery to the political center. This distinction underlies criticism of many petitions, such as a December 1642 peace petition, which, "though it were not delivered by any of the subscribers into the House, yet it was read there last week & is now in print." Earlier that year a Kent Royalist encountered petitioners on the road to London, who, he claimed, had a petition drawn up in London. "They were only to deliver it when it should be printed."[93] Acknowledging a break with tradition, a Royalist petition cites political necessity as the reason why, in 1648, it had been "published without . . . formal presentment to the Parliament." That year a hostile observer called attention to plans to print three thousand copies of a Leveller petition: "if it be a petition to the House, why is it printed and published to the people, before the presenting of it to the House?

---

[93] *MSS Tanner* 64, fol. 109; "Roger Twysden's Journal," p. 201. Lending credence to Twysden's report is the unusual demand in this Sussex petition (see above, n. 42). At the delivery of the Surrey petitions to Parliament, D'Ewes observed, "These will, I believe, be imprinted," *PJ* 1:402.

Is it to get the approbation of multitudes?"[94] If, indeed, "the approbation of the multitudes" was the goal, then printing was essential. Plans for a Presbyterian petition from London in 1646 included coordination of its printing and presentation to Parliament. "They had printed it the day before, & dispatched it by 3 o'clock in the afternoon, though they had not their answer until 7."[95]

Evidence of the intent to print petitions as an appeal to public opinion by putting them before an audience of readers is often explicit. It appears in a pamphlet that commends a July 1643 petition, the first manifesto of a nascent Independent party whose arguments would be "useful to the less knowing sort of men."[96] It also appears in the practice of printing copies of petitions for use in gathering signatures, often in a crude, unembellished edition, and then publishing another edition to the public at large (see figs. 13 and 14). This practice was followed by Royalists,[97] Presbyterians,[98] Independents,[99] and proponents of the "good old cause."[100] The printer of a 1649 Leveller petition, *The Second Part Of Englands New-Chaines Discovered*, used the same form for two title pages that differ only in one passage, one version directed to potential subscribers, the other to the reading public.[101] Other features of printed petitions also announce the intent to appeal to public opinion and not merely the petitioned authority. A petition from an Essex parish against their superstitious vicar was printed as a broadside, with a notice at the bottom, "To the Courteous Reader," that describes, for readers too dim to grasp the point, how this case supports the general proposition that "Prelates have been the original cause of all the divisions and schisms in the church" (see fig. 15). At the bottom of a broadside petition from Presbyterian inhabitants of a ward to their court moot is a notice that "like petitions were presented in other wards in London." It and the supportive petition it sought to elicit from the London Common Council were printed in one edition.[102]

Though supporters and leaders of the Long Parliament initiated the practice of rushing petitions into print, it was not limited to Puritans and Parliamentarians. The other side quickly became adept at this practice,

---

[94] *Humble Petitions of the Eastern Association*, p. 30; *Declaration of Some Proceedings*, p. 25.

[95] *MSS Williams* 24.50, fol. 79v.

[96] *Remonstrance Redivivus* (E61[21], 1643), sig. A2v.

[97] 669f.11[47] (1647); E518[11] (1647).

[98] 669f.10[58] (1647); 669f.10[63] (1647).

[99] 669f.12[63] (1648); E452[7] (1648); E452[38] (1648).

[100] 669f.20[71] (1657); E936[5] 1658.

[101] E548[16] (1649) is bound with both title pages.

[102] 669f.4[28] (1641); 669f.10[41] (1646); E316[20] (1646).

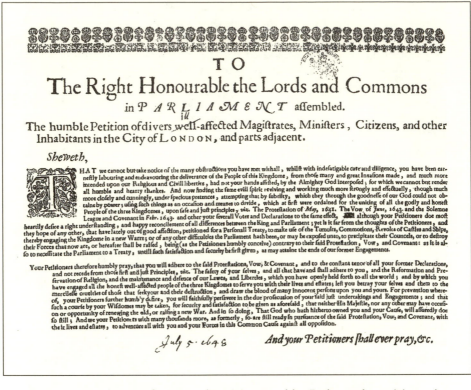

TO

The Right Honourable the Lords and Commons

in *PARLIAMENT* assembled.

The humble Petition of divers well-affected Magistrates, Ministers, Citizens, and other Inhabitants in the City of LONDON, and parts adjacent.

Sheweth,

THAT we cannot but take notice of the many obstructions you have met withall, whilst with indefatigable care and diligence, you have been earnestly labouring and endeavouring the deliverance of the People of this Kingdome, from those many and great Invasions made, and much more intended upon our Religious and Civill liberties, had not your hands assisted, by the Almighty God interposed; for which we cannot but render all humble and hearty thankes. And now finding the same evill spirit reviving and working much more strongly and effectually, though much more closely and cunningly, under specious pretences, attempting that by subtilty, which they through the goodnesse of our God could not obtaine by power; using such things as an occasion and meanes to divide, which at first were ordained for the uniting of all the godly and honest People of the three Kingdomes, upon safe and just principles; *viz.* The Protestation of *May*, 1641. The Vow of *June*, 1643. and the Solemne League and Covenant in *Febr.* 1643. and other your severall Votes and Declarations to the same effect, although your Petitioners doe most heartily desire a right understanding, and happy reconcilement of all differences between the King and Parliament; yet is it far from the thoughts of the Petitioners, and they hope of any other, that have lately out of good affection, petitioned for a Personall Treaty, to make use of the Tumults, Commotions, Revolts of Castles and Ships, thereby engaging the Kingdome in a new Warre; or of any other difficulties the Parliament hath been, or may be exposed unto, to precipitate their Councels, or to destroy their Forces that now are, or hereafter shall be raised, being (as the Petitioners humbly conceive) contrary to their said Protestation, Vow, and Covenant: as it is also to necessitate the Parliament to a Treaty, untill such satisfaction and security be first given, as may attaine the ends of our former Engagements.

Your Petitioners therefore humbly pray, that you will adhere to the said Protestations, Vow, & Covenant, and to the constant tenor of all your former Declarations, and not recede from those first and just Principles, *viz.* The safety of your selves, and all that have and shall adhere to you, and the Reformation and Preservation of Religion, and the maintenance and defence of our Lawes, and Liberties, which you have openly held forth to all the world; and by which you have engaged all the honest well-affected people of the three Kingdomes to serve you with their lives and estates; lest you betray your selves and them to the mercilesse cruelties of those that seeke your and their destruction, and draw the blood of many innocent persons upon you and yours. For prevention whereof, your Petitioners further humbly desire, you will faithfully persevere in the due prosecution of your said just undertakings and Engagements; and that such a course by your Wisdomes may be taken, for security and satisfaction to be given as aforesaid, that neither His Majestie, nor any other may have occasion or opportunity of renewing the old, or raising a new War. And in so doing, That God who hath hitherto owned you and your Cause, will assuredly doe so still; And we your Petitioners with many thousands more, as formerly, so are still ready in pursuance of the said Protestation, Vow, and Covenant, with their lives and estates, to adventure all with you and your Forces in this Common Cause against all opposition.

July 5. 1648   *And your Petitioners shall ever pray, &c.*

Fig. 13. An edition of a printed petition used by Independent citizens in London to gather signatures.

prompting a complaint by a Puritan member of an Oxford college about a 1641 petition issued in the name of several university colleges in support of Royal prerogative and the established church. "The petition, which . . . was sent to our hall and other houses, was printed in our names before we know and is now presented in our names, though of our hall but eleven subscribed, and above twenty now resident refused."[103] When a Royalist activist, Sir Thomas Aston, assembled a collection of mostly county petitions that sided with Charles I against the Long Parliament and advocated repression of sectaries, his intent in publishing them was to "show that the way is open. And since noise and number are taken into consideration, the forwardness of assailants [i.e., Puritan petitioners] will . . . put shame upon the defendants to be so far behind." This inspired a proposal in *An Appeale To The World In these*

[103] *MSS Add* 70003, fol. 127.

The humble

PETITION

OF

Divers well affected Magiſtrates,
Miniſters, Citizens and other inhabitants in the City of *London*,
and parts adjacent.

Preſented to the Houſe of Peeres, on
Wedneſday the 12 of *July*, 1648.

With their Lordſhips Anſwer thereunto.

Die *Mercurii*, 12. *Julii*. 1648.

ORdered by the *Lords Aſſembled in Parliament*
that this Petition and Anſwer be forthwith
printed and publiſhed.

Joh. Brown, Cler. Parliamentorum.

London Printed for *John Wright*, at the
Kings Head in the Old-Bayley. 1648.

Fig. 14. Another edition of the same Independent petition, this one destined for readers.

TO THE RIGHT

HONOVRABLE

THE KNIGHTS, CITIZENS AND BVRGSESES OF
THE COMMONS HOUSE OF PARLIAMENT.

The humble Petition of some of the Parishioners in the Parish of Chigwell *in the County of* Essex *and divers others.*

Humbly Sheweth,

 THat Dr. *Emanuell Vtey* now Vicar of the Parish Church of *Chigwell* aforesaid hath erected an Altar in the said Church, and doth use frequent and offensive bowing and cringing thereunto , compelling others to doe the like , and hath kissed the Altar three times in one day, and doth constantly read the Prayers in the Divine Service with his face toward the Altar and backe towards the people, so that many of them cannot heare what is said.

That the said Vicar, openly in the Pulpit of the said Church, hath spoken these ensuing words, or words to the same effect, viz.

1. That his Fathers Soule was in heaven, making intercession for his, and that it was lawfull to pray unto Saints if the time would permit.

2. That the Commands of the Arch-bishop of *Canterburie* (whom he compared unto the high Priest) were equally to be obeyed with Gods command in his word.

3. That the said Vicar hath said, that the King is not Supreame head of the Church next under Christ, and being demanded who then was he answered, the Bishops and said further, that no Minister, who understood himselfe, would pray for the King as Supreame head of the Church under Christ, and that there hath been no true Religion in *England* these 40.yeares, and being then told he was a friend to the Pope, answered, that he loved the Pope with all his heart, and affirmeth that the Pope is not *Antichrist*, whosoever he is.

4. That the said Vicar hath declared, that whatsoever any person (who had entred into holy orders) did speake, he spake by Divine Inspiration, and being urged, that then they differed not from those that wrote the holy Scriptures, he made no answer to that, but impudently and blasphemously persisting in his former opinions said further, that, if the Divell could have orders put upon him, whatsoever he should say, should be by Divine inspiration.

5. That the said Vicar hath said, that if a man usually meet with occasions of Drunkenesse or Fornication and be actually overcome by them, yet such a man doth not sin, because he sought not the occasion.

6. That the said Vicar hath beene oftentimes seene drunke, and his wife hath reported that he was a Papist in heart, and did weare a Crucifix in his bosome and kept one in his study, and that hee so bitterly threatned her for not bowing to it, as she was constrained to cry out for helpe and hide herselfe.

7. And lastly, the said Vicar hath said, the house of Parliament hath nothing to doe in matters of Religion, but if any things were amisse, complaint ought to be made to the Bishops, and they were to reforme it, and hath also uttered many other words tending to the dishonour of the High and Honourable Court of Parliament.

All which premises containing Popish and superstitious Ceremonies, corrupt and dangerous opinions and Tenents contrariant to the established Doctrine and Discipline of the Church of *England,* scandalous and blasphemous words tending to the dishonour of Almighty God, and (as they conceive) the subversion of his Majesties Royall Supremacy, and the abridgment of the power and authority of the High and Honourable Court of Parliament.

Your Petitioners humbly implore the suddaine removeall of the said Vicar, with a reformation of the said Innovations and such censure upon the offender, as to the grave Wisedome of this Honourable assembly shall be thought meet. And your Petitioners shall ever pray, &c.

To the Courteous Reader.

IT is obvious to the judicious, that the Prelates have beene the originall cause of all the divisions and schismes in the Church, as well since the Reformation as before, as may appeare by their withstanding of it in the beginning, and also ever since by their imposing things upon mens consciences , contrary to Gods word, and to the uttermost of their power persecuting all zealous and Godly Ministers, because they would not be obedient to their ungodly commands, and in the meane time maintaining and countenancing a dumb idle and scandalous Ministry, so long as they would be conformable to them, yea Popish Ministers and Popishly addicted, as may appeare both by this Petition and many other presented to this Parliament, and to divers former Parliaments, but the Prelates have such a sway that no good could be effected. Wherefore let every good Christian pray earnestly unto God, that he would put into the hearts of his Majestie and this Parliament, utterly to abolish this Antichristian Hierarchicall Govement, which hath beene the chiefe hindrance of a through Reformation.

Printed in the Yeare, 1641.

Fig. 15. A petition from parishioners against their cleric. Note the notice to the reader at the bottom.

Times of Extreame Danger for publishing a collection of pro-Parliament petitions in one printed edition.[104]

Publication of political petitions was stimulated by the alliance of commerce and controversy in print culture. Ideological conviction was a motive for printing petitions, but so was the pursuit of profit by printers who eagerly sought hot items for their presses. Richard Oulton and Gregory Dexter printed many petitions for themselves, as a private venture, and others for other booksellers. To satisfy popular interest, they kept type standing in order to reprint petitions or to include a recently presented petition in a new edition of otherwise old news. *Six Great Matters of Note* became *Seven Great Matters of Note* when Oulton and Dexter printed a recent petition on the blank verso of the title page to *Six* and altered the title page accordingly. For another bookseller, Oulton and Dexter printed Pym's speech to the Lords on January 25, 1642, and the petitions from Essex, Hertford, London, and Middlesex that he presented to this conference. For this they reprinted all six pages of the London petition, using type left standing from an edition of the petition they printed for themselves and page 1 of the Hertford petition from standing type used to print it for another bookseller.[105] The reading public's interest in petitions explains why Henry Parker's invocation of popular sovereignty in defense of the Long Parliament initially appeared in mid-July 1642 as *A Petition or Declaration* putatively intended to be presented to Charles I. The type was also left standing and the text reissued at the end of the month, but now the title page— *The Danger To England Observed*—dropped the pretense that it was a petition.[106]

This last example shows how printers used popular interest in petitions to trick readers into buying newsbooks. A hastily composed newsbook of events in Sussex at the onset of the second civil war in 1648 contains only a fleeting reference to "a very presumptuous petition out of Sussex," yet its title, *A Petition Presented . . . By The Royal Party in Sussex*, seeks to exploit public interest in Royalist petitions for a treaty with the king.[107] Forged petitions are another manifestation of commercial motives in political printing. In 1642 a stationer paid a

[104] Thomas Aston, *A Collection of Sundry Petitions* (E150[28], 1642), sig. A2v; E107[26] (1643), p. 3.

[105] Bradford Swan, *Gregory Dexter of London and New England* (Rochester, NY, 1949), pp. 24–27. In the Thomason collection, the edition with Pym's speech and the petitions is bound in two places, E200[21] (1642) and E200[23] (1642). Cf. E134[7] (1642), sig. A4–B2 and E200[21], pp. 3–8; also, E133[15] (1642) and E200[23], sig. B3. The two Hertford petitions in E133[15] were printed for another bookseller by unidentified printers who I assume are Oulton and Dexter.

[106] E107[29] (1642); E108[17] (1642).

[107] E522[38] (1648), p. 5; and see E449[35] (1648).

Cambridge student, the going rate, 2s. 6d., for forging a petition from Hertford.[108] In September and November 1641, another printer used the same forged text to publish two petitions from political opposites, *A New Petition Of The Papists* and *The Humble Petition Of The Brownists*.[109] The economic interest of printers in producing multiple editions of texts they thought had great public interest helps to explain why more than two hundred printed petitions and collections of petitions appeared between April 1641 and April 1643.[110] Printers ordinarily met popular interest in petitions by publishing them in multiple formats, often first in a broadside edition, designed to be affixed to a public place or used to gather signatures, then in a quarto format, either alone or with other petitions, and finally in the next weekly edition of a newspaper.

Commentary on petitions in newspapers reflected the partisan alignment of editors and publishers. In 1643, when conflict between Royalists and Parliamentarians produced a spate of rival petitions for peace and war policies, the *Kingdomes Weekly Intelligencer* reprinted a London petition from the war faction to counter "malignant" reports, sent "into all parts," that covered "only petitioning for peace."[111] News reports might be brief and circumspect for highly controversial petitions, but readers would find something about them. For example, they read about important petitions-in-progress by Independents in London, even in papers aligned with other factions. When conflict escalated between Independents and Presbyterians, the *Scotish Dove*, a partisan Presbyterian diurnal, reported on a Presbyterian petition in London and observed, "There is a cross-petition . . . by another party in and around the City. . . . There are many thousand hands gathered all about the suburbs . . . especially at conventicles and private meetings."[112] In the *Kingdomes Weekly Intelligencer* readers learned that activists in the New Model Army were aggrieved "that their humble and innocent address unto the Parliament by way of petitioning was interpreted to tend to a distemper and a mutiny." *Perfect Occurrences* in 1649 informed readers that "a petition was promoted at several congregational meetings . . . for women to subscribe" in support of imprisoned radical leaders. "In some

[108] A. D. T. Cromartie, "The Printing of Parliamentary Speeches, November 1640–July 1642," *HJ* 33 (1990): 39; and see *PJ* 1:326.

[109] E169[7] (1641); E178[10] (1641).

[110] Fletcher, "Petitioning and the Civil War," p. 42.

[111] E65[11] (1643), p. 227.

[112] *Scotish Dove*, May 28–June 3 (E339[13], 1646), p. 676; see also *Mercurius Civicus*, July 6–13 (E60[9], 1643), p. 5; *Weekly Account*, May 27–June 3 (E339[14], 1646), sig. Z4.

places many signed it, in other places none at all, and in some places it was disputed."[113]

Initially, scribal reproduction was the principal mode of transmission for political petitions in the early 1640s. In late-August 1640, the newsletter writer Edward Rossingham reported but did not reproduce a petition against the billeting of soldiers from Yorkshire gentry to the king. Writing from London, Rossingham told Lord Conway he omitted to do so "because it may be already at Newcastle," where Conway was stationed. Rossingham did copy out the substance of a petition presented by the grand jury at the assizes in Berkshire, though it, like the Yorkshire petition, circulated as a separate, as did contemporaneous petitions over the oath enjoined in the Book of New Canons, which London booksellers lent out to patrons who wished to copy them.[114] Up and down the social ladder contemporaries relied on these scribal practices for information on political petitions connected to the invasion of the Scots and desires for a Parliament. In September 1640, a member of the king's household informed a wealthy landowner in Suffolk, "If you desire to see the Scot's petition and the King's answer, my Lady May, to whom my wife has sent them, will let you have them." That month a steward of Northampton recorded in his diary that, on a journey, he saw (probably in a tavern) a copy (extant only in manuscript) of the Twelve Peers Petition. Also that month a future member of the Long Parliament, Sir Simonds D'Ewes, wrote from Suffolk to a Puritan alderman in London, requesting copies of petitions drawn up by the City in support of the Twelve Peers Petition. The alderman was unable fully to comply: "I have here sent you a true copy of the City's petition. I was driven to have it written out in haste. The ministers' petition I could not get." Later that year, D'Ewes, now an MP, sent manuscript copies of petitions presented to the Long Parliament to his wife, "desiring you, after you have perused them, and suffered our friends that will to copy them, you lay them up safe for me."[115]

Printing quickly supplanted scribal modes of transmission for petitions and their reliance on personal connections. Evidence of the transition appears in an episode of petitioning in 1642, when four county petitions were presented to the king, then in York at a critical point in the struggle over the militia. The petitions urged him to return to London and seek an agreement with Parliament. Popular interest was heightened

[113] *Kingdomes Weekly Intelligencer*, May 18–25 (E389[3], 1647), p. 534; *Perfect Occurrences*, March 30–April 27 (E529[21], 1649), p. 990.

[114] *CSPD* 1640, pp. 553, 554, 619–20.

[115] *MSS Tanner* 65, fol. 112v; *MSS New College* 9502, September 9, 1642 [unfoliated]; *MSS Harl* 383, fol. 88; D'Ewes, *Autobiography and Correspondence* 2:252.

by a midnight "attack" at a lodging house where twenty petitioners
from Lincolnshire awaited the king's response. The Nottinghamshire
petition was printed along with a letter by one of the petitioners in York,
who wrote to tell his brother in London, "I have copies of them all [pe-
titions], but they are too long for me to copy out at this time." The
petitioner then informs his brother whom to contact in London for
manuscript copies of all the petitions, and he encloses a copy of the
king's reply to one of them. A badly plagiarized version of this letter
later appeared in another news pamphlet, *Terrible Newse from York*, issued by a printer eager to take advantage of public interest in these
events.[116]

The routinization of printing for petitions not only made them more
accessible to readers but also to subscribers. This facilitated petition
campaigns that, on short notice, covered London or an entire county. In
1645, Presbyterian activists in London circulated a printed petition for
gathering signatures, with blank spaces in the title where the name of
different wards could be inserted. Marginal notations on a printed copy
of this petition indicate that they were "handed up and down in the re-
spective wards within the city . . . the promoters endeavoring to get
them subscribed by as many hands as is possible."[117] This use of printing
made petitions a flexible weapon that could respond rapidly to unfolding political developments. It also facilitated more popular participation
in petitioning. From printing presses issued small "tickets," such as one
in July 1643 from a nascent Independent party that informed "well affected persons" that they could sign a petition for more active prosecution of the war against the king at the Merchants Tailors Hall from
4 A.M. until 8 P.M (see fig. 16). An account of this petition-in-progress,
which substantially reproduced the ticket, was available to readers of the
newspaper *Special Passages*.[118]

Petitions printed for use by petitioners often came with instructions
on how to gather signatures and meet to present the signed petitions in
a procession to Parliament. Broadside copies of the *humble Petition of
many thousand poore people* were "for the use of the petitioners who are
to meet this present day in More Fields, and from thence to go to the
house of Parliament with it in their hands." A petition from women Levellers in and around London, who called for the release of six imprisoned radicals, announced, "All those women who are approvers hereof
are desired to subscribe it, and to deliver in their subscriptions to the

[116] E143[8] (1642), p. 4; E143[12] (1642). For a similar letter printed with another
petition, see 669f.8[41] (1643).

[117] 669f.[10]37 (1645); *MSS Nalson* 22, fol. 131.

[118] E61[3] (1643); E61[9] (1643), p. 7; for another ticket announcing a petition, see
E83[46] (1643).

ALL forts of well-affected Perfons, who defire a fpeedy End of this Deftructive Warre ; Are intreated to meete at *Marchan-Taylers-Hall* to Morrow, being *Wednefday* the 19. of *July*, 1643. At any houre of the Day, from 4 of the Clock in the Morning, till 8. in the Evening, there to heare, and fubfcribe a *Petition* to the *Parliament*, (to which Thoufands have already fubfcribed) for raifing the whole *People* of the *Land* as one *Man*, againft thofe Popifh-blood-thirfty Forces raifed, to Enflave, and Deftroy *Us*, and our *Pofterity*.

The *Wednefday* above mentioned, is the Laft, and Onely day appointed to Compleat the *Petition*. Wherefore all *Gentlemen* that have any Copies thereof in their hands, are Defired to bring them In, at the Time and Place above faid.

Fig. 16. A Printed announcement that informs London residents where and when they can sign a petition for more active prosecution of the war against Charles I.

women who will be appointed in every ward and division to receive the same; and to meet at Westminster Hall upon Monday the 23 of this instant April 1649, betwixt 8 and 9 of clock in the forenoon." Similar instructions appear on other petitions by Anabaptists, Levellers, and, in 1648, insurgent Royalists.[119] The utility of printing for massive petition

[119] 669f.4[54] (1642); E551[14] (1649), p. 14; and see 669f.8[27] (1643); 669f.11[126] (1648); 669f.12[20] (1648); 669f.12[39] (1648); 669f.13[89] (1649).

campaigns should not be underestimated. In 1648 Royalist insurgents in Essex and Surrey had five hundred copies of a petition printed for use in gathering signatures.[120] But this practice could backfire. Adversaries might learn about a petition-in-progress and attempt to head it off with a counterpetition. This was the fate of an early Leveller petition: "Divers printed copies thereof being sent abroad to gain subscriptions, one whereof was intercepted by an informer." The result was a counterpetition from London's Common Council that prompted Parliament to condemn the Leveller petition.[121]

Content

In addition to heightening access to petitions for subscribers and readers, printing led to change in the content of messages conveyed by petitions. In order to understand this development we must return to a theme discussed in the last chapter, printing's imposition of dialogic order on political conflict. There we saw that petitions, like other political texts, encouraged readers to view politics as an ongoing debate in which texts responded to prior texts, simultaneously referring to, excerpting from, and commenting on them. By the middle of the 1640s, factional politics pushed this development in new directions. Printing's technical potential for rapid reproduction of texts allowed activists to publish petitions from adversaries and to add their own critical commentary, often with the intent to head off a favorable reception in Parliament. Of course, this violated traditions that made petitioning a privileged form of communication and led contemporaries to regard commentary from third parties before receipt of a petition as an obstruction of justice. Such intervention was as inappropriate as ex parte lobbying of a judge on a pending case. Yet this did not deter a preemptive strike against a 1646 petition from Lancashire Presbyterians, when Independents in London printed critical commentary and what Presbyterians said was a "false copy" of their petition. But this refers less to accuracy than to unauthorized publication—the pirated version in the Independent pamphlet is accurate; nearly all differences, except one, between it and the edition published by Presbyterians appear to be the result of transcription error.[122] This may explain why Presbyterian petitioners in Norwich refused to allow copies to be made of their petition when they read a scribal copy before that City's Common Council—the

---

[120] 669f.12[20] (1649); *HMC Portland* 1:453.

[121] E392[19] (1647), p. 1; *CJ* 5:112.

[122] *A New Birth Of The City Remonstrance* (E350[12], 1646); Tilsley, *A true Copie of the Petition.*

clerk's wife was an Independent.[123] Yet Presbyterians were equally adept at these preemptive practices. In *A Sectary Dissected, Or, The Anatomie of an Independent Flie, still buzzing about City and Country . . . a scurrilous Petition, intended to be obtruded upon the Parliament,* they printed an Independent petition then circulating in London for signatures and subjected it to scathing criticism.[124]

Additional evidence of printing's imposition of dialogic order on political conflict comes from cross-petitions, which challenged prior petitions, often on the issue of their validity as a representation of local opinion. "We have better ground and warrant to represent the sense of the gentry and commons of Yorkshire," asserts a cross-petition, framed in opposition to a prior petition issued by Yorkshire Royalists.[125] The Kent petition that stridently upheld the cause of Royalism and episcopacy was promoted at the April 1642 assizes in opposition to earlier expressions of support from Kent for the Long Parliament. If it was a cross-petition, it quickly prompted a cross-cross-petition in May that, in turn, cited Parliament's "gentle acceptance" of London's 1640 Root and Branch Petition and the January 1641 "parrot" petition from Kent.[126] Cross-petitions first appeared in 1641, when supporters of the Church responded to the Puritan petition campaign against bishops and ceremonial "corruptions." Subsequent cross-petitions gave voice to rival views over the issue of who would control the militia in the spring and summer of 1642, and later that winter over peace and war policies. During 1645–48, cross-petitions emanated from complex, multifaction politics that involved Presbyterians, Independents, the New Model Army, Levellers, and resurgent Royalists whose petitions protested "arbitrary authority" in the centralized controls imposed by Parliament via county committees. This complexity appears in *Plain English,* whose defense of a London Presbyterian petition includes negative references to a radical anti-tithe petition from Hertford, a 1642 pro-war petition from London citizens, a Leveller petition and an Independent cross-petition, and praise for Presbyterian petitions from London citizens and Essex and Suffolk ministers.[127]

Printing's imposition of dialogic order on political conflict went beyond responses to petitions and extended to grievances and requested

---

[123] *An Hue-And-Cry after Vox Populi,* pp. 22–24.

[124] E384[17] (1647).

[125] 669f.6[9] (1642).

[126] E142[10] (1642); 669f.5[13] (1642).

[127] Captain Jones, *Plain English: Or, The Sectaries Anatomized* (E350[11], 1646); E338[7] (1646) is the Presbyterian petition; negative references are to E382[2] (1647); E130[26] (1642); E343[11] (1646); either E339[12] (1646) or 669f.10[57] (1646); positive references are to 669f.10[58] (1646); E339[11] (1646).

remedies in printed petitions. The consequence was another sharp break with tradition: petitions were now a vehicle for placing political discussion and debate before the reading public. This occurred when grievances in a petition referred to prior petitions from the same party that had met with a less-than-favorable reception, a source of the self-referential quality in many Leveller petitions. Title pages to several in 1649–50, including one from women Levellers, describe them as petitions from "presenters and promoters of the late large petition of September 11," which advanced many radical requests, including abolition of the House of Lords, toleration in religion, and a trial for Charles I.[128] Thus, one consequence of routine printing of political petitions was references to unmet requests in former petitions, further moving the practice of petitioning in the direction of what we now call lobbying. The title page of another Leveller petition in 1649 refers to requests advanced in three prior petitions, dating back to 1647, intended to secure "the people's rational and just rights and liberties, against all tyrants whatsoever, whether in Parliament, Army or Council of State."[129]

References in petitions to other printed materials, such as speeches, declarations, ordinances, and laws, were another consequence of printing's imposition of dialogic order on political conflict. Widespread availability of these texts facilitated an immanent mode of political criticism in petitions that cite and reproduce texts by opposing parties. In 1643, London apprentices defended a petition for peace with excerpts from a May 1642 parliamentary declaration and a printed speech by a member who, in February 1642, upheld the right of a "multitude" to subscribe and present a petition. A Royalist petition in December 1647 against free quarter and high taxes cited the 1628 Petition of Right and other parliamentary declarations.[130] Parliament inadvertently facilitated this immanent criticism because it had ordered the printing and distribution of many political texts referenced by Royalist petitioners. Of course, Parliament's actions also promoted petitions that went along with prevailing political winds in Westminister. Just prior to the outbreak of civil war, one of the king's judges traveling the summer assize circuit received county petitions that were too favorable, in his opinion, to Parliament's position on control over the militia. This, and the alacrity with which such petitions were framed, he attributed to the widespread availability of printed materials on the militia issue "so generally well known, posted up upon all public places."[131]

---

[128] 669f.13[73] (1649); E551[14] (1649); E579[9] (1649); 669f.15[50] (1650); 669f.13[16] (1648) is the September petition.

[129] E574[15] (1649); and see E470[32] (1648), p. 4.

[130] *An Humble Declaration of the Apprentices* (E245[2], 1643), p. 7; 669f.11[104] (1647).

[131] *CSPD* 1641–43, p. 375; for the petitions see E112[14] (1642).

Printing was thus an important source of change in the nature of grievances conveyed by petitions. This communicative change was not an extension of specific ideological commitments, for it appears across the spectrum of religious and political positions. Discourse oriented to an anonymous audience of readers is as much a part of petitions from Puritans as petitions from those who advocated repression of "sectaries," from Royalist critics of Parliamentary tyranny as from Independents and Levellers. The same holds for immanent criticism in petitions, which presupposes popular access to other political texts. These discursive developments, then, did not arise from ideological commitments but from the impact of printing on traditional forms of communication. What unites innovations in petitions that advance contrary points of view are economic and technical aspects of printing, respectively, commercial motives that ensured a plentiful supply of printed political materials and the ease with which texts could be reproduced. To be sure, printing was not the sole source of a capacity to construct public life in terms of ideological conflict. We saw in chapter 5 that this occurred under conditions of scribal transmission of political texts. But printing is the sine qua non for explaining a transformation in petitioning that replaced communicative norms of secrecy and privilege by open appeals to public opinion. Printing not only provided vastly greater access to petitions but also reoriented their production so that their framers addressed themselves to public opinion, which, as we shall see, was increasingly presumed to consist of readers capable of rational thought—that is, able to understand and arrive at sensible judgments on rival political claims advanced in petitions.

Two additional issues must be examined in order to conclude this study of links between change in communicative media and the "invention" of public opinion that constituted a democratic model of the public sphere in politics. First, the claim that appeals to public opinion flowed from printing's imposition of dialogic order on political conflict, and not ideological principle, implies that this development was inadvertent, that it developed initially at the level of unreflective practice. Beyond the observation that this development cut across political and religious divisions, evidence for this claim exists in contemporary reluctance to acknowledge or embrace it, which is as widespread as the innovation itself. Political petitioning is, then, a signal instance of the paradox of innovation. Second, it remains to be shown that the authority attributed to public opinion in printed petitions during the Revolution has a discernible relationship to liberal-democratic ideology. For this it is necessary to find links between practice and theory, to locate points at which cumulative, pragmatic developments in the practice of petitioning inspired novel ideas on public opinion and the nature of political authority.

THE PARADOX OF INNOVATION IN PETITIONING

Ambivalence bordering on denial best describes contemporary responses to innovations in petitioning practices during the Revolution. Though we may be inclined to celebrate innovative petitioning and laud the printing press as democracy's handmaiden, that was not the reaction of most contemporaries. Some saw it as a sign of spiritual and political failure. "Let us all make it our practice to serve God cordially, and we shall need no more petitions."[132] Reluctance to acknowledge the legitimacy of political petitioning flowed not only from traditional norms of secrecy and privilege in political communication, but also from more general precepts about deference and hierarchy in politics. The absence of a formal philosophic or ideological rationale for placing public opinion at the core of political practice also explains this reluctance. Only in later stages of the Revolution, after innovative petitioning had become an established political tactic, do we find principled expressions of support for democratic ideas on the centrality of public opinion in politics.

Though they imitated Parliament's early success in using printing to publicize petitions, Royalists disclaimed the innovation and attacked its appearance in petitions from adversaries. A Royalist pamphlet defends its author's decision, in 1642, not to sign a petition against the bishops because "the making and repealing of laws . . . is a special and peculiar power, privilege and right, proper only to Parliaments, therefore not to be forced or coacted by me, being no parliament man. . . . This is rather to be a tyrannical judge than a legal witness." In addition to using juridical metaphor to highlight the illicit move from conveying information to lobbying, the author criticized novelty in organizing petitions: "that which is to go under the name of a county or town ought to be first asserted unto by the sheriff, justice of peace, or other magistrates . . . then the matter may be publicly propounded and condescended unto or contradicted." Instead, Puritan petitions emerged from "clandestine and surreptitious actions, going about from house to house by no commission of authority, to engage people . . . and to make it as an act of a county or a town."[133] Sir Thomas Aston, whom we encountered previously as the editor who published a collection of Royalist petitions because he thought "noise and number" were important, nonetheless decried this development in Puritan petitions. Similar contradictions exist in declarations by Charles I as conflict escalated between him and the Long Parliament. The king bitterly criticized innovation in petitioning,

---

[132] *Scotish Dove*, May 28–June 3 (E339[13], 1646), p. 675; and see E351[7] (1646).
[133] J. W., *Petitions Against Bishops* (E133[10], 1642), pp. 3, 4.

but shifts in royal views show the growing importance of petitions as propaganda. One declaration denies legitimacy to petitions that "carried not the style of all" because they did not maintain the fictive unity presented by petitions from officials on behalf of a corporate entity and "implied no other consent than such as went visibly along with it." But in another declaration the king chides Parliament for refusing to receive petitions from his supporters, "as if you were only trusted by the people of one opinion," thereby sanctioning partisan petitions.[134]

Ambivalence and contradiction also marked reactions to innovative petitioning by those who sided with Parliament against Charles I. After the king rebuked petitioners who urged him to defer to Parliament—"as in particular, His Majesty says, He never intended you to be judges betwixt him and his Parliament"—the petitioners acknowledged "our unfitness to become judges betwixt your Majesty and Parliament in anything."[135] Like Royalists, Parliamentarians disclaimed innovation in their own petitions and found it in those of their opponents. A cross-petition in March 1642 from London citizens denounced the "bold publishing in print" of a petition organized by the Royalist mayor and recorder, "purposely done, wickedly, seditiously, to make divisions." The previous December Denzil Holles, the future Presbyterian leader in the Long Parliament, cited the potential for creating "divisions" when he urged impeachment of bishops for issuing a petition protesting popular intimidation. The presumption that politics—for example, making divisions, lobbying Parliament—tainted petitions by adversaries appears in a pamphlet, a county petition, and a declaration by Parliament, all published in 1642. These texts criticized petitions in support of the king and episcopacy for being "of a very strange nature," "prescribing rules to the Parliament," and presuming "to interpose their advice contrary to the votes of both Houses of Parliament."[136] Puritans and Parliamentarians thus reacted no differently from Charles I to the novel use of printed petitions to appeal to public opinion. Similar reactions to innovative petitioning later appeared in the conflict between Independents and Presbyterians, even though use of printed petitions as propaganda was by then a routine political practice. To fend off criticism of Presbyterians who violated traditional strictures on petitions, one writer scarcely avoided affirmation of unwanted novelty: "though they petition for

[134] Thomas Aston, *A Remonstrance Against Presbytery* (E163[2], 1641), sig. B4; *Rushworth* 4:597, 635.

[135] E148[4] (1642), sig. B4; 669f.6[15] (1642).

[136] 669f.3[58] (1642); *Densell Hollis Esquire, His Worthy and learned Speech* (E199[48], 1641), p. 4; *A Letter Sent By a Yorkshire Gentleman* (E150[5], 1642), p. 3; *The Somerset Petition* (E155[16], 1642), p. 17; *A Remonstrance Or Declaration of Parliament* (E148[23], 1642), p. 13.

nothing but what the Parliament have voted and granted, just things in case of necessity may be unseasonably asked, and yet the fault is pardonable, but audacious bold threats deserve censure."[137]

The leading Presbyterian polemicist of the time, Thomas Edwards, deflects criticism to its source, when, in the first volume of *Gangræna*, his sensationalistic account of sectarian religion and politics, he accuses Independents of "practicing that themselves which they condemn in others . . . interposing in anything before [Parliament] by way of petition, or having meetings for that end."[138] The near admission by Edwards about "meetings" is revealing. Independent petitions and pamphlets often cite private political activities and, invoking traditional strictures on petitions, warn Parliament against Presbyterian petitions that "prescribe unto them."[139] The same pattern holds in 1647. Confronted by a petition against a Presbyterian settlement, the county committee in Kent framed a declaration against sectarian religion in which it observes "that several petitions are set on foot" in Kent "wherein they take to themselves a liberty of venting their own private thoughts . . . in matters concerning the public . . . which can produce no other effect than the raising and countenancing of contrary parties and factions within the country." This episode did not escape the vigilant eye of Edwards, whose catalogue of Independent villainy now spilled over into volume 3 of *Gangræna* and included references to the Kent petition hostile to his faction and other Independent initiatives against Presbyterian petitions."[140] Denunciation of "clamorous" and "unusual" and "dangerous" petitions also came from radical groups when their political ambitions seemed threatened by counterrevolution or by Parliament's reluctance to put the king on trial. Levellers, Independents and activists in the New Model Army often disclaimed innovation in their petitions, which did not seek to "put condition on the Parliament" but came "wholly with submission to your honors' wisdom and determination."[141]

---

[137] E339[6] 1646, p. 11; see also *A Glass For Weak ey'd Citizens* (E341[5], 1646), p. 5.

[138] Edwards, *Gangræna*, p. 44, and see pp. 67–68; see also *A Glass For Weak ey'd Citizens*, p. 6.

[139] E339[12] (1646), sig. A3v; and see *Toleration Justified* (E319[15], 1646), p. 2; *The Interest Of England Maintained* (E340[5], 1646), pp. 3–4; *A New Petition* (E340[24], 1646), pp. 7–8; *An Hue-And-Cry after Vox Populi*, p. 14.

[140] *A Declaration Set Forth by the Presbyterians within . . . Kent* (E3370[25], 1647), sig. A3v; Edwards, *Third Part of Gangræna*, pp. [93], [259].

[141] *A Narrative And Declaration Of the Dangerous Petitions* (E446[25], 1648), p. 5; *The Copies of Two Petitions From . . . Fleetwoods Regiment* (E468[32], 1648), p. 4; *The Petition And vindication Of the Officers* (E385[19], 1647), sig. A1; 669f.12[104] (1648); and see *Letters From Saffron-Walden* (E383[24], 1647), p. 12; *Declaration of Well-Affected Non-Subscribers*, p. 3.

Thus, writers and promoters of petitioners who represented all shades of prevailing political and religious opinions published printed petitions that appealed to public opinion as a means to lobby Parliament. Yet they preferred not to acknowledge this innovative use of petitions. Opportunism and political necessity are not irrelevant for understanding this response to innovative petitioning; but this response also exhibited a pattern, shaped by communicative practices that ran ahead of political and social theory. No principled defense then existed for that which is implicit in innovative petitioning, namely, invoking the opinion of a public to justify a legislative agenda. Instead, contemporaries relied on traditional rhetoric and hierarchical ideas to justify their petitions and attack those by adversaries. At the same time, however, novel practices led some contemporaries to tentative new ideas that expressed a surprisingly robust conception of public opinion in political life.

THE AUTHORITY OF OPINION

What remains to be assessed is the authority attributed to opinion in politics. Out of practical experiences with political petitioning emerged new ideas that attached unprecedented authority to public opinion in politics. Initially, this appeared in debates over the representative quality of petitions, in tactical efforts that defended or attacked opinions invoked in rival printed petitions. This led some commentators to adopt remarkably modern ideas on the importance of consent and reason in opinions submitted for public consideration. In addition, limitations of petitions as an inherently reactive device led some to see the need for constitutional reforms that would institutionalize the authority of the public sphere. At this point, practical experiences with petitioning led to speculation that took political theory in a liberal-democratic direction.

When petitions competed to claim the authority of public opinion, contemporaries confronted the issue of numbers versus social status. Did numbers or social status of supporters convey more authority for opinions advanced in rival petitions? Tradition favored the latter, which one cleric invoked when confronted by a hostile petition from his parishioners. A cross-petition on his behalf "was subscribed by most of the gentry and divers other persons of quality, honesty and ability in the parish. And many more hands I might have had, had I regarded the number of men above the integrity and worth of the persons." A few years later the Long Parliament rejected the claim that many signatures on a petition from London citizens was a sufficient reason for Parliament to reconsider its refusal to accept the Presbyterian discipline

recommended by the Assembly of Divines.[142] But contemporaries sometimes cited the number of signers to justify or discredit a petition.
Against Digby's dismissive remarks on thousands of signatures presented along with the Root and Branch Petition, "all that could be got
to subscribe," the alderman who presented it responded, "If there were
any mean men's hands to it, yet if they were honest men, there was no
reason but their hands should be received." A cross-petition from a
grand jury in Worcester, in August 1642, disavowed a petition from a
previous grand jury "as not agreeable to the intents or desires of us, or
any considerable number of the said county." It had been "contrived
and prepared" for the jury "by some few persons." In 1647, when petitions began to flow to the New Model Army, one MP, William Waller,
discounted radical petitions sent to the army because they "were at-
tested only by a few inconsiderable hands."[143] The importance of numbers appears in petitions with few signatures that refer apologetically to
constraints of time. One from London Presbyterians in 1646 had many
signatures, but at its presentation to the Common Council its promoters
averred that "many thousands more of citizens of quality might have
been had to subscribe the same if time had permitted."[144]

Still, much ambivalence existed over invoking numbers as the ground
of legitimacy for an opinion. Promoters of petitions might seek a favorable spin by attributing virtue to a few signers. Unable to match three
thousand signatures on a petition favoring the moderate earl of Den-
bigh, the Warwickshire committee ingenuously declined "to get up
a counter petition . . . not wishing to foment differences."[145] Cross-
petitions opposed to Puritan petitions for reform inconsistently referred
to numbers and social composition. The importance attached to numbers in them appears in reports to the earl of Leicester, who received a
copy of the London Root and Branch Petition and information about
plans for "a counter petition which is much labored, that the hands to
this may over number those of the [the Root and Branch Petition]."
Readers of Rossingham's newsletter learned that, in response to anti-
Episcopal petitions, "the clergy say again that they can procure ten
hands for the continuing of episcopal government for every one hand
that subscribes against it." This was the boast of a Cornwall cleric, when

[142] Edward Finch, *An Answer to The Articles* (E175[11], 1641), p. 26; *HMC Portland*,
1:297.

[143] *Rushworth* 4:171; *D'Ewes I*, pp. 339; 699f.5[65] (1642); Ashton, *Counter-Revolution*, p. 131.

[144] *MSS JCC* 40, fol. 184; and see 669f.8[41] (1643); 669f.11[15] (1647); E452[38]
(1648), p. 3.

[145] Hughes, *Politics, Society, and Civil War in Warwickshire*, p. 236; *HMC 6th Report*,
p. 27. See also E714[8] (1653), p. 3; 669f.21[55] (1659).

debate in a tavern over a Puritan petition led him to claim "they would get thirty thousand hands in Cornwall to cross that petition."[146] Yet the persistence of traditional habits of thought that upheld deference as a prime virtue in politics upheld the importance of social status for these petitions, which often grouped signatures by the rank of signers. Contemporary reaction to petitions for and against Puritan reform in the early 1640s often took account of the status of subscribers. Reports "of many hundreds and thousands who have subscribed their names to Parliament" on anti-Episcopal petitions led one cleric to conclude, "It is an argument that the episcopacy is pleasing unto God because the multitudes so much distaste it." On the other side, Puritan activists in Hereford complained about a pro-Episcopal petition: "Much pains have been taken to get hands, no matter how foul or mean." Toward the end of 1642 peace petitions were attacked by allegations that they commanded disproportionate support from the London's lowlife.[147] Subsequently, when promoters presented a petition to the Common Council from Presbyterian citizens in 1646, they noted that its subscribers "are all citizens of the best rank and quality." Presbyterian and Independent polemicists attacked each other's petitions in references to the gender, age, and occupation of their subscribers.[148]

In addition to discussions about the number and social status of subscribers, debates over rival petitions grappled with the role of consent and reason in the public sphere. Out of these debates emerged a rough consensus on the importance of informed consent, an open exchange of ideas, and reason as the ground of opinions in political petitions. The issue of informed consent appears in debates occasioned by rival petition campaigns in 1641 between opponents and proponents of Puritan reform. Brilliana Harley, the staunchly Puritan spouse of a prominent MP, asked her son "whether those that have put in the petitions against bishops have taken the hands of all such as do not understand what they have put their hands to. I am told that it is the way in all counties. . . . To me it does not sound reasonable; for, in my opinion, such hands should be taken as understand it."[149] Lucy Hutchinson later affirmed the importance of informed consent for petitions circulating in Nottingham, whose validity, she thought, was undermined by fraud and the use of force to gain subscriptions. Economic threats and inducements also

---

[146] *HMC De L'Isle* 6:371; *MSS Add* 11045, fol. 135; *MSS Tanner* 63, fol. 22.

[147] *MSS Rawl* D134, fol. 152; *MSS Add* 70003, fol. 204; Lindley, *Popular Politics and Religion*, p. 342.

[148] MSS. JCC 40, fol. 184; *An Hue-And-Cry after Vox Populi*, pp. 11, 25; Jones, *Plain English*, p. 12; *New Birth Of The City Remonstrance*, p. 4.

[149] *Letters of Brilliana Harley*, pp. 113–14; see also *The Somerset Petition* (E155[16], 1642), p. 17.

violated the ideal of informed consent. Parliamentarians hurled this allegation against Royalist peace petitions.[150] Independents argued that, in evaluations of Presbyterian petitions, the impressive number of subscribers should be heavily discounted "if one considers that influence, the activity, subtlety, promises, threats of some rigid persons." Plans for "an anti-petition" by Independents included the promise that it would be supported by "free and voluntary subscribers."[151]

Informed consent was not a novel idea. Traditional views on petitioning discounted the need for massive petitions, but required that signatures, few or many, be given freely. In prerevolutionary England, petitions with support from powerful aristocrats could be called into question by a revelation that signatures had been obtained by "undue pressure."[152] Hence, a Kent minister in 1641 followed tradition in seeking evidence of circumstances that impeded informed consent when subscribers signed a petition hostile to his ministry. A few were drunk; another thought he had been "bewitched"; others spoke about economic threats and inducements.[153] Novelty arose when thinking on informed consent implicated the importance of a free, open exchange of ideas in petitioning. Reinforcing this implication was the perception that, unlike a public petition campaign, one conducted in secrecy facilitated manipulation or fraud. This point surfaces amidst factional petitioning in the mid-1640s, when it was invoked by promoters of Presbyterian petitions in Norwich, Lancashire, and London. The Lancashire petition "is not the clandestine whisper of a few contemptible ones in corners, but the true sense of the Parliamentary party in that county, in which the pulse of the people may be felt." In London a supporter observed that a Presbyterian petition "was read publicly, which was, I conceive, the best way, so that if any had aught against it, they might understand of it." The Common Council rebuked Independent citizens who organized a cross-petition because they did so "in a clandestine manner."[154] One year later, Independent activists alleged this against an anti-army petition from Essex Presbyterians who quietly sent printed copies from London for distribution to clerics. This "clandestine" procedure facilitated efforts by Presbyterian clerics to coerce parishioners into signing a document that had no popular input. "That which is to go under the name of a county or corporation ought to be first publicly

[150] *Memoirs of Colonel Hutchinson*, pp. 149, 153; Lindley, *Popular Politics and Religion*, p. 344 n.
[151] *A New Birth Of The City Remonstrance*, pp. 4–6.
[152] *Letters of John Holles*, 1:xxxiv.
[153] Larking, *Proceedings in Kent*, pp. 168, 171–73.
[154] Tilsley, *A true Copie of the Petition*, p. 5; Ale, *A Brief narration Of The Truth*, p. 3; MSS JCC 40, fol. 183v; and see *An Hue-And-Cry after Vox Populi* p. 18.

propounded to all the inhabitants of that county or corporation, that there may be a general meeting, debates & consultation about the matter."[155] Toward the end of this era, a petition on behalf of the "good old cause" noted that the "petitioners did not carry on their business in a secret underhand way, but openly as to all circumstances of time, place and persons."[156]

Innovations in petitioning also led contemporaries to cite reason as the basis for their opinions. Precedents for this came from prior invocation of reason by Parliamentarians who appealed to public opinion against Charles I at the beginning of the decade.[157] When this later occurred in popular petitions that opposed the importance attached by tradition to the social composition of subscribers, we have an important historical precedent for "people's public use of their reason," the hallmark of the public sphere that Jürgen Habermas assigns to the eighteenth century. In response to pro-Episcopal petitions that claimed support from "the better sort of inhabitants," defenders of petitions against bishops, in 1641, held the relevant issue to be not the petitioners' social standing but "their considerations, what they publish." The next year women petitioners offered "their several reasons, why their sex ought thus to petition, as well as the men."[158] Amidst subsequent debates during factional petitioning in the middle of the decade, a Presbyterian petition was the topic of an Independent pamphlet with a dialogue in which a churchwarden urged a parishioner to sign the petition. After the churchwarden declared, "It is as harmless a petition as ever was subscribed unto, and many honest and understanding men have subscribed it," the parishioner replies, "I will not make other men's examples, but my own reason the rule of my actions. . . . I look upon it as a very dangerous petition." Readers of a Leveller petition encountered arguments about recent political developments, followed by the claim that "this our understanding was begotten in us by principles of right reason."[159]

A perennial request of Levellers, abolition of mandatory tithes, was advanced in 1646 by radical petitioners in Hertford and adjacent counties, who invoked reason to justify their petition in a subsequent pamphlet whose title page proclaims that it was conceived "by some of the

---

[155] *A New Found Strategem* (E384[11], 1647), p. 7; and see *Declaration Of Well-Affected Non-Subscribers*, p. 3.

[156] E936[5] (1658), p. 8.

[157] Andrew Sharp, "John Lilburne and the Long Parliament's *Book of Declarations*: A Radical's Exploitation of the Words of Authorities," *History of Political Thought* 9 (1988).

[158] *The Petition For The Prelates Briefly Examined* (E160[2], 1641), p. 7; *A True Copie Of The Petition of the Gentlewomen* (E134[17], 1642).

[159] *A New Petition . . . to back the late City Remonstrance* (E340[24], 1646), p. 3; 669f.13[16] (1648).

said petitioners . . . for the vindication of themselves and their fellows" (a term indicative of humble social status). They defended their petition "by good reasons from the word of God, and by evident demonstration of sound reason, sufficient to convince any rational man, unless he have a resolution that he will not be convinced."[160] Petitions and other Leveller texts strongly upheld the centrality of reason as the ground for opinions advanced in public. Political petitioning demanded a specifically critical reason; what was needed for deliberation on public issues was "advised deliberate consideration (such as few in this nation are accustomed unto), without which that which is called knowledge or understanding is not true knowledge of understanding."[161]

TOWARD LIBERAL DEMOCRACY

Debates over representation, consent, and reason in petitioning led to novel claims for the authority of public opinion in politics. This cumulative, pragmatic development was the unintended consequence of the competitive use of printed petitions, prompted initially not by principle but by short-term political pressures and tactical considerations that confronted managers of the Long Parliament and their Royalist adversaries. Later, use of printed petitions as propaganda in highly partisan petitioning in the mid 1640s precipitated debates over the relative merits of competing petitions and new ideas on the authority of public opinion. When they confronted the problem of competition between rival petitions, some contemporaries invoked consent, openness, and reason as criteria of the validity of opinions. A very thin line separates this and democratic principles on the importance of free speech in politics, which some Levellers crossed after their experience with political petitioning led them to include communicative rights among the liberties of the subject. In a petition presented to Parliament on January 18, 1649, that opposed new licensing requirements, these radicals demanded of the Long Parliament "that you will precisely hold yourselves to the supreme end, the freedom of the people; as in other things, so in that necessary and essential part of speaking, writing, printing, and publishing their minds freely." Animating this claim is the rationale that government must "hear all voices and judgments, which they can never do but by giving freedom to the press."[162]

---

[160] *The Husbandmans Plea Against Tithes. Or, Two Petitions* (E389[2], 1647).

[161] William Walwyn, *A Word in Season* (E337[25], 1646), p. 2; and see *Walwyns Just Defense*, p. 356.

[162] Wolfe, *Leveller Manifestoes*, pp. 328–29.

Of course, this was not an entirely novel point. The open exchange of ideas in public as the likeliest source of sound policies was a theme in John Milton's *Areopagitica*, which was published in 1644. But Leveller views on petitioning and freedom of the press were not fixed and had evolved toward a broader conception of communicative freedom than that advanced earlier in the decade, when controls on the press were met with narrowly construed objections. In 1644, William Walwyn denounced licensing requirements because Presbyterians used them against "honest men," that is, radical sectarians. Two years later a Leveller petition prompted by the imprisonment of John Lilburne criticized the Commons because they "open the printing press only unto one," namely, the Presbyterians.[163] Like Milton, most Leveller leaders did not think that communicative rights in public life were universal, for these extended no farther than an ecumenical assessment of the breadth of England's Protestant consensus.[164]

Leveller arguments for a not inconsiderable extension of communicative freedom at the end of the decade drew upon experience with political petitioning that provoked new ideas about the authority of public opinion. For example, a Presbyterian petition instructs Parliament not to be offended by its reiteration of points in a prior petition that Parliament had rejected. Even greater presumption later appears in Leveller petitions that bluntly affirm a right to petition "against things established by law."[165] Though petitioning against specific laws violated traditional strictures on petitions, it occurred and was upheld as a fundamental right, not only by Levellers, but by Royalists as well. Surrey petitioners for Royalist peace proposals defended, against fierce opposition from Parliament, the right to petition "for redress of grievances, nay, for the removal of things established by law."[166] This development emerged alongside the immanent mode of criticism that printing facilitated in petitions. The authority for opinions in petitions expanded as petitioners cited prior laws or general principles thought to have overriding validity in order to advocate alterations in current laws and policies. Royalists, Levellers, and army agitators issued petitions in support of divergent proposals that cited texts such as the 1628 Petition of Right. Citing its provisions for the rule of law, a Royalist petition from

---

[163] *The Compassionate Samaritane* (1644), in J. R. McMichael and B. Taft, eds., *The Writings of William Walwyn* (Athens GA, 1989), p. 113; Wolfe, *Leveller Manifestoes*, p. 121.

[164] Christopher Hill, *John Milton and the English Revolution* (New York, 1978), pp. 152–57.

[165] E338[7] (1646), p. 7; 669f.11[98] (1647); and see *Rash Oathes unwarrantable* (E393[39], 1647), p. 28.

[166] *A Declaration . . . of Surrey: Concerning their late Petitioning* (E443[8], 1648), p. 3.

Hereford decried the "arbitrary government" of the Long Parliament in matters such as suppression of the 1642 petition from Kent. Subsequent Royalist petitions lobbied Parliament to disband the New Model Army and enter into a treaty with Charles I, advancing these proposals "not as a favor, but [as] our undoubted right and hereditary freedom, which you have faithfully engaged in sundry Remonstrances."[167] On the other side, radical petitions used immanent criticism, citing and reprinting excerpts of the 1628 Petition of Right, laws, and ordinances, in order to argue against policies and actions by Parliament—for example, its refusal to receive petitions from female Levellers.[168]

At the same time, some radical participants in competitive petition campaigns began to perceive limitations in petitioning as a means to subject politics to public opinion. Debate over the right to petition led some petitioners to think about the duty of Parliament to heed petitions. In 1647 one Leveller asks, "To question [by petition] any act done in the House was a breach of the privileges of Parliament; but . . . tyrannically to suppress and reject it, and illegally to imprison some of the petitioners . . . was no breach of the privilege of the subject?"[169] One year later this train of thought led some petitioners to perceive a need for constitutional remedies. A radical petition from a regiment of Northumberland troopers in 1648 observes how, since the king's defeat, Parliament had become the oppressor: "we find that they increase and multiply our oppression . . . reject and slight the just directions and petitions of the people . . . persecute the promoters and presenters, and burn their petitions." Accordingly, in this and other petitions for the current radical agenda—for example, a purge of Parliament and a trial for Charles I—references to suppression of petitioners are followed by requests for "a solemn contract" based on "principles of common right" to "be drawn betwixt the people and the representers."[170] This flows from growing awareness among some radicals of the inherently reactive nature of petitions as a device to organize and invoke public opinion. The experience of political petitioning in the 1640s thus led to new political ideas, prompted by the perception that legitimation of even an expanded role for petitioning would not ameliorate structural problems of governance. This point appears in Leveller writings, whose authors confront it when they advance arguments about how petitions ought to

[167] 669f.6[49] (1642); 669f.11[104] (1647); and see E441[25] (1648), p. 3; 669f.12[44] (1648).

[168] 669f.14[27] (1649); and see 669f.11[98] (1647); 669f.11[109] (1647); E402[11] (1647), p. 3; 669f.14[20] (1649); 669f.14[31] (1649); 669f.15[50] (1650); 669f.15[54] (1650); 669f.17[24] (1653).

[169] Amon Wilbee, *Plain Truth Without Feare or Flattery* (E516[7], 1647), p. 14.

[170] E475[13] (1648), pp. 2, 9; and see 669f.12[97] (1648); 669f.13[61] (1648).

be evaluated by those in authority. Some argued that "it will not be thoroughly well in England, till Parliaments make answers to petitioners according to the rule of fundamental law."[171] Fundamental law, in Leveller thought, refers imprecisely to an amalgam of natural and constitutional law. An even more explicit turn to constitutional reform as an alternative to petitioning appears in arguments associated with *An Agreement of the People*, set forth by Levellers and army agitators as the basis for a constitutional settlement. Lilburne and others advocated constitutional reform, "conceiving it to be an improper, tedious, and unprofitable thing for the people to be ever running after their representatives with petitions for redress of such grievances as may at once be removed by themselves."[172]

Here we are on the brink of a formal platform for a liberal-democratic model of the political order as experience with political petitioning stimulated new ideas about the centrality of public opinion as the ultimate ground of legitimacy for a legislative agenda. Use of printed petitions to constitute and invoke public opinion in the mid-to-late 1640s led some radicals to doubt that this was an adequate means for coordinating legislative politics and public opinion and consequently to speculate on a variety of reforms in the franchise and mechanisms for electing representatives. Though this development appears in Leveller writings just before and after the execution of Charles I, it occurred elsewhere as well, when, as I note in the epilogue, political petitioning influenced constitutional schemes in the 1650s and again during Whig agitation that preceded the Glorious Revolution of 1688. At this point we encounter contemporaries advancing liberal-democratic principles to justify a political agenda. Yet such principles did not precipitate the Long Parliament's conflict with the Stuart monarchy. Precedents for democratic principles pertaining to public opinion emerged from innovative communicative practices by political factions that sprang up in the wake of the inability of Parliament and Charles I to negotiate a settlement of their differences. For many participants and observers, traditional rhetoric dampened perceptions of innovation as it applied to petitions. But for some radical supporters of Parliament, experience with political petitioning highlighted the obsolescence of traditional norms of secrecy in political communication.

[171] *The Onely Right Rule For Regulating Laws and Liberties* (E684[33], 1653), p. 13; and see E936[5] (1658), p. 5.

[172] John Lilburne, *Englands New Chaines Discovered*, in Haller and Davies, *Leveller Tracts*, p. 160; see also *An Agreement of the Free People of England*," in Haller and Davies, *Leveller Tracts*, p. 324.

CHAPTER NINE

Epilogue

IT SHOULD NOW be evident why communicative practice and not intellectual precedent holds the key for understanding the origins of liberal-democratic philosophies and the role of the English Revolution in that development. Democratic principles for politics did not influence Parliamentary opposition to Stuart policies in prerevolutionary England or at the outbreak of revolution. When conflict between Charles I and the Long Parliament led to fighting, threats to property and the rule of law by the Stuart monarchy were the overriding issues, as they were, after the Restoration, for the early Whig opposition to Charles II. Democratic innovations in political thinking by John Locke, the earl of Shaftesbury, and Algernon Sidney thus did not derive or extend from intellectual principles that animated earlier episodes of opposition to Stuart rule, for these involved assumptions about the ancient constitution, native birthrights, and other aspects of a political legacy whose recovery, not abolition, was the manifest goal.

Neither was the invention of public opinion propelled by other doctrines that shaped political perspectives among opponents of the Stuart monarchy, such as millenarianism and classical republicanism. Millenarian beliefs were stimulated by the summoning of the Long Parliament after the eleven years of personal rule by Charles I. Among many supporters of Parliament, millennial expectations about imminent, drastic change pointed toward establishment of a Christian commonwealth. Moderate versions of millenarianism, which were widespread, and radical ones among militant sectarians had only negative implications for public opinion in political life. At the core of proposals for a Christian commonwealth was a coercive, intolerant politics of moral control, which saw public enforcement of piety, however broadly conceived, as the means by which the elect honored their God.[1] Decoupling the Puritan dream of a Christian commonwealth and oppositional politics facilitated democratic philosophies by writers like Locke who made public opinion, not tenets of a specific denomination, the arbiter of political legitimacy. Republican theories of government appeared later in the 1640s in the context of widespread speculation on vox populi in politics

---

[1] For more on this, see David Zaret, "Religion and the Rise of Liberal-Democratic Ideology in Seventeenth-Century England," *ASR* 54 (1989).

and salus populi as its goal. At many points, republican thinking on the purposes of government was entangled with religious issues, most notably millennial aspirations for a society free from moral corruption. But because it attached little importance to open debate, classical republican theory, too, has limited relevance for our purposes. Presuppositions about the rationality of public opinion are nearly as foreign to classical republicanism as to religious millenarianism. Neither provided for a public sphere in which the pluralist pursuit of utility was held to optimize the aggregate social welfare. During the English Revolution Harrington, Marten, Milton, Neville, Nedham, and Sidney reworked different traditions of classical republicanism and arrived at different conclusions. Harrington, who was not an active politician, abhorred the popular turbulence that he associated with subordinating politics to popular rule and advocated constitutional devices to limit popular participation. Sidney and Nedham, though, had vast experience with practical politics, and they defended "tumults in a commonwealth as not only preferable to tyranny but positively beneficial."[2]

Another line of thought holds that intellectual precedents for democratic ideas existed in subterranean radical traditions. In spite of nearly continuous censorship and repression, these traditions preserved and transmitted radical ideas in religion, then politics, from fifteenth-century heretics to seventeenth-century Levellers and thence to Locke. Rhetorical properties of this tradition include "a vernacular plain style," developed by Lollards, transformed in the 1640s into journalism, and later adopted by William Blake.[3] But this line of reasoning relies more on suggestive parallels between ideas and less on hard evidence that describes the precise nature of their connections, especially between the Levellers and Locke.[4] Whatever the merits of the thesis of an underground radical tradition, it does not advance our understanding of the early public sphere any more than do efforts to link it to principles advanced in anti-Stuart politics prior to 1640, or to millenarianism or classical republicanism. Ideas seldom exist apart from practice. Instead of constructing a great chain of ideas, we should explore how political conflict prompted innovative communicative practices that became precedents

[2] Jonathan Scott, *Algernon Sidney and the English Republic, 1623–1677* (Cambridge, 1988), p. 111, and see pp. 32–42, 110–12; J. C. Davis, "James Harrington's Republicanism," in I. Gentles, J. Morrill, and B. Worden, *Soldiers, Writers, and Statesmen of the English Revolution* (Cambridge, 1998), pp. 231–33.

[3] Christopher Hill, "From Lollards to Levellers," in *Collected Works* (Amherst, MA, 1985–86), 2:85–116; *The World Turned Upside Down* (New York, 1972), pp. 21–26; Joad Raymond, *The Invention of the Newspaper* (Oxford, 1996), pp. 129, 140–41.

[4] G.E. Aylmer, "Locke no Leveller," in Gentles, Morrill, and Worden, *Soldiers, Writers, and Statesmen*, pp. 304–22; J. C. D. Clark, *Revolution and Rebellion* (Cambridge, 1986), pp. 93–111.

for innovative thinking on democratic principles for English politics. In the previous chapter we followed these causal links and saw that innovations in practice were unanticipated, that they violated established norms of secrecy and privilege in political communication, and that experience with innovative practices prompted Leveller writers in the late 1640s to speculate on constitutional arrangements that would institutionalize the authority of public opinion.

Further evidence for this thesis exists in developments in the 1650s and after the Restoration in 1660. Despite the abrupt reversal of political fortunes in the Restoration, many continuities in political communication spanned the middle and later decades of the century. The Restoration brought back the monarchy, bishops, the House of Lords, and strict licensing requirements for printing, ably administered by the Surveyor of the Press, Sir Roger L'Estrange. Yet this did not extinguish the illicit side of political communication. Scribal and print publication of political news and commentary remained closely intertwined up to the end of the seventeenth century. The raucous journalism of the 1640s was not entirely suppressed by successive licensing acts, first in 1649 and then after the Restoration. Although licensed newsbooks—*Mercurius Politicus* in the 1650s, the *London Gazette* beginning in 1666—had a near monopoly on printed news, news also circulated in coffeehouses by scribal modes of publication as well as by illicit printing. Charles II tried to close the coffeehouses when it became evident that censorship of the press was circumvented by scribal publication of critical political literature, which included republican commentary and railing verses on the sexual practices of the king and his bishops.[5] During periods of acute political crisis, publication of printed news resembled the explosion of political literature in the 1640s. This occurred at the end of the Protectorate and after the Restoration, when the Popish Plot and the Exclusion Crisis generated press wars from 1678 to 1682 with many of the same features that we surveyed in the 1640s: political news and commentary in printed newsbooks, pamphlets, broadsides, and ballads, accompanied by debate over the propriety and implications of these texts.[6]

Communicative continuities also extended to petitioning and speculation on democratic models of government. Political petitioning was prominent in the political crises provoked by the Popish Plot and the Exclusion Crisis. In response to prorogations of Parliament by

[5] Tim Harris, *London Crowds in the Reign of Charles II* (Cambridge, 1990), pp. 92, 94; Harold Weber, *Paper Bullets: Print and Kingship under Charles II* (Lexington, KY, 1996), pp. 158–61; see also James Sutherland, *The Restoration Newspaper and Its Development* (Cambridge, 1986).

[6] Raymond, *Invention of the Newspaper*, p. 14; Weber, *Paper Bullets*, p. 164.

Charles II, Whig organizers mounted massive petition campaigns in 1679–80 that defended the Protestant identity of the nation and the privileges of Parliament. Tories saw this as a return to the "principles of 1641," though this did not preclude them from organizing their own petitions. In 1681 Tory apprentices in London presented one with eighteen thousand signatures to Charles II, which provoked Whig apprentices of the City to produce a cross-petition with twenty thousand signatures. In addition to the process of petition begetting petition, many other features of political petitioning that we observed for the 1640s reappeared at this time. As Whig political tactics radicalized London politics, Tory attacks on Whig petitioning were deflected with claims on behalf of petitioning as "the undoubted right of subjects of England." A majority in the House of Commons upheld this as a "common natural right."[7] Like his father, Charles II attacked popular petitions by pointing out that they came not from corporate entities but from "a company of loose and disaffected people."[8] Petitions with blank spaces facilitated local efforts to gather signatures (the tactics of 1645), which often occurred in inns and taverns. So did correlative political pamphlets that, along with petitions, poured from illicit presses, one of which allegedly was kept by Shaftesbury.[9] Practical experience with political petitioning also stimulated ideas about the centrality of public opinion in politics in republican and Whig speculation on democratic models of governance. This has been shown for constitutional schemes by Harrington, whose materialism placed him outside the mainstream of classical republicanism, and for Sidney, who was very much within it. Central to Sidney's later political views and those of the preeminent Whig theorist John Locke was the massive petition campaign mounted by Whig activists in 1679–80. It left its mark, for example, on Locke's thinking about popular consent and conditions under which a government could lose legitimacy.[10] Locke did not provide his political philosophy with an explicit defense of freedom of expression and of the press in the *Two Treatises of Government*, yet his confidence in the rational potential of public opinion—it was ultimately the arbiter of when revolt was justified against an

[7] Richard Ashcraft, *Revolutionary Politics and Locke's Two Treatises of Government* (Princeton, 1986), p. 212, and see p. 239; Harris, *London Crowds*, pp. 174–77; Jonathan Scott, *Algernon Sidney and the Restoration Crisis, 1677–1683* (Cambridge, 1991), p. 66, and see pp. 58–59, 65;

[8] Harris, *London Crowds*, p. 173.

[9] Ashcraft, *Revolutionary Politics*, p. 174; Harris, *London Crowds*, p.172.

[10] J. A. W. Gunn, *Politics and the Public Interest in the Seventeenth Century* (London, 1969), p. 122; Mark Knight, "Petitioning and the Political Theorists: John Locke, Algernon Sidney, and London's 'Monster' Petition of 1680," *P&P* 138 (1993); Scott, *Sidney and the English Republic*, pp. 15, 32–35; Scott, *Sidney and the Restoration*, p. 66.

illegitimate regime—nearly inverted prior assumptions that had governed political discourse in England. Locke, too, worried about the demagogic trends in popular politics. But, for Locke popular irrationality was historically contingent and not a necessary state of affairs.[11]

DEISM, SCIENCE, AND OPINION

Practical innovations in political communication preceded and prepared the way for democratic principles. But this does not adequately explain how Locke and other proponents of liberal democracy were able to put public opinion at the core of politics. Recall that the paradox of innovation sprang from the persistence of traditional assumptions about the nature of social order, a key tenet of which was that irrationality inversely correlated with social rank, that the masses were a "many-headed monster." Reinforcing this assumption were specific religious commitments of Puritanism, which emphasized the corruption of human nature and reason. The severely pessimistic assessment of human nature flowing from these social and religious sources was a principal reason why, during the English Revolution, adversaries of the Stuart monarchy were unwilling to acknowledge innovative claims about subjecting politics to public opinion. In contrast, a political philosophy that embraced appeals to public opinion required an optimistic assessment of human abilities. Liberal confidence in the capacity for individual self-help and reason separated Lockean liberalism from the broad Puritan tradition that emphasized the corruption and limitations of reason.[12]

The rise of toleration, Deism, and natural religion, along with confidence in natural science as a means for overcoming religious differences, were key developments after the Restoration that facilitated the creation of liberal-democratic philosophies by Locke, the earl of Shaftesbury, Algernon Sidney, and other writers. Proponents of these political and religious doctrines were united not only by ideas but also by social background and shared experiences. Most reached adulthood during the English Revolution, attended Oxford or Cambridge, and came from Puritan families. They rejected Calvinist theology and its ideal of a holy commonwealth, and were also united by complex interpersonal ties.

[11] Peter Laslett, "Introduction," in *Locke's Two Treatises of Government* (Cambridge, [1690] 1960), p. 85 n; John Dunn, *The Political Thought of John Locke* (Cambridge, 1982), pp. 185–86.

[12] On the reformed tradition and reason, see John Morgan, *Godly Learning: Puritan Attitudes toward Reason, Learning, and Education, 1560–1640* (Cambridge, 1986), pp. 43–61.

Shaftesbury, the leader of the early Whigs, was Locke's aristocratic patron and political mentor. Though Shaftesbury and Sidney were not
friends, they shared many of the same supporters.[13] Not all proponents
of tolerance, natural religion, and Deism were Whigs, but most Whig
theorists, such as Locke, supported novel developments in religious doctrines which, in spite of other differences, held in common that there
could be nothing in religion that was not compatible with reason.

In these new religious doctrines, *reason* denoted a specifically public
reason that derived from experience; hence the term *natural religion*. Its
advocates argued that reason was vested in the individual by nature, not
grace. Religion, wrote Benjamin Whichcote, "is no stranger to human
nature," a point commended to the public by the earl of Shaftesbury."[14]
At a stroke this demolished pessimistic doctrines about the corruption of
reason that were central to Puritan religion. Natural reason was sufficient in itself to reveal the existence of Providence and its designs. In this
view, religious fanaticism and intolerance were inevitable when religion
rejected reason for revelation. Thus, Locke argued that "to this crying
up of faith in opposition to reason, we may . . . ascribe those absurdities
that fill almost all the religions which possess and divide mankind."[15]
But adherents of this position were not atheists who sought to replace
religion with reason, for they saw natural religion to be the capstone of
the broad tradition of English Protestant dissent. This view was advanced by leading thinkers affiliated with many religious, intellectual,
and political movements: not only Whig writers but also members of the
Royal Society, Cambridge Neoplatonic philosophers, and Latitudinarian clerics and bishops. When Locke and other Whig authors asserted
that there were "no suggestions of the holy spirit but what are always
agreeable to, if not demonstrable from, reason,"[16] they did so in concert, and often word for word, with Henry More, Bishop Wilkins and
the Latitudinarian churchmen, and Robert Boyle and other members of
the Royal Society.[17]

[13] Ashcraft, *Revolutionary Politics*; James R. Jones, *The First Whigs* (New York, 1961);
Douglas R. Lacey, *Dissent and Parliamentary Politics* (New Brunswick, NJ, 1969).

[14] Benjamin Whichcote, *Works* (Aberdeen, 1751), 3:5–7, 181.

[15] John Locke, *An Essay Concerning Human Understanding* (Oxford, 1894), 2:426.
See also *The Correspondence of John Locke* (Oxford, 1976), 2:500.

[16] Locke, *Correspondence*, 2:504; and see Thomas Hunt, *The Great And Weighty Considerations* (*Wing* G1660, 1680), p. 13; James Tyrrell, *A Brief Disquisition Of The Law of
Nature* (*Wing* T3583, 1692), sig. A7.

[17] Henry More, *Enthusiasmus Triumphatus*, in *A Collection Of Several Philosophical
Writings* (*Wing* M2646 1662), p. 39; Richard Westfall, *Science and Religion in Seventeenth-Century England* (New Haven, 1958), p. 175; Barbara Shapiro, *John Wilkins, 1614–
1672* (Berkeley, 1969).

This appeal to reason had at least two sources. One was a negative response to conflict and religious radicalism during the English Revolution, when the collapse of official control and emphasis on inward faith produced an explosion of sectarian activity in which the tenets of any one group were seen by others as further instances of the worldliness that oppressed the saints. In this context, sectarianism was fertile ground for radical politics that assumed the form of a charismatic revolt against all worldly institutions—including the church, universities, the law, and the state—seen as impediments to creation of a holy commonwealth. One response to the evident failure of this goal was Quaker quietism, which rejected the political agenda of sectarianism. Another was natural religion, which rejected sectarianism by banishing revelation and other forms of religious enthusiasm that did not accord with reason and promote tolerance.[18]

Yet more than a negative response to sectarianism animated innovations in natural religion. They also sprang from growing confidence in public reason, a product of well-publicized triumphs of experimental science, whose promoters saw it as a model for rational discourse in both religion and politics. Robert Boyle and others advanced the amiable idea that "the proper study of nature bridges religious and political divisions among men."[19] Proponents of the Royal Society, such as Thomas Sprat, lauded knowledge produced by experimental science as "public knowledge." Printing not only facilitated publication of this knowledge but also its production, making the laboratory a public space by surmounting limits in scribal publication in order to communicate vast amounts of data, designs of scientific instruments used for data collection, and mathematical tables for data analysis.[20] This development transformed hitherto private, idiosyncratic practices by experimenters, which now occurred in a public sphere constituted by laboratories linked by printing.

> Experimentalists like Boyle and his Royal Society colleagues in the 1660s were engaged in a vigorous attack on the privacy of existing forms of intellectual practice. The legitimacy of experimental knowledge, it was claimed, depended upon a public presence. . . . If experimental knowledge did in-

[18] For more on this development, see Zaret, "Religion and Liberal-Democratic Ideology," pp. 171–72.

[19] James R. Jacobs, *Robert Boyle and the English Revolution* (New York, 1977), pp. 117–18; and see Isaac Barrow, *Theological Works* (Cambridge, 1859), 3:399; Joseph Glanvill, *The Vanity of Dogmatizing* (*Wing* G834, 1661), pp. 229–31; Steven Shapin and Simon Schaffer, *Leviathan and the Airpump: Hobbes, Boyle, and the Experimental Life* (Princeton, 1985), p. 301.

[20] Elizabeth Eisenstein, *The Printing Press as an Agent of Change* (Cambridge, 1980), pp. 520–74, 668–70.

deed have to occupy public space during part of its career, then its realization as authentic knowledge involved its transit to and through a public space.[21]

Within this space, the rule of reason in the formation of scientific knowledge overrode traditional social restrictions. In laboratories, unlike in schools and universities, participants deferred to "the meanest, so he can plead reason for his opinion."[22] To be sure, experimental science was not the sole source of growing confidence in public reason at this time. It was also promoted by increased mastery over the physical and social environment, for example, in agriculture and reliance on statistics for actuarial calculations. And its connection to experimental science sprang as much from publicity by its promoters as from its concrete achievements.[23]

The appeal to reason in religion had immediate and far-reaching consequences for political speculation. Banishing revelation from religion made divinity largely irrelevant to politics because it jettisoned nearly every specific doctrinal tenet that distinguished not only Protestantism from Catholicism, but Christianity from other religions. Beyond a belief in the existence of Providence and an afterlife, the core tenets that reason validated for proponents of natural religion constituted an innocuous, utilitarian creed, leavened by a few ethical maxims, such as the Golden Rule. "The laws of God," said Archbishop Tillotson, "are reasonable, that is, suitable to our nature and advantageous to our interest." Bishop Wilkins thought it was "not possible to contrive any rules more advantageous to our own interest than those which religion does propose."[24] This is very nearly the outlook of the Enlightenment, where the union of morality and utility explained this best of all possible worlds. Natural religion made divinity irrelevant to political philosophy because, in the end, it held that utility, not revelation, should guide thinking on the politics.

Locke and other Whig writers had little difficulty with the precept that any adequate doctrine on political authority must encompass

[21] Steven Shapin, "The House of Experiment in Seventeenth-Century England," *Isis* 79 (1988):384.

[22] Charles Webster, *The Great Instauration* (New York, 1976), p. 60; and see Shapin, "House of Experiment," p. 397.

[23] Margaret C. Jacob, *The Newtonians and the English Revolution* (Ithaca, 1976); Keith Thomas, *Religion and the Decline of Magic* (Harmondsworth, 1973), pp. 781–85; Barbara Shapiro, *Probability and Certainty in Seventeenth-Century England* (Princeton, 1983); Webster, *The Great Instauration.*

[24] John Tillotson, *Works* (London, 1728), 1:57; John Wilkins, *Of The Principles and Duties Of Natural Religion* (London, [1675] 1693), p. 393. See also Westfall, *Science and Religion*, pp. 118–25, 134, 157, 161.

religion because their religious thinking lacked specific commitments beyond the bland proposition that Providence had created a potentially wonderful world. To be sure, political magistracy was ordained by God, but because God "confined such as shall be chosen rulers, within no other limits in reference to our civil concerns, save that they are to govern for the good of those over whom they come to be established, it remains free and entire to the people . . . to prescribe and define what shall be the measure of the public good."[25] In *Court Maxims* Algernon Sidney, too, declared that government was instituted by God but that God had "left us a liberty of choosing and constituting such a government as according to the time and nature of the place and people we find most convenient." Against Filmer, he argued that civil liberties derived not from divinity, but from nature inasmuch as utility is the measure of politics. Earlier, in *Mercurius Politicus*, Nedham advanced a similar argument.[26] Locke also had little difficulty in reconciling belief in Providence with a political doctrine that subordinated government to natural rights that were revealed by reason, not revelation. "I find no difficulty to suppose the freedom of mankind, though I have always believed the creation of Adam." Hence, Locke wrote, "There is absolutely no such thing . . . as a Christian commonwealth," yet he recommended against extending full toleration to atheists. The irrelevance of all divinity other than the simple affirmations of natural religion underpins Locke's confidence that "men of different professions may quietly unite . . . under the same government and unanimously carry the same civil interest, and hand-in-hand march to the same end of peace and mutual society, thought they take different ways to heaven."[27]

Thus, religious developments in Restoration England facilitated a decoupling of religion and politics, an entanglement that had animated contemporary reluctance to acknowledge innovations in communicative practices and that had been an obstacle to formulating democratic political philosophies. After elevating reason over revelation, Whig writers, unlike their Puritan predecessors, were no longer obligated to assign divinely privileged status for any political arrangement. Locke and other writers could more openly embrace the authority of opinion in politics

[25] Robert Ferguson, *A Representation Of the Threatening Dangers* (*Wing* F757, 1689), p. 6; and see Hunt, *Great And Weighty Considerations*, p. 8; James Tyrrell, *Patriarcha non Monarcha* (*Wing* T3591, 1681), p. 243.

[26] Algernon Sidney, *Discourses on Government* (New York, [1698] 1805), 1:313–14, 423; Scott, *Sidney and the English Republic*, p. 197, and see pp. 111–12.

[27] Locke, *Correspondence* 1:110; John Locke, *A Letter Concerning Toleration*, in M. Montuori, ed., *John Locke on Toleration and the Unity of God* (Amsterdam, [1689] 1983), pp. 73, 93; Locke, *Two Treatises of Government*, pp. 169, 375–36.

because their religious commitments, though nominally Protestant, upheld an optimistic appraisal of human nature and did not preclude the
priority of tolerance over revelation as a precondition for the pluralist
pursuit of utility.

CONTEMPORARY IMPLICATIONS

In chapter 2 I observed that theories of the early public sphere have
strong implications for debates over the current public sphere's status
and prospects. This observation holds as well for the account offered in
this study, though it leads to conclusions that militate against theoretical
currents in contemporary sociology and cultural studies which flow from
the deepest impulses of modern academic life, namely, to cultivate an
antagonistic relationship to the larger society. In so doing, this study of
communicative change in the early-modern era provides a corrective to
pessimistic assessments of the contemporary public sphere's potential
for sustaining the critical use of reason in the political life of advanced
industrial societies. Long a hallmark of critical theory, this pessimism has
been extended in new directions in postmodernist social theories. What
is especially striking about both theoretical positions is the exaggerated
sense of novelty attached to communicative developments in the twentieth century—commercialism and the growing capacity for textual reproduction—that are held responsible for the eclipse of reason in public life.

In chapter 2 we surveyed change and continuity in older and more
recent accounts by Habermas of the rise and fall of the public sphere.
There we saw that since publication of the historical-institutional account in *Structural Transformation*, the opposition between culture
and capitalist civilization has ceased to be central to Habermas's analysis
of cultural dynamics in modernization. Subsuming and revising it is a
categorical distinction between instrumental and communicative reason. Yet an important continuity links both phases of Habermas's writings, as well as those by the first generation of critical theorists: a model
of cultural dynamics in modernization that resembles a parable of rise
and decline, of differentiation and dedifferentiation. In this model the
rise of the public sphere—or, more broadly, emancipatory tendencies
toward greater universalism—is traced to differentiation of thought or
discursive processes from societal contexts such as media, money,
power, and so on. This development flows from a key precept of critical
theory, exemplified long ago by Horkheimer's dictum, "The opposition
of philosophy to reality arises from its principles." In *Structural Transformation* Habermas analyzes the differentiation of reason and society,

which earlier critical theorists had read into the history of philosophy, in terms of the bourgeois public sphere's acquisition of autonomy from capitalist civilization and the sovereign state. We also saw in chapter 2 that this had led Habermas to argue that printing "had evolved out of the public's use of its reason," reversing what we have seen was the causal relationship between the two. The same line of reasoning in more recent writings underlies Habermas's remarks on the "spontaneous" nature of the public sphere in civil society. In both instances, critical thought in the public sphere arises from immanent principles, formerly from those of philosophic reason, more recently from those of communicative reason. Continuities also exist in the analysis of dedifferentiation in modernization, which is held to threaten critical use of reason in the public sphere. In earlier critical theory it was technological rationality that effected an alignment of philosophy and reality; in contemporary critical theory, this alignment is brought about when discursive processes are dedifferentiated from instrumental reason.[28]

Not only does this model of cultural dynamics guide other contemporary accounts of critical theory,[29] but, oddly enough, it is central to many strands of postmodernist theorizing, whose principal proponents, such as Lyotard, dismiss the idea of critical rationality as a logocentric language game that constructs metanarratives on growing universalism as the "unitary end of history." Hence, "postmodernists abandon the language of large publics and transformational politics."[30] In their writings, dedifferentiation takes two related forms. Postmodernists use dedifferentiating deconstruction to unmask as a fiction the modernist ideal of reason's autonomy, whereas critical theory views the initial differentiation of reason from society as a real, however imperfect, historical development. Dedifferentiation also appears in postmodernism as a historical trend propelled by the accelerated pace of textual reproduction in electronic media. This leads to the collapse of boundaries that are isomorphic to those delineated by critical theory between culture and civilization, now described in semiotic terms. Baudrillard contrasts

[28] Max Horkheimer, "The Social Function of Philosophy," *Studies in Philosophy and Social Science* 8 (1939), p. 325. On the eclipse of reason, see Theodor Adorno and Max Horkheimer, *Dialectic of Enlightenment* (New York, [1944] 1972); Herbert Marcuse, *One-Dimensional Man* (Boston, 1964). See above, chap. 2, for Habermas's arguments.

[29] E.g., S. Benhabib, *Critique, Norm, and Utopia* (New York, 1987); Craig Calhoun, *Critical Social Theory* (Cambridge, MA, 1995); David Held, *Introduction to Critical Theory* (Berkeley, 1980); Douglas Kellner, *Critical Theory, Marxism, and Modernity* (Baltimore, 1989).

[30] Jean-François Lyotard, *The Post-Modern Condition* (Minneapolis, 1984), pp. 72–73; Robert Antonio and Douglas Kellner, "The Future of Social Theory," in D. Dickens and A. Fontana, eds., *Postmodernism and Social Inquiry* (New York, 1994), p. 142; see also Douglas Kellner, *Postmodern Theory: Critical Interrogations* (London, 1991), p. 283.

modernism, in which "a signifier referred back to a signified," and post-modernism, in which "the code no longer refers back to any subject or objective 'reality,' but to its own logic. The signifier thus becomes its own referent." Thus, textual reproduction in the postmodern simula-crum dissolves boundaries between the real and the imagined.[31]

The eruption of signification that denotes the postmodern condition has been traced not only to change in media, the hypertextuality of electronic communication, but also to the commodification of discursive production in "late" capitalism. Some strands of postmodernism subscribe to this view, as do many proponents of critical theory and other neo-Marxist theories. Considerable disagreement exists over the relative causal importance of change in media and in the political economy, and over the degree to which the postmodern condition represents an intensification of key trends in modernization, *pace* Jameson, or, as Baudrillard avers, a radical departure from them. Versions of postmodernism that stress historical discontinuities induced by novel developments in electronically mediated communication are least amenable to critical theory.[32] Other versions offer opportunities for synthesis, even though proponents of critical theory cannot subscribe to the postmodernist dismissal of universalism as a logocentric language game. Treating the heightened capacity for textual reproduction as an extension of the logic of commodity production makes it possible to incorporate postmodernist themes in critical theory[33] or in related schools of neo-Marxism based on Gramscian notions of hegemony.[34]

In postmodernist social theories, however, dedifferentiation is not, as in critical theory, an invasion of commerce or instrumental rationality into discursive processes, but an eruption of signs that moves in the reverse direction. In place of Habermas's account of the decline of "the relative autonomy" formerly enjoyed by bourgeois culture, a critical theory infused with postmodernism asserts that "the dissolution of an autonomous sphere of culture is rather to be imagined in terms of an explosion: a prodigious expansion of culture throughout the social

---

[31] Jean Baudrillard, *The Mirror of Production* (St. Louis, 1975), p. 127; and see also Jean Baudrillard, *Simulations* (New York, 1983).

[32] E.g., Mark Poster, *The Mode of Information* (Chicago, 1990).

[33] Ben Agger, *Fast Capitalism* (Urbana, IL, 1989); Best and Kellner, *Postmodern Theory*; David Harvey, *The Condition of Postmodernity* (Cambridge, MA, 1990); Frederic Jameson, *Postmodernism* (London 1992); Douglas Kellner, "Boundaries and Borderlines: Reflections on Jean Baudrillard and Critical Theory," *Current Perspectives in Social Theory* 9 (1989); Scott Lash, "Discourse or Figure? Postmodernism as a 'Regime of Signification,'" *Theory, Culture, and Society* 5 (1988).

[34] For links to theories of hegemony, see Mark Gottdiener, *Postmodern Semiotics* (London, 1995), pp. 165–87; Angela McRobbie, *Postmodernism and Popular Culture* (New York, 1994).

realm."[35] In the ensuing postmodern condition, signification run riot effaces distinctions between image and reality and leads to a total dissipation of objectivity, which is succeeded by floating modes of signification, a continuous crisis of narratives that formerly sustained modernist claims to reason. Whereas critical theory attributes the eclipse of reason to commercialism—or, more broadly, instrumental rationality—that invades the public sphere, for postmodernists the culprit is textual reproduction, the hypertextuality of electronically mediated communication. In critical theory, dedifferentiation leads to a one-dimensional world that precludes appeals to reason in public life. In postmodernism, an explosion of signification dedifferentiates signifiers and the signified, and thereby creates n-dimensional worlds, each with its own particular truths.

Yet both the one- and n-dimensional theses of critical theory and postmodernism suffer from similar misapprehensions of communicative change. Both theses credulously accept a pristine view of communicative realities in the early-modern era, a viewpoint whose origins are the self-promoting claims of representatives of the early-modern public sphere. Critical theory assumes that commercialism did not permeate the print culture that sustained the early-modern public sphere. Postmodernism assumes that signification run riot was not an important feature of mediated communication in the age of the printing press. That these are bad assumptions is only one general conclusion to be drawn from this study of communicative change in the early-modern era. More importantly, we have also seen how commerce and textual reproduction imposed dialogic order on political conflict, an immanent style of criticism in political debates, and reoriented production of petitions and other printed texts to the tasks of constituting and invoking public opinion as a political tactic. Communicative change propelled by commerce and textual reproduction led to novel political practices that constituted a public sphere in which participants issued reasons to defend opinions on setting a legislative agenda. In short, liberal-democratic modernism was a practical accomplishment that sprang from the very developments that critical theorists and postmodernists hold responsible for the dissolution of modernism and liberal faith in reason as a progressive force in politics. The force of this observation might be lessened if it could be shown that the magnitude of communicative change, in terms of increased commercialism and capacity for textual reproduction, is far greater in the twentieth than in the seventeenth century. Yet this seems unlikely when one considers the point of departure for communicative change in the early-modern era: scribal modes of transmission and norms of secrecy. A his-

---

[35] Jameson, *Postmodernism*, p. 48.

torically balanced assessment of communicative change forces us to acknowledge the intrinsically positive features of commerce and the growing technical ability to reproduce texts. Historical study of communicative change thus provides a corrective to one-sided views of its negative consequences that fuel unwarranted pessimism on the modern public sphere.